A Critical Collection on Alejandro Morales

University of New Mexico Press / Albuquerque

Edited by Marc García-Martínez
and Francisco A. Lomelí

A Critical Collection on Alejandro Morales
Forging an Alternative Chicano Fiction

© 2021 by the University of New Mexico Press
All rights reserved. Published 2021
Printed in the United States of America

First paperback printing 2025 | ISBN 978-0-8263-6808-9

Library of Congress Cataloging-in-Publication Data
Names: García-Martínez, Marc, editor. | Lomelí, Francisco A., editor.
Title: A critical collection on Alejandro Morales: forging an alternative Chicano fiction / edited by Marc García-Martínez and Francisco A. Lomelí.
Description: Albuquerque: University of New Mexico Press, [2021] | Includes bibliographical references and index.
Identifiers: LCCN 2021032884 (print) | LCCN 2021032885 (e-book) | ISBN 9780826363091 (cloth) | ISBN 9780826363107 (e-book)
Subjects: LCSH: Morales, Alejandro, 1944– Criticism and interpretation. | LCGFT: Literary criticism. | Essays.
Classification: LCC PS3563.O759 Z64 2021 (print) | LCC PS3563.O759 (e-book) | DDC 813/.54—dc23
LC record available at https://lccn.loc.gov/2021032884
LC e-book record available at https://lccn.loc.gov/2021032885

Founded in 1889, the University of New Mexico sits on the traditional homelands of the Pueblo of Sandia. The original peoples of New Mexico—Pueblo, Navajo, and Apache—since time immemorial have deep connections to the land and have made significant contributions to the broader community statewide. We honor the land itself and those who remain stewards of this land throughout the generations and also acknowledge our committed relationship to Indigenous peoples. We gratefully recognize our history.

Cover photograph courtesy of Alejandro Morales.
Designed by Mindy Basinger Hill

CONTENTS

1   **INTRODUCTION** / Alejandro Morales / An Errant Maverick Faces the Literary Canon and History / *Marc García-Martínez and Francisco A. Lomelí*

13   **ONE** / Submersion, Suffocation, and Entombment of the Mexican and Immigrant Body in *River of Angels*—Probing Figurations of Violence and Isolation / *Marc García-Martínez*

35   **TWO** / The Analogous Correspondence of an Extreme Poetics between Stanley Kubrick's *A Clockwork Orange* and Alejandro Morales' *Barrio on the Edge* / *Francisco A. Lomelí*

53   **THREE** / Alejandro Morales' *The Captain of All These Men of Death* and Philip Roth's *Nemesis*: Parallels and Contrasts / *Stephen Miller*

71   **FOUR** / Tropes of Ecothinking and the Spatial Imaginary in Alejandro Morales' *River of Angels* / *Sophia Emmanouilidou*

89   **FIVE** / History, Spatial Justice, and the *Esperpento* in Alejandro Morales' *Pequeña nación* / *Jesús Rosales*

109   **SIX** / Heterotopia and the Emergence of the Modern *Ilusa* in *Waiting to Happen* / *Margarita López López*

127   **SEVEN** / City History and Space Politics: Los Angeles in Morales' *River of Angels* / *Baojie Li*

143   **EIGHT** / *Pequeña nación* / Big (Feminist) Revolution / *Amaia Ibarraran-Bigalondo*

161 **NINE** / Bodies in Motion in *The Place of the White Heron*, Volume Two of the Heterotopian Trilogy / A Glance through the Panopticon / *Adam Spires*

179 **TEN** / Race, Space, and Magical Realism in *The Brick People* and *River of Angels* / *Adina Ciugureanu*

197 **ELEVEN** / Mestizaje, Cultural Identity, and Environmental Degradation in Alejandro Morales' *The Rag Doll Plagues* / *Manuel M. Martín-Rodríguez*

213 **TWELVE** / Translation as Rewriting and Resituating / The Two English Versions of *Caras viejas y vino nuevo* by Alejandro Morales / *Elena Errico*

227 **THIRTEEN** / History and Fiction in Alejandro Morales' Narratives / *Luis Leal*

247 **FOURTEEN** / Epidemics, Epistemophilia, and Racism: Ecological Literary Criticism and *The Rag Doll Plagues* / *María Herrera-Sobek*

263 **FIFTEEN** / A Dialogue with the Writer Alejandro Morales / *Francisco Lomelí, Marc García-Martínez, and Daniel Olivas*

285 Bibliography / *Donaldo W. Urioste*

307 Contributors

311 Index

A Critical Collection on Alejandro Morales

INTRODUCTION / Alejandro Morales /
An Errant Maverick Faces the Literary
Canon and History / MARC GARCÍA-MARTÍNEZ
AND FRANCISCO A. LOMELÍ

Literature is not merely language; it is also the will to figuration, the motive for metaphor that Nietzsche once defined as the desire to be different, the desire to be elsewhere ... to be different from oneself ... to be different from the metaphors and images of the contingent works that are one's heritage: the desire to write greatly is the desire to be elsewhere, in a time and place of one's own, in an originality that must compound with inheritance, with the anxiety of influence. —Harold Bloom, *The Western Canon*, 1994

Alejandro Morales has been a steady presence in the thematic diversification of the Chicano/a novel that followed the first wave of fiction writers sparked by the Chicano Movement, referred to as the Quinto Sol Generation (between 1967–1974) and known for its openly cultural nationalist aesthetic agenda. Novels from this first wave included Tomás Rivera's ... *Y no se lo tragó la tierra* (... And the Earth Did Not Part [1971]), Rudolfo A. Anaya's *Bless Me, Ultima* (1972), Oscar Zeta Acosta's *The Autobiography of a Brown Buffalo* (1972), Rolando Hinojosa's *Estampas del Valle y otras obras* (Sketches of the Valley and Other Works) (1973) and Miguel Méndez M.'s *Peregrinos de Aztlán* (1974), among others. In a watershed moment in 1975, however, Alejandro Morales composed *Caras viejas y vino nuevo*, a work that marked a definite shift away from epic and cultural nationalist representations in favor of depicting an unforgiving, hard-core barrio.

Rather than offering burnished or romanticized views of a relegated cultural history or environment, Morales focused on discerning the inner—and occasionally ambiguous—qualities of characters steeped in the contradictions of a raw and even savage reality. Along with a small group of other writers such as Ron Arias (*The Road to Tamazunchale* [1975]), Isabella Ríos (*Victuum* [1976]), Phil Sánchez (*Don Phil-O-Meno sí la mancha* [1977]), John Rechy (*The Sexual Outlaw* [1977]), and Aristeo Brito (*El diablo en Texas* [1976]), Morales emphasized craft and far-reaching novelistic experimentations through largely unconventional means. Chicano/a culture no longer had to be mirrored, or even reinvented, because what mattered most was zeroing in on the capabilities of the genre in order to further probe or capture Chicanos/as in their multiple and widespread sociocultural manifestations.

The work of Alejandro Morales constitutes a bold alternative, both to the Quinto Sol Generation and to the newer group of authors with whom he had an affinity. His literary representation of the mentioned sociocultural manifestations is so persistently unconventional that it challenges and at times even effaces the much-affirmed panoply that is Mexican American and Chicano/a letters. Morales stands out for his audacious and dauntless incursions into explorations of subject matters that others either outright avoid or shy away from in this literature, in great part because they require not only meticulous research into their respective backdrops and sociohistorical contexts but also a willingness to face the wholesale rawness of human existence. His breadth and range are remarkable, as he does not restrict himself to what is fashionable for the sake of popularity or marketability. Indeed, his works present a wide spectrum of thematic and metaphoric representations, extending from an almost monomaniacal dedication to recovering and revisioning history to exploring the disturbing role of epidemic diseases. Morales not only looks at what might have happened within the annals of history and its corresponding backdrop—oftentimes understood as the views and experiences of Chicanos/as below Anglo-America's radar—but also focuses on purported documents that authenticate a social history that has otherwise remained unknown, or "invisible." This Chicano author wants us to contemplate that a significant group of Mexican descendants were not only subjugated but were virtually erased by the majority society after the Mexican-American War of 1848. His works evince a predilection for the intrahistorical and the fanciful, as he seeks to extricate meaning and validation on behalf of a full-fledged, culturally informed subset that has struggled to survive within a hegemonic system. In his writing Morales ruminates on both the past and the future, offering incisive reflections to help the reader better understand how a conquered people may constitute a reality of new possibilities. Still, he sometimes writes as if he and his readers have an old score to settle, challenging their complacency through the unusual plot twists he hurls at them. In some cases, we are overwhelmed with bizarre characters of noir narratives and speculative imaginations, visceral figurations, overlapping symbologies, somatic encodings, and other elements that produce a shock that is hard to ignore.

There is something undeniably challenging and alternative about Morales' literary methods, which have been characterized by Antonio C. Márquez as "interlaced with surrealism, dream-narrative, magic realism, ample touches of the grotesque, and elements of the fantastical" (1995, 79). Others, like José Antonio Gurpegui, fittingly stress "la riqueza imaginativa de Alejandro Morales"—the richness of his creative vision and the wealth of imagination found in his work (1996, 43). While his writings never fail to produce verbally and visually rich incantations, they nonetheless always manage to form an intense assemblage of plot, voice, motif, complex metaphor, and stirring diegesis, arousing a genuine unease in the reader. The presence of these elements exerts considerable leverage on the way in which we come to understand both the author and the man. No doubt due to the aforesaid shock and unease, publishers initially rejected Morales' manuscripts—literary testimonials deemed painfully crude, disturbingly exotic, and just a bit too surreal. Even so, to this day his works firmly and unapologetically comprise a veritable library of crude counterhistories, exotic metanarratives, and surreal "flesh-and-blood" aesthetic experimentation.[1]

In doing so, Alejandro Morales' inimitable works contest and confront the present-day literary canon, both Chicano/a and international. Through innovative iterations of power struggles and strange, unvarnished apocalyptic renderings, and atmospheres and interrelations of considerable strife, his fictional works represent an ongoing experimentation with form, time, characterization, and geography. There arises from his novels a distinctive narrative voice that articulates a fascination with both the omnipresent trope of the metonymic barrio around East Los Angeles and the ever-changing geo-demographic developments in Los Angeles as a zone of intense hybridities and cultural admixtures, which he positions within a factual and fictionalized region that extends all the way to Mexico City. In engaging with his prolific library of work, the reader must contend with dynamics of realism versus the magical real, infrarealism versus "mystic realism," ethnohistory versus official history, intrahistory versus antihistory, chronicle versus testimonial, biography versus autobiography, myth versus legend, science versus popular medicine, surrealism versus hyperrealism, contemporaneity versus futurism, ambiguity versus speculative allusions, colonialism versus postcolonialism, dystopia versus heterotopia, race versus eugenics, "extreme poetics" versus sanitized portrayals, and natural diseases versus apocalyptic epidemics.[2] Because he freely and creatively indulges in the construction of metanovels that breach the gap between Chicano/a lived experience and how Anglo-America has attempted to define and ensnare Chicanos/asas a recycled, ahistorical living stereotype, Morales' work breaks the canonical shackles of space, history, unilingualism, character normativities, narrative modalities, and conventional approaches. He often refers to his characters' migratory patterns but does not necessarily limit himself to coming-of-age immigrant tales or to the sociopolitical polemics of the border. He prefers to unearth through aesthetic means troubling and problematic systemic constructions that have built barriers tending to hinder and encircle not only Chicano/a but *human* existence.

Thus, Morales does not fit neatly into a single classification in literary terms, due to his unprecedented eclecticism, worldview, and cutting-edge imaginary of emerging vanguard creations. Though he is a harsh, confrontational iconoclast who creates works that some readers and critics avoid, Morales nonetheless won UC Santa Barbara's prestigious Luis Leal Award for Distinction in the Arts in 2007. Moreover, 2020 marked the forty-fifth anniversary of the publishing of *Caras viejas y vino nuevo*, his first and most pivotal novel that made a major splash in Chicano/a letters. Nine novels and a collection of three novellas later, his work has been published worldwide and translated into Spanish, Italian, Dutch, and German. He is indeed an ethnic writer, but this should not be understood in reductionist terms situating him within one specific trend or category, for there is always something intranational and extranational about him.

And yet despite all this, it must be affirmed that Morales' literary art is cognate to literary art that came before; indeed, he admits a connection to and respect for past writers that inform his work. He possesses a vast knowledge of Chicano/a literature, of course, and yet is also influenced by the Latin American Boom writers (Carlos Fuentes, Gabriel García Márquez, José Donoso, Julio Cortázar, Mario Vargas Llosa), by the Mexican La Onda group (José Agustín, Gustavo Sáenz), by key North American voices (John Dos Passos, William Faulkner, Ernest Hemingway), and by prominent European writers (James Joyce, Alain Robbe-Grillet, Camilo José Cela). Chicano/a literary historians—namely, Luis Leal, Genaro Padilla, María Herrera-Sobek, Ramón Gutiérrez, and Francisco Lomelí—have sensed and often noted this knowledge and influence operating in his works. Nonetheless, Morales offers much beyond this influence, synthesis, or rematerialization, because he actively engages in creating new representations in order to visualize all literary possibilities, particularly when applied to his concepts of the future and what it might hold. Simply put, he has a persistent penchant for innovation.

This includes not repeating literary formulas, instead favoring trailblazing tales on unusual topics as well as multifarious experimentations, ranging from obscure or noir fictional worlds, backward plots, totalizing novelistic ventures of crisscrossing stories, the novel within a novel framework, echoes of resurrected protagonists or monster characters, and expansive personifications of geographies (i.e., the Los Angeles River, Irvine, Texan towns, the Simons Brickyard Factory, and a realm that he refers to as "Lamex") to the role of plagues as an atavistic reminder of past human struggles that somehow reemerge in modern and future times. We are convinced that attending to these histories, distressing ventures, character constructs, personifications, and innovative representations best permits us to isolate and measure the force that propels his literature. It would be a fallacy to deem this force as purely residing in Morales' natural talent or coming from a deep craving to express himself, or to claim that it is solely sourced in the author's personal history as son of Mexican immigrants growing up in a relatively stable working-class environment yet witnessing the harsher and poorer realm of the surrounding East L.A. barrios. It cannot be necessarily found in any of these reasonably predictable sources, but rather stems from what he himself calls "not being in one particular place at one specific time . . . where I see myself traveling through the past, present and future. I refuse to be limited to space, time or topic. Writing should always be a site of complete and unconditional freedom. I have always been a maverick, nonconformist writer who prefers to work independently unencumbered by outside expectations. . . . I can be anywhere in the expanding sphere of knowledge and, most importantly, of the imagination and creativity."[3] Morales speaks here of a will to create otherworldly temporal chronicles and to fashion original work mirroring unlimited and universal experiences. Asserting the existence of a resolve to regard but differentiate himself from his predecessors and contemporaries, exploring head-on uncharted dimensions of time, place, content, and form, his words send a clear signal that one of the most reliable ways to isolate and measure the power propelling Moralesian literature is to chart his determination to be "nonconformist" and "unencumbered"—that is, to probe his craving to be free in aesthetic imagination and unencumbered by reader expectations or canonical categories.

Morales' unrepentant individualism invites an explicit affirmation that he may arguably be in a category all his own, though paradoxically within and somehow beyond the genus of Chicano/a letters. The latter is characterized by Ramón Saldívar (1990, 5) as not only provocative, demanding, and strategic but also as one of the most striking, ambiguous, and demanding literature forms produced in the United States (10). Such a characterization, we believe, accurately pertains to Morales' vast and varied writings. Yet there is another compelling categorization of Chicano/a literature pertinent to Morales' work, namely, Luis Leal's claim that such texts ought to readily connect with Mexico, Mexican culture, or various content- and aesthetic-based works related to that country (Rosales 2014, 115). This is more or less true. Leal highlights the "many connections" that organically exist between Chicano/a and Mexican literary production, contending that "Chicano literature's roots are in Mexican literature" (116). His interconnection premise might be categorical, perhaps even controversial, but it is apropos to Alejandro Morales—fulfilled and well substantiated by much of the latter's literary output. If Mexico is not always in the foreground of Morales' tales, it is indeed a significant part of the background, or a subtle reminder, and/or a combination thereof.

Case in point, he has actively sought validation and support from Mexican publishing houses for his literature. His first two works were both written in Spanish and published in Mexico City by Joaquín Mortiz—*Caras viejas y vino nuevo* in 1975 (translated a few years later by Max Martínez as *Old Faces and New Wine* and two decades later by Francisco Lomelí as *Barrio on the Edge*), and *La verdad sin voz* in 1979 (translated nearly a decade later by Judith Ginsberg as *Death of an Anglo*). For the latter, Morales chose the novel's title from a quote by twentieth-century Mexican writer, essayist, and political activist José Revueltas. In addition, *La verdad sin voz* makes direct and indirect references to contemporary Mexican history, specifically, to the Mexico City Tlatelolco student massacre in 1968, the various guerrilla actions of the 1970s, and the myriad institutional and political violence perpetrated by the Mexican government. Morales' third work was the novel *Reto en el paraíso*, a bilingual and complex book centering on the social, historical, cultural, geopolitical, and (especially) emotive dynamics of Mexicans who lost their land in old California. *Reto en el paraíso* focuses on the progeny of these Mexicans, and all the sociocultural and psychosexual dynamics at work in their much-fragmented Mexican American identities. *The Brick People*, his subsequent effort from 1988, tells a story of Mexican migration and immigration, highlighting Mexican small-town realties via the example of

Quiseo de Abasolo in the central Mexico state of Guanajuato. In the novel, this Mexican town serves as the origin of most of the immigrant workers who appear in its overarching narrative.

The publication of *The Rag Doll Plagues* (in 1992) significantly altered the narrative landscape of Morales' writings. It is a novel composed of three interdependent cross-temporal and cross-geographic books that range from (past) colonial Mexico to (present-day) Southern California, and then to a (future) Mexico City-Los Angeles monolithic geopolitical corridor. His subsequent and exceedingly intricate work *Waiting to Happen* (2001) depicts the conditions and dynamics of Mexico and its often-warped sociopolitical relationship with the United States, while his novella compilation *Pequeña nación* (translated from the 2005 Spanish version as *Little Nation and Other Stories* by Adam Spires in 2014) presents a minichronicle entitled "Quetzali" about an Aztec mother encountering the brutal effects of the conquest of Tenochtitlán.

His next novel, *The Captain of All These Men of Death* (2008), takes us back from this relationship to the Mexican homeland and into a Southern California cosmos, distinguishing itself for its unusual and unexpected exploration of the effects of tuberculosis as a disease that impacts the Mexican American community. And his most recent novel, *River of Angels* (2014), weaves an epic narrative of immigrant and then first- and second-generation Mexican American families who interact within the immediate space of the Los Angeles River. It is a novel that masterfully unveils the tapestry of cultures and histories that interface throughout time.

Finally, in his aforementioned novella collection (*Pequeña nación*) Morales presents new experimentations that push the limits of some of his narrative imagination: a moving narration (in "Pequeña nación") about a group of L.A. barrio women who find the social agency to safeguard their neighborhood; a story ("Los jardines de Versalles") about a French emigrant couple who become marginalized within their community; and a tale ("La penca") told from the point of view of *esperpento* or gross exaggeration, in which an artist imposes his sordid desires onto a painting of the venerated Virgin de Guadalupe. Though many other Chicano/a and Mexican American writers do, in fact, proficiently reference Mexico, Mexican culture, and various content- and aesthetic-based works of that country in their prose and poetry, Morales appears most consistent in doing so, indisputably fulfilling Leal's aforesaid criterion of an undeniable Mexican connection.

There is no doubt that Morales' exception within Chicano/a literature is steadily becoming recognized, as his multihued works continue to receive attention by the general reader and critical scrutiny by various scholars. To read and grasp the aesthetic ingredients as well as the experimental strategies of his tales can be a rewarding exercise for the reader. For the scholar, however, demonstrating the full force of Morales' inimitable oeuvre by analyzing its persistent willful figurations, tense narrations, mysterious characterizations and imagery, and allusive coded sociocultural ironies may seem a nearly unworkable task. Even so, it has been attempted in ways that have achieved a nicely critical and textual equilibrium up to this point. There are, for example, Marc García-Martínez's and Jesús Rosales' full-length critical tomes, *The Flesh-and-Blood Aesthetics of Alejandro Morales: Disease, Sex and Figuration* (2014) and *La narrativa de Alejandro Morales: Encuentro, historia y compromiso social* (1999), respectively. There is Max Martínez's aforementioned translation of *Caras viejas y vino nuevo*, Judith Ginsberg's rendering of *La verdad sin voz* into *Death of an Anglo*, and Francisco Lomelí's and Adam Spires' cited translations of *Caras viejas y vino nuevo* and *Pequeña nación*. There is moreover José Antonio Gurpegui's mini-Festschrift from 1996, peculiarly titled *Alejandro Morales: Fiction Past, Present, Future Perfect*, which also contains poetry and an essay by Morales. The new, comprehensive bibliography by Donaldo W. Urioste presented in this compendium is also an authentication of Morales' prolific five-decade long production in terms of assorted novels, a collection of novellas, sporadic short stories, and a book of poetry; it also includes interviews and numerous scholarly essays on Morales' work. Accolades from an ever-expanding academy of contemporary critical circles have accumulated notably, placing Morales at the zenith of Chicano/a novelists in recognition of his relentless aspiration to tell stories that others have not been so able or prepared to do. As evidence of such notoriety, Stanford University formally acquired his personal papers and manuscripts in 2008, establishing an Alejandro Morales archive. Far from retiring, as of this writing Morales finds himself working on three works at initial stages of development. One is a biographical novel tentatively entitled *Rainbow of Colors*, which takes place in Japan from the 1920s to the beginnings of World War II. A second one, tentatively entitled *The Place of the White Heron*, deals with Mexico City, as well as Los Angeles and related sites in the near future, while the third is an ambitious speculative work that challenges widespread scientific beliefs. He is also working on a collection of short stories, tentatively called *The Integrals*, as well as *Zapote Tree*, a volume of poetry. The full force of his production, and the production of scholarly criticism, is therefore steadily swelling; indeed, it is intensifying, and there seems no end in sight.

Regarding the scholarly criticism, all endeavors to unearth important insights related to this author's historical, rhetorical, narratological, and experimental innovations open up new thematic understandings and consideration of his work—work that, once again, must be addressed for its stylistic nonconformity, as Daniel Schreiner underscores, "the socio-critical prose and the literary techniques of the Californian writer and scholar Alejandro Morales are unique within the canon of Mexican American literature of the last decades. Morales's style and variety of themes differs significantly from other contemporary Chicana/o authors, influenced as it is by his education in Latin and world literatures at US universities. . . . Being positioned more or less outside the mystic-Marxist-Chicano nationalist discourse, Morales hence must be considered as an important international author of contemporary world literature who masters various techniques of style and narration" (2017, 171).

Morales' aesthetic more often than not frees itself from such discourse, especially from such predictable ideological or political binds. As Schreiner observes, Morales exemplifies a global artistic vantage point, producing narrative exegeses and enigmas that challenge international readers and scholars to decipher all of his stylistic codes of meaning and systemic patterns of word phrasings. In order to fully appreciate the nuances of the narrative intricacies in his work, it is necessary for readers and (particularly) scholars to keep in mind that Morales' literature—to apply Roland Barthes' phrase—is "coded to a very high degree" (Barthes and Duisit 1975, 265). Even then, it remains in certain ways mysterious, convoluted, and difficult to apprehend, sometimes so intensely metaphorical as to almost thwart any attempt to reliably judge or adequately explicate it. And yet, the respective chapters constituting this compendium seek to do just that.

Keeping the above in mind, we have attempted to capture and suggest the expansiveness, richness, intricacy, and far-reaching nature of Morales' literary imagination in this volume, which offers the most recent crop of scholarly perspectives on the subject. By "intricate," we mean how each chapter explores Morales' pages by focusing on a singular explicative phenomenon and then broadening the lens to a more panoptic perspective. We mean "far-reaching" both literary and figuratively, as we included in this collection not only critical articles that more or less cover Morales' novels and short stories but also critical articles from around the globe—produced by scholars from China, Spain, Canada, Romania, Italy and Greece, as well as by various specialists on the author's writings working in the United States. This assemblage of intra- and international critical articles comprises a nonchronological effort to probe the temperament and singular complexities of Alejandro Morales' literature. It is a scholarly and approachable presentation of diverse methodologies that elucidate and demystify his unrelenting literary labor. Though distinct, these perspectives intersect as they confront the content of his novels and short stories both as acute renderings of Mexican, Mexican American, and Chicano/a experiences and as ideological works that forge definitive statements about history, ethnicity, race, and our aberrant yet enduring human condition.

All in all, the thought-provoking chapters that follow ultimately form a united heuristic voice, with which we argue that *listening to* is how one best measures the full force, impact, and promise that have driven this unyielding author throughout his long lifetime of writing.

NOTES

1. For further explanation, see García-Martínez (2014).

2. See Francisco Lomelí's article in this compendium, "The Analogous Correspondence of an Extreme Poetics between Stanley Kubrick's *A Clockwork Orange* and Alejandro Morales' *Barrio on the Edge*."

3. See the chapter "A Dialogue with the Writer Alejandro Morales" in this compendium.

WORKS CITED

Acosta, Oscar Zeta. 1972. *The Autobiography of a Brown Buffalo*. San Francisco: Straight Arrow Books.

Anaya, Rudolfo A. 1972. *Bless Me, Ultima*. Berkeley, CA: TQS.

Arias, Ron. 1975. *The Road to Tamazunchale*. Reno, NV: West Coast Poetry Review.

Barthes, Roland, and Lionel Duisit. 1975. "An Introduction to the Structural Analysis of Narrative." *New Literary History* 6, no. 2 (Winter): 237–72.

Bloom, Harold. 1994. *The Western Canon: The Books and School of the Ages*. New York: Harcourt Brace.

Brito, Aristeo. 1976. *El diablo en Texas*. Tucson: Editorial Peregrinos.

García-Martínez, Marc. 2014. *The Flesh-and-Blood Aesthetics of Alejandro Morales: Disease, Sex, and Figuration*. San Diego: San Diego University Press.

Gurpegui, José Antonio. 1996. *Alejandro Morales: Fiction Past, Present, Future Perfect*. Tempe, AZ: Bilingual Press / Editorial Bilingüe.

Hinojosa, Rolando. 1973. *Estampas del valle y otras obras / Sketches of the Valley and Other Works*. Berkeley, CA: Editorial Justa Publications.

Márquez, Antonio C. 1995. "The Use and Abuse of History in Alejandro Morales's *The Brick People* and *The Rag Doll Plagues*." In *Alejandro Morales: Fiction Past, Present, Future Perfect*, edited by José Antonio Gurpegui, special issue, *Bilingual Review / Revista Bilingüe* 20, no. 3 (September–December 1995): 76–85.

Morales, Alejandro. 1981. *Old Faces and New Wine*. Translated by Max Martínez. San Diego: Maize Press.

———. 1988. *Death of an Anglo*. Translated by Judith Ginsberg. Tempe, AZ: Bilingual Press/ Editorial Bilingüe.

———. 1998. *Barrio on the Edge / Caras viejas y vino nuevo*. Translated by Francisco A. Lomelí. Tempe: Bilingual Press / Editorial Bilingüe.

———. 2014. *Little Nation and Other Stories*. Translated by Adam Spires. Houston: Arte Público Press.

Méndez, Miguel M. 1974. *Peregrinos de Aztlán*. Tucson: Editorial Peregrinos.

Rechy, John. 1977. *The Sexual Outlaw: A Documentary: A Nonfiction Account, with Commentaries, of Three Days and Nights in the Sexual Underground*. New York: Grove Press, 1977.

Ríos, Isabella. 1976. *Victuum*. Ventura, CA: Diana-Etna.

Rivera, Tomás. 1971. . . . *Y no se lo tragó la tierra* (. . . And the Earth Did Not Part). Berkeley, CA: Quinto Sol Publications.

Rosales, Jesús. 1999. *La narrativa de Alejandro Morales: Encuentro, historia y compromiso social*. New York: Peter Lang.

———. 2014. *Thinking En Español: Interviews with Critics of Chicana/o Literature*. Tucson: University of Arizona Press.

Saldívar, Ramón. 1990. *Chicano Narrative: The Dialects of Difference*. Madison: University of Wisconsin Press.

Sánchez, Phil. 1977. *Don Phil-O-Meno sí la mancha*. San Luis, CO: Sánchez.

Schreiner, Daniel. 2017. "The Once and Future Chicano—World Literatures between Intra-History and Utopian Vision: An Interview with Alejandro Morales." In *Symbolism 17: Latina/o Literature: The Trans-Atlantic and the Trans-American in Dialogue*, edited by Rüdiger Ahrens, Florian Kläger, and Klaus Stierstorfer, 171–84. Boston: Walter de Gruyter.

ONE / Submersion, Suffocation, and Entombment of the Mexican and Immigrant Body in *River of Angels*— Probing Figurations of Violence and Isolation / MARC GARCÍA-MARTÍNEZ

> Water is nebulous, it has no shape, you can pass your hand right through it; yet it can kill you. The force of such a thing is its momentum, its trajectory. What it collides with, and how fast.... —Margaret Atwood, *The Blind Assassin*, 2001

> ... it was discovered, when they attempted to remove him, that the water which had dripped upon him for ages from the crag above, had coursed down his back and deposited a limestone sediment under him which had glued him to the bed rock upon which he sat, as with a cement of adamant.... —Mark Twain, "Petrified Man," 1862

In Alejandro Morales' saga *River of Angels* (2014), the early twentieth-century conurbation of Los Angeles is at a precarious crossroads with its ethnic populace. The novel charts the winding, generations-long course of the Mexican American Rivers family in the growing and often volatile City of Angels. Encroaching tides and shifting currents of people from diverse cultural backgrounds and castes are transforming the restless city's milieu, spawning social anxieties, Aryan ideologies, and eugenics schemes, as well as economic competition and worker exploitation. Morales renders this transformation by constructing gripping metaphorical exemplars and connotative moments to reveal the ever-cruel toil of the subordinate working class, the assorted ruptures of overwhelming racism, and the heartrending dispossession of human dignity and life. *River of Angels* is hermeneutically structured by a series of harsh and evocative instances involving bodies that are submerged, entombed, lacerated, and liquified. These episodes involve dramatis personae who become encased in asphyxiating tombs. There are those who drown in the savage flow of river water or lose their mobility in paralyzing mud. Some end up collapsed and submerged in their own bodily fluids and waste, while others lie beaten, castrated, and fractured by forces outside their control. There are also characters who become engulfed both in indelible love and in savage odium. The aesthetic power of the novel—its remarkable capacity to secrete unexpected degrees of figuration and far-reaching emotional complexion into the overall reading experience—lies in this progression of metaphorical exemplars and connotative moments.[1]

One of the more emotive, horrific moments in this progression involves the entombment of a "mongrel," "retarded," "docile," and "stupid" unnamed Mexican worker, buried alive in a pit of smothering concrete (86). Preparing foundations for an immense water tank facility for the wealthy railroad entrepreneur Samuel P. Huntington's personal cattle herd on the edge of Los Angeles' renowned Griffith Park, Mexican workers are measuring and pouring copious amounts of fast-drying concrete into massive forms. As they measure and pour, the workers cautiously position themselves in and around the ponderous machinery. Suddenly, calamity strikes, the aesthetic overtone of which exposes the tragic futility of monolingualism alongside the disposability and disappearance of helpless immigrants:

> Ernest, the foreman and several young Mexican workers watched as two men squatted under the huge scoop shovel to check the locks. Ernest could see only one of the men, while the other man checked the lock on the other side of the scoop. The man whom Ernest could see signaled that his side was secure. Ernest immediately ordered the foreman to carry on the pour. While the crane slowly lifted the scoop, shouting broke out from the far side. Ernest did not understand Spanish. He ignored the workers' screams and motioned to the crane operator to position the fully loaded scoop over the pit.... At that instant Ernest saw a worker hanging by his arm, trapped in the latch release lock that was almost fully opened. The cement started to pour, the worker's arm freed as he screamed, falling to the bottom of the foundation. Five hundred pounds of fast-drying Portland cement entombed the Mexican worker. The crane shut down. Silence fell on the site. (86–87)

Ernest makes a hasty choice "between deadline and life," an impulsive decision that causes the luckless Mexican worker to be horrifically buried alive. The reader's reaction certainly must run the range from quiet surprise that this could happen to outright shock that it did and in this particular manner. Yet with this incident Alejandro Morales pushes the reader further past their surprise or shock, forcing them to grasp its savage irony. As the poor laborer's entombed body becomes one with the molten mineral grave, it fatefully becomes one with the edifice to be completed within the affluent landscape. The man is no doubt also buried evermore in the minds and memories of his fellow laborers, and any individual or collective taphephobia they already suffer as a result of their jobs must be amplified by this atrocious incident.

Such an incident is rife with Moralesian overtones of near-homicidal injustice, reverberating with a mournful emotional dimension. Resisting some reductive example of racial discrimination or clichéd antipathy (such as a landlord wrongfully evicting their ethnic tenant or some inflamed gang street brawl), Morales creates a more sophisticated episodic connotative device that resonates deep inside the reader. This device undercuts Ernest the foreman's apparent matter-of-fact indifference toward his drowned, crushed laborer. From this we perceive not just the author's intimation of our woeful mortality but his verification of how wealth entitlement and business economics converge to create hardships for the cross-racial classes in his intensifying literary setting of Los Angeles:

> Everyday at the lumber yard and at the construction sites a parade of mixed-race workers, mostly Mexicans, reported to work. Ernest had to consider the budget, had to deal with the reality of business economics. The only way he could make a substantial profit was to employ Mexicans eager to work for him in dangerous working conditions and for substandard wages. . . . He saw his worker at the last second. There was nothing he could have done; it was over in seconds. Ernest's thoughts came fast. He looked up to see the crane operator still staring at him, now surrounded by the Mexicans who had shut down the crane. Ernest looked down into the pit. He took his hat off and ran his hand through his hair, walked off the scaffolding, got to his car thinking that the job was simply too difficult for some men. (Morales 2014, 86–87)[2]

The death of this Mexican laborer is not just a denoted case in point of occupational hazard. It is a transfixing metaphorical death associated with inferior human worth, with the impossibility of shared sensibilities between overseer and drudge, with affluence that figuratively and literally builds on the corpses of an ethnic stratum. Through this metaphorical lens we witness the sacrifice of "mongrel," "retarded," "docile," "stupid," and "foolish" souls for a greater purpose that in turn parallels the virtual death of the indigenous Los Angeles River by the ensuing erection of its concrete tomb. Morales writes in the novel of powerful interests striving "to bury, disfigure, and control the Los Angeles River . . . to smother, oppress the natural waterways" (xi), and those same interests sadly do the same to mortal lives. The disfiguring entombment of the hard-working Mexican worker connotes cultural humiliation and exploitation to the extent that he is permanently prevented from ever openly speaking his name in the story and from ever overcoming the tenacious caste boundaries imposed on him by industrialist forces building all around the venerable Southern California city.

The tragedy is also brilliantly allusive, for this harrowing moment in the narrative evokes a powerful echo of a bygone era, namely that of gruesome superstition and subjugation in the ancient legendary Japanese ritual of *hitobashira*. Known as the "human pillar" (Frédéric 2005, 337), "person-post" (Mitchelhill 2003, 8), "human foundation" (Blake 1902, 586), or "man-pillar" (Munro 1908, 640), hitobashira was by all accounts a ritual that necessitated a human being buried alive directly within or right underneath solid complex edifices such as large-scale dams, castles, fortresses, and especially bridges. William Aston's *Shinto: The Way of the Gods* (2013) explains that "there are several indications of the existence of this practice in still older times. Human sacrifices to river-Gods have already been mentioned. We have seen that when a Mikado died a number of his attendants were buried alive round his tomb, from which it may be inferred that considerations of humanity would not have prevented similar sacrifices to the Gods. Cases are also recorded of men being buried alive in the foundations of a bridge, a castle, or an artificial island. These were called *hito-bashira*, or human pillars" (29).

Noritake Tsuda's 1918 exploration of human sacrifices in Japan corroborates Aston's report:

> The tradition of human sacrifices is also concerned with the building of large bridges. For example, in the *Yasiitomi-ki*, a diary of the fifteenth century, a famous tradition is contained, called Nagara-no Hito-bashira (*hitobashira*, "human pillar"). According to the tradition, a woman who was carrying a boy on her back was caught while she was passing along the

river Nagara, and was buried at the place where a large bridge was then to be built (763).... The Hito-bashira or "human pillar" traditions are always connected with some important enterprise and mostly with water. In large enterprises human lives are often lost in the work itself, therefore in some cases such loss of human life would have been looked upon as a human sacrifice. (763–67)

It is generally accepted that these sacrificial beings included debased servants, sick or indigent women, and as one might expect, actual hapless laborers constructing those very edifices. According to Munro, "under the name of *Hitobashira* (man-pillar) the practice of human sacrifice by burying alive at the foundations of buildings and especially bridges to ensure their stability by placating the soil or river god, was prevalent in Japan" (641). Aston emphasizes that the hitobashira practice was a bold offering of souls for a greater purpose—not so much outwardly commercial or economic as strictly religious. This ritual practice disturbingly operated as an appeasing "prayer" to supernatural deities to protect against physical disaster or attack on the newly constructed works (Tsuda 1918, 763–64). Running counterpoint to construction or creation, hitobashira is paradoxical in all respects. Given its dependence on death, this so-called human foundation is contrastive to creation, and with regards to the Mexican worker's sacrificial entombment it connotes a pure irony as Keller's construction site undeniably becomes a destruction site.[3]

In crafting his fictional twentieth-century version of the savage rite of hitobashira, Morales launches this irony squarely at the reader. Remarkably, there is a nonfictional twentieth-century version providing a measure of alarming realism to the episode in the novel. In 1944 a dangerous conflagration ignited in a number of subterranean passageways of the Miike Plant Coal Mine in Japan. Many of the miners at the plant were actually Chinese conscript laborers. In order to shield unmined coal in adjoining tunnels, the mine company directors ordered the erection of a huge cement wall to plug the path of the fire and prevent a detrimental financial loss. The Chinese laborers—dispensable lives in contrast to valuable ore—were entombed and buried alive. Referred to as the "Miike Coal Mine Hitobashira" (Kozaki 1973), it was a death sentence imposed on those ill-fated workers by the dictatorial industrialist forces leading the Miike Plant Coal Mine.[4]

For our purposes, both the poor Mexican worker's body and the draftee Chinese workers' bodies are interred in a dialectical space entrapped by industrial labor and corporate plantation values. This dialectic can never resolve itself, for within the cement and unforgiving earth the fictional worker and nonfictional coal miners become immobile statues incapable of ever thinking or speaking again. As statues they posses no agency, effectively metamorphosed from a once-dynamic animal state into a static mineral one. They bear out Ollivier Dyens' claim that the body is at all times tenuous and susceptible to natural and unnatural forces beyond its control. In *Metal and Flesh—The Evolution of Man* (2001), Dyens stresses how the body can be readily transformed into any figure or shape due to "its materiality and its essence, hav[ing] no absolute integrity, being nothing more than malleable and flexible material" (58). This reinforces a poignant theme in *River of Angels*, namely that Mexicans are a malleable and dispensable utensil used in certain settings toward certain entrepreneurial ends. Whatever justifications exist for the gruesome hitobashira, whatever its cultural-corporeal abstractions, it registers the existence and effect of a powerful form of caste schism that Morales develops throughout his novel. As such, the *River of Angels* becomes a compelling social critique and literary grievance concerning a schism in early twentieth-century Western society, in which *el cuerpo de la gente* toils, dies, and then transforms and disappears for the benefit of purported superior beings and loftier economic purposes.

Further addressing this schism, or rift, along with how the corpus is vulnerable to the smothering doctrines of superiority, *River of Angels* forces its reader to witness a gruesome lynching and castration. Occurring amid an enveloping and choking mélange of watery mud and bloody cement, these gruesome acts are enacted upon Albert Rivers, a young, bright, hard-working Mexican American and devoted lover of the young German American girl Louise Keller. Their passionate cross-ethnic/cross-racial/cross-class relationship, marriage, and eventual progeny cause severe dissension among headstrong Keller family members—most notably Louise's incensed uncle Philip. As a steadfast Aryan supremacist he despises Albert, considering him as nothing more than an "mixed lower-race . . . social undesirable" (181). The culmination of this racist hatred results in Albert's grisly beating and laceration at the hands of Philip and his outraged fellow sectarians:[5]

> Three faucets leaked badly, dripping water onto the small concrete platforms in front of each water basin. He reached over to the first faucet and turned it shut. His hand moved over to the second and turned, when a heavy object struck his back and knocked him down to the cement slab. His body rolled

to one side, only to be punched and kicked from many directions. Sharp sudden pain entered his ribs for an instant, shutting down his breathing. Albert's hand scraped mud from his eye that had closed after the blow to his back. A few more sharp kicks to his chest and shoulder brought him around on his back where he could not scream, not say a word. (215)

Against an unambiguous watery backdrop, Albert's body is knocked down and violently shoved from side to side, pummeled, and suffocated. Like Ernest's Mexican worker, Albert becomes a voiceless being, unaided and plunged into darkness. It is here that Morales suddenly veers his novel's established third-person descriptive narration head-first toward a hallucinatory free-indirect discourse. He unveils the continuation of the Mexican American's thrashing by blending the voices of the enraged Aryans with the thoughts of the helpless Albert, resulting in a remarkable narrative singularity. Weaving a sensuous, kaleidoscopic rhetoric that teems with eddies of hate and rapid violence, as well as overlapping currents of voices and thought, Morales stitches together numerous elliptical caesuras to unite the discourses and allow for the dynamic passage of time and movement between word and action. It is an extraordinary passage that must be considered in its full length:

> Albert tried to respond, help me, he thought, maybe three, four voices screamed, hands grabbed at his body, ripping his shirt off . . . back to Mexico . . . pulling at his shoes, his pants down . . . half-breed . . . a knife cut through his pants . . . the belt . . . warm liquid, blood covered his arms . . . Albert felt for his nose . . . he sensed laughter . . . flat nose against his mouth . . . you won't fuck . . . the voices dragged his body half way off the cement slab . . . white girl again . . . voices grabbed his legs . . . a voice cut off Albert's underwear . . . this knife on my hogs . . . laughter . . . loud laughter . . . Albert twisted his shoulders violently . . . get up, get up . . . several hands fondled his genitals . . . it all off . . . only his balls . . . just like your pigs . . . the voices broke out in great laughter . . . a celebration . . . his balls . . . pain . . . terrible pain . . . he lost his breath . . . his hands clutched his penis . . . blood came from below . . . he screamed . . . the voices kicked him again and again . . . you ain't going to sin anymore boy . . . no more mongrel moron children . . . he won't run . . . just to make sure . . . several boards crushed a knee . . . opened his eyes . . . only mud . . . crawled through the mud . . . pushed damp mud between his legs . . . cool relief . . . under the leaky pipes . . . dripping

water valves ... stuffed mud into his crotch ... screamed ... screamed
again ... mud-smeared eyes widened ... felt light ... floating away ...
short breath ... breathing ... pain faded ... into mud. (215–16)

Morales strategically inserts these chilling, seemingly empty caesuras to signify a sense of the quick-moving, lung-collapsing, bone-crushing, skin-tearing, and near-deafening vortex of being beaten. They also suggest a sense of being engulfed and drowning in the fast, pre-concrete Los Angeles River rapids. In the most ferocious rapids there is at all times a boiling interplay between the velocity of the water, the surface of the riverbed, the shape of the channel, and the amount of mineral or arboreal debris present. There is a dynamic interplay of the disoriented senses of hearing, seeing, smelling, and touching. Morales captures in this passage the act of falling victim to harsh water forces, replicating what Bell and Lyall describe as being thrust into a "dynamic" and "accelerated" violent terrain. In *Accelerated Sublime*, they consider how many landscapes maintain exceedingly "kinetic" and "immersive" properties that involve rapidity, flow, steep falls, rises, declinations, rush, and power (2002, 60). Bell and Lyall classify the relationship between the body and the landscape as "dangerous, not only because of the forces brought to bear on the body ... but also because dynamic systems are inherently unstable" (61).

This corresponds both in rhetorical terms and in meaning to poor Albert's beating, for his is an episode ingeniously crafted to fling the reader into the blend of sequence and simultaneity; we are tossed into the whirlwind ferocity of elemental liquidity. This ferocious beating reminds us that though a water current has a sequence and progression, in its uncontrollable destructive state all movement or directive flows become haphazardly overlapping and simultaneous. Thus, Morales skillfully transcribes the multidimensional phenomenon of liquid force onto a flat two-dimensional page—an aesthetic folding technique or rhetorical origami transforming his book's pallid sheet of paper into a bloody-muddy dimensional form. Morales' endeavor to simultaneously represent Albert's fluidic bodily ooze, his mental sensations, and emotional dynamism is successful beyond doubt. The lengthy passage plays with our sense of time and sequence, transcending both movement *and* moment within the slowing overlapping action. Albert Rivers cannot escape. He is rupturing and drowning.

Such a bodily-mental rhetorical interplay of a hatred that injures and drowns, of the disorientation and resultant dynamism of chaotic movement, is affirmed by an analogue from Ambrose Bierce's "An Occurrence at Owl Creek Bridge"

([1890] 1989). In this tale, through inner fantasy, the forsaken prisoner of war Peyton Farquhar escapes a hostile Union lynching party and firing squad by dropping into a river. Dodging bullets and enduring punishing currents, he is swept away by harsh rapids from homicidal men who seek to catch him and hang him for his seemingly illicit deeds:

> Keen, poignant agonies seemed to shoot from his neck downward through every fiber of his body and limbs. These pains appeared to flash along well-defined lines of ramification and to beat with an inconceivably rapid periodicity. They seemed like streams of pulsating fire heating him to an intolerable temperature. As to his head, he was conscious of nothing but a feeling of fullness—of congestion. These sensations were unaccompanied by thought. The intellectual part of his nature was already effaced; he had power only to feel, and feeling was torment. He was conscious of motion. . . . he swung through unthinkable arcs of oscillation, like a vast pendulum. Then all at once, with terrible suddenness . . . a frightful roaring was in his ears, and all was cold and dark. (13–14)

Bierce's and Morales' stories share thematic configurations of sociocultural conflict, loathing, and warped ideological superiority. They both reveal how contradictory currents collide (an Aryan force hunting down Mexicans, a Union Army force hunting down Confederates), the way undercurrents of time get distorted through trauma, and how those abstract and elemental forces pummel and play havoc on the human senses. Peyton's and Albert's capacity to think is compromised, so that they can now pretty much only feel. What the reader witnesses in these portrayals are brilliantly explicative representations of the blunt-force simultaneity and disarray that accompany a lynching (in Peyton's case it is a literal and inevitable hanging). Yet Morales differentiates himself from his predecessor by taking us further, to the extent that his description of Albert's execution also becomes its form. He formally portrays on the page—that is, folds onto it—a rippling psychosomatic rhetoric that is *broken-up* (as are Albert's skin and bones), *convoluted* (as are Albert's awareness and feelings), *continuous* (as are the tortuous beatings and insults to Albert's body), *overlapping* (as are Albert's sensations and the voices of his hangmen), and *flowing* (as are the muddy water and Albert's blood).

These rhetorical patterns, however, go further still as Morales gathers all the forces brought to bear on Albert's body and describes its beating through not so much an aural but a verbal onomatopoeia. Equal to and yet beyond Bierce's word patterns, Morales imitates the prevailing "kinetic" and "immersive" movements and senses of the terrible racist assault itself. We may discern his rhetorical arrangement in Bruce Dean Willis' terms as a "kind of radical onomatopoeia, expanded beyond the rage of mere sound such that the word is the image" (2013, 11). In the cited passage from *River of Angels*, word formations act as structural imagery exposing the anguish or vertigo of the Mexican corpus hit by a devastating force of Anglo-Aryan odium. Our author summons all his innovative power to essentially mimic the "occurrence" that he describes, evoking near drowning and suffocation, thereby making said description much more interactive and intense for the increasingly uneasy reader.

This metaphorical interconnection of life, landscape, and senses, of the feeling of being beaten, buried, and submerged, is profound. Ironically, Albert studies design engineering and construction at a prominent local university, but Morales twists his character out of order, deconstructs him and violently submerges him in the elements so that his bodily integrity is disintegrated to the point that he is virtually liquefied—or in Dyens' terms, rendered (59) into his surroundings. The effects of xenophobic antipathy are figuratively measured through the lessening of bodily and landscape cohesion and through an image of sorrowful disintegration. What is more, as Albert's anguished body is disintegrated among the elements it lies upon (and within), his body in turn objectively measures the desperate moral disintegration of the Aryans themselves. This collision-disintegration metaphor, where the Mexican body is battered by Anglo force, richly correlates to Arturo Islas' *The Rain God* (1984)—specifically, to the character of Felix, whose fear of desert canyon sandstorms always "made him feel buried alive" (136). At one point in Islas' tale, Felix is in fact buried alive, not by some literal sandstorm but by forces of fear and hatred. Driving in the desert with no storm in sight, Felix tries to seduce a young white midwestern soldier from a nearby camp:

"Ah don't think ah want to go into the canyon," the boy said.

"Oh, come on, only for a few minutes. It's real nice in there."

Felix took the boy's silence as an indication of consent and he began the slow drive up the canyon road. . . .

Felix said and put his hand on the boy's knee. The boy sat rigidly on his side staring at the windshield and not the landscape. Felix sensed his preoccupation with the hand as it stroked his thigh.

"Don't do that," the boy said in a quiet, even tone.

"Don't be scared. I'm not going to hurt you. Let's have some . . ." The blows began before he finished. They were a complete surprise to him, and the anger behind them stunned and paralyzed him. He began to laugh as he warded off the attack. . . .

"Hey, come on. I was just kidding." He was vaguely aware that he spoke through a mouthful of stones. It did not occur to him to struggle or to fight back. He forced his door open and fell to the ground, kicked sharply in the kidneys from behind. (136–37)

Here Felix is also being beaten to death. In the story, he sexually exploits young men who have entered the country illegally to work, requiring them to have "physical examinations" that he tenderly performs when they first arrive at their jobs. Yet Felix is now paying for these manipulations with his life. Like Morales and Bierce, Islas intermingles previous elements of a character's life, the terrain they fall upon, their senses, and the robust liquid element. Islas' scene, in other words, depicts the occurrence of being trampled, choked, and submerged into the rough desert sand and into abstract fluidity:

The stones in his mouth looked like teeth as he spat them out, and he turned to avoid the blows to his back. The boy stood over him. The kicking continued and he felt great pain in his groin and near his heart. Then his mouth was full of desert and then it was not. He could no longer see the boy. The pain in his loins and along his side seemed distant . . . He tasted the dust. . . .

The biting ache began to recede and it seemed odd to be falling from a great height while lying on the desert floor. The sound of walking on stones puzzled him because he was surrounded by water. Its reflection and the luster of the boots flashed before him in an irregular, rhythmic motion . . . Felix had time to be afraid before he heard his heart stop.

The desert exhaled as he sank into the water. (137–38)

Islas describes Felix fighting "irregular, rhythmic" motions and currents, "falling from a great height" that does not exist in physical actuality. His description captures the aforesaid violent dynamics of landscape and force and the resulting disorientation of a sensual vertigo. Though one could reasonably argue that the frightened young man was defending himself from Felix's sexual assault, he nonetheless murderously pummels a pitiable man into the tough desert topography. Laying there, Felix transitorily feels enveloped in a bizarre runny realm. This metaphorical illustration of landscape and senses, of the perception of being enshrouded and submerged, signifies both consequence and confluence of sociocultural conflict, clashing identities, and revulsion against the sexual, political, or cultural Other.

While Bierce's prisoner of war and Islas' sexually conflicted man die on the spot, Albert in fact survives the beating and castration, if only barely.[6] Like Felix, Albert is not prepared for the attack. Like Felix, he finds himself stunned and suffocating within the filthy mineral setting. Albert's unbelievably vile assault, however, is taken to a higher level than Felix's. Alex submerges into something fluid and viscous, ending up swollen, broken, and cut, but it is only as he lays stricken at hospital that the reader comes to understand the increasingly figurative enormity of his assault:

> Mr. Rivers, your son was severely beaten. He sustained a broken nose, several broken ribs and his right knee is swollen to the point that we cannot assess the damage. And he suffered a glancing blow to the head. Whatever they hit him with struck him mostly in the back . . .
>
> Mr. Rivers, the cowards that did this to your son, Albert, also attempted to castrate him . . .
>
> They tried, but they did a bad job of it. There's no other way to say this but to tell you that your son lost one of his testicles. The other one is slightly damaged. They cut one testicle out and slightly cut the other one. (2014, 219)

Albert Rivers thus becomes a particular text to be read in the context of passive Mexican ethnicity and violent white dominion. He is a character-maneuver employed by Morales to exemplify the brutal dialectical collision between these two entities. In this fictional story, just as they do in actual reality, Aryans hold an excessively credulous belief in their own superiority (peruse pages 181 through 183 in the novel). They maintain a widely held and near-superstitious belief in causation leading to unwanted consequence that must be stopped by any means: the miscegenation and wholly damaging dilution of their race *and* their city by lesser bloodlines.

The attack on poor Albert is a culmination of these pairings and conflicts, of these vicious contests for control and separation. For Morales, lynching and castration are a legible aesthetic-rhetorical trope for the reality of racial confrontation and struggle within Los Angeles. In employing it in the novel he substantiates Melissa Stein's principle that "lynching and castration served the same ideological and practical functions: intimidation, containment, and social control" (2015, 239). In *Measuring Manhood—Race and the Science of Masculinity*, Stein demonstrates how this manner of assault powerfully symbolizes white supremacy in its agenda to thwart crossbreed, immigrant, biologically inferior, and low-morality peoples (239). What Stein claims and how she claims it are apposite to Morales' novel. When the unreasonable Aryan mob cuts Albert, the victim clutches at his bloody genitals, screaming until he loses his breath. He is punished by the mob for his immorality ("you ain't going to sin anymore boy"), kicked in the groin to thwart copulation ("you won't fuck"), and thrashed to the point of permanently stopping his ability to generate "mongrel moron children." Preventing procreation, putting a violent halt to the ability to have sex in any form and with anyone, does not stem merely from a general "anxiety" about the ethnic body; rather, according to Catherine Clinton and Michele Gillespie it is a control mechanism over what they fittingly call a "bonded labor force" (1997, 82). Though considered in respect to ownership, sex, generation, and cost burden, Clinton and Gillespie stress that castration is ultimately a "means of retribution and punishment" (78). It is a sick, hostile rite connected to a certain division of people, by a certain division of people, and woefully done to a certain division of people.

So we must consider these connotative maneuvers of lynching, punishing assault, and bloody slicing as enhanced Moralesian attempts to provoke his reader. Such attempts not only succeed at doing so—they underscore a wholesale ethnic, political, geo-cultural (and in some respects, sexual) rivalry taking place in the city of Los Angeles. This rivalry reflects past outcries over the supposed threat to pure American homogeneity by the representative dirty Mexican (Gómez-Quiñones 1994, 65), and as we have seen, the novel chronicles this with a variety of figuratively laden connotative scenarios. The drama composed in *River of Angels* is real, and its author prompts the reader to recall that many industries like Ernest's construction company historically sought to maximize profits by bringing in Mexican labor, even though there were countervailing efforts to eventually suppress, deport, and repatriate the migrants (Gómez-Quiñones 65). Indeed, the novel reminds us how immigrants were "forced into cycles of movement based on their economic need that place them into a bare life that renders them invisible with respect to rights then marks them as criminals whose bodies need to be eradicated from the land while they are also being sought for their labor" (Manzella 2018, 157). Such efforts to eradicate the Mexican body are darkly portrayed in *River of Angels*, whether by unsafe working conditions, by indifferent and dismissive attitudes as seen with the smothered and entombed unnamed Mexican worker, or by hateful racist violence represented by the attack on poor Albert.

The connotative depictions of the submerged, flattened, and wounded racial-ethnic body within elemental textures of tough cement, oozing immersive mud, drips and splotches of water, and an enveloping blood are powerful and revealing. But in the novel these depictions pertain to others as well. For instance, further indications of being emblematically beaten, broken, submerged, bloody, and delirious are unearthed when the "mean" and "hard-headed" Philip Keller falls victim to the 1929 stock market crash (145). Badly hurt by this nationwide disaster, something awful befalls this terrible character before he is found by his nephew Ernest, face-down in in his bedroom. Cautiously, Ernest comes upon his uncle, who was somehow assailed and injured and is now lying in vomit, blood, shit, and urine:

> Ernest walked into the bedroom. Uncle Philip, wearing a shirt and nothing else, lay face down in the middle of his bloodied bed. The stench was even more repulsive. At the side of the bed on an expensive Indian rug, Ernest found a pan half-filled with urine and lumps of feces.
>
> "Uncle Philip," Ernest called in a whisper to his uncle, but there was no response. He moved closer. "Uncle Philip?" He lay in a puddle of vomit and urine.
>
> Ernest turned him over. What he saw horrified him. His uncle's face was unrecognizable. His left ear was hideously enlarged, his nose flattened, his eyes swollen shut, his lips split open. But he was breathing. (146)

This moment is a flawlessly expressive one and not devoid of striking imagery. It is disturbing to read. There is nonetheless metaphorical import as Keller lies (deservedly) immobile, drenched in his own fluids—an anguished living carcass altered into a trodden and twisted pile of goo. Bodily transformation of this sort once again verifies Dyens' idea regarding the materiality of the body, how our frail physical being at all times remains malleable and ultimately transformable (58). While we acknowledge this frightening scene as an exquisitely connotative moment, we become sensitized not just to its visuality but to the manner in which Keller's puddling excrement, vomit, and blood associate with abject violence, failure, and isolation—a violence, failure, and isolation that he is plainly drowning in:

> Ernest jumped on the bed, crouched behind him and wrapped his arms under Uncle Philip's armpits. His uncle yelled when Ernest pulled him up. Ernest was finally able to button the shirt and put a jacket over Uncle Philip's shoulders. With a soaked cloth he gently wiped the sweat from Uncle Philip's face. His uncle winced with pain every time Ernest dabbed at the crusted blood. Ernest stopped when a trickle of blood ran from a deep cut on his cheek. Ernest noticed that many deep cuts covered Uncle Philip's face, as if his face had been slashed repeatedly with a sharp object. (147)

River of Angels aesthetically bonds Keller's body to forces of intolerance, fear, class, race, geography, and insensitive business. Morales superimposes figurative imagery and connotative devices onto these forces as follows: (1) Keller is fully immersed in his hideous racist beliefs, so he is portrayed suffocating in his own vomit and feces; (2) Keller is full of uncontainable anxiety and fear, so he is portrayed incontinent and submerged in his own urine and blood; (3) the man reeks of a nasty dogma, so he is portrayed surrounded by and emitting a stinking odor; (4) he is a sadistic Aryan bully who is guilty of beating others to a bruised and bloody condition, so he is portrayed beaten, bruised, and blanketed in blood; (5) Keller is a chauvinistic and sometimes ruthless businessman, so he is portrayed in the very state of the early twentieth-century municipal and national economy—that is, warped, slashed, and flattened.

Thus, as he lies there petrified and secluded in his filthy bed, Philip Keller becomes an allegorical personification on the written page. What is more, he presents a lesson in the dynamics of choking and liquefaction. To choke is to be deprived of air, to become constricted and obstructed by an intractable force. With liquefaction, a solid is made liquid in response to an applied stress or shock. Whether caused by an acute collapse of solidity, a drowning, or subsequent necrosis of landscape and bodily structure, liquefaction and choking operate as emblematic constructs in Morales' novel to portray the wholesale breakdown of a guilty man's mind and body. If we liken this to "A Subtle Plague" by Alejandro Murguía (1992), we grasp a comparative portrayal of the breakdown of one man's avarice and his contemptable chauvinistic business tactics. Murguía's character John Shaker, a corporate developer long coveting the sacred homeland ranch of the very old Mexican citrus farmer José García, takes over all of the parcels surrounding García's land, Rancho Maravilla. Shaker's eventual takeover of Rancho Maravilla occurs after the old farmer's mysterious death. Arrogantly inspecting his newly acquired property, Shaker inventories what must be discarded and torn down to make way for the inevitable condominiums to be built. He walks all around the Mexican farmer's home, where his sense of smell is assaulted by an unbearable hidden force:

> While standing on the porch admiring the site, Shaker noticed the overpowering army of smells assaulting him from within the house. The stink of pungent Mexican cigarettes permeated the walls; the smell of grease and chilies and jerked deer meat stormed from the kitchen, and emanating from the bedroom came the sad odor of loneliness and stale farts. (322)

The horrendous smells entering Shaker's nose start to grow into something more material. With every step he takes from the porch and inward through the rows of citrus trees, he is overtaken by an odd "white dust" made entirely, he realizes, of "minute, triangular-shaped white flies" (322). Growing thicker, the wave smothers Shaker, blinding his eyes and clogging his nose. Running back and forth in the yard and then into the García house, frightened and panicked, the selfish developer finds himself trapped. The flies, along with a hurricane wind forming in that space, force him to flee from what he realizes must be a curse. Making a desperate rush to escape the ghostly force into his parked car he descends into more dust:

> By the time he reached his car, the white powder was up to his waist and the door handles were buried and impossible to reach. He flailed at the mounds of white but succeeded only in stirring up the flies. Turbulent clouds of white rose up against him and clogged his ears, blinded his eyes, choked his throat. Shaker stumbled through the moonlit orchards in a blind rage—howling, spitting, choking, and lost . . . they found Shaker lying in a mud puddle face down in the turkey water. A grotesque, agonized expression of terror twisted his stiff features. (324)

Murguía executes a figuration of the collision of class struggle, personal ownership, and unfriendly business—and a haunting retribution for the contempt one character in his story displays for another family's venerable abode. Undeniably, there is pain in José García losing Rancho Maravilla to Shaker, so the author creates a fantastic suffocating vengeance for its takeover. This pain is represented by the elemental textures of a choking matter, in addition to an encasing muddy water that creates image-driven connotations of a justifiable punishment.[7] Still, though "A Subtle Plague" also employs the device of a man found face-down in a puddle, and though both Shaker and Philip suffer artistic measures of the same relative fate (isolated, in agony, smothered, face-down, punished, and discovered by others), it is Morales' dramatic flesh-and-blood details that augment the explicit racist ethos of Philip Keller.

Unlike Murguía with Shaker, Morales highlights not so much Keller's overly avaricious or tyrannically self-seeking traits but rather his Aryan racist character—one that despises nonwhites, the members of the Mexican Rivers family in particular. An intolerant xenophobe, he angrily thinks of the Riverses as low and essentially "mongrel." We have already observed how, when his niece Louise falls in love with Albert, Keller fiercely attempts to prevent the two families from ever coming together by directing wild rapids of aggression and violence against Albert. In doing so, Keller shields both himself and his heirs from proximate racial mixing and degenerative social flux. His aggressive hatred for Albert is both as silent as a shallow brook and as savage as a river torrent, setting up significant tensions and wholesale dissension within the novel as a whole. All of his words and deeds, in fact, directly lead to significant strife and resulting tragedies. It is remarkable, then, that in this scene Uncle Philip Keller himself becomes the ugly, paralyzing, foul-smelling manifestation of strife and tragedy.[8]

The reader thus registers both revulsion and curiosity at seeing him laying glued to his bed, at witnessing him submerged and nearly drowned in his own swollen flesh, blood, and waste matter. Is this the result of a savage beating meted out by his fellow Aryans for failing to tear down Albert and Louise's bond? Was the assault committed by despicable bankers, cruel mobsters, or merciless creditors to whom he owed money when the market crashed? Some common wretched home-invading robbers, perhaps? Did Uncle Philip perhaps do this to himself as self-flagellation or maybe an abortive suicide? Is this an act of revenge? The reader will come to agree that the reason for the beating, exactly who did it and how, is not made clear by Morales. What is clear is that a hypergraphic flesh-and-blood moment such as this is, in a way, a microcosm of the initially seeping, then overrunning effects of the 1929 stock market crash and the resulting national depression.[9]

Indeed, the crash was earth-shattering and far-reaching, fascinatingly described by historian Howard Zinn with this curiously relevant diction:

> The capitalist system was by its nature unsound: a system driven by the one overriding motive of corporate profit and therefore unstable, unpredictable, and blind to human needs. The result of all that: permanent depression for

many of its people, and periodic crises for almost everybody. Capitalism, despite its attempts at self-reform, its organization for better control, was still in 1929 a sick and undependable system. [. . .] After the crash, the economy was stunned, barely moving. Over five thousand banks closed and huge numbers of businesses, unable to get money, closed too. Those that continued laid off employees and cut the wages of those who remained, again and again. (2001, 387)

Zinn's progression of select words attach fittingly to Philip Keller's beaten, bleeding, and prostrate self. The historian employs such evocative words as "unsound," "driven," "unstable," "blind," "crises," "sick," "stunned, barely moving," "unable" and "cut . . . again and again" (387). In the novel Keller is a singularly *driven* ideological man, mentally *unsound* as well as emotionally *unstable*, somewhat *blind* to the unstoppable realities of the multicultural realm of Southern California. He is deep in fiscal and personal *crises*, physically *sick*, lying there on the bed *stunned, barely moving*, obviously *unable* to protect himself—and most assuredly and brutally *cut again and again*. Thus, how the historian Zinn literally describes the event of the market crash coincides with how the novelist Morales describes the event of Keller's near-death state. In both Zinn's representative rhetoric and in Morales' representative imagery the crashed economy *and* the crushed man become emblematically connected in a most amazing way. Such is the unmistakable relevance of Alejandro Morales' well-conceived, innovative literature to various episodes of human history and society.

All in all, to probe the ways in which Morales painstakingly grafts connotative devices and rhetorical figurations onto torrents of history, racial enmity, and disposals of human rights and life is necessary to help his reader better comprehend particular intangibilities in particularly tangible ways. Call it his style of artistically criticizing early Los Angeles' social injustices and controls in addition to racist dogmas. In this regard, Melanie Pooch is spot-on when she declares, in "The Poetics of DiverCity," that "stylistic devices, such as metaphor, irony, alliteration, simile, or parody, are often used as a tool to overtly or covertly criticize certain ideologies or conventions" (2016, 58). Yet, Morales' artistic style comes at a price, for it produces very severe sprains in an otherwise stable novel, and these sprains elicit undeniable reactions and tense emotions from the reader. Because of this, critics who may regard *River of Angels* as an affirmative or optimistic turn away from his past works of death, pain, and decay will find themselves mistaken. This novel lays bare numerous thematic ideas, but it especially lays bare its author's conception of ethnic stratification and social animosity not as a natural phenomenon but as a contrivance—just like the controlled "man-made" Los Angeles River itself.

It therefore may be the model Chicano novel in that it portrays the sadly all-too-human states of intolerance, fear, and sociocultural fracture while attempting to set the record straight regarding the value of the Mexican, which Morales confesses is the very motivation for writing the book: "to show the reader that Mexican labor, not the U.S. Army Corps of Engineers, not history, not Los Angeles, was responsible for building the bridges over the L.A. River. *They* did it and have a right to be recognized" (Morales 2020). All things considered, we are left with an arguably menacing literary testimony, with a rhetorically charged, aesthetically emotive rendering of bodies that are submerged, broken, entombed, suffocated, lacerated, and liquefied. It is through such testimonial rendering that the reader may better fathom the fierce conflicts that develop when racialist Anglo discrimination and its often horrific and hegemonic social rites angrily collide with Mexican cultural ethnicity and its self-determinant rights.

NOTES

1. *Connotation* is a slippery term, complicated by critical conceptions and esoteric theoretical revisions. In its basic sense, connotation means a semantic phenomenon involving perceived ideas, emotions, and relative interpretations of word or phrase. Frye et al. consider it in an emotive context as ideas, attitudes, or emotions associated with a word in the mind of the reader, a range of "feelings aroused by the word" (1977, 127). Muffin and Ray explain it as associations evoked by a word beyond a literal intention, a word-driven reflection of recognized or understood "broad cultural associations" (2009, 73). I prefer Barthes' consideration, in which he puts forth that illustrative imagery or narrative moments in a text can indeed be connotative—what he calls an "aesthetic signified" that suggests a broader range of interpreted possibility (1997, 34–35). What I interpret in Morales' novel, then, involves ideas, emotions, senses, and associations arising out of particular acts: occurrences in his novel must be read for their overtones, emotional coloring, tenor, and sudden figurative import.

2. Ernest is an anagram for *resent*, employed conceivably to signal his annoyance with his responsibilities or circumstances, or perhaps indignation at having (for financial reasons) to deal with these people. Though indifferent here, Ernest ultimately comes to represent principled tolerance and friendship later in the novel.

3. The novel also references the disposal of bodies, along with the disposal of objects, via the asphyxiating encasements of children in a junkyard. The childrens'

deaths are prevented by the River Mother, a mystical descendant of the indigenous Tongva culture and Yangna settlement that was to become Los Angeles. She keeps a vigilant watch for children who become trapped in old ice boxes at the junkyard: "Several men finished loading old rusty ice boxes. The River Mother had the doors removed before sending the boxes to the metal chopper. She had dealt with too many tragedies concerning abandoned ice boxes with doors that locked playing children inside to suffocate. Few paid much attention to these killers of children" (Morales 2014, 175). A domestic container becomes a deadly coffin in this instance, a terrifying suffocation made all the more heartbreaking due to human life prematurely shortened.

4. Some old castles in Japan are also connected to hitobashira: Maruoka Castle in Fukui Prefecture is said to contain a hitobashira in its pillar, and Matsue Castle in Shimane prefecture is said to contain one buried under its stone wall. Matsue Ohashi Bridge is believed to have human sacrifices built into its base, as is the Hokkaido Jomon tunnel, located on the Sekihoku Main Line. In the aftermath of a 1968 earthquake, several skeletons were said to be found buried upright in the walls of that tunnel. For additional information online, see Matthew Meyer's *Illustrated Database of Japanese Folklore* and *Online Database of Japanese Ghosts and Monsters* (yokai.com/hitobashira/); Lafcadio Hearn's *Unfamiliar Glimpses of Japan*, 142–43 (http://www.gutenberg.org/ebooks/8130?msg=welcome_stranger); and *SlappedHam*'s "Creepiest Urban Legends Around the World" (slappedham.com/creepiest-urban-legends/2).)

5. Note that this is actually the second time that Albert Rivers is beaten by Philip and his xenophobe comrades. His first beating is relatively short and quite violent, but meant only as a warning (Morales 2014, 204–6). This subsequent attack and beating is planned, prolonged, and much worse.

6. Only to sadly die later on in the novel by direct, willful murder (238–37).

7. Though Shaker goes on to perish, note a less lethal retribution for incursion into a venerable abode that transpires in Morales' tale after the matriarch Toypurina's death: "Oakley's parents' home, for at least four or five years, had one renter after another and not one stayed a year. The last renter stayed for only two weeks. It was Toypurina, according to Sol, who returned to make life miserable for the renters. She haunted every room, every object that was in the house. It happened over and over again: pots and pans rattling, chairs levitating, babies moved at night, ice freezes in the middle of warm rooms, bed covers torn off the bed while the renters made love, screams and sighs coming from within the walls, dishes and glasses falling off shelves and tables. The last renters complained about not being able to get out of their clothes, then their rooms, then the house. The renters left when the house finally allowed them to leave" (Morales 2014, 57).

8. A manifestation, that is, until the novel's surprising conclusion, where Uncle

Philip undergoes what can only be described as an evolution of conscience. The reader encounters in the book's final pages a changed Keller who seeks to atone for his sinful words and deeds. Finding God, his change is personal, social, geographic, religious, financial, and legalistic—and generational, as descendants of the Rivers family are positively affected by the alteration in more ways than one.

9. See my book *The Flesh-and-Blood Aesthetics of Alejandro Morales* (2014) for compelling explications of Morales' visceral, hypergraphic representation and its artistic metaphorical significance in nearly all of his works to date.

WORKS CITED

Aston, William George. 1905. *Shinto: The Way of the Gods*. ATLA monograph preservation program. Issues 1188–92 of *Western Books on Asia: Japan*. London: Longmans, Green.

Atwood, Margaret. 2001. *The Blind Assassin—A Novel*. New York: Random House.

Barthes, Roland. 1977. *Image/Music/Text*. Translated by Stephen Heath. New York: Hill and Wang.

Bell, Claudia, and John Lyall. 2002. *The Accelerated Sublime: Landscape, Tourism, and Identity*. Westport, CT: Praeger.

Bierce, Ambrose. 1989. "An Occurrence at Owl Creek Bridge." In *The Collected Writings of Ambrose Bierce*, 9–18. New York: Citadel Press.

Blake, Beverley. 1902. "Every-Day Japan." *Chautauquan Magazine* 35, no. 1 (April): 582–89.

Branch, Edgar M., and Robert H. Hirst, eds. 1979. *Twain's Early Tales and Sketches, 1851–1864*. Berkeley: University of California Press.

Clinton, Catherine, and Michele Gillespie. 1997. *The Devil's Lane: Sex and Race in the Early South*. New York: Oxford University Press.

Dyens, Ollivier. 2001. *Metal and Flesh—The Evolution of Man*. Translated by Evan J. Bibber and Ollivier Dyens. Cambridge, MA: MIT Press.

Frédéric, Louis. 2005. *The Japan Encyclopedia*. Translated by Kathe Ross. Cambridge, MA: Belknap.

Frye, Northrup, Sheridan W. Baker, George B. Perkins, and Barbara M. Perkins. 1997. *The Harper Handbook to Literature*. 2nd ed. New York: Longman.

Gómez-Quiñones, Juan. 1994. *Mexican American Labor*. Albuquerque: University of New Mexico Press.

Kozaki, Fumito. 1973. *Iwarenaki Miike tanko no hitobashira*. Edited by Massaki Hiraoka. Tokyo: Ushio Shuppansha-Showa.

Manzella, Abigail G. H. 2018. *Migrating Fictions: Gender, Race, and Citizenship in U.S. Internal Displacements*. Columbus: Ohio State University Press.

Mitchelhill, Jennifer. 2003. *Castles of the Samurai: Power and Beauty*. Tokyo: Kodansha International.

Morales, Alejandro. 2014. *River of Angels*. Houston: Arte Público Press.

———. 2020. Guest lecture presentation for the course Chicano Authors (Chicano Studies 182). University of California, Santa Barbara, February 4, 2020.

Muffin, Ross C., and Supryia M. Ray, eds. 2009. *The Bedford Glossary of Critical and Literary Terms*. 3rd ed. Boston: St. Martin's Press.

Munro, Neil Gordon. 1908. *Prehistoric Japan*. Yokohama. eBook.

Murguía, Alejandro. 1992. "A Subtle Plague." In *Mirrors beneath the Earth: Short Fiction by Chicano Writers*, edited by Ray González, 321–25. Willimantic, CT: Curbstone Press.

Pooch, Melanie U. 2016. "The Poetics of DiverCity." In *DiverCity–Global Cities as a Literary Phenomenon: Toronto, New York, and Los Angeles in a Globalizing Age*, 57–78. Bielefeld, Germany: Transcript Verlag. eBook.

Stein, Melissa N. 2015. *Measuring Manhood: Race and the Science of Masculinity, 1830–1934*. Minneapolis: University of Minnesota Press.

Tsuda, Nortake. 1918. "Human Sacrifices in Japan." *Open Court—A Monthly Magazine* 32, no. 740 (January): 760–67.

Willis, Bruce Dean. 2013. *Corporeality in Early Twentieth-Century Latin American Literature: Body Articulations*. New York: Palgrave-Macmillan.

Zinn, Howard. 2003. *A People's History of the United States: 1492–Present*. Updated edition. New York: HarperCollins.

TWO / The Analogous Correspondence of an Extreme Poetics between Stanley Kubrick's *A Clockwork Orange* and Alejandro Morales' *Barrio on the Edge* / FRANCISCO A. LOMELÍ

> Utopia is a place where everything is good; dystopia is a place where everything is bad; heterotopia is where things are different.
> —Walter Russel Mead, "Trains, Planes, and Automobiles," 1995

The novelist, short story writer, poet, and essayist Alejandro Morales is considered something between an anomaly and a rarity within the field of Chicano/a letters. He has penned a sizable production of eight landmark novels, one collection of short stories, various theoretical essays, and several poems, yet he has, almost inexplicably, not been regarded as a trendsetter or innovator. Morales has certainly embarked on a broad variety of provocative as well as sophisticated narrative techniques, approaches, and experimentations that well illustrate a fiercely independent originality and uncanny inventiveness in broaching what might be considered unorthodox, even odd ideas. His work often tackles controversial and taxing subjects head-on, such as diseases, plagues, monstrosities, and hyper-real depictions. It is difficult to point out any direct disciples of Morales, although the argument could be made that he launched the subgenre of the hard-core barrio novel with *Caras viejas y vino nuevo* (1975) and its translation *Barrio on the Edge* (1998),[1] which other authors such as Luis J. Rodríguez, Yxta Maya Murray, and Danny Santiago later refashioned.[2] In other words, he introduced the barrio theme to the Chicano novel after it had already become widespread in poetry, theater, and to some degree in short stories as a reflection of protest and social angst. Morales' main contribution consists of interrogating the barrio as a permanent element of the Chicano lifestyle, inviting the reader to examine and decode it in order to better understand its predicaments, entrapments, and shortcomings. Per Morales, Chicanos have had to confront their demons and the corrosive nature of the barrio, which has lost its way (or has it been subverted?) from a pastoral setting to a degenerative, death-filled, and alienating milieu comprising a series of symbolic and ambiguous inversions. The gnawing issue remains: how to survive, change, or transcend such a place that also functions as home?

Morales' signature aesthetics stands out for its narrative innovations, its thematic audaciousness (another form of extreme poetics), its boundary-breaking topics, and its eerie intimations about disease, antihistory, and the future. Specifically, he dedicates considerable attention to the interpretation or revisionism of intrahistory among Chicanos/as in relation to how their respective social sphere establishes and lives by its own rules. Morales indeed stands out as an author profoundly committed to the act of writing: not simply for exploring new topics but for engaging with a wide array of subjects that more often than not rattle entrenched or complacent sensibilities. His writings are self-referential, often constructed as an antiesthetic that goes against the grain of the mainstream American canon while also challenging the trends of Chicano/a writings in vogue since the mid-1970s.[3] His place in the field has been well chronicled in terms of not necessarily conceding to strictly favorable representations of the people and environments he portrays.[4] Succinctly put, he advances various works with a rawness and sometimes crudeness of unorthodox ruminations, as Marc García-Martínez (2014) compellingly proves, thereby offering visceral and unfiltered depictions.[5] A number of critics, including the novelist himself in his critical essays, have stipulated that his aesthetic project corresponds well with the social order of a heterotopia, as originally proposed by Michel Foucault in "Different Spaces" (1998), given that the Chicano writer often harnesses reigning hegemonic circumstances, forcing characters to confront or oppose the status quo's legitimacy. Others argue that Morales is well rooted in conceptualizing what Edward Soja terms a "thirdspace" or Homi Bhabha calls a "hybrid zone," in which invented space fuses with reality.[6] The metonymic barrio in *Barrio on the Edge*, a unique Chicano construction, unfolds as ripe with an underground swell of dissent and bottled-up rage, in the process becoming a contorted representation of a heterotopia uneasy with its own social conditions and raison d'être.

I still recall my first reading of *Caras viejas y vino nuevo* in 1976 as a venture into a dark, sordid style, since most of the novel takes place at night and discernible descriptions and movements are blurred or indistinct. Greatly influenced by an all-encompassing neorealism, the most advanced style par excellence of the latter part of the twentieth century—with repeated hints of an extreme surrealism—every page is contoured by way of airbrushing characters with imprecise features, much like an incomplete graffiti mural; at the same time, the narrative anecdote figures in a minimalist rather than mechanistic manner. Its neonaturalist bent suggests a distinct dystopia, seen via Morales' intrepid and honest efforts to capture what hard-core barrio life is like for forsaken characters who are not only trapped in their environment but also molded and defined by it. They are essentially trapped within an environment driven by vices and self-negation. Ultimately, the internal structural elements of the novel are brought together by a definite neobaroque impulse that encapsulates the spirit of the milieu, the arrangement of the components of the action within a kaleidoscopic simultaneity, and the multiplicity of layers of meaning inherent to a cross-sectional narrative. Here we encounter a complex web of interconnected elements that defy simplicity for the sake of emphasizing underlying connotations of chaos and disorder. The work disrupts any sense of an orderly aesthetics appropriate to an unfinished modernity. This discourse of rupture corresponds well to a literary enterprise that captures marginalized characters ensnared (and perhaps victimized) in vices that are either self-created or assimilated from the surrounding environment. The almost absent central plot is characterized by impressionable flurries of backward action as if deliberately designed inside out. Furthermore, the novel suggests much more than it actually tells, enhanced by qualities of ambiguity, fragmentary internal and external structures, dreamlike iterations, and calculated disfigurements that put a premium on deciphering and connecting floating dots—notice, for example, the extensive use of semicolons to stitch predicates and clauses as jointed sentence fragments. At times, the novel appears to present a radiographic or X-ray image of a barrio environment more than the barrio itself. Here we encounter a carefully articulated representation of an atavistic social setting driven by habit and preconditioned practices that only an extreme poetics can capture in order to personify the visceral nature of such an intense place.

With these preliminary observations, I attempt to unpack and then confront a nagging concern about genealogy or origins in certain enigmatic pages of *Barrio on the Edge*. The novel seems to appear out of nowhere in 1975—in Spanish, which contributed to its prolonged imperceptibility—because no one before Morales had focused on the barrio as a viable subject within narrative fiction. He essentially undermined prevalent idealizations of this milieu to remind us of its complications and the need to confront its negative baggage. A philosophical question seemed to haunt readers at the time: Why write about a barrio in the first place? For one, the Chicano publishing company Quinto Sol located in Berkeley, California, led by editor Octavio Romano-V., rejected the manuscript of *Caras viejas y vino nuevo*, proving that even Chicanos at the height of the cultural nationalist Chicano Movement were not prepared for portrayals of a hard-core barrio in the face of the long-standing history of social stigma, stereotyping, and vexing views of their community. With the exception of John Steinbeck's *Tortilla Flat* (1935), which touched on subaltern populations, mainstream American literature up through the 1970s did not consider the barrio a relevant or worthy topic of representation; it was simply either a nonsubject or an invisible one—although most Chicanos were fully cognizant of living a version of it every day. For that reason, Morales opted to target the Mexican mainstream publishers Fondo de Cultura Económica and Siglo Veintiuno and the unconventional publisher Joaquín Mortiz as possible venues, but they in turn found the novel too unusual, even exotic, bizarre, and somewhat strange. These publishers sympathized with a youthful generation of Mexican literature from the 1960s known as La Onda, which attempted to "modernize" the previously mythologized trends of Mexican nationalism into a more experimental, craft-oriented, and concerted search for renovating thematics. Finally, Joaquín Mortiz proved willing to gamble on such an obscure and risqué subject matter, attracted by the novel's unconventional syntax and convoluted style. The abstruse subtextual underpinnings of Morales' work probably reminded Mortiz of both the linguistic and political reverberations of other short Latin American text packed with connotations, for example the interpersonal and disparaging violence in Mario Vargas Llosa's *La ciudad y los perros* (1967), the deep-rooted sense of despair in Juan Carlos Onetti's *El pozo* (1939), the interior action and overriding moral crisis in Alejo Carpentier's *El acoso* (1957), and perhaps hints of the stark alienation and psychologically entrapped characters in Ernesto Sábato's *El túnel* (1947).

While we can directly detect in Morales the compelling influence of such *Nouveau roman* aesthetics that had in great part helped shape the Latin American literary boom as a school of fiction dedicated to style and especially craft, in his work this acquires a new function and purpose. Laying out the novel's basic plot in reverse serves as a brilliant technique to challenge readers who might wish to find facile social renderings or solutions to hard-core barrio predicaments, while reminding us that complexity and intertwining factors characterize postmodern reality. In fact, Morales' barrio becomes a central metonymic metaphor in the Chicano novel, similar to how authors such as Alurista, Rodolfo "Corky" Gonzales, and Ricardo Sánchez had earlier established it as a common trope in poetry, except that Morales does not mythologize or romanticize. This is because he does not view it as a redemptive aspect of Chicano life but sees it rather as the cross to bear and an experiential motive to overcome. The barrio for him is our best friend—if we understand it as community—but also our worst enemy, which functions as a framework of encirclement, entrapment, and cannibalization that turns inhabitants into interchangeable objects. The natural conclusion is that the barrio falls under what sociologists Tomás Almaguer (1994) and Mario Barrera (1979) classify within the framework of dependency theory as an internal colony in terms of its marginal condition and degree of exploitation.[7] Frankly stated, the barrio was both cruel and merciless, in fact a pivotal marker in 1960s and '70s Chicano life of our underprivileged and underclass social conditions, requiring deep reflection, interrogation, and possibly doing something to at least overcome or, better yet, transcend it.[8] The novel's central action confirms that this story is no boy scout or girl scout outing, with death flanking it in the beginning and the end: this is harsh, graphic, unsentimental, violent, oppressive, eschatological, fanatically obsessive, pent-up anger and subjacent rage that is easy to penetrate but difficult to escape. In many ways, this kind of representation embodied what Chicanos saw as their inevitable sociohistorical backdrop, or as their main experience in negotiation with their relegated urban environments that typically ended in either bare survival or being swallowed up by them. The fact that the repeated references to the outside world ("over there" or "on the other side") seem obscure and almost unidentifiable speaks to the barrio's insularity, lost within an urban jungle. Morales captured it in a timely fashion to try to rescue both this environment and its inhabitants from themselves.

By focusing on the second narrative fragment of the novel, which consists of only three pages near the "beginning" (out of a total of thirty-four segments that resemble chapters), we discern that this cutting-edge work, which initially caught us off guard, has more influences and intertextual points of contact than it lets on. Indeed, its publication by Joaquín Mortiz in Mexico City subtly decoded and consequently cloaked it within the Latin American Boom. There is something highly intuitive about the way the story unfolds, in that the beginning is really the end and the end is really the beginning of this cumulative chaos that moves like the collision course of a train wreck. Interestingly, there is a gap, a pause, a ventriloquism of introspective flashes that resemble attitudes and images out of such a seemingly dissimilar work as Stanley Kubrick's 1971 film *A Clockwork Orange*—and probably older antecedents such as Luis Buñuel and Salvador Dalí's *Un Chien Andalou* (1929) and José Camilo Cela's *La familia de Pascual Duarte* (1942)—suggesting a social time bomb ticking in the midst of unbridled violence around the world or at least insinuating an extreme environment of inverted values of contradictions and paradoxes.[9] These works encompass or reflect violent times of the twentieth century as lived during the Great Depression, World War II, the turbulent period of the civil rights struggle of the 1960s, and the period of intense sociocultural experiments of the 1970s. They hint in each case at historical watershed moments when aesthetic niceties or decorum become targets of an affront, with each attempting to reach out to the viewer/reader to shock, alarm, and leave an unforgettable impression. Likewise, in *Barrio on the Edge* something is clearly off kilter, as if the barrio were an incongruous and isolated social ambience, precariously devoid of a destiny, as an anonymous narrator observes: "Here only the lights tried to shine, sparkling as if the stars had disappeared" (Morales 1998, 34).

Barrio on the Edge advances as if in a gestational state, open to possibilities and intertextual renderings in search of an extreme form and content. In the novel's second narrative fragment, we find some odd references peppered with critical assessments about the development of the modern world in a cryptic and enigmatic prose. Instead of discovering the natural evolution of progress, the reader encounters the exact opposite. Should we presume that there is a secret coded message embedded as a cautionary tale with numerous reverberations throughout the murky narrative of disjointed objects? If not, why are there repeated peculiar and discordant allusions to objects that appear hidden as if inert in dark closets, such as the 1968–1969 calendar within a grungy bathroom; the confusion between sirens as ambulance alarms, *lloronas*, or wailing women and mythological figures who mesmerized sailors; the bonfires around which the barrio men congregate to warm up but which seem to multiply exponentially from a rooftop view; a crucifix that sometimes suggests something beyond religiosity; and the drug hallucinations that directly affect both the narrative style as well as the perception of reality for most characters? Certain allegorical qualities seep through the text by assembling counterpoints of meaning: for example, through the contrast of the calloused, self-destructive, and self-indulgent drug-alcohol-sex addict named Julián (a budding Julius Caesar, potentially capable of exerting power and leadership, but who goes awry) to Mateo, who symbolically functions as a disciple of an indirect religiosity or social order, signaling a fundamental change from this tawdry Chicano Sodom and Gomorrah; the bus driver with his Jewish medallion as a sign of committing to a specific religion and the prevalence of the mystical number "3" throughout the novel; Christmas time, which marks the birth of a savior in contrast to the barrio's many deaths; and finally the issue of a mystical experience to reach a higher level of transcendence (be it God or a pseudogod), but which metamorphoses into what I call "mystical realism." The latter implies the portrayal of an environment consisting of distortions via stimulants, sexual encounters, hallucinations, rage, and unidentified sentiments that overwhelm characters, illustrating their fallibilities and vulnerabilities. Even the father, Edmundo, a misguided family figurehead, echoes the "world" ("*mundo*" in his name) while the mother, Margo (short for "*amargo*," or sour), reflects bitterness as a mother and wife. Then we have the Buenasuerte brothers, who hold the keys to perdition by serving as the drug suppliers for the barrio inhabitants—hardly representing good luck or good fortune, in ironic contrast to their last name.

After describing in considerable detail the failed, rampantly decadent landscape of a barrio surrounded by "famished dogs" and "mangled automobile carcasses," rotted or "skeletal" structures, "threatening warehouses," crying children, and "foreboding black lethal chimneys [that] puff pollution into the air," Morales equates Western civilization to an enslaving orgasm, wherein "the crucifix is both used as a cane and a condom through youth's delirium" and "strange familiar sounds . . . [blend] with the jungle" [an urban one?] (34). The analogy between *Barrio on the Edge* and *A Clockwork Orange* is not found in explicit terms related to the physical landscape as described in Morales' novel, but rather in the social depravity that exists within this urban space of aimless characters. Extreme descriptions of endless ruins abound and populate the landscape like ominous reminders of their predictable and exorable corrosion.

The barrio is a Chicano ground zero of a degenerating urban jungle situated in plain view, that is, a place that is fast regressing backward to the point of self-ruin—in parallel to the way the story unfolds. A clarification is required: this is hardly the stuff of a cultural nationalist literary agenda, which up until the mid-1970s preferred culturally positive and near-sanitized representations of Chicanos. On the contrary, we encounter a disturbing setting on the verge of bursting at the seams, that is, an environment that cannot take the pressures hinted at by Morales any longer. Morales creates a Chicano *Guernica*, echoing one of Picasso's maximum cubist expressions that deals with its own horrors from an undeclared war within an unspecified cause-and-effect framework. The barrio landscape resembles an outright war zone, except that the bombs and artifices of war are not easily discernible because they are multidirectional. Yet the effects of evoking what *Guernica* connotes are comparable: human and social tragedies seem to accumulate exponentially due to invisible forces that have exerted their might and dominance over this Chicano space, seen as a dumping ground of humanity where people are barely remnants of themselves, as effectively represented in the cubist style. At the same time, the barrio is a bastion of insularity (a lost urban island), a singularity and the "last" line of defense for its inhabitants, who are unable to escape the onslaught of outside forces, many of which have been internalized—a sense of quick gratification via drugs or sex, male prowess as the ruling social order over women, poverty and its social symptoms, education as a futile exercise, religion as a questionable vehicle for spiritual renewal, and sanctified cultural archetypes (family, church, kinship) as worthless and ineffectual sources of community cohesion. This *Guernica*-like space also provides the inhabitants with a semblance of a fortress of temporary protection, which then becomes a mirage or what Morales calls "un mundo torcido" (a twisted world) (17).[10] The tone that reigns is logically one of desolation, gloom, and hopelessness, suggesting the barrio is at a point of no return when it comes to seeking redemption from its own self-destruction. A foreboding ambiance is consequently emerging that appears to presage either a collapse or a reckoning.

Hints of *A Clockwork Orange*'s bizarre and sometimes wacky but opaque morality narrative begin to surface in Morales' text, making themselves manifest through obscure tropes and stylistic devices. They take on a visceral quality in the second narrative fragment (or chapter?) of the novel, while historically placing the action in 1968 and 1969 when Chicano barrios were historically on the brink of exploding in the midst of a social movement slowly transitioning from a rural to an urban setting, that is, from a labor movement of human rights to a student movement of civil rights. In the novel, an anonymous, freewheeling narrator with a dystopian lens (who seems to be oblivious to the characters' actions) pauses to pontificate, criticize, and indict in vague terms: "The fires of people burning the past, protesting the present, and fornicating the future can be heard in the streets of the nation" (36). The fires are both signs and harbingers of things as they were, have been, and will become. We detect a veiled call to arms, or a rallying cry to face the full spectrum of history and what it has done to the barrio itself as a Chicano space and its people as victims. The surroundings indicate a boiling point of no return, expressed by a place raging with anguish and on the brink of exploding. The barometric pressure of this barrio appears to be intensifying.

In a parallel but conspicuously distinctive fashion, the film *A Clockwork Orange* raises the ante by exhibiting gratuitous violence to an extreme, for example, when Alex and his three "droogs" or delinquents wander the streets of London in the form of tricksters, always ready to mischievously or subversively carry out—in their minds—half-hearted cruel "jokes" by beating a homeless tramp and then later gang-raping the wife of a writer while "innocently" singing "I'm Singing in the Rain." In contrast to the zany and sensationalized sense of unbridled brutality toward defenseless victims in *A Clockwork Orange*, in Morales' novel brutality takes on a more serious note due to the effects of the oppression of modern society in a Chicano barrio; there is no gaiety here, but rather muffled thoughts and muted actions. In the film, the first home invasion appears to be a sardonic game of sexual assault in which the perpetrators prance to Beethoven's music in the background while using phallic-shaped masks with a mindful justification of participating in what are purportedly young men's playful pranks. In a second home invasion, Alex indiscriminately kills a woman by smashing her head with a giant-sized penis sculpture. We witness the use of violence for violence's sake as a subversive weapon against the social establishment, supposedly "acting" playfully while harboring antisocial hostilities in the form of farcical or eccentric revelry. Alex is later arrested and subjected to behavioral conditioning in a rehabilitation center, with the objective of recovering a sense of social morality, except that he learns to fake his cure in front of psychologists. At one point he admits to his inherently violent tendencies by ironically acknowledging "I want to do good," which sounds disingenuous and vacuous when uttered. On another occasion, he notes, "My mind is blank," a symbolic statement that indicates the degree of his hollowness. He is essentially an empty individual devoid of well-intentioned sentiments, for whom morality is a foreign concept (reminding us of Julián in Morales' novel). At the end of the film, Alex confesses, "I was cured all right," after dreaming of a sexual rendezvous with a nude woman—the moral message being that he cannot heal because he doesn't have anything inside to mend. Kubrick's 1971 film, based on Anthony Burgess' homonymous novel from 1962, had a more lasting influence than the book, by capturing a historical juncture of intense sociocultural tensions and bizarre behavior as the norm through inversions. The film operates between a parody and a satire while implying a definite ethical overtone in trying to purge the protagonist's twisted sense of behavior and social order. It also depicts an impression of the modern world gone askew, thanks to unbridled violence, a decaying social fabric, and arbitrary actions against others—the very world narrated in *Barrio on the Edge*. Both Morales and Kubrick, therefore, offer correspondences aimed at shocking their respective social sensibilities, but the latter also intends to insult by hyperbolizing the droogs' actions to an extreme point. The Chicano author, on the other hand, leans more toward a subtle commentary on social conditioning and scruples, even suggesting that drug- or sex-induced actions become akin to a religious or mystical experience. Morales strategically prefers to unveil the complexities of his main characters as they struggle with a sense of fate gone astray while at the same time posing a stinging denunciation of the way the barrio has deteriorated. Either way, both works are clear expressions of a hyperpoetics aimed at rattling the senses. María Herrera-Sobek points out this particular effect in *Barrio on the Edge*: "The society in which they live has usurped their soul, their spirituality and left them bereft of any tender human feeling. The man and woman in this society, aware of this horrendous vacuum, seek to fulfill themselves through alcohol, drugs, sex and violence. In this state of 'numbness' they 'forget' some of the pain" (1977, 149).[11]

The second narrative fragment of Morales' novel contains an exceptionally enigmatic paragraph worth examining in order to fully establish its correlation with *A Clockwork Orange* and other comparable texts. Only in this way can we confirm the presence of an extreme poetics that serves to contextualize, and by extension, rationalize the Chicano characters' predicament. The first part of the paragraph, serving almost as a preamble or quasi manifesto, consists of a series of extraneous reflections by an omniscient narrator who makes value judgments about contemporary life in metaphorical terms, alluding to modernity as "the menstrual period of time" (using "period" as a double entendre) and society as the "jackass of humanity." The nihilistic overtones are inevitably comparable to *A Clockwork Orange*'s overt anarchism, with both fostering a sense of an underlying rebellion. This is followed by references to explicit sexual acts and power differentials in relation to countries that succumb, acquiesce, or surrender to greater nations or authorities:

> Padded with sanitary napkins for negotiating the menstrual period of the time, the bloody jackass of humanity appeared last night on television. In countries inundated with mouths, the cock is apt to be eaten. And in still others we can see silk ties on top of gorged bellies supported by leather belts. (36)

Later in the same the paragraph, descriptions become appraisals and beliefs more than judgments, expressly articulated through a free-flowing surrealism of uninhibited associations aimed at provoking more than explaining while situating the action historically at the end of the l960s. The "bull testicles" conjure up the emblematic image of the cubist representation of the bull in *Guernica*, invoking bottled-up sentiments of apprehension, sexual suppression, and a beheaded nation that treats its minorities and other countries similarly via a system of impositions. In other words, these are efforts to capture what is almost ineffable and certainly difficult to articulate. Here we also find explicit sexual references so prevalent in *A Clockwork Orange*, such as the incongruous, yet abstract, correlation between a clitoris and revolutions. The sentence "Films show erections of breasts and trouser flies" smacks of numerous scenes in Kubrick's film, where the droogs not only use pointy masks in the form of erections but also wear conspicuous plastic jock straps to conceal what would be equivalent to their "trouser flies." In addition, while a comment about pornography is inserted to reinforce the idea of 1968 as a year of historical changes, the year 1969 can be understood as a masked symbol of the conversion of hypersensibilities: extreme social tensions related to the Vietnam War, the exploding hippie movement, and the open generational and cultural conflicts. The year "nineteen sixty-nine" could also suggest a symbolic pun and covert reference to rampant sexuality (again, something common in both the film and the novel):

> Art expresses the yanking out of bull testicles with which to illustrate the school-like lessons of how to suck the clitoris of modern revolutions. Films show erections of breasts and trouser flies. The year nineteen sixty-eight is not so significant, but in nineteen sixty-nine more pornography will be sold. (36)

In addition, the reference to pornography here conveniently corresponds to the year "sixty-nine," which in part applies to elements in both works by Kubrick and Morales if viewed superficially and with a decontextualized lens. Sexuality as an uninhibited form of expression here parallels what in the 1950s was called the "pornography of violence."[12] The overt sexual acts or references correspond more to expressions of personal validation, a desperate reaching out for companionship and potential affection, which the characters seem to lack in their respective ambience. However, their self-indulgence does not permit them to make authentic connections with others because of their obsession with immediate self-gratification; their actions ultimately appear as sensationalized acts of violence that do not pretend to stimulate erotic feelings. In both cases, sex is utilized as a weapon of conquest, victory, and subjugation, not as the mutual communion of spirits but simply as temporary carnal imposition.

The paragraph in question continues with provocative statements that go unqualified and would appear to be more bizarre than some of the scenes in *A Clockwork Orange*. The narrator's utterance "Psychiatrists masturbate horses and scream: The Russians are coming!" (36) is as striking as Luis Buñuel and Salvador Dalí's iconic scene in *Un Chien Andalou* in which someone cuts across a large eye with a blade in full view, with blood gushing out. The objective is to evoke actions that evoke strange deeds. The first part of the sentence suggests a hypersexualized act committed by scientists—an explicitly exaggerated or irrational action leaning toward sensationalism—but the second part embodies a slogan from the height of the Cold War warning Westerners of a Russian invasion. Incompatible ideas are somehow fused together as if their connections were seamless, but the opposite is true. The interpretation can be left to the eye of the beholder. The point is that the references initially seem nonsensical, except that their disparate nature lends itself to greater connotation for a shock effect into disbelief. Given the explosive content of *Barrio on the Edge,* these free associations of disconnected realities further suggest a surrealistic composition, which at times is enhanced by cubist synecdoches that figure as fragments of abstract movements in the dark tinged with nihilistic overtones (e.g., hands that strike, arms that flail, feet that move into a room, "mouths with bites and painful grimaces," that is, parts of the body acting and reacting independently as if they have a mind of their own). Consequently, the paragraph reads more like a codex meant to be deciphered about a place and characters that share acute issues, thanks in great part to the stream of metaphors that give a restrained impression of existing social tensions without providing specificities. As depicted in the paragraph, Morales' expressive violence cannot be reduced to ideology, as the various fragments speak for themselves. At the same time, such violence can be subtle, overt, sublime, arbitrary, or take the seductive form of counteracting inhibitions—but the degree of sensationalism here does not match *A Clockwork Orange*, where it is in fact the norm and arguably the ultimate goal. Nonetheless, both texts leave decidedly long-lasting impressions.

In addition to echoing *A Clockwork Orange*, the central ideas in the paragraph intertextually bring to mind other works with a strong surrealistic bent influenced by the inherent skepticism of nihilism, such as Buñuel and Dalí's highly provocative *Un Chien Andalou* and Cela's disturbing *La familia de Pascual Duarte*. The unnerving surrealism in Buñuel's film is followed by the emergence of *tremendismo* in the midst of World War II—and the beginnings of the Franco dictatorship—a particular style whose name was coined by Cela to express the unbridled violence unleashed in his novel, giving the sensation that anything goes because human beings do not possess an inherent value. Tremendismo, then, manifests as uncontrollable pain and anguish on the part of Pascual Duarte, who provokes outright violent destruction among others wherever he is, killing family members in the process and ending up committing a horrific matricide. The implication is that, much like in *A Clockwork Orange* and *Barrio on the Edge,* violence is the only recourse, suggesting an extreme realism with existentialist overtones. Alienation among urban youth also plays a role in Buñuel/Dalí's, Cela's, Kubrick's, and Morales' creations, as in each case the characters exist outside the realms of a bourgeois society. A common denominator among them is that each work emerges during a peak of social tensions and upheavals: the Great Depression, World War II, an antiestablishment era characterized by cultural wars, the civil rights movement, and the Vietnam War, and the emergence of barrios as the new battleground for Chicanos. Morales' novel is similar to the other three works in depicting the deep angst experienced within barrios as a depository of human degeneration. These authors turn to an inexplicable irrationality within surrealism that challenges conventions while unleashing suppressed emotions through sometimes grotesque imagery, distortions, and hyperrealism. In most cases they present a subversive potential thanks to the sardonic undressing of gratuitous violence because there does not seem to be another alternative. In other words, extreme conditions invite extreme measures, while inducing extreme portrayals and poetics.

Barrio on the Edge seems to possess common links with the other works mentioned, but it also stands out on its own. While all four seek an immediate shock effect on very different sociohistorical stages, Morales does not seek gratuitous violence. Violence in the barrio is not engendered randomly; rather, it emerges organically within a context of long-standing oppression that has evolved through time while not offering the characters alternatives (with the one exception being the protagonist Mateo). Consequently, we find "*veteranos*" as survivors of past undeclared wars (more turf wars than actual combat?), roaming *lloronas* looking for their "lost children" (both literally and figuratively), sirens blaring to warn of an impending catastrophic occurrence, fires burning to signal an explosive situation, and satanic elements that hover like demons, which together form an apocalyptic ambience that has been ignored for far too long. Morales addresses opportunities and free will through a cause-and-effect framework by forcing the reader to rewind the plot back to the point of its idyllic origins in the general area of East Los Angeles. Many questions emerge in the process: What happened to this place over approximately two decades? How did Julián, a young man of tremendous physical talent, go wrong to become such a dissolute individual? Why does a pecking order exist in relegating women to sexual objects of unnegotiated desire? And, ultimately, is death the fundamental equalizer, as we see Julián perish in a car crash at the beginning of the novel and Mateo die from leukemia at the end? As we can appreciate, the novel spurs more questions than answers. What is nevertheless made clear is that the barrio is unrelenting, pervasive, smothering, destructive, and nonredemptive, as witnessed by the drug peddling Buenasuerte brothers, whose ironic name rings throughout the barrio streets. The characters do not have much of a chance of surviving the barrio, being much like mice lost in a maze in pursuit of the elusive "*vida loca*." Mateo is the only character who attempts to transcend this place, which he somehow considers redeemable, describing its potential on various occasions when he climbs to the top of buildings to have a broader view—except, ironically, he is the one who dies of a blood disorder. The final moral of the story would appear to be an unsubtle indictment of the barrio setting, despite its seductive qualities that allow its inhabitants to experience temporary "mystical" illusions through a fleeting indulgence in drugs, alcohol, and sex. Although not totally self-created, the barrio's cannibalistic tendencies of self-hate and endogenous violence are portrayed as self-perpetuating and institutionalized, as if lost within a dark cyclical space.

All these works offer commonalities, sharing ideological warnings of worse times to come by deliberately going against the grain of sanitized representations of their respective eras. Morales in particular felt compelled to portray the barrio as an invisible Chicano outside space that contains a sense of community. Instead of resorting to an easy and realistic portrayal of the barrio, he chose an oblique representation filled with ambiguities through the extensive usage of synechdoches, fragmentation, truncated images, counterpoints, and an almost plotless story of signifiers, all couched within a hyperrealist style appropriate to the neobaroque narrative construction, comprising reverberating connotations as part of a multilayered narrative.[13] Anarchy becomes a mode of self-reflection in order to instill a greater consciousness about the vulnerable barrio, which is ultimately the protagonist in *Barrio on the Edge,* along with its kissing cousin:

Death. The novel shares certain points of contact with previous artistic representations that became key landmarks of innovation and experimentation in the twentieth century by sending aesthetic shock waves against what before them were avant-garde frameworks. *Barrio on the Edge* sought what it considered its own legacy by promoting the hard-core barrio subgenre, except that in the process it also discovered its affinities and intertextual underpinnings with previous works that likewise attempted to establish a fundamental shift in vision or literary projects. Morales, thus, confirms that his novel is comfortably couched within previous trends of experimentation while renewing Chicano sensibilities in order to have the reader confront chaos and disarray.

In sum, *Barrio on the Edge* projects some of its origins, antecedents, and influences that give a whole new meaning to how it came about: not as a literary accident or isolated case, but rather as a carefully calculated novel of links and a priori points of contact. If some of these points appear as critical conjecture, I nonetheless find echoes of Buñuel and Dalí's *Un Chien Andalou*, Cela's *La familia de Pascual Duarte*, and especially Kubrick's iconoclastic and anarchistic *A Clockwork Orange* in Morales' *Barrio on the Edge* in the capturing of a particular zeitgeist that manifests itself in contemporary Chicano terms. When all is said and done, Morales presents a highly intense social environment on the verge of exploding, but the medium to express that reality neither matches nor needs to resort to overly bizarre representations despite employing modern modes of hyperrealism. Surrealism is indeed prevalent in Morales' aesthetically constructed barrio in order to render the bizarre "craziness" and intensity of such a setting, thanks to the stylistic modalities of surrealism and what I call "mystical realism." However, this barrio is not simply an extension of the author's imagination, because he focuses on it as the Chicanos' next battleground in the mid-1970s en route to finding liberation from the urban spaces that contain and imprison their populace. He effectively recreates the barrio's inherent nature of extreme proportions, including downtrodden lives, self-perpetuated violence, and misdirections and fatality. Such a depiction is intended to make it unforgettable as a place requiring urgent consideration by its inhabitants in order to defy the alternatives of its demise. The film *A Clockwork Orange* inspired many authors—at the time Morales was completing *Barrio on the Edge*—to pursue subjects, narrative forms, and a new language to capture characters who felt trapped in their social environment and sought ways to break the shackles of their humdrum existence, thus giving them a rightful place within the spectrum of their alienation. Both works, fundamentally controversial in nature, opened up innovative constructs of expression within their respective cinematic and literary mediums, crafting gripping new subgenres in the process.

NOTES

1. The usage of this classification for a Chicano novel was first proposed by Lomelí and Urioste (1976, 44). Nota bene: From here we will use the translation *Barrio on the Edge* by Francisco A. Lomelí (Morales 1998) as the basis for our study, with its corresponding pagination.

2. A rubbing-off or residual effect of influence is easily detected in Rodríguez's *Always Running: La Vida Loca, Gang Days in L.A.* (1994), Murray's *Locas* (1997), and Santiago's *Famous All Over Town* (1983). The phenomenon of writing about the barrio as a place and a mentality has been somewhat trendy in fiction, serving as a thematic launching pad for much of the Chicano Movement poetry in the l960s and l970s, because the barrio functioned as both a source of fascination and our curse for social, economic, and political reasons.

3. Morales' first introduction into the field of Chicano letters can be explained, in part, by what I have described as a small group or generation of writers that I call the Isolated Generation of 1975 (1975–1980) because Morales, Isabella Ríos in *Victuum* (1975), Ron Arias in *The Road to Tamazunchale* (1975), Aristeo Brito in *El diablo en Texas* (1976), Berta Ornelas in *Come Down from the Mound* (1975), Rudy S. Apodaca in *The Waxen Image* (1977), and Phil Sánchez in *Don Philo-O-Meno, sí la mancha* (1977) all came into Chicano letters via different routes: from a Latin American basis, or a folkloric one, and even science-fiction and the magical real. They focused less on epic stories than did the Quinto Sol Generation of 1967–1975 that preceded them; rather, they concentrated more on technique, circumstantial viewpoint, and craft, avoiding cultural nationalist thematic overtures. They preferred to open up new avenues of expression, including women's explorations into the novel genre and the first mystery novel.

4. Consult my introduction to the translation of *Barrio on the Edge* (Morales 1998).

5. García-Martínez (2014).

6. See Soja (1966) and Bhabha (1994).

7. Consult Almaguer (1994) and Barrera (1979).

8. We can't help but contemplate Camarillo's (1979) hypothesis regarding the emergence of barrios by the end of the nineteenth century after the disenfranchised Californios slowly lost their lands in the wake of the Mexican-American War of l848.

9. While Kubrick's 1971 film *A Clockwork Orange* had an immediate impact, we are operating under the assumption that Anthony Burgess' novel from 1962 with the same title did not.

10. Consult Morales (1996, 17).

11. Herrera-Sobek (1977).

12. *Merriam-Webster*, s.v. "pornography (*n.*)," accessed October 23, 2018, https://www.merriam-webster.com/dictionary/pornography.

13. What García-Martínez refers to as "signs of strife, that is, semiotic depictions of "cruel violence, vile sexuality, and innate human excesses" (2014, 70).

WORKS CITED

Almaguer, Tomás. 1994. *Racial Fault Lines: The Historical Origins of White Supremacy*. Berkeley: University of California Press.

Apodaca, Rudy. 1977. *The Waxen Image*. Mesilla, NM: Titan.

Arias, Ron. 1975. *The Road to Tamazunchale*. Reno, NV: West Coast Poetry Review.

Barrera, Mario. 1979. *Race and Class in the Southwest: A Theory of Racial Inequality*. Notre Dame, IN: University of Notre Dame.

Bhabha, Homi. 1994. *The Location of Culture*. London: Routledge.

Brito, Aristeo. 1976. *El diablo en Texas*. Tucson: Editorial Peregrinos.

Buñuel, Luis, dir. 1929. *Un Chien Andalou*. Co-written by Buñuel and Salvador Dalí.

Burgess, Anthony. 1962. *A Clockwork Orange*. New York: W.W. Norton.

Camarillo, Albert. 1979. *Chicanos in a Changing Society: From Mexican Pueblos to American Barrios in Santa Barbara and Southern California, 1848–1930*. Cambridge, MA: Harvard University Press.

Carpentier, Alejo. 1956. *El acoso*. Barcelona: Editorial Losada.

Cela, José Camilo. 1942. *La Familia de Pascual Duarte*. Madrid: Aldecoa.

Foucault, Michel. 1998. "Different Spaces." In *Aesthetics, Method, and Epistemology: Essential Works of Foucault, 1954–1984*, vol. 2, edited by James Faubion and translated by Robert Hurley, l75–85. New York: New Press.

García-Martínez, Marc. 2014. *The Flesh-and-Blood Aesthetics of Alejandro Morales: Disease, Sex, and Figuration*. San Diego: San Diego State University Press.

Herrera-Sobek, María. 1977. "Review of *Caras viejas y vino nuevo*." In "Chicano Literature," special issue, *Latin American Literary Review* 5, no. lo (Spring): 148–50.

Kubrick, Stanley, dir. 1971. *A Clockwork Orange*. Polaris Productions.

Lomelí, Francisco A. 1998. "Hard-Core Barrio Revisited: Violence, Sex, Drugs, and Videotape through a Chicano Glass Darkly." Introduction to Morales, *Barrio on the Edge*, 1–21.

Lomelí, Francisco A., and Donaldo W. Urioste. 1976. *Chicano Perspective in Literature: A Critical and Annotated Bibliography*. Albuquerque: Pajarito.

Martínez, Max. 1981. *Old Faces and New Wine*. San Diego: Maize Press.

Mead, Walter Russell. 1995. "Trains, Planes, and Automobiles: The End of the Postmodern Moment." *World Policy Journal* 12, no. 4 (December): 13–31.

Morales, Alejandro D. 1975. *Caras viejas y vino nuevo*. Mexico City: Joaquín Mortiz.

———. 1996. "Dynamic Identities in Heterotopia." In *Alejandro Morales: Fiction Past, Present, Future Perfect*, edited by José Antonio Gurpegui, 14–27. Tempe, AZ: Bilingual Press / Editorial Bilingüe.

———. 1998. *Barrio on the Edge / Caras viejas y vino nuevo*. Translated by Francisco A. Lomelí. Tempe, AZ: Bilingual Press / Editorial Bilingüe.

Murray, Ixta Maya. 1997. *Locas*. New York: Grove Press.

Onetti, Juan Carlos. 1939. *El pozo*. Montevideo: Ediciones Signo.

Ornelas, Berta. 1975. *Come Down from the Mound*. Phoenix: Miter Publishing.

Ríos, Isabella. 1976. *Victuum*. Ventura, CA: Diana-Etna.

Rodríguez, Luis. 1994. *Always Running: La Vida Loca Gang Days in L.A.* Willimantic, CT: Curbstone Press.

Sábato, Ernesto. 1948. *El túnel*. Buenos Aires: Editorial Sudamericana.

Sánchez, Phil. 1975. *Don Phil-O-Meno, sí la Mancha*. San Luis, CO: Sánchez.

Santiago, Danny. 1983. *Famous All Over Town*. New York: Simon and Schuster.

Soja, Edward W. 1966. *Thirdspace: Journeys to Los Angeles and Other Real-and-Imagined Places*. Oxford: Blackwell.

Steinbeck, John. 1935. *Tortilla Flat*. New York: Covici-Friede.

Vargas Llosa, Mario. 1962. *La ciudad y los perros*. Barcelona: Editorial Seix Barral.

THREE / Alejandro Morales'
The Captain of All These Men of Death
and Philip Roth's *Nemesis* / Parallels
and Contrasts / **STEPHEN MILLER**

Despite being well-known diseases, neither polio nor tuberculosis are much discussed because their occurrence is so notably infrequent in the United States. It is therefore remarkable that two established, pre–Baby Boomer novelists—the New Jerseyan Philip Roth (1933–2018) and Californian Alejandro Morales (1944–)—chose to focus their respective literary works on polio and tuberculosis. Unlike the exotic and even invented diseases or genetic conditions found in the best-selling fiction of Michael Crichton, Stephen King, and Stephanie Meyer, Morales' *The Captain of All These Men of Death* (2008) and Roth's *Nemesis* (2010) explore what occurs when the lives of everyday people are altered by the onslaught of these dreadfully real diseases.

Roth's novel—hailed in some obituary pieces as his masterwork—was his last novel, marking the conclusion of his career as a writer. Morales, however, continued to write after *Captain*, publishing *River of Angels* in 2014—his masterwork so far. There has never been, as far as we know, any personal connection between Morales and Roth, though their lives have decided parallels. Morales was raised in an East Los Angeles barrio, the son of immigrants from Mexico, whom he portrayed in *The Brick People*.[1] Roth was reared in what was, literally speaking, the Jewish Weequahic ghetto of multiethnic Newark, the grandson of Jewish immigrants from Eastern Europe.[2] While Morales completed his PhD at Rutgers University, Roth did his graduate work at the University of Chicago, where he had formative contact with novelist and creative-writing professor Richard Stern, as well as some interaction with his future great friend Saul Bellow. Moreover, Morales, having made his subsequent career and life in Southern California, turns that area and the Mexico of his parents into the fertile ground of his novelizing. In a like way Roth, while living between England and the northeastern United States, most especially Manhattan, makes his and his family's home in Newark the home turf of his characters' lives. Added to these parallels, all public pronouncements by these two writers from the opposite ends of the United States indicate that on the conservative-to-liberal scale in politics, they tend to express themselves on the liberal side. After all, as members of two formally recognized minority groups in the United States and significantly shaped by the civil rights era, both authors emerged from circumstances that called for liberalizing measures to aid their respective groups, long accustomed to being the objects of racial/ethnic prejudice.

So, the question that offers itself is how, if at all, did these respective biographies lead their subjects to center their individual literary fictions on two serious diseases that are scarcely in the news in the Western world today. For unlike cancer, cardiovascular issues, HIV-AIDS, Ebola, or even hypothesized lycanthropic conditions, polio and tuberculosis are not necessarily the concern of large numbers of people. Are, then, Morales' focus on infectious tuberculosis and Roth's on polio considered denotatively in and of themselves, or should they be considered metaphors for broader societal issues? The comparative study that follows hopes to answer this question.

MORALES, TUBERCULOSIS, AND
THE CAPTAIN OF ALL THESE MEN OF DEATH

Morales' path to tuberculosis in *Captain* is clear. In the acknowledgments to the book he explains, "The inspiration for [this novel] I owe to my son Dr. Gregory Stewart Morales, who suggested and encouraged me to write [it] based on his UCLA Medical School thesis on the treatment of tuberculosis" (2008, xi). For when his son was doing his research, he "asked if I knew any surviving tuberculosis patients" and that led to "my tío Roberto Contreras" (xi). Contreras, we learn, was diagnosed with tuberculosis as a nineteen-year-old in 1944, when he walked into the recruiting office "to volunteer to go to war" to join family and friends already fighting in the European and Pacific theaters (8). Yet the youthful Contreras was subsequently rejected for military service and recommended to civil authorities for treatment. This process eventuated in two institutionalizations. The first was at the dystopic "Monrovia Consumptive Rehabilitation Center [which was] nestled against the foothills" with "a magnificent view of the Los Angeles basin" (26). The center was "located in an old mission-style three story building," with a total of "ten good-sized, one-story cottages flanking the main building" (26). During the ten months he lived there with physically and psychologically wounded Pacific combat veterans, as well as with acute tuberculosis patients who typically left Monrovia in the feet-first position, Roberto's own condition did not worsen. Once judged to be noncontagious, he was allowed to return to his parents' home under a strict regime of separate eating and living arrangements. However, since his TB was not cured, his mother, receiving counsel from Roberto's health-care worker and doctors at the Long Beach Health Center, pushed to get him into the higher-level TB center at the historical Olive View-UCLA Medical Center in Sylmar, California (45, cf. xi). This sanatorium became the site of a nearly four-year stay, during which he underwent two operations; it also became the site of a virtual guided tour, which a septuagenarian Uncle Roberto gave to his nephew Alejandro Morales and great-nephew Dr. Gregory Morales. Moreover, it (along with the East L.A. barrio and the outwardly attractive, but dangerous Monrovia "death trap" [45]) became the principal of the three extended locales of *Captain*'s overarching action.

The base narrative mode of the novel is a first-person narration by Roberto that covers the January 1944 to 1950 period. It is framed by author Morales' paratextual explicatory acknowledgments and author's note (xi–xii). Together both sections oblige the reader to consider the relation between fact and fiction in the narrative that follows.[3] After emphasizing that *Captain* is, "like my other novels" a "work of fiction," Morales goes on to define his fictive activity in this novel in problematic, suggestive, and perhaps even paradoxical terms. For Morales, his novel is "an attempt to conjure a fantasy of accuracy inhabited by those persons living or dead who intentionally, by their own free will, with pleasure or torment, read and identify themselves in the story. What they see of themselves is probably not far from the truth, however fictional" (xii).[4] That said, neither Morales nor his son are actual characters in the fiction. Their extratextual role is to foment Uncle Roberto's decision "to begin my story" of the 1944–1950 TB period of his life. This happens sometime after Roberto's first return "in over thirty years" to the Olive View Sanatorium, which by then is in ruins, on February 24, 1996 (1). The terms of Morales' fiction then stimulate Roberto, as he says in his prologue (1–3), to begin to remember everything connected with his

Olive View experiences when "accompanied by my nephew Alejandro Morales ... and my nephew Gregory Morales, who was writing a case history on me as an ex-TBer" (1). This is because Roberto finds himself interiorizing the process, as—in light of the complete narrative—strangely "*many fond memories about the place* were rushing back to me" [my emphasis] (1). Among these were those of the equally young fellow patient Mayte ("I saw her in the many places and times that we spent at the sanatorium"), who we learn succumbed not to TB but, as some critics stress, to the questionable treatments that she received (see Jirón-King [2008–2009, 12]). Though Mayte "stayed with me throughout my life" because she "truly was my one and only love" (1),[5] her role in *Captain* is much more complex than merely standing as Roberto's love interest.

While waging her own personal and ultimately unsuccessful fight against death, Mayte becomes the editor and lead contributor of the *Olive View Point*, an in-house publication serving the sanatorium's patients. Offering articles related to tuberculosis, ten of these *O.V.P.* pieces appear in *Captain* as short narratives, many written by Mayte. They are intercalated at regular intervals into Roberto Contreras' main narrative and wind up constituting veritable episodic or anecdotal histories of tuberculosis.[6] Beginning with stories of the Greek physician Hippocrates in 460 to 370 BC (16–21), these intercalated narratives reach forward chronologically to bacteriologist Robert Koch's identification of the *tubercle bacillus* in the late nineteenth century (201–7) and, in response to the 1931 case of Alire Ford, to the creation and implementation in Los Angeles (and eventually all of California) of strict protocols for the obligatory, lawful isolation and treatment of "tuberculosis patients and victims of irresponsible tuberculants" (232). In accord with the five principal divisions of Roberto's narrative ("Prologue," "The Disease," "Olive View Sanatorium," "The Cure," and "Prognosis"), these intercalated materials include one six-page section written by Roberto's great-nephew Dr. Gregory Morales. Perhaps taken and somewhat adapted from Gregory's UCLA Medical School thesis, the section, printed in a unique type face, represents chapter 6 of *Captain*, simply titled "Olive View Sanatorium." This chapter forms a kind of bridge from Roberto Contreras' pre–Olive View treatment to his long time spent there, and more concretely from the section "The Disease" (5–73) to the somewhat subjective and intercalated history entitled "Olive View Sanatorium" (75–180). For from the perspective of the post-1996 family visit to the ruins of Olive View, Dr. Morales' six pages end with the comment that despite the natural beauty of the sanatorium's setting, carved out from a seventeenth-century Spanish land grant tract, the place, not unlike the Monrovia facility, was "still only the backdrop, the battlefield of a deadly disease" (73). Furthermore, Dr. Morales adds that on his April 12, 1945, date of entry to Olive View, "Robert [sic] Contreras understood that he was about to enter a place where," despite the attractive Sylmar grounds, life was synonymous with death" (73).[7]

In ways not dissimilar, then, to such novels as *Don Quixote* (1605/1615) and *Moby Dick* (1851), *The Captain of All These Men of Death* is structured upon two narrative planes: that of the first-person narrator Robert Contreras telling his story; and that of the sometimes far-ranging secondary, intercalated narratives that frequently purport to be historic and serve to contextualize in time and place the story of Robert's personal experience. In *Don Quixote*, the intercalated, supposedly real-life narratives offer sometimes obvious, and other times not-so-obvious comparisons, contrasts, and even alternatives to protagonist Alonso Quijano's mad or purposely playful adventures.[8] But in Melville's first-person story it is the main character Ishmael who regularly intersperses his narrative with secondary material concerning the anatomy and natural history of sperm whales or of whaling and whalers themselves. Morales' *Captain*, however, while employing the technique of intercalated, secondary narratives that harkens back to *Don Quixote*, is more closely like *Moby Dick* in supplying intercalated materials that more directly bear on the novel's thematic core: whales and whaling in the case of Melville, tuberculosis and its treatment in the case of Morales.[9] In a genuine sense, then, what *Moby Dick* and *Captain* both share beyond their incorporation of intercalated narratives is their narratives of lives that dramatically end with the telling of disasters of destruction and disease, and only cursory hints about the narrator's/survivors' afterlives.

So the reader of the first plane of *Captain* experiences the history of the six years Robert Contreras lives as a person with TB, from diagnosis through the different stages in his treatment and, finally, recovery following an operation that comes after his release from the sanatorium.[10] The reader subsequently processes the second narrative plane involving intercalated materials that function within themselves and reflect upon or bear on Robert Contreras' autobiographical narrative. This kind of multilevel text obliges the reader to decenter from Robert's story, transfer their attention to multiple other narratives, discern their relevance to Robert's, and then re-engage directly with Robert.

Between the end of his first institutionalization at the Monrovia Consumptive Rehabilitation Center and entering the sanatorium at Olive View, the twenty-year-old Robert "found a job not far from home" that "was in a furniture shop" (62). And even though he then was at Olive View for nearly four years, he did need a complicated, but successful surgery for TB in his collar bone a short time after his discharge. With this last hurdle having been overcome forty-six years in the past, Robert concludes that "once more my life became routine," which meant he returned "to work at the furniture company doing the same job as before" (262; cf. 279). Morales' reader also learns that back when he emerged from tuberculosis, life was good for Robert's four veteran-brother siblings; most of them and their sisters were married and getting on with generally acceptable lives (see 220, 262). At the same time "routine" for Robert, twenty-five years old in 1950, included continuing to live with his parents and palling around with his old friend Cuke. And while he and Cuke "joined the Catholic Youth Social Club" where they "met lots of girls in church and at the socials" (262), Robert's past dragged on him. He writes that "after Olive View I just couldn't get close to any woman" (262). Why? Because he "was always afraid she would find out, consider me infected for life . . . and leave me" (262). So while Robert "socialized" he "never really got serious" because none of the women, he "became convinced," would ever be like his platonic, life-inspiring, true Olive View love, Mayte (262; cf. 219–20).

When the reader finally finishes *Captain*, it is upon reading the last words of Robert's narration, last words that repeat essentially those just quoted above: "As far as what I did after getting out of the sanatorium, nothing exciting, nothing to brag about: I went back to work for the furniture company" (279). No paratextual materials await, just a few blank end leaves. But so devastating are these words in their postulation of a kind of death-in-life description of decades lived without warmth, without meaning, that it is natural to return to the beginning of the novel to see if there are materials there that shed more or better light on Robert's life. But there is nothing of that sort. The "Prologue," for instance, anticipates *Captain*'s ending: "You see, nothing really exciting happened in my life. I led a normal life" (1). By "normal" he means never marrying and having children, and continuing to work for the rest of his life in the furniture factory, albeit in time reaching the rank of "biller" working directly with the company accountant (248). In such a "normal" life it is not surprising that, as Robert writes toward the end of the "Prologue," the "strangest thing that happened" in that life of some forty-six more years "was when my nephew [Alejandro Morales] came to visit with his son [Dr. Gregory Morales], who asked me for an interview" based on his being "a surviving TBer and about my stay at Olive View Sanatorium" (1). The strangeness of the visit then leads to Robert's first-person narrative, which, as complemented especially by the intercalated materials on the history of TB found in the pages of the *Olive View Point*, contextualizes and amplifies the pathos of his and his fellow patients' TB histories. In the very last part of the "Prognosis" Robert experiences a kind of epiphany: "Now [in the 1990s] I understand that Olive View was a battlefield and I was simply [by visiting] a soldier returning to the scene of the battle, a victor who had lost many comrades on this site" (3). Robert is indeed a survivor, but the reader, who now rereads the last page, wonders if Robert's resumption of his routine "normal" life—a kind of half-life without Mayte—really constitutes a victory.

In the context of relative levels of being victorious, one last aspect of *Captain* requires attention before we move on to Roth's *Nemesis*. While forwarding Robert's narrative about his treatment and Mayte's role in it, chapter 17 holds a certain formal dimension in common with the ten intercalated sections on the history of the how, what, and where of the treatment for TB. This chapter is overwhelmingly concerned with the arrival of and outcome for a new patient at Olive View, one Sandro Díez (known as "el Coloso" because of his great height and weight). Perhaps as a kind of homage to his own native Montebello, California, and to the memory of the Simons Brick Factory of the same town that plays a central role four years earlier in his novel *The Brick People*, Morales has Sandro hail from Montebello. There, Sandro works among Mexican or Mexican American workers in the prospering, three-shift Pacific Pipe Clay and Cement Company (a version of which seems to be as historical as Simons). After enduring and observing many abuses of himself, his fellow workers and, in a company town, their families, Sandro starts to agitate for unionization. After some difficulties, the owners, desperate not to find their plant unionized, make concessions and Sandro is given some special considerations as the workers' leader. Management is nonetheless mistrustful and suddenly Sandro finds himself and his family being diagnosed with tuberculosis and himself being with great force confined to Olive View Sanatorium. After some good and well-meaning doctors there determine Sandro has no TB (and probably never did), they begin to try to get him discharged, but a visit by his wife and children sends a sad and desperate Sandro into a rage. This is met by overwhelming police force and Sandro is a beaten to pulp, his presence in *Captain* essentially over. This semi-intercalated account demonstrates how authorities charged with controlling and treating TB at the highest level—as opposed to the frontline physicians—can be corrupted. As part of the overarching power structure, they can use facilities under their control to "handle" or "manage" people and matters unrelated to sickness that they, all the same, judge to be within their competency.

As chapter 17 is the last one of the novel's section titled "Olive View Sanatorium" (75–180), the next section, "The Cure" (181–245) and its first chapter, the eighteenth in the novel, reasserts the primary narrative of Robert Contreras about himself, Mayte, and their fellow patients. In conjunction with the intercalated story of Sandro Díez that fills chapter 17, it is important to note that chapter 16 concludes with Mayte's piece from the *Olive View Point* on the eighteenth-century French TB specialist Marcel Triguer. In *Captain*'s telling he became caught up in the terror of the period of the French Revolution. While jailed and before his execution, Triguer is obligated to examine a small, ten-year-old boy who turns out to be the incarcerated orphan-king Louis XVII. Following years of purposeful neglect and mistreatment, and Triguer's own execution, the poor child dies of tuberculosis in 1795. The chronology of the Triguer/Louis XVII story immediately preceding that of the Olive Point doctors/Sandro Díez one lets the reader come to their own conclusions about the unfortunate way that tuberculosis has historically been mistreated and manipulated by out-of-control civil authorities for their own political ends. In that context the great abuse of Sandro Diez and the family he leaves without its breadwinner is perhaps worse than what Triguer and Louis XVII suffered. That such a cold, calculating, and violent manipulation takes place nearly two centuries later and, worse, in the democratic United States is sobering at best and, at worst, no words can be found to describe it.

ROTH, POLIO, AND *NEMESIS*

Nemesis maintains no sociopolitical dimension similar to *Capitan*'s tuberculosis-related stories of the brutalities of revolutionary Paris in the early 1790s or of Los Angeles in the post–World War II period. While *Capitan*, despite the recovery of Robert Contreras and his long post-TB afterlife, conveys through its intercalated stories and main narrative a great and justified mistrust for civil authorities, ignorant and manipulative by turns, *Nemesis* does not advance such historical anecdotes about the treatment of polio. Much more simply, it accounts for the reality of polio as a crippling and, for those who contracted it, death-dealing scourge in the decade or so before Dr. Salk's vaccine. The book concentrates on how the crippling consequences of the disease affect over the years its two principal characters, Arnold Mesnikoff and Bucky Cantor.

In this novel, first-person narrator Mesnikoff tells his own story of polio but principally relates the story of Cantor, another sufferer who years before was the younger Arnold's idolized, stalwart, and athletic Newark playground director.

Like Morales' Robert Contreras, Roth's Bucky Cantor was rejected for service in World War II, albeit at the beginning of the war and for poor vision rather than the polio that struck him years after he was classified as a 4-F candidate for military service. While Robert Contreras is doubtlessly the first-person narrator and protagonist of *Captain*, Roth's first-person Mesnikoff, despite centering his narration on Cantor before and after he is struck with polio, is arguably the protagonist of *Nemesis*. The Mesnikoff narrative however may be more complex than that of Morales' narrator because its primary victims from the narrative viewpoint—Bucky and Mesnikoff—survive their polio, but with significant physical impairments that mark, to different degrees, their subsequent lives. In *Captain*, on the other hand, the primary tuberculosis victim, Robert, survives, but as we already addressed he has very little to say about his life during nearly the next half century. In contrast to his Olive View years, during the decades before his 1996 visit to a ruined Olive View he appears to have lived alone. And worse still, this nearly half century was passed without life-giving purpose because Mayte, who "truly was my one and only love," died at the same Olive View Sanatorium from which he emerged successfully in 1950. Both Mesnikoff and Bucky, albeit impaired for life, survive the immediate consequences of falling victim to their polio, unlike others they knew on that Newark playground. It is in the third part of *Nemesis*, twenty-seven years after the onslaught of their disease, that the polio-crippled Mesnikoff chances to meet a crippled and almost unrecognizable Cantor in the street.[11] And that is when the most important part of Mesnikoff's story begins: first, his account of Bucky's blunted afterlife as a grievously disabled polio victim whose suffering is more psychological and emotional than physical; and, second and somewhat implicitly, his own story of acceptance of what could not be changed while continuing on to a quality personal and professional life.

Nemesis indeed gives more stress to the characters' afterlives than to the life-marking disastrous events that lead to Mesnikoff's first-person narrative, which includes his telling about Cantor as well as including a record of Cantor's own words in his conversations with his former playground charge. For *Captain* to be more like *Nemesis*, Mayte would have had to have survived Olive View, not returned Robert's love, and then for Robert to have met her, much changed and not for the better, many years later (and, of course, for him then to have narrated that entire story). For *Nemesis* to be more like *Captain*, Roth would have had to intentionally move toward the encyclopedic dimensions of *Captain*, vis-à-vis tuberculosis, by intercalating sociohistorical materials telling of polio through the millennia. Reference to polio is at the very least made in relation to "the country's greatest prototype of the polio victim," President Franklin Delano Roosevelt, who died in early 1945 after Arnold and Bucky contract the disease and are in their respective periods of hospitalization, though more for overall contextualization than as point of departure for political or characterological discussion and extended comparisons and contrasts with the protagonists of *Nemesis*.[12]

A further prominent difference between Morales and Roth is the personal dimensions to Morales' interest in tuberculosis: how his medical doctor son's professional interest in the disease becomes intertwined with Uncle/Great Uncle Roberto Contreras being a TB survivor with a story to tell, and how that story reveals specific cases of authorities' ethnic prejudice against Mexican Americans. Roth's interest, on the other hand, seems to have no personal or ethnic dimension. Despite the scene with which the novel begins, the one where some young Italian street toughs say they have come to spread among the Jews the polio that has struck their own poor neighborhood (see 12–16; cf. p. 1), *Nemesis* postulates no connivance among any groups or the authorities to use polio as a direct or indirect weapon against Jewish ethnicity or culture. In the novel polio is an ethnically blind scourge that authorities, for fear of it spreading, deal with as best they can in the days before Salk's vaccine. Moreover, neither in any interviews known to me, nor in the paratextual materials of *Nemesis* (i.e., the acknowledgments on an unnumbered leaf between the title page and the numbered first page of the novel) does Roth make polio a personal or ethnic matter. Instead he mentions two or three reference works used to increase his knowledge of the disease. And this because, as would have been typical for a person of his generation who did not contract the disease or have close relations with someone who did, Roth's first-hand knowledge of polio may well have been rather limited. That is probably why Roth, who is closer in age to his narrator and something like ten years younger than his protagonist Bucky Cantor, gives the overall idea of having been a passive observer of the effects of polio in a few individuals known to him during his formative years in Newark.

These impressions, of a kind the author of this study and his generation also had on Long Island, were supplemented with more understanding by chance interactions in adulthood with polio survivors who suffered varying degrees of paralytic loss from their polio. And in that same free-flowing way, Roth's college years at Bucknell University in rural Pennsylvania may have been the real-life objective correlative for the Pocono Mountains summer camp where Bucky Cantor and his fiancée feel protected from Newark's fictional polio outbreak. For despite the novel beginning with the words "The first case of polio that summer [of 1944] came early in June, right after Memorial day, in a poor Italian neighborhood crosstown" from Bucky and his narrator Arnold Mesnikoff's "Jewish Weequahic section" (1), no critic consulted or research conducted by me indicates that there was anything in 1940s Newark like the epidemic of polio that is the premise on which *Nemesis* is based. Beyond that the other cited references in the paratextual acknowledgments have much more to do with the way summer playgrounds and camps were managed. Documenting these activities is important since Bucky Cantor, with his late 1941 4-F draft rating because of his extremely poor vision, earns his living in 1944 as a neighborhood playground supervisor in Newark. Yet, at the urging of his fiancée, Marcia Steinberg, who fears him becoming a victim of the polio raging—at least according to Roth's fiction—that summer in Newark, Bucky leaves his playground and the boys who idolize him to work as a counselor at the same summer camp as Marcia, located in the clean air of the Pocono Mountains and removed from the hot "Equatorial Newark"—the title of chapter 1—and its disease-prone urban population (1). In the end Bucky's tragedy is double, for by the time he joins Marcia, and unbeknownst to him, he has already contracted the disease to which he has seen some of his young playground charges fall. Worse, from his own point of view, he goes on to bring polio to the summer camp after having abandoned his playground charges to their fate, albeit not passing it on to the daughter of Dr. Steinberg, M.D. He views his polio-stricken self as unworthy of Marcia and, despite all her protestations to the contrary in the name of the love she bears him, he breaks off their engagement once and for all.

This is a parallel to the love relationship in *The Captain of All These Men of Death*, one underpinned by disease and essentially severed by socio-medical forces more or less beyond the protagonists' control. A work whose connections with the rest of Morales' oeuvre are more subtle, *Nemesis* belongs to an identified subgrouping within its author's thirty-one published books.[13] In the unnumbered fore-pages of the first, hardback edition, one page before the title page of *Nemesis* there is the listing (customary for Roth) of his work divided into thematic subgroupings. But only with the listing found in the 2010 edition do *Everyman* (2006), *Indignation* (2008), and *The Humbling* (2009) migrate from the last, miscellaneous category of "Other Books" (not a "slouch" category, since it includes such key Rothian titles as *Goodbye, Columbus* and *Portnoy's Complaint*) to form, with *Nemesis*, a new, penultimate subgrouping titled "Nemeses: Short Novels." Uncharacteristically among these volumes, the blurb for *Nemesis* extends beyond the inside of the front flap of the dust jacket onto the rear inside flap. Doubtlessly with Phillip Roth's blessing, if not active collaboration, those six lines from the rear flap read, "Through this story run the dark questions that haunt all four of Roth's recent short novels [including] *Nemesis*: What kinds of choices fatally shape a life? How does the individual withstand the onslaught of circumstance?"[14]

This kind of sharp thematic focus proper to the novella genre is the exact opposite of encyclopedic novels such as *Captain*. Its center is TB, but its range in space and time is greatly expanded by including the millennium-spanning anecdotal intercalated narratives. Ten in all, they break into the narrative of the principal and secondary characters' direct experience of disease in 1944–1950 and their treatments for it. Hence, while *Captain* is to tuberculosis what the longer-still novel *Moby Dick* is to whaling, Roth's short novel or novella *Nemesis* is to polio what Melville's short novel *Billy Budd, Sailor* is to British naval warship discipline in the early nineteenth century.[15] Not at all encyclopedic, the short novels *Nemesis* and *Billy Budd* concentrate on how their protagonists, Bucky Cantor and Billy Budd, react to having to "withstand the onslaught of [the] circumstance" of becoming the powerless victims, respectively, of ineluctable disease and the unappealable provisions of martial law (which require Billy's summary execution for—no matter the provocation—having merely struck, let alone killed, a British officer in time of war).[16] *Captain*'s Robert Contreras, on the other hand, actually withstands the onslaught of tuberculosis, is left physically unscathed, and, something that cannot be said of all TB survivors, goes on to a long life. Yet he is left emotionally diminished and even spiritually atrophied by the loss of Mayte, who succumbs while being treated against TB's onslaught. Roth's Bucky Cantor conversely suffers both physical and psychological trauma at the hands of polio, which leaves him as emotionally lessened as Robert but also physically crippled for life.

The difference in *Nemesis* between the narrator Arnold Mesnikoff and his subject Bucky Cantor is more similar to Contreras' case than to Budd's. For the latter dies before the onslaught of his circumstances while Arnold and Bucky, like Uncle/Great Uncle Roberto, physically survive their diseases. Significantly in *Captain* there is no real probing of why Robert lives and Mayte dies. Yes, it is said that she dies not of her tuberculosis (if she ever had it, which the novel questions) but as the consequence of some kind of failed experimental treatment in the La Loma annex of Olive View, a place where Robert also is experimented upon. So the real question in light of details about the respective experiments is: did Mayte die and Robert live simply because it was so fated?[17] The most that can be said, it seems, is that his condition was more susceptible to treatment at Olive View and the off-site collarbone operation afterward than was hers. And while, as is consonant with his entire literary aesthetic as identified and vigorously investigated by Marc García-Martínez, Alejandro Morales goes deeply into the gritty details of the history of treatments for tuberculosis, as well for some, but not all of those which Roberto and Mayte and Roberto's entire cohort at Monrovia and Olive View receive, Phillip Roth shuns that investigation and exposition as respects polio. It is almost as if Roth assumes the reader has seen enough polio-contorted bodies to not need details from him on the failed treatments those ruined bodies received before reaching their present state of something like equilibrium. More interesting for Roth are first the fact of the crippling transformations caused by their polio in Arnold and Bucky and then his exploration of how each man looks back on that fact and evaluates it in light of the life he led before they meet by chance in Newark twenty-seven years later.

FINAL POINTS

We began by asking if Morales' tuberculosis and Roth's polio were being considered in themselves as denotative diseases or as connotative medical metaphors for more broadly societal matters—perhaps in the manner of the plague in Camus' existentialist novel of the same time published in 1947. It is helpful that Morales took up such matters in his 1995 interview with José Antonio Gurupegui about the existence of the "informative or literal level" of his narrations, as well as their "symbolic level" (13). Both levels are more or less under his control, but more interesting to him, in the name of the reader, is the question of whether there also exists a potentially richer "third meaning" beyond his—or, indeed, any writer's—conscious control, but to which the reader accedes (13).

From the exposition and analysis of *Captain* and *Nemesis* it seems clear both Morales' Robert Contreras and Roth's Bucky Cantor are characters whose sickness, even when conquered in the most basic way of physically surviving it, kills their affective selves. We have cited and commented on Robert's words to the effect that after Mayte, he could never relate to another woman and proceeded to live what once was called in the Catholic Church to which Roberto belonged a life of "single blessedness." But in Robert's version, it is at best an arid life. In his polio afterlife Bucky is not so different. He tells Arnold that, after the death of his grandmother long ago, "no loved one from the past remained in his life" (247), that the sports he once loved so much no longer hold interest for him, and that, excepting a weekly meal at one of Newark's Portuguese restaurants, he does little besides watch TV news and sit in the park on nice days as he goes between his apartment and job at the central Newark Post Office. Only the chance meeting with Arnold and their subsequent weekly diner lunches changes this routine. But even after hearing from the thirty-nine-year-old Arnold how he, disabled and all, turned his life around following the suicide of his bitter, brilliant, but polio-afflicted Jewish college roommate at Rutgers (267–69), the fifty-year-old Bucky remains unmoved. While he seems happy for Arnold, he can only ruminate constantly on what could have been had polio not ruined his life twenty-seven years before.

The reader of *Nemesis* learns many more specifics about Bucky Cantor's life than the reader of *Captain* does about Robert Contreras'. But it is not certain that Bucky's details are any more positive than the lack of the same in Robert's case. So, while it is easier to picture the dimensions of Bucky's life's ruin, nothing suggests it to be less arid or better than Robert's. The death of Mayte and of Arnold's college roommate on the one hand, and Arnold's successful polio afterlife on the other, are kinds of "bookend" alternatives to Bucky and Robert's lives. The particular power of both characters and their novels is that the reader is drawn into considering how and why these two characters react to the onslaught of disease in their lives the way they do. That reader may also consider whether and how she or he would be more like them, like Arnold's roommate, or like Arnold himself. And in that process the reader in dialogue with the books creates his or her own "third" meaning.

Perhaps the biggest difference between the two works is that of the encyclopedic dimensions of *Captain*. Its greatly enhanced "informative or literal level" of narration multiplies both symbolic and meaning-creating possibilities. Yet, as in Aristotle's comparison in the *Poetics* of how dramatic and epic poetry produce their effects on the audience (26.1–8), the shorter form (i.e., in our study the novella form chosen by Roth) produces stronger emotion by making plot and character focus attention more specifically and intensely than can the epic or, in our case, the encyclopedic novel form. But the effect of Morales' epic/encyclopedic novel embraces and makes present wider vistas of human experience. In the end the reader can have both *Captain* and *Nemesis* and take from each its unique way of creating literary experiences around the phenomenon of infection and illness. However, as readers we most certainly go beyond either work's thematic topics and create our own specific or broader meanings by comparing and contrasting all the characters and their fates that bringing these two related works together accordingly fosters.

NOTES

1. A short, substantive, biographical introduction to Morales as a Latino Southern Californian and writer may be found in Thompson (2015). For the biographical dimension of Morales' parents found in *The Brick People* see his 1995 interview with Gurpegui (10, 13).

2. Historical views of Newark and Roth, including Newark's ethnic neighborhoods and diversity, can be found best in the chapter "Safe at Home" of Roth's episodic biographical memoir (1988) and in Malanga (2017).

3. Jirón-King (2008–2009) dedicates more attention to the fiction-fact relation than is within the scope of this paper.

4. The novelist Javier Cercas (b.1962) has subsequently made the concept of the "novel of real life" very familiar for Spanish readers in such works as *Anatomía de un instante* (2009) and *El impostor* (2014). The title piece of his collection of essays *El punto ciego* (2016) also deals extensively with the kind of fiction or novel of real life that Morales pioneers in *Captain*.

5. Another dimension to Mayte's relation with Robert and other young men at Olive Grove arises toward the end of the novel. While she does form some very close relationships with male patients other than Roberto, and a very good one with Roberto also (see 149), her motivation seems inseparable from the fact that they are all facing imminent death from TB. Notable in this overall context: Mayte forms a particular, one-on-one relationship with the French medical doctor Annique Demore. And while Mayte makes sure that Dr. Demore takes increasing and probably life-saving interest in Robert's case, she spends more time with the doctor than with Robert. This includes long walks, going to her house for dinner, and his staying the night there with her (177).

6. For a different, complementary discussion of *Captain*'s intercalated narratives see Jirón-King.

7. Lines like these in *Captain* lead critic Roberto Ayala to use the Foucauldian concept of "heterotopia" to describe the sanatorium spaces of the novel as places to marginalize and isolate Latinos, whether they be sick as is Roberto, or, perhaps more dangerously, politically problematic for Anglo authorities.

8. Those who endorse the theory of Alonso Quijano as a role-playing sane person versus a man driven crazy by his reading of chivalric romances include Mark Van Doren in *Don Quixote's Profession* (1958) and Gonzalo Torrente Ballester in *El Quijote*

como juego (1975). Gustave Doré's influential and oft-reproduced illustrations (370 of them) for the French folio edition in two volumes (1863) can stand in with all their graphic force for those who consider Quijano to be crazy.

9. Although not his main focus (he comments more on the characters than on the structure of *Captain*), García-Martínez also astutely notes a Mevilleian dimension to the novel (see 2014, 135 n. 41).

10. Most frequently Roberto or Robert Contreras is referred to as "Robert" in the volume *The Captain of All These Men of Death*. However, just as Morales sometimes inserts phrases in Spanish into his base English-language text in order to create a particular, desired effect, sometimes the name "Roberto" is used here instead of the much more prevalent "Robert." In this article I use "Robert" or "Roberto" as my references to Morales' occasionally code-switching text indicates to be more in keeping with the spirit of the relevant section of Morales' and my own text.

11. The figure of "twenty-seven years" is based on Mesnikoff's direct statement on page 241.

12. It should be stated that FDR died of a cerebral hemorrhage and that what was then considered his polio today is thought to have been Guillain-Barré syndrome. Roth must have known this, but the hypothesis is anachronistic as regards the timeline of *Nemesis*.

13. García-Martínez's demonstration of what he calls "the flesh-and-blood aesthetics" of Morales' work is a prime example of a critic making such connections (particularly about Morales' pre–*River of Angels* oeuvre).

14. Given his stature as that rare combination of esteemed and much-awarded literary author, and sometimes a best-selling one, New York native Roth saw his *Nemesis* recognized with immediate reviews in the *New York Times*. In "Newark, 1944, When Polio Disrupted the Playground," Michiko Kakutani, the long-term chief critic for the paper as well as the 1998 winner of the Pulitzer Prize in Criticism, panned the novel. Four days later, on October 8, 2010, in "Summer of '44," Leah Hager Cohen, an author of fiction, nonfiction, and criticism, began by rehearsing the aversion women of her generation felt for Roth's work on grounds that it was the product of a notorious misogynist. Nonetheless, the *Times* assigned the book to her, she read it, and was won over by the novel; this led her to read more by Roth and to her growing admiration for his production. Both Kakutani and Cohen give prominence to the polio theme of the novel, and not because of personal experience of a disease they both were too young to have had. Both were born and raised in the United States after polio's virtual elimination thanks to the Salk vaccine. Unlike the children and youth of Roth's Depression-era birth, or even children born in the earliest years of the Baby Boom, Kakutani and Cohen's generation were never forbidden by polio-fearing parents to enjoy the delights

of public swimming pools; nor did they interiorize a nearly manic fear of the germs carried by "poor kids." Among these "germs" were ones not mentioned by Roth but in the minds of parents at that time—those that could give their kids lots of bad diseases, maybe even tuberculosis.

15. My purpose is to make formal comparisons with no intention of entering into the odious terrain of discussion of literary rankings. For it is clear that making anything like quality or importance comparisons of *Moby Dick* and *Billy Budd* would be as inappropriate and useless as comparing the works by Melville and Morales, or Melville and Roth, or Morales and Roth that are under analysis here.

16. Melville (1962a, 111).

17. Giannopoulou's reading of *Nemesis* in relation to Sophocles' *Oedipus* is convincing. One thing, though, she does not really take up: while Oedipus is partly the victim of his own hubris, that is a condition from which draft-reject Bucky never suffers. No matter his accomplishments, being rejected for military service in wartime both humbles and shames him; in turn, contracting polio destroys what is left of his feelings of self-worth.

WORKS CITED

Ayala, Roberto. 2013. "The Space of Disease in Alejandro Morales's *The Captain of All These Men of Death*." In *Landscapes of Writing in Chicano Literature*, edited by Imelda Martín-Jones, 151–60. New York: Palgrave Macmillan.

Cercas, Javier. 2009. *Anatomía de un instante*. Barcelona: Mondadori.

———. 2014. *El Impostor*. Barcelona: Literatura Random House.

———. 2016. *El punto ciego*. Barcelona: Literatura Random House.

Cervantes, Miguel de. 1987. *El ingenioso hidalgo don Quijote de la Mancha*. Edited by Luis Andrés de Murillo. Madrid: Editorial Castalia.

García-Martínez, Marc. 2014. *The Flesh-and-Blood Aesthetics of Alejandro Morales: Disease, Sex, and Figuration*. San Diego: San Diego State University Press.

Giannopoulou, Zina. 2016. "Oedipus Meets Bucky in Philip Roth's *Nemesis*." *Philip Roth Studies* 12, no. 1 (July): 15–31.

Gurpegui, José Antonio. 1995. "Interview with Alejandro Morales." In *Alejandro Morales: Fiction Past, Present, Future Perfect*, edited by José Antonio Gurpegui, special issue, *Bilingual Review / Revista Bilingüe* 20, no. 3 (September–December 1995): 5–13.

Jirón-King, Shimberlee. 2008–2009. "Illness, Observation, and Contradiction: Intertext and Intrahistory in Alejandro Morales' *The Captain of All These Men of Death*." *Bilingual Review / Revista Bilingüe* 29, no. 1 (January–April): 3–13.

Malanga, Steven. 2017. "Philip Roth's Newark: The City at Its Peak and in Its Decline Are the Novelist's Greatest Characters." *City Journal*, Spring 2017. https://www.city-journal.org/html/philip-roths-newark-15132.html.

Melville, Herman. 1962a. *Billy Budd, Sailor (An Inside Narrative)*. Edited by Harrison Hanford and Merton M. Sealts Jr. Chicago: University of Chicago Press.

———. 1962b. *Moby Dick, or The Whale*. New York: Holt, Rinehart and Winston.

Morales, Alejandro. 1988. *The Brick People*. Houston: Arte Público Press.

———. 2008. *The Captain of All These Men of Death*. Tempe: Bilingual Press / Editorial Bilingüe.

Roth, Philip. 1988. *The Facts: A Novelist's Autobiography*. New York: Farrar, Straus and Giroux.

———. 2010. *Nemesis*. Boston: Houghton, Mifflin.

Thompson, Nicole Akoukou. 2015. "Palabras: Alejandro Morales, Professor and Author of *River of Angels*, Explores Fiction, Bilingualism." *Latin Post*, September 10, 2015. https://www.latinpost.com/articles/78030/20150910/alejandro-morales-professor-and-author-of-river-of-angels-explores-speculative-fiction-bilingualisim.htm.

Torrente Ballester, Gonzalo. 1975. *El Quijote como juego*. Madrid: Ediciones Guadarrama.

Van Doren, Mark. 1958. *Don Quixote's Profession*. New York: Columbia University Press.

FOUR / Tropes of Ecothinking and the Spatial Imaginary in Alejandro Morales' *River of Angels* / SOPHIA EMMANOUILIDOU

We make no distinction between man and nature: the human essence of nature and the natural essence of man become one within nature in the form of production of industry, just as they do within the life of man as a species. ... [M]an and nature are not like two opposite terms confronting one another ... rather, they are one and the same essential reality, the producer-product. —Deleuze and Guattari, *Anti-Oedipus*, 1983

The influence of nature on human societies and the ways different cultures have responded to their places in the natural world are crucial elements of historical understanding and basic to the ways in which cultures explain their pasts. Studying these relationships also increases our understanding of the past as process. Seeing human historical events in the context of long-term ecological or geological time produces a perspective on human history and a set of historical concerns very different from one based on single historical events or the accomplishments of individuals.
—Goucher, LeGuin, and Walton, *The Balance*, 1998

PROLOGUE: ENVIRONMENTAL DISCOURSE AND CHICANO ECOTHINKING

In *Anti-Oedipus: Capitalism and Schizophrenia* (1983), Gilles Deleuze and Félix Guattari attempt a coherent claim to the reciprocity between humankind and nature. These two cultural critics assert that humankind and nature interpenetrate and are of "the same essential reality" (5). Although European poststructuralist theory can be a treacherous inclusion in a study of Chicano ecowriting, the first epigraph above serves as an apt preamble to an ecocritical analysis of Alejandro Morales' *River of Angels* (2014). Morales' novel unfolds the conjoined histories of urban development and racial discrimination within the context of construction work in general and the building of bridges over the Los Angeles River in particular. As for the subtle connections between French philosophy and Chicano literary writing, while Deleuze and Guattari postulate the codependence between nature and human essence, Morales in a similar way explores the social relationships that are formed in the context of humanity's mechanical endeavors to control the natural world. The analogy employed in this study supports the definition of selfhood in ecological terms, and at the same time highlights some of the power relations that contour the interactions between human societies and the nonhuman world. In this regard, *River of Angels* can be read as an ecodiscourse, or as a literary insight into the spatial and environmental imaginary of the Los Angeles River basin area.

River of Angels construes humanity's interactions with nature in regard to a twofold abuse: the exploitation of natural resources and the maltreatment of indigenous populations. In contrast to the use of abstract concepts, especially those that obstinately disengage experience from the significance of nature, Morales' ecothinking foregrounds nature as a catalyst in human history. The novel employs ecowriting in order to explicate the history of Los Angeles via the incorporation of environmental consciousness in the hermeneutics of otherness and identity.[1] Accordingly, this study examines the historical presence of cultural identity in Los Angeles through the lens of ecology. *River of Angels* explores the development of numerous ethno-racial communities since before the Spanish conquest of Southern California. Morales composed an epic novel that redefines the formation of human societies as a natural process of creating spatiocultural niches, each one inextricably connected with the landscape's geomorphology and its distinct biota (the plant and animal life of a region). The ecocritical viewpoint of this study welcomes the examination of the environmental processes of partitioning and interaction. These two processes take place concurrently, involve the existence of multiple identities in Los Angeles County (such as Euro-Americans, Native Americans, and Mexicanas/os, Chicanas/os), and shed light onto the varied aspects of cultural presence in the landscape.

Written against the backdrop of mainstream politics that endorse social partitioning and implement strategies for ethnic marginalization, *River of Angeles* prompts an ironic reversal of the intentional demarcation of space and selfhood.[2] In fact, Morales' epic novel takes the form of a backlash against the dogmas of discrimination and explores cultural empowerment in the peripheries of the United States. In other words, *River of Angels* reveals how white America's rampant exclusionary politics have in effect assisted the creation of a marginal social milieu that resists cultural extinction within the barrios of Los Angeles. This kind of barrio localism becomes a defense mechanism against the rhetoric of superiority that is designed to encourage acceptance of racial-cultural difference.

River of Angels unveils the developed world's methodical violation of the natural laws of adaptation and evolution in both sociopolitical and ecological terms. The book tackles the desecration of the environment parallel to strategies systematically annihilating of localized cultures. These two interpretive functions of the novel are fundamentally informed by two key ecological concepts, *the association* and *the ecotone*. In community ecology, an association underscores the existence, endurance, and versatility of biodiversity. It also serves the interests of an organic community as a whole, becoming part of a larger biotic equilibrium, preserving diversity, and evolving the physiognomic characteristics of a spatial enclave. Moreover, nature's global forces generate numerous areas of transition that gradually and evenly blend adjacent ecosystems into each other. During such processes, nature creates spaces of intersection that retain the biological characteristics of both systems.[3] These intermediary locales, more importantly, create unique biotic and abiotic factors within their own territorial boundaries. In ecology, ecotones stand for exceptionally useful interfacial zones between different ecosystems. They are geographical formations that enrich our awareness of natural hybridities. As liminal areas they abide by the rules of evolution and adaptation, upholding a nonturbulent rite of passage from one level of existence to another. Within this framework, what is ecological becomes predominantly cultural and political in Morales' epic novel.

Moreover, as the concept of the ecotone effectively pertains to the novel, it also recasts definitions of borderland spaces as safe zones appearing as dissimilar environs and as cultural realms of in-betweenness. Associations and ecotones are fundamental segments of an ecologist's scientific interest, but in this study they transmute into tropes for understanding humanity as historicized in Morales' work. It is my ecocritical contention that associative relations and ecosystem intersections can best explain the multilayered experience in the geocultural borderlands between twentieth-century Anglo and Mexican Los Angeles.

CULTURAL ASSOCIATIONS AND ECOTONAL SPACES IN THE BORDERLANDS

Cultural theories largely focus on a complex web of abstractions to elucidate self-identity. However, since the mid-1990s literary criticism has highlighted the environmental perspective to discuss our cultural productions and/or practices. More particularly, in the introduction to *Nature in Literary and Cultural Studies: Transatlantic Conversations of Ecocriticism* (2006), Catrin Gersdorf and Sylvia Mayer probe the linkages between nature studies and the numerous cultural manifestations across the globe. The interdisciplinary angle that these two ecoscholars take explores the correlations between the natural sciences and academia's abstract codifications. Gersdorf and Mayer posit a series of tentative questions with the aim of foregrounding the natural environment as a definitive factor in the creation of self-identity: "How and to what effect is nature conceptualized in various cultural, critical, and disciplinary contexts? How and to what effect are concepts of the natural and the human related to each other? What is the relationship between nature, language, art, and literature?" (13). Answers to such questions are aptly offered by Devon G. Peña, whose ecothinking redefines Chicana and Chicano studies as an inherently environmental field of research, one that implements a straightforward attack on our present techno-scientific fixations. He asserts that pairing up the study of nature with cultural theories brings forth the issue of power. More specifically, the Chicano ecothinker contends that if the "socially constructed category of Other, [i.e.] nature" is omitted from scholarly endeavors and/or university curricula, then the world of academia turns a blind eye to the reciprocity between environmental deterioration and sociopolitical injustice (1998, 7). Peña holds that self-cognizance is attainable through a wholehearted scrutiny of our spatial surroundings and the life-forms inhabiting it. His environmental standpoint creates an innovative, philosophical matrix that validates the consolidation of the humanities with the material cosmos.[4] Peña holds that "knowledge is power, and truth is thus situated; it is a by-product of whatever social group is positioned to impose its own version of the truth. This philosophical problem has haunted Chicano Studies since the questions of identity and subjectivity were cast out among the intersections of race, class, gender, and sexual difference. But much of this discourse seems cut off from collective expressions of struggle in our home communities" (7). Peña's nuanced statement aligns with the theoretical turn taken toward the study of localism and/or translocalism, a turn suggesting that place-based knowledge or "the truth [that] is situated" can provide effective solutions to global ecodestruction (7).[5]

Drawing from the above brief reference to the valid linkages between natural sciences and cultural studies, *River of Angels* offers a historical insight into a dual suppression that has taken place in Los Angeles: repression of the physical world and of several other-than-white communities. Along with the two anecdotes that appear in the prologue and epilogue, the novel covers a temporal span of approximately two centuries. It explores the ecological history of the area and traces the transformation of the landscape from a state of untouched natural beauty into extended urbanization. Moreover, this epic novel reels out the coercions endured by the native population, immigrants, and the grassroots residents. The political forces and doctrines that determine Los Angeles' post-Conquest history include Spanish colonialism, Euro-American settlement, capitalist tactics of surveillance, Nazism, the doctrines of eugenics, and neonativism. All these authoritarian formulations legitimize the agendas of expansionism, exercise the (in)famous Cartesian dualism, and disdain the categories of Other on the grounds of their alleged "deficiency . . . social, cultural, religious and personal diversity" (Plumwood 2003, 55). The main plot of *River of Angels* centers on the lives of two families, the indigenous Riverses and the white American Kellers, two families whose initial, cordial relationship is complicated by manifold ethical and dogmatic predicaments. Along with his paratextual sections and the intermittent short stories, anecdotes, and vignettes included therein, Morales relays a historical overview of the moral crises emerging in the heart of American society, some of which include cultural annihilation, historical oblivion, and disruption of the ecosystem.[6] From the ecocritical angle, American despotism comprises the gripping central theme of the text, which corresponds to anthropogenic interventions in the natural environment and to the concomitant threats to the well-being of local communities.[7]

River of Angels redresses the history of Los Angeles by looking into the fallout of Euro-American politics over local life, culture, and ecological landscape use. The narrative presents Los Angeles as "a city with history buried underneath its present face. It is a palimpsest with archives layered one on top of the other by human beings crossing into this vortex since the ancient people settled here near the river" (xi). In the prologue, Morales is apprehensive of borderlines and accentuates the negative effects of cultural and spatial segmentation. In fact, the narrative voice is strikingly concerned with hegemonic centrism and the mighty powers of what the narrator ingenuously refers to as the "Anglo political machine" (xii). For Morales, Anglo-American politics of discrimination forge impervious bisections of both self-identities and ecospaces. So, the Chicano author openly espouses interculturalism as the most effective tactic for the democratization of the greater L.A. society. He considers the existence of borders as part of an authoritarian political pact, a misjudgment that has resulted in extended ecodestruction and the expropriation of indigenous cultures. Thus, he pinpoints the inherent flaws of geographical boundaries when they are drawn by those in power and hails cultural intermingling as a natural process of adaptation. Morales writes:

> Borders cannot be controlled-shut down by the military or by a great wall or technological devices—simply because inherent human migration cannot be stopped, detained, held back by artificial means. Attempts to control borders, to stop the movement of people, have and will cost lives and billions of dollars. Human migration is a natural phenomenon, as natural as the migration of birds, fish and butterflies. It will cease when there is no need to move. Language is a living dynamic system whose process must be learned, supported, and whose existence must be encouraged. . . . A stable culture is an anachronistic idea, a silly demand that advances nativism, racism and discrimination. . . . Cultures . . . constantly impact, change and support each other. Continuous cultural negotiation is the future. (x)

River of Angels presents colonization as a protracted conquest, part of an expansionist scheme that forcefully controls cultural identity and the physical environment. The novel offers insights into the colonizers' prejudicial mindset and the propagandistic jargon that facilitate the complete subjugation of an invaded space. In fact, it reveals the repercussions of the Eurocentric separation of mind and body, interpreting this disjunction as the outcome of a dual approach to experience, one that has sparked a series of discontinuities in the New World. Val Plumwood terms this process "hyper-separation," a term signaling "an emphatic form of separation that involves much more than just recognizing difference. Hyper-separation means defining the dominant identity emphatically against, or in opposition to, the subordinated identity, by exclusion of their real or supposed qualities" (2003, 54).[8] In *River of Angels* the notion of "hyper-separation" emerges in the construction of bridges over the Los Angeles River. From a pragmatic perspective, the watercourse is a natural resource that sustains life and facilitates the creation of settlements in accordance with natural patterns of land surface development.⁹ In the prologue to the novel, however, the taming of the water flow and the construction of bridges transpire with ethno-racial divisions. Morales elaborates on this awareness by recording an intense conversation with his friend Mark. While driving to a Los Angeles Central Library reading event, Mark expresses his awe at the magnificent structures crisscrossing the river. But Morales responds to his interlocutor's words of praise with a thoughtful instruction on the offensive intents that launched the erection of the Los Angeles bridges:

> [the bridges] were built in the twenties and thirties. The gringo city fathers built the bridges so that the Mexican laborers who worked in the city on the Westside could leave. . . . The rich didn't want Mexicans living with them or anywhere near them, so the East-side, known as "East LA," was developed for Mexican workers to inhabit. . . . That's what the Anglos wanted, and that's what they got. East LA was designated for Mexicans and industry. They did not want Mexicans living in Hancock Park, West Los Angeles, Hollywood, Brentwood, Beverly Hills. They built the bridges to get those Mexicans, that labor force, back over to the other side. (xi–xii)

The prologue of *River of Angels* is a solicitous introduction to the interaction between autocracy and the ecosphere, an interaction that is often reproduced in interdisciplinary writings of a cultural, sociopolitical, and ecological interest.¹⁰ This thematic concern is further amplified in part 1, which introduces the reader to a temporal vista of the area, reviving life in the nineteenth century and also recreating some of the injustices endured by the local indigenous populations. The presence of the conquistadores appears in *River of Angels* as vague memories of a distant past where ancient peoples were forced to stay "at what they called *the missions*, but many native people resisted and ran to the mountains or into the chaparral on the hills and lands leading to the sea" (7). The overall historical experience of the "people of Yanga" in Los Angeles, however, is ultimately one of cultural appropriation (7).¹¹ Morales records the Spanish onslaught as the original cause of wretchedness for the indigenous populations, as "their way of life [was] brutally disrupted and threatened, [and] the Indians had lost almost complete control of their land, language, religion and bodies" (7).

River of Angels charts the text's chronotope within a matrix of imperialism. At the onset of the novel, the temporal ecocontext is set in 1842, prior to the signing of the Treaty of Guadalupe Hidalgo in 1848. Morales attributes Eden-like qualities of symmetrical species' distribution to the river basin. The prevalent feature of the landscape recreates a harmonious assembly, where human and other-than-human species coexist in a spiritual, ecological coalition. In this natural equilibrium, Morales claims that

> the Indians knew how to listen to the trout that had travelled the length and depth of the river, the trout that had swum against currents and around every turn of lush vegetation crammed with wild roses, grapes and spices that perfumed the air and calmed the spirit, the trout who had explored the underground beginnings of the river's natural sources. (6)

The field of community ecology explains the equitable association between the varied elements of an ecosystem as a precondition for sustainability. Similarly, cultural ecology avows the presence of indigenous groups as the backbone of egalitarian societies. Morales' description of life along the banks of the river details an ecocultural community that does not disconnect any species population from the general physiognomy of the landscape. For instance, the trout is anthropomorphized and assumes the role of a wise character. In fact, the trout embodies the sole bearer of the exact locations of the water source. And while not fully deified, the trout becomes the recipient of the Indians' respect because it can safeguard environmental continuation.

River of Angels thus explores the associative channels that the autochthonous populations develop with their physical surroundings. The Indians "listened to plenty of water, to plenty of trout, to plenty of animals, and to plenty of vegetation, and to plenty of wind and rain, to all that combined to understand the river's voice, to sing the river's cycles, to know the river's space and to sense the river's movement" (6). In this light, the text is an enriching account of ecoawareness, one that delves into the interconnections between self-identity and environmental being. The novel commences with only a sketchy description of the Pueblo of Los Angeles, eloquently recounted as "nestled next to its Río de la Porciúncula" (2). Apart from the natural border, with its eastern and western banks, the basin area is one of an integrated social life. The land by the river hosts a number of cultural groupings, and the watercourse symbolizes a rejuvenating element for the livelihood the basin area. Yet despite Los Angeles County being an unspoiled environment that has sustained native populations for centuries, it soon becomes a hostile space because of the intrusion of settlers. In fact, the river transmutes into a site that engenders humanity's efforts for economic growth and development. Soon, an antagonistic dynamic ecocontest happens near and over the river for the extraction of natural resources, a conflict that unsettles the ecological balance that the indigenous populations had always honored. First, the gold nuggets in the water lure numerous *mineros* (miners) from Mexico to inhabit the area, "working different sections of the streams and deep arroyos" (2). But the river is both a source of wealth and an agent of adversity, one that "did not give up its stones easily" (3). Morales complicates the pious life on both banks of the river with calamity via the fickle flow of its waters, "the powerful flash floods," and the treacherous muddy waters (3). Furthermore, the spatial imaginary Morales delineates is of a harsh environment for the ignorant settlers from the East, because only the Indian populations fostered place-consciousness for survival purposes. And although a practical outlook would construe life by the river as hazardous, the Indians believed in the sublime quality of the watercourse. In fact, the novelist juggles with the literary tradition of magic realism when he describes the Indians' veneration for the waters. In support of their symbiotic relationship with the natural world, the local people revered the watercourse and

> believed that the river spirit considered all that existed in its waters living precious objects, sending out its river energy to bring them back. The native people know that in some way, some time, all things from the river would return to the river. The river's spirit would never be controlled; it was unpredictable; it was greater than man. (3)

River of Angels presents human geography in Los Angeles as an assortment of settlers "from the interior of Mexico and from the southern and northeastern areas of the United States" (2). But discriminatory politics slash the locale by imposing social borders, the aim of which is to separate the dominant culture from nonwhite communities. In a way, the novel exposes how the Spanish maltreatment of the Indians was intensified by white Americans, ultimately leading to the barring of all racially Other populations from the cityscape of Los Angeles (Peña 1998, 7). Nevertheless, the text reassesses the effectiveness of prejudicial policies in terms of spatial marginalization. So, instead of representing places for the distressed and disenfranchised, barrio locales become social sanctuaries. The book describes Mexican neighborhoods as geographical patterns that do not function purely as antihegemonic or unruly arenas in the United States. Instead, these peripheral spaces become the fertile soil for social solidarity, whereby dwellers create the conditions for cultural invigoration and carve out a safe passage from social exigency to conviviality. For example, in part 3, *River of Angels* traces the economic collapse of the Great Depression. In a striking antithesis to the euphoric aura of the rising economy in parts 1 and 2 due to urban growth and industrial development, part 3 echoes the negative consequences of being caught up in the lures of the stock market and the frenzy of affluence. The economic collapse of October 1929 causes an unprecedented social downturn that eventually deprives people of the promises of the American Dream. We encounter hordes of bankrupt investors and laid-off "men and women . . . who . . . got up in the morning to walk the streets in hopes of finding work for a couple of hours, half a day" (154). The stock market slump wrecks the nation's social web and generates a series of dramatic effects in people's lives. Morales remarks that the economic collapse leads to

> drastic consequences: jail for the husband and possibly the wife. The children would be taken by the County Child Protection Services, which meant an orphanage or a foster home. Deportation was a possibility for those who were from abroad. The third possible result was living in a car or truck, waiting for the next government handout. (144)

The Great Depression triggers a major crisis in the heart of the nation's laissez-faire economy, a crisis that paradoxically backfires against its most fervent advocates. But *River of Angels* alleviates the lingering memories of the Crash with a powerful juxtaposition, wherein the repercussions of the stock market's collapse are counterbalanced with vivacious descriptions of barrio life. The narrative collates home economy practices in East Los Angeles as the antidote to the capitalist ideal of prosperity. So, after the Crash, "once in a while, white men walked into Mexican barrios . . . more than willing to work for a few handfuls of beans, some rice, a couple of ears of corn, some tortillas" (154). Like paradisiacal apparitions, the gardens of Mexican housewives give "the tired, sad-eyed men . . . a look at the rows of vegetables, pots with tomatoes, green beans, peppers and many more vegetables" (154). The barrio represents an alternative way of living, which lauds the ownership of small plots of land and the benefits of tending one's own vegetable garden. In short, the text shifts our attention from the desolate urbanites to the serene barrio dwellers. *River of Angeles* also conveys the charitable ethics of barrio living. The Mexicans treat the occasional white visitors with generosity and approach them with "a grocery bag [with] [t]ortillas, *frijoles, calabacitas y tomates para* . . . [la] *familia*" (55). As a differential space against the bleak post-Crash wasteland of the main city, the barrio represents an eco-utopia "that was thriving there in the middle of East Los Angeles" (155). The Mexicans "held together and survived the economic times . . . The Depression equalized and made every man vulnerable . . . [People] took any kind of labor. Pride was not needed during this time of desperation when the priority was to feed their children and themselves" (156).

Morales' novel creates a sharp antithesis between the vulnerable landscape of Anglo-American individualism and an ecosystem of barrio cohesion through collectivity. Indeed, by the turn of the twentieth century the political elite had crafted the mindset of social egotism. But quite ironically and amid the turmoil of economic demise during the Great Depression, white American decision-makers devalued the interstitial ecobarrio. So, "White calls increased not to hire Mexicans, to cut them off from any kind of public help, and to repatriate or deport the aliens who took jobs away from the real Americans, [while] the gardens in the Mexican barrios became more productive" (156). In a sense, the political mise-en-scène described by Morales turns Mexicans into scapegoats for the failure of its fiscal policies and propounds the exclusion of nonwhite people from the governmental relief benefits, or even worse, the repatriation of "the aliens" (156).

A central event in *River of Angels* is the love relationship between Albert Rivers and Louise Keller. The emotional bond between a Mexican American young man and an Anglo-American girl symbolizes the viable connections that can come into being among different racial identities. The honest devotion that the two characters have for each other is rejected by Louise's uncle, a fanatic supporter of the "master race" and an ardent devotee of eugenics (182). Philip Keller is an evil person who epitomizes the entrepreneurial principles of extreme capitalism, the colonization of the landscape, the mistrust of Mexicans, and the removal of the indigenous populations. In short, this character reflects the neonativist dictum that excludes all nonwhite social groups from the American national identity. Uncle Philip supports social demarcation based on people's racial identity and repeatedly "warns his family about the innate inferiority of dark-skinned people and the physical dangers and genetic risks of associating with unfit humans" (182). The complication in the plot structure arises when Louise realizes she is with child, but the consummation of the young couple's marriage is thwarted as Albert is cast among the "biologically defective, mentally inadequate sub humans" (184). Fearful of confronting the normative attitudes of the time, Albert and Louise elope in order to defend their interracial affection, and the barrio of Simons Town becomes their chosen hideout, a crevice-like space that can protect the union of the two young lovers:

> [The barrio] people were understanding, generous and helpful. [Albert] was grateful for the women who had accepted Louise and invited her to their gatherings, to church. They invited Albert and Louise to come to celebrate baptisms, marriages, family dinners and fiestas. They made them feel welcome and comfortable. (179)

The barrio turns into a liminal zone or a spatial haven that protects the young lovers from the eugenicists' austere codifications.[12] Simons Town becomes an ecotonal, intermediary space where a transitional consciousness is facilitated for the couple. The enclave of the barrio is an intermediary space between two antithetical cultural positions: the white American and the Mexican. In *River of Angels* the barrio is a cultural space that welcomes racial difference as an associative paradigm of social life and offers the opportunity to ameliorate the animosity sparked by racist theories. Finally, although Louise and Albert's hideaway in the Mexican barrio appears as a responsive move away from the dire notions of racial cleansing, it soon allows the two young characters to reclaim their upper-class social status from the maladies of racism. Indeed, except for Uncle Philip both families consent to Albert and Louise's relationship by welcoming their union and the birth of their child.

CONCLUSION: OF BORDERLANDS, ECOTONES, AND LOCAL CULTURES

In the *Borderlands / La Frontera: The New Mestiza* (1987), Gloria Anzaldúa construes human existence as a vacillating or unpredictable passage to self-understanding. Anzaldúa claims that identity cognition entails an esoteric struggle: "Chicano, indio, American Indian, mojado, mexicano, immigrant Latino, Anglo in power, working class Anglo, Black, Asian—our psyches resemble the border-towns and are populated by the same people. The struggle has always been inner, and is played out in outer terrains" (87). Her insightful approach to identity formation incorporates both our inmost "struggles" for self-definition and our associations with "outer terrains" (87). In this context, self-understanding is part of a community's and/or an individual's natural passage to maturation, which happens in relation to the physical world surrounding us. This process does not always imply a tumultuous rite to identity formation, but it may be a phase of change that effectuates one's introduction to a new state of being, whether it is of a conformist or nonconformist kind. As for the material world, the discipline of ecology examines similar intermediate conditions of ecosystem formation in the study of ecotonal spaces. Forming between two different ecosystems, an ecotone is a spatial pathway to organic and inorganic change. The function of an ecotone is to regulate and safeguard a tranquil passage from the physical characteristics of one terrestrial zone to an adjoining one. Both Anzaldúa's notion of identity negotiation between different cultures and the biogeographical formation of numerous ecotones around the world explain transition as a natural stage toward social and ecological replenishment and balance. In other words, the renewal of a social setting and/or an ecological environment does not threaten existing conditions of being; rather, change abides by the laws of natural evolution, mitigates inaction, and hinders decay. *River of Angels* in this regard charts numerous interim spaces and transcodes them as locales that maintain environmental and cultural harmony through the use of associative tropes. Above all, the use of spatial fissures like Simons Town enriches the allegorical elements of Morales' compelling work and underscores the existence of borderline regions as a valuable asset in the preservation of sociocultural accord.

The connections between the borderland metaphor and the laws of nature are most illuminating in the integrative study of ecology and Chicano literature. The literal and figurative exchange of environmental characteristics and national identities in Morales' novel reassesses the existence of all intersection areas (the borderlands and ecotones) as vigorous spaces that maintain stability and ordinariness in times of an ecological and/or historical crisis—in this case represented by the essential raping of indigenous land by invading Euro-Americans and the 1929 stock market crash. In fact, the novel interrogates evolutionary processes and associative coexistence as the antidotes to a stagnant mentality that promotes the production of a single guardian class (i.e., the master race according to the principles of eugenics) and cultural centrism. In all, Alejandro Morales reconsiders supremacist notions of whiteness by expounding on them with an emphasis on ecobeing, all the while arguing that institutionalized racism coincides with ecocide and that the anthropocentric or technocratic agendas of the West endorse the defilement of nature as the ultimate victory of imperialist onslaught. *River of Angels* accordingly nullifies the paradisiacal ideal of building the city-upon-the-hill for white settlers only. In an ironic reversal, the original strategy for the obliteration of Mexican communities actually aids in the formation of vibrant barrios. The political strategies of carving bounded areas and crafting social frames in the novel start off as a praxis of discrimination that in turn gives rise to a cultural antipraxis of grassroots existence in the barrios. In this light, *River of Angels* recasts the history of Los Angeles, imparts multilayered, empowering tales of resisting culture-cide, and relates racial diversity to ecological and/or natural diversity—and beyond.

NOTES

1. One of the major premises of ecothinking is to highlight the importance of inclusivity and diversity in our study of the world. For example, Simon Estok maintains that ecothinking withstands the "pathological inability to see connections" between humanity's sets of significance and those of otherness, be they human or nonhuman (2009, 9).

2. Ecowriters often articulate the unnatural aspect of bounded areas and the ethical irregularities of geographic division and border patrol. More precisely, the ecophilosophical perspective holds that the nation is a fictitious condition of self-identification, one that can be as easily wiped out as initially created. For example, Wai Chee Dimock claims that "the nation is revealed to be what it is: an epiphenomenon, literally a superficial construct, a set of erasable lines on the face of the earth. It is no match for that grounded entity called the planet, which can wipe out those lines at a moment's notice, using weapons of mass destruction more powerful than any homeland defense" (2007, 1).

3. At this point, the distinction between place and space is pending. For example, Lawrence Buell maintains that place and space are parallel but also divergent, geographic concepts. For Buell, place and space explain our sociocultural connections with the material world. He contends that "place entails spatial location, entails a spatial container of some sort. But space as against place connotes geometrical or topographical abstraction. . . . Those who feel at stake in their community think of it as their place. . . . Up to a point, world history is a history of space becoming place" (2005, 63).

4. Devon G. Peña (2010) claims that "university-based Chicana/o studies has steadily lost much of its concern for participatory, community-based social action research. However, the infatuation with discursive politics appears to be running its course. It seems to be in stasis as an epistemological project, largely because students and community activists are losing interest in the stale form of discourse fetishism that characterizes much of the so-called cultural studies Left in academia" (149). According to Peña, scholarly preoccupation with reflective thinking brings about alienation from the material cosmos surrounding us.

5. The translocal or glocal rapport of Chicana/o literature is an intriguing, critical proposition for the reconsideration of the canon. In fact, Chicana/o scholars have repeatedly attempted to evade the political register of El Movimiento, and since the 1960s Chicana/o writings have applied the experiences of Mexican Americans as a paradigm of being-in-the-world beyond the realm of ethnopolitics. For instance, Luis Leal points out that "the identification of Chicano literature has progressed from the narrow, sociological definition to the broad, humanistic, and universal approach. Chicano literature, by lifting the regional to a universal level, has emerged from the barrio to take its place alongside the literatures of the world" (2007, 32).

6. Candice Goucher, Charles LeGuin, and Linda Walton (1998) maintain that our perceptions of the world are amalgams of abstract negotiations and material concreteness. The three ecothinkers argue that "the cultural relationship between humans and their environment varied according to people's perceptions of the landscape. In this way, technology and culture altered both the inner landscape of the individual and the physical landscape of the natural world. Though in the modern world, influenced by the powerful impact of industrialization, we tend to see nature as something to be dominated and controlled by human effort, early human cultures were shaped and informed by an awareness of the power of nature" (3).

7. Ecocritical thinking looks into the intersections of politics, culture, and nature with the purpose of creating an interdisciplinary juncture that will eventually curb biogeographical destruction. For example, Greg Garrard (2012) maintains that in order "to confront the vast, complex, multifarious agglomeration of ecological crises . . . the apparently flimsy tools of cultural analysis must be seen by the ecocritic as a moral and political necessity" (16).

8. Val Plumwood historicizes dualism and traces the political hues in our definitions of culture. For Plumwood, "the function of hyper-separation is to mark out the Other for separate and inferior treatment. . . . Colonizers exaggerate differences—for example, through emphasizing exaggerated cleanliness, 'civilized' or 'refined' manners, body covering, or alleged physiological differences between what are defined as separate races. They may ignore or deny relationship, conceiving the colonized as less than human. The colonized are described as 'stone age,' 'primitive' or as 'beasts of the forest,' and this is contrasted with the qualities of civilization and reason that are attributed to the colonizer" (2003, 54).

9. My comment here reflects the ecocritical perspective that the natural world cannot be separated from humanity's endeavors, especially when considering the negative effects anthropogenic interventions may have on a bioregion. According to Bruno Latour, "the name of the game is not to extend subjectivity to things, to treat humans like objects, to take machines for social actors, but to avoid using the subject-object distinction at all in order to talk about the folding of humans and nonhumans. What

the new picture seeks to capture are the moves by which any given collective extends its social fabric to other entities" (1998, 93–94).

10. There are five basic types of ecological relationships that in conjunction define species coexistence, resource allocation, and reproduction. These types are classified as predation, competition, mutualism, commensalism (long-term symbiosis), and parasitism. Ecological relationships are interactions that may have positive or negative effects on the biota of a specific landscape. My ecoperspective in this study discusses competitive relationships (i.e., the Anglo-American paradigm of the inner city) and symbiosis (i.e., Indians and Mexicans on the banks of Río de la Porciúncula, in the forests, and in barrios). For more on ecosystem synergism and/or antagonism, see Dickinson and Murphy (1998).

11. The Tongva are the Native American inhabitants of Los Angeles County. They were later referred to as Gabrieliño- or Fernandiño-Tongva, names corresponding to the Spanish missions in the region. To this day, the Tongva tribes have not received legal recognition by US legislation, and their land use rights have become a controversy of legal interest. For an insightful discussion of the genocide of the Gabrieleño-Tongva, see Jurmain and McCawley (2009).

12. It is of critical interest to compare Albert and Louise's escape from mainstream codes of conduct and Uncle Philip's breakaway from the democratic ideal. Both decisions are acts of defiance and/or emancipation, which may lead to moral advancement or, on the antipodes, to social collapse. From the psychoanalytical standpoint, Fred Alford (2002) points out that the two major categories of emancipation are "negative and positive freedom [and both] reflect the poles of borderline experience, the poles of losing and fusing. Negative freedom risks becoming 'me and my will is sovereign over the world,' and so losing the human connections that make life worthwhile. Positive freedom risks becoming the fusion of my will all that is powerful and good, be it my higher self, God or the Party. Needed is a concept of freedom that sees negative and positive freedom not as competing definitions, but the ends to which freedom may be pursued, and so lost. Freedom is neither a place nor a possession. Freedom is a delicate balancing act" (115).

WORKS CITED

Alford, C. Fred. 2002. *Levinas, the Frankfurt School and Psychoanalysis*. London: Continuum.

Anzaldúa, Gloria. 1987. *Borderlands / La Frontera: The New Mestiza*. San Francisco: Aunt Lute Books.

Buell, Lawrence. 2005. *The Future of Environmental Criticism: Environmental Crisis and Literary Imagination*. Malden, MA: Blackwell.

Deleuze, Gilles, and Félix Guattari. 1983. *Anti-Oedipus: Capitalism and Schizophrenia.* Minneapolis: University of Minnesota Press.

Dickinson, Gordon, and Kevin Murphy. 1998. *Ecosystems: A Functional Approach.* London: Routledge.

Dimock, Wai Chee. 2007. "Planet and America, Set and Subset." In *Shades of the Planet: American Literature as World Literature,* edited by Wai Chee Dimock and Lawrence Buell, 1–16. Princeton: Princeton University Press.

Estok, Simon. 2009. "Theorizing in a Space of Ambivalent Openness: Ecocriticism and Ecophobia." *ISLE* 16, no. 2 (Spring): 1–23.

Garrard, Greg. 2012. *Ecocriticism.* London: Routledge.

Gersdorf, Catrin, and Sylvia Mayer. 2006. "Nature in Literary and Cultural Studies: Defining the Subject of Ecocriticism—An Introduction." In *Nature in Literary and Cultural Studies: Transatlantic Conversations of Ecocriticism,* edited by Catrin Gersdorf and Sylvia Mayer, 9–24. Amsterdam: Rodopi.

Goucher, Candice, Charles LeGuin, and Linda Walton. 1998. *The Balance: Themes in World History.* Boston: McGraw-Hill.

Jurmain, Claudia, and William McCawley. 2009. *O, My Ancestor: Recognition and Renewal for the Gabrieliño-Tongva People of the Los Angeles Area.* Berkeley: Heyday Books.

Latour, Bruno. 1998. *Pandora's Hope: Essays on the Reality of Science Studies.* Cambridge, MA: Harvard University Press.

Leal, Luis. 2007. "The Problem of Identifying Chicano Literature." In *A Luis Leal Reader,* edited by I. Stavans, 28–32. Evanston, IL: Northwestern University Press.

Morales, Alejandro. 2014. *River of Angels.* Houston: Arte Público Press.

Peña, Devon G. 1998. *Chicano Culture, Ecology, Politics: Subversive Kin.* Tucson: University of Arizona Press.

———. 2010. "Environmental Justice and the Future of Chicana/o Studies." *Aztlán: A Journal of Chicano Studies* 35, no. 2 (Fall): 149–57.

Plumwood, Val. 2003. "Decolonizing Relationships with Nature." In *Decolonizing Nature Strategies for Conservation in a Post-Colonial Era,* edited by William M. Adams and Martin Mulligan, 51–78. London: Earthscan.

FIVE / History, Spatial Justice, and
the *Esperpento* in Alejandro Morales'
Pequeña nación / JESÚS ROSALES

Alejandro Morales is without doubt one of the most prolific and respected Chicano novelists of our generation. He began publishing in the mid-1970s, initiating a second wave of novelists stemming from the Chicano Movement of the 1960s. Morales' body of work can best be described as *totalizador*, a term connoting an entity's overwhelming and absolute "completeness."[1] In Morales' narrative, totalizador pertains to how his novels present a reality consisting of fragments of lived experiences that seem to closely portray a broader Chicano worldview. In his case, these translate to fragments of Chicano history that introduce glimpses of past and present, with hints of the future. As far as pinpointing a particular spatial epicenter, the preferred location of Morales' historical fiction generally takes place in California, the Los Angeles metropolitan area more specifically. In addition, there is the ubiquitous de facto Mexican and Mexican American barrio of Simons, a corporate township within the city of Montebello.[2]

As of this writing, Morales' fiction consists of nine novels and one collection of short stories that includes a novella.[3] His first two novels, *Caras viejas y vino nuevo* (1975) and *La verdad sin voz* (1979), were written entirely in Spanish and published in Mexico by Editorial Joaquín Mortiz. *Reto en el paraíso* (1983), his third novel, was written in both Spanish and English, no doubt preparing his readers for the exclusively English-language narrations that followed: *The Brick People* (1988), *The Rag Doll Plagues* (1992), and *Waiting to Happen* (2001). Morales briefly returned to writing in Spanish with his collection of stories *Pequeña nación* (2004) but switched to English with his last two novels to date, *The Captain of*

All These Men of Death (2008) and *River of Angels* (2014). Morales' use of these two languages in his narrative is consistent with a prevalent Chicano sense of urgency to express oneself in Spanish, a crucial component of their cultural character, as most Mexican Americans and Chicanos desire to maintain their Mexican ties or identity.

The purpose of this study is to present a general interpretive reading of three tales from *Pequeña nación* and focus on the dynamic role that history, spatial justice, and the concept of the *esperpento* play in them.[4] History has persistently demonstrated that those in power often disrupt communities, thereby creating heterotopias, spaces of constant change and mobility that damage the spatial identities of such communities.[5] With this in mind, it can be argued that in *Pequeña nación* Alejandro Morales raises spatial and existential concerns necessary for understanding the complexity of his characters. For Morales, these concerns present themselves as troubling and sinister esperpentos that distort his characters' reality.

"LOS JARDINES DE VERSALLES": HISTORY AND SPATIAL INJUSTICE

When one considers Morales' profound interest in history and his outspoken desire to present Chicano life in the most realistic and, at the same time, fantastical manner, it is fitting that he commences *Pequeña nación* with "Los jardines de Versalles," a novella comprising a number of the elements that characterize his overall fictional landscape. Such elements involve a plot and setting that take place in specific historical spaces. In addition, we see here both the use of the oral tradition honoring the folkloric backgrounds of Chicano literature and the Chicanos' struggle with spatial and historical displacement and identity erasure. And, in a unique Moralesian way, we note an obsession for presenting a literary world in carnivalesque and supernatural *embrujos* that allows past, present, and future spaces to converge and coexist. In more ways than one, these characteristics surface not only in "Los jardines de Versalles" but also in "La penca" and "Pequeña nación," two other stories that comprise his collection. The existence of these characteristics in *Pequeña nación* presents a microcosm of the totality of Morales' overall narrative, thus impelling readers to ponder whether the collection is actually one novel written in three parts that remain linked by the barrio Simons, that ever-present and emotive protagonist of Morales' narrative world.

"Los jardines de Versalles" introduces Plácido Beaugival and his wife, a French couple who established their roots within the borders of a Los Angeles area Chicano barrio. Their world changes one day when the city notifies all local residents that an electrical substation will be constructed there and that they are mandated to sell their property. The couple of course refuses to comply, but the electric company disregards their grievances and proceeds to build the substation around their house. A fire then burns the substation down to the ground, including the Beaugivals' home, after which the city decides not to build a new substation and callously sells the property. Eventually, the Beaugivals' property is abandoned and no trace of the French couple is ever found. Strangely, in an ironic twist of fate, a brief "Nota" at the end of the story reveals that catacombs are eventually uncovered under what was the Beaugivals' home with two human skeletons embracing one another.

The narrator's account of the skeletons embracing each other is telling, for it introduces the element of orality in the story: Mr. and Mrs. Beaugival's narrative rests on a mother narrating it to her son, who in turn narrates it—as an adult—to the reader. The mother of the son serves not only as the community's virtual *corridista* but, more importantly, as a local folkloric historian who conserves and fortifies the barrio's oral history.[6]

The mother recounts to her son that Mr. and Mrs. Beaugival resided quite close to Simons, the aforementioned Mexican and Mexican American barrio formed as a direct result of the founding of the Simons Brick Company in the early twentieth century.[7] "Los jardines de Versalles" revolves around the Beaugival couple and their importance not just to their Los Angeles historical storyline but to a broader Mexican historical background, namely the fact that the French army invaded Mexico in 1862, establishing a monarchy headed by Maximilian I, which lasted five years. After the French withdrew from Mexico in 1867, it is more than plausible that some of their soldiers remained in the country and fathered children with Mexican women, thus legitimizing a Beaugival ethnic background and its later existence in California. In the story, Mr. Beaugival proclaims himself French yet is fluent in Spanish and sympathizes with the Simons residents.

Mrs. Beaugival, on the other hand, does not speak Spanish or English and is most likely French. However, her added ties to Mexico are implied through the narrator's mother, who relates that the only time Mrs. Beaugival ever left the house was when she visited her brother in the Simons barrio, where he usually stayed during his visits from Mexico City.

Morales' employment of the cultured French couple within the story is consistent with the representation of the *Californio* characters he previously introduces in *Reto en el paraíso*. In both narratives, the characters are considered *gente de razón*, educated and powerful people who regrettably lose their material holdings and privileged social status due to an overpowering Anglo-American hegemony that took over their lands. Though the Anglo-Americans viewed Californios as inferior, they at least held them superior to mestizos, African Americans, and indigenous peoples. In the Beaugivals' case, the couple is seen as superior to the barrio residents—and they evidently believe it themselves. This belief is manifested through the exclusive private life they live, and through the ostentatious growth of their property. For example, in a symbolic manifestation of this superiority, Mr. Beaugival enlarges the house and his meticulously kept gardens. The couple's property soon becomes a local tourist landmark, advertised as the "Beaugival Estates," the "Beaugival Ranch," or in an appropriate Hispanic context, the "Beaugival Hacienda."

This last description is of upmost importance, for it speaks to the exceedingly romanticized "Spanish Fantasy Heritage" conception that scholars like Carey McWilliams have tried to discredit. McWilliams (1948) argues that the idea of New Mexico as the Land of Enchantment and of California as the idyllic paradise of window-serenading caballeros and tempting señoritas of pure Spanish lineage was just self-serving propaganda to attract Anglo-Americans to settle the Southwest. As McWilliams points out in regard to the racial makeup of the original settlers of Los Angeles, these were far from being of pure Spanish blood. On the contrary, they were a motley group made up mostly of mestizos and indigenous peoples.[8] To negate this reality, it is not surprising that in the story the mayor of Montebello affirms that the Beaugival couple are an excellent example of the locals' "Spanish French heritage." This affirmation speaks to concerns over distorted, romantic representations of the Southwest, specifically in Los Angeles. In his study of barrio displacement, Raúl Villa voices a comparable concern:

> Los Angeles was initially transformed into an Anglo city and illustrates the physical, repressive, and ideological strategies—the landscape, law, and media effects—through which Chicanos were subordinately located in the dominant social space. These strategies principally consisted of urban-planning practices, police vigilance and containment methods, and hegemonic representations of the "Spanish romance" and the "Mexican problem."
> (2000, 16)

Villa's statement is an added case in point revealing that the mestizo and indigenous ancestors of the present-day Mexicans and Mexican Americans were mapped out of the city's history and that gente de razón eluded this fate primarily through their Spanish heritage.⁹ Tragically, however, as history proves, the gente de razóns' survival is illusionary and ephemeral, for eventually their cultural predominance also yielded to the power of new Anglo-American gatekeepers.¹⁰

In one sense, the Beaugivals serve as fine examples of these gente de razón. Within the boundaries of the barrio community they embody a powerful group of people who, like the disenfranchised and marginalized working class, are also victimized by the dominant culture. Comparable to the fate suffered by the residents of the Chavez Ravine barrio who were forced to sell their homes for the assumed common good of the city, the Beaugivals are also forced out of theirs.¹¹ By stressing the Beaugivals' fate, Morales literally and figuratively unearths buried pieces of Chicano history to clarify and expose its past reality. It is also worth noting that in the literal meaning of "Los jardines de Versalles," or the gardens of Versailles, Morales explores the French couple's symbolic function in the barrio. Through the title of the story the reader senses a trace of irony and even *burla* (mockery) connected to their introverted lifestyle. Mr. and Mrs. Beaugival live a very private life, and their self-imposed isolation from their neighbors creates an ambience of mystery and assumption, accentuating their proud "jardines" as a metaphor to depict their illusional and inaccessible world.

Indeed, the Beaugivals' story plays on the power of the myth and of the fallacy, for their reality dwells on a romanticized past that is unreal and unattainable. The title of the story alludes to the world-famous gardens of Versailles constructed for the French king Louis XIV between 1662 and 1700. These were majestic gardens accessible only to royalty, which covered vast acres filled with thousands of strategically planted trees along the confines of the gardens, creating self-imposed physical and symbolic borders. Inside its enclosure, splendid fountains decorated the grounds and thousands of flowers were delicately planted. The gardens were constructed under an axis that pointed from the east to the west, which followed the course of the sun. At a certain time of day the sun would shine its light into a specific section of the palace—in the Court of Honor area—where it slowly shed its light into the king's bedroom and into a hall of mirrors where its multiple reflections overwhelmed the senses. The gardens of Versailles were constructed with the intent of proving man's will over nature. Of foremost importance in their master plan was the manipulation of symmetry, including trees planted in straight lines and trimmed to a certain height. The palace was the central point of the gardens. From its balcony the king would stare beyond the horizon, contemplating the strength of his infinite power.

It goes without saying that in Morales' story, the Beaugivals' gardens are far from representing the grandeur of their French counterpart. The periphery of their property is made of uneven adobe bricks and landscaped with tall and short *nopaleras* (cactus plants) and treacherous *magueyes* (succulents) planted on dusty and dry stony ground. Their "jardines" lie within the confines of a tight-spaced working-class urban barrio populated by Mexicans and Mexican Americans and controlled by the tight-fisted dominance of a company town. In the eyes of the dominant culture, this fact makes Mr. and Mrs. Beaugival closer in kin to the barrio's residents than to Anglo-Americans and consequently sharing in essentially the same limitations and disadvantages as Chicanos. This is clearly seen when the mayor of the city of Montebello at first celebrates the Beaugivals' home as an important tourist attraction, only to later change his mind and call it "a house made with mud balls that any Greaser could have built" (10) when the city wants to appropriate it.

In this regard, the Beaugival couple were victims of what Villa defines as "creative destruction" and "dominant strategies of sociospatial repression [barrioization]" (2000, 17) imposed on them by a dominant politico-corporate culture. "Los jardines de Versalles" presents a kind of mythical couple whose faded story resurfaces thanks to the skill of the aforementioned corridista mother and son storytellers. Their world, similar to the fate suffered by the powerful gente de razón who ruled over the common population during the Spanish colonial days, was obliterated by stronger forces. What Morales' tale affirms is that what *did* survive this obliteration was the palpable presence and culture of the storytellers' Mexican American or Chicano descendants. These descendants experience the same fate placed upon them as the French couple; yet the difference here is that they did not fade into history—on the contrary, they survived it to perpetuate their story. It is true that "creative destructions" and barrioization still exists today for many Chicanos, but they share solid cultural bonds that help to often overcome these displacements. The Beaugivals could not overcome, and their introverted and sheltered world impeded them from foreseeing the spatial injustice that tragically culminated in them becoming sequestered in the hollow core of a self-constructed grave.

"PEQUEÑA NACIÓN": HISTORY AND SPATIAL JUSTICE

In an effort to perhaps authenticate the Spanish historical presence in California, the novella "Pequeña nación" presents a number of historical facts pertinent to the founding of the city of Los Angeles. One of the most important and symbolic, as far as identity is concerned, is that associated with the city's original founding name. Most people nowadays refer to it as "City of Angels," though Morales challenges this widespread semi-translation by reviving the city's original Spanish colonial name of "El Pueblo de Nuestra Señora la Reina de Los Angeles de Porciúncula." To reinforce this nomenclature, Morales also includes the exact date of L.A.'s founding, 1781. This date is significant because it underscores the era of the Spanish mission system in California, a tool in the conquest, colonization, and pacification of the indigenous populations. From this historical authentication, Morales introduces specific present-day Mexican and Mexican American spaces that gradually developed into Chicano barrio spaces. These include Boyle Heights and Geraghty Loma, the city of Montebello, Los Angeles' first cemetery, and Chávez Ravine. The story also includes the aforementioned barrio Simons.

In addition to unearthing these places and pieces of Chicano history, Morales presents the reader with harsh realities faced by the modern Chicano barrio.[12] He concentrates on a geographic space that is neglected and plagued by violence, alcoholism, and drug-dealing controlled by cynical thuggish gang members who victimize neighborhoods (associated with them is a hostile and untrustworthy police department that is seen as a peripheral, de facto gang itself). The gang's control over barrio life is so absolute that it almost bleeds with arrogance. This is evident in how the gang leaders identify their home turf as an autonomous nation, proclaimed by one of its *cholo* members:

> The only thing we can do is build our little nation. We know that we have complete control of our community. It's like we're making our stand . . . We're all brothers and nobody fucks with us. We take pride in our little nation and if any intruders enter, we get panicked because we feel our community is being threatened. The only way is with violence. And nobody, not even our own, can stand in the way of protecting our little nation. (96)

With the cholos' self-proclaimed land ownership and a barrio nation apparently in place, the crucial question underlying the story is how to overturn this control of power and eradicate the gangs to produce balance and positive outcomes for the innocent neighborhood residents.

For possible answers, Morales turns to more spiritual and collective nation-building by contemplating the principles of the Chicano Movement—specifically, those dealing with self-determinism and empowerment, including the forming of a Chicano nation as envisioned through the concept of Aztlán. In the 1960s

Chicano community leaders like Rodolfo "Corky" Gonzales and José Angel Gutiérrez founded organizations that fostered cultural pride, spirituality, and political empowerment among Chicanos.[13] Student groups demanded curriculum changes that resulted in monumental academic gains, exemplified by the Plan Espiritual de Aztlán and the Plan de Santa Bárbara, which not only inspired and initiated Chicano and Chicana studies programs across the nation but further deepened the already developing sense of Chicano nationalism. The fundamental purpose of this Movimiento was to empower Chicanos and motivate social change. In this context, the barrio served as a microcosm of a Chicano homeland. It is not surprising, then, to see that the barrio Geraghty—where the story takes place—was more or less perceived as a truly autonomous Chicano space.[14] The problem, however, was that it did not represent the utopian space that Chicanos hoped for. On the contrary, the barrio became a perilous battleground where only the strong survived, a representative combat zone employed by Morales in this story (and in other works) to highlight the decadence of the barrio.[15] Morales is not completely apocalyptic, for he does offer a glimpse of optimism and hope by introducing a group of organized community leaders who seek spatial justice and betterment for barrio residents.

Several geographers, including Edward Soja, use the expression "spatial justice" to define the interaction between space and society in order to understand injustices and construct policies to correct them. In his exploration of spatial justice as a theoretical concept, Soja explains that spatial justice is "consequential geography," which he defines as

> a spatial expression that is more than just a background reflection or set of physical attributes to be descriptively mapped.... The geography, or "spatiality," of justice... is an integral and formative component of justice itself, a vital part of how justice and injustice are socially constructed and evolve over time. Viewed this way spatial justice becomes fundamentally, almost inescapably, a struggle over geography. (2010, 1–2)

Furthermore, he adds that

> these consequential geographies are not just the outcome of social and political processes, they are also a dynamic force affecting these processes in significant ways... An assertive and explanatory spatial perspective helps us make better theoretical and practical sense of how social justice is created, maintained, and brought into question as a target for democratic social action. (2)

In "Pequeña nación," Morales' Chicano nation-building and self-determinism is led, not by misguided and violent gang members or the much more preferable and idealistic 1960s-type male leaders, but by a group of organized women community leaders who take over the "consequential geography" in order to remove the evils that harm the barrio. These women are directed by Micaela Clemencia, a college-educated Chicana who works as a teacher and serves as the local historian; doña Paca, another historian who documents barrio history through the art of photography; and doña Felícitas, the reliable vigilant of barrio affairs. They name their movimiento the Federación Mujeres de las Tijeras, an organization that pledges to "act" against the threatening forces of the barrio gangs by using love, intimidation, and practical strategic force as their main weapons. In addition, they believe that a divine path is needed to eradicate injustices, as outlined by the principles of liberation theology: "El Ver . . . El Analizar . . . El Actuar" (61)—to be alert to the existence of a social injustice; to analyze the cause of the problem and present a solution; and most importantly, to assume responsibility to act upon the problem to eradicate it. Guided by these beliefs, the Federación sets out to strategically apprehend and castigate their aggressors, using *tijeras* (scissors) as their main weapon. Not surprisingly, this eye for an eye, tooth for a tooth resolution brings positive outcomes for the residents, which soon changes the barrio:

> Con el desarme de las pandillas a la vez se eliminaron las drogas. Cada vez que la Federación tomaba una casa pandillera, también se llevaban o destruían las drogas. El valor de los narcóticos que la Federación destruía se contaba en millones de dólares. Sin drogas y sin armas, el barrio despertaba de la pesadilla de las pandillas.[16] (124)

In the narrative, the Federación mujeres' control of the barrio brings, as Soja would say, a "more effective actions aimed at changing the world for the better" (2), which is the ultimate goal of spatial justice. Of utmost importance to them is the fostering of self-worth and empowerment instilled in the residents of the barrio, proving that women leaders could hold their ground in the hostile confrontation with their gang member enemies.[17]

The positive results of the Federación's activism in "Pequeña nación" involves strong community action and support that raises funds to buy land for the common good, including the building of a successful school for girls.[18] The Federación promotes peaceful strategies to obtain their goals. They punish and humiliate the barrio's thugs, but they also show compassion and forgiveness by welcoming back those expelled from the barrio when they repent their wrongdoings. However, what seems like a promising and fruitful future for the barrio soon takes a negative turn due to internal and external forces that weaken the Federación's achievements: gang members' mothers refuse to support the Federación, the press is unsympathetic, and the police see them as a deadly menace.

It is not surprising that the success of the Federación mujeres, who in effect create their own pequeña nación (a utopian nation that offered better working and living conditions for its people), would be considered a national security threat that demands its immediate destruction. At one point in the story, without warning, the Federación members wake up to find that the police had blocked all entrances to the barrio. Soon the barrio's water supply is shut down and the area surrounded by the military, instigating an all-out war on its residents. This brings death to many of them, including those sheltered in the home of the Federación when a helicopter crashes on the roof of the building. To justify the military force applied in the Chicano barrio, the federal investigators report that the leaders of the Federación were drug dealers from a Mexican cartel who used the barrio as a shield to protect their lucrative business.

Fortunately, the local residents believe in the Federación's cause and see the women leaders as regional heroes who are elevated to martyr status after their deaths. This recognition is nevertheless short-lived, for time erases their heroic accomplishments. As with the Beaugivals and Chávez Ravine residents from the previous tale, the land where the barrio once stood is sold and new houses are constructed over the ashes of the previous ones. New people occupy the structures and plant flowers and trees in their gardens, *cobijando* (covering up) the memories that quickly transform themselves into faded recollections, as chronicled at the end of the story: "con el tiempo, el público se olvidó de las víctimas de la masacre" (135).[19] It is important to note that the Federación's leader Micaela's body is not found in the area's debris, an extraordinary circumstance similar to the Beaugivals' in "Los jardines de Versalles" after their house burns down.

In the end, what Morales seems to offer with the Federación mujeres is the Chicanos' human desire to improve their social condition, but not through the extreme of creating divisive pequeñas naciones within the barrio. In this story the pequeñas naciones are represented in two extremes—the negative created by the *pandilleros* and killer thugs, and the positive founded by the women of the Federación. Both extremes imply isolation and exclusion, not compromise and integration—two components required for inclusion into mainstream society. When all is said and done, what remains in Morales' "Pequeña nación" is a faded memory that is both part fact and part fiction. What is real are the historical facts presented in the story. In this sense, Morales renders spatial justice for the residents of the barrio. Soja would describe it as a promising possibility that "can open new sources of insight and innovative practical and theoretical applications" (2010, 3), translating into a hope within a hope, a possibility within a possibility. Spatial justice is served, but only within a short illusory fragment of time. La Federación Mujeres de las Tijeras is successful, but only for a fleeting moment, yielding rapidly to the will of a higher power. What remains is the promise to rebuild a barrio and open spaces for others to penetrate and renew the process of change. Such is the wisp of hope that Morales leaves us in this novella.

"LA PENCA": *ESPERPENTO A LO CHICANO*

The obliteration of the Beaugivals in "Los jardines de Versalles" and of la Federación Mujeres de las Tijeras in "Pequeña nación" attest to Morales' consistent preoccupation with the Chicanos' place in history and its dismal spatial circumstances. In "La penca," the third novella of *Pequeña nación*, Morales does not dwell on history or spatial (in)justice to call attention to the social concerns of Chicanos. Instead, he relies on a powerful Mexican cultural icon—la Virgen de Guadalupe—to express their complex relation to their *mexicanidad*.

In Mexico, the image of the la Virgen de Guadalupe is untouchable and people are discouraged from portraying her image in any unconventional way that might denigrate her. In the United States, however, the Chicano operates under a different set of cultural rules that allows the flexibility to interpret cultural icons—including la Virgen—as one desires.[20] In "La penca," Morales allows David, the main protagonist of the story, to practice such flexibility and use la Virgen to fulfill his sexual desires, an *atrevimiento* (daring act) that is risky and gritty for both Morales and his protagonist.

In "La penca," the use of the oral tradition returns when an inquisitive son questions his mother about the existence of *curiosidades*, or anomalies, in their barrio's history. The mother responds affirmatively, saying that she knew many of them, including the peculiar stories of characters such as the "Jorobadito," the "Terremoto," "La Bigotes," and "La Penca." La Penca, the subject of Morales' story, was a man who as a boy lived a normal childhood but as a teenager suffered immensely due to physical abnormalities that changed his life. As an adult his unfulfilled love life was also attributed to his grotesque physical condition, ultimately triggering the polemical oddities of his art.

Reviewing the term *esperpento* helps to discuss aspects of these abnormalities and aberrations. Defined by the Real Academia Española dictionary as a "persona, cosa o situación grotesca o estrafalaria," esperpento describes a grotesque/eccentric person, thing, or situation. In literary terms, it is closely associated with the work of the Spanish writer Ramón del Valle-Inclán and his celebrated *Luces de Bohemia* (1978). In this play, Valle-Inclán metaphorically highlights concave and convex mirrors that distort the images of people who gaze at them.[21] In Valle-Inclán's literary context he uses the absurd and satirical implications of the term to express the tragic circumstances of Spanish life, which in the historical context of its time (late nineteenth, early twentieth century) he interpreted as decadent. In Morales' story the term is transposed to the story of David, the gifted artist nicknamed La Penca (a fleshy cactus leaf with thorns) whose physical abnormalities dictate his life as an artist, and in the process deconstructs the image of la Virgen de Guadalupe.

In "La penca," David lives with his mother in Simons, the all-pervading barrio mentioned in all three of the stories in *Pequeña nación*. As a boy, David suffers from a rare physical deformity that causes the abnormal growth of pointed protruding bones in his body. This fantastic abnormality haunts him early in his school years, as he is identified as the school's freak. His intellect and artistic gift lead him to survive those trying years, but unfortunately he comes to feel that he could never be intimately involved with a woman. This frustrating truth culminates when one day he witnesses the women he secretly loves having sex with her partner in his own art gallery. In desperation, and feeling defeated, he releases his sexual anxieties by aggressively making love to one of his paintings of la Virgen de Guadalupe, cutting his protruding bones and causing blood to spill all over the canvas.[22] The blending of the paint colors and the blood over the freshly painted Virgen creates unique abstract results that excite the art community, making David an overnight sensation.

For his part, David feels that he has finally found a beloved soul mate. The sexual encounter with la Virgen not only gratifies him sexually but, in a way, avenges the *maleficio* (or curse) that God has conferred upon him through the physical deformity. As he embraces la Virgen, David speaks to her, humanizes her, and then questions her:

> ¿Me quieres Virgencita? Madre de Jesús, tu hijo, otro desgraciado, sacrificado, que no podía fornicar con las mujeres que él quería y quienes lo seguían esperando que se las echara una noche a escondidas.[23] (35)

David consequently believes that la Virgen answers his questions, as the narrator of the story recounts that he, La Penca, "sintió que ella le respondía, le acariciaba cada tumor de su cuerpo ... la Virgen le exprimió toda la energía de su cuerpo" (felt that she responded to him, that she caressed every tumor of his body. ... The Virgin squeezed all the energy from his body) (35).

And then later:

> Su hambre carnal y espiritual se dirigía a la Virgen que se aparecía en los lienzos para luego dejarlo amarla y crear nuevas imágenes de ella y sobre ella, productos puros del amor divino y de su hambre insaciable por ella. Deseaba más y más su precioso cuerpo.[24] (40)

What results from this encounter is an extraordinary painting that is immediately sold at a high price. This sexual encounter repeats itself nightly, producing a number of unique pieces of art for hankering buyers. Many members of a more conservative community of course do not find joy in La Penca's paintings. To them, the artist's paintings of la Virgen are blasphemous acts created by the devil himself. David's work indeed stirs the local communities, who either praise his work or demonize it. David is considered an atheist by members of the community who believe that he has disrespected Mexico's most precious religious icon. They refer to him as a *vendido*, a sell-out to his culture who must be excommunicated, not only from the Catholic Church but also from his Mexican heritage.

In an ironic twist of fate, David's "atheist" and blasphemous images of la Virgen lead to an improbable paradox. For example, in the story, Morales presents a man who is lying dead in a dark alley; nearby, an abstract painting of la Virgen is soon after found in a dumpster, suggesting that an overzealous objector killed the man and dumped the sacrilegious painting in the trash, seeking to obliterate both the man and the image. Yet, when the painting is removed from the dumpster and it accidentally touches the dead man's body, he comes back to life, mesmerizing the believers who witnessed the miracle. Without vacillating, the people immediately build an altar on the site where the miracle occurred and properly name it "El callejón de los milagros" (Alley of Miracles). In this sense, David's painting was never sacrilegious after all; on the contrary, his art becomes the creation of a holy

Chapter Five **101**

man whose painting is the result of the consummation of his love for la Virgen. Because of that, David indeed becomes a virtual miracle worker.

Here, then, is where Valle-Inclán's esperpento plays a role in Morales' story. La Penca's physical deformity helps create his artistic esperpento by distorting the image of la Virgen de Guadalupe and humanizing it without depriving it of its divine power. David's creation, seen as monstrous by the conservative Catholic community, rapidly turns into a divine wonderment worthy of both praise and sanctification. Valle-Inclán used the esperpento to aptly define the broken spirit of a Spain that, in the late nineteenth century, lost its last colonies in America. In Morales' story the concept is applied to uncover the dark side of the Chicano/a ethos to *escandalizarnos* (to scandalize or provoke), in other words, to test our will and question how far the Chicano/a is willing to challenge the traditional concepts of mexicanidad without jeopardizing cultural identity.

When the boy's mother finishes narrating the story of La Penca, the story is actually left open-ended. There is no solid conclusion to David's fate, and the boy simply retires to sleep in the living room. As he observes the family's own painting of la Virgen hanging on the wall, he realizes that the traditional small cherubic angel nestled beneath the image has changed into something drastically different:

> Dormí en la sala, bajo un cuadro de la Virgen de Guadalupe en el que nunca me había fijado. Por primera vez descrubrí la finura de la obra. Me acerqué para gozar del rostro sublime de la Mujer Sagrada y me di cuenta de que el angelito debajo de los pies de Ella tenía la cara y el cuerpo lleno de cuernos y en la frente llevaba escrito el nombre de *La Penca*.[25] (53)

So the main question in this context that esperpento puts forward is whether the term presents a deformed image of reality or an accurate image of a deformed reality. In the case of Morales' "La penca" it can go either way, for one can conclude that reality distorted David, and that by painting abstract images of la Virgen and converting her into his platonic lover, he in turn repaid the favor by deforming reality. When Max Estrella, the main protagonist in *Luces de Bohemia*, tells don Latino that "las imágenes más bellas en un espejo cóncavo son absurdas," and don Latino answers by asking him "¿Y dónde está el espejo?," Max responds, "En el fondo del vaso" (Valle-Inclán 1978, 106).[26] For our purposes, one can consequently surmise that Valle-Inclán's concept of the esperpento—"España es una deformación grotesca de la civilización europea" (106)—can be rephrased to imply that "el chicano es una deformación grotesca de la civilización nortemericana."[27]

In sum, all three tales in *Pequeña nación* are affected in one way or another by the imperfect warped reality seen through the lens of the esperpento (most specifically, "La penca"). All three highlight either Chicano and Mexican history ("Los jardines de Versalles," "Pequeña nación"), or Mexican cultural icons ("La penca"). They touch on figurations where spatial justice is both reachable and deceptive ("Los jardines de Versalles," "Pequeña nación"). What the trio also have in common is the element of an unresolved present and an uncertain future. Moreover, the tales do not necessarily seek to romanticize their Chicano/a characters. On the contrary, their humanity comes across just like any other—though they are situated as more or less heroic entities living in a surreal, unpredictable, and rather abominable Moralesian world where, in Marc García-Martínez's words (2014), flesh-and-blood figurations abound.[28] Such figurations lead readers into a variable realm of aesthetic and ideological representations that converge with past, present, and future spatial realities and possibilities. This is the cutting-edge function of Morales' literature. It is a literature that indeed presents a harsh and jarring world that Francisco Lomelí describes as "a depository of human degradation" (1998, 17), but one that seems purposefully created by Morales to rattle our senses and to avoid complacency in our analysis of his rather extraordinary imagination.

NOTES

1. This totalizador concept stems from the "novela total." These novels tend to present a complex and total reality, with all its details and subtleties, for example, the world of Gabriel García Márquez's Macondo in *Cien años de soledad*, or Carlos Fuentes' Mexico City in *La región más transparente*.

2. Reference to Simons is more or less a given in nearly all his works.

3. His new novel *White Heron* is forthcoming in 2022.

4. *Esperpento* is defined as a literary style that deforms reality as a means to criticize it. It relies on the grotesque and the belittlement of humans to achieve its purpose. The term was introduced by the Spanish writer Ramón del Valle Inclán, a member of the Generación del '98.

5. According to Morales, heteropia is used to describe "a perplexing urban area constituted by a continuum of shapeless cities with no center, no core of a single identity" (1996, 24) where people need to develop new strategies of survival.

6. The narration of the mother's story of her barrio is fundamentally akin to the *corridos* of the nineteenth and early twentieth centuries, in which the *corridistas* sang stories that told of the local history and culture of the people.

7. The Simons Brick Company sold millions of its bricks to large urban cities like San Francisco, which used them to reconstruct its buildings after the 1906 earthquake. In Los Angeles, many buildings built with Simons bricks still exist today. See "Los Angeles Revisited: Simons Brick Company," *Los Angeles Revisited* (blog), https://losangelesrevisited.blogspot.com/p/simons-brick-co-album.html, accessed June 2, 2021.

8. In *North from Mexico*, McWilliams (1948) writes, "Los Angeles is one of the many cities in the borderlands which has fed itself on a false mythology for so long that it has become a well-fattened paradox . . . of the original settlers of Our City of the Queen of Angels, their wives included, two were Spaniards; one mestizo; two were Negroes; eight were mulattoes; and nine were Indians. None of this would really matter except that the churches in Los Angeles hold fiestas rather than bazaars and that Mexicans are still not accepted as a part of the community. When one examines how deeply this fantasy heritage has permeated the social and cultural life of the borderlands, the dichotomy begins to assume the proportions of a schizophrenic mania" (36).

9. The "Old Spanish Days" Fiesta is a cross-dressing event celebrated in Santa Barbara, California, every August. The three-day gathering is both a cause of McWilliams' concern and the motivation for his "Fantasy Heritage" argument. Interestingly, the eminent Mexican American journalist for the *Los Angeles Times* Rubén Salazar mentions Santa Barbara's "fiesta" in his 1970 seminal work, "Who Is a Chicano? And What Is It the Chicanos Want?" In the article, Salazar addresses Chicanos' resentment at the fact that "when the governor dresses up as a Spanish nobleman for the Santa Barbara Fiesta he's insulting Mexicans because the Spanish conquered and exploited the Mexicans" (*Los Angeles Times*, February 6, 1970).

10. For example, the popular Seguín family from San Antonio, Texas, who were supportive of Moses and Stephen F. Austin's settlers in the first decades of the nineteenth century, and the celebrated Mariano Vallejo, who collaborated with Hubert H. Brancroft by narrating his experience as a native Californio, became powerless heroes to the native Tejanos and Californios, respectively, both surrendering to the dominance of the Anglos and supposedly fading into historical oblivion. Juan N. Seguín fought by the side of the Texans against Mexican general Antonio Santa Anna. Seguín was not present at the Battle of the Alamo, hence his survival. He and his family lost political clout and soon were forced to leave Texas and fight for the Mexican army. His book *My Memoir* documents his complicated issues with identity, concluding that he felt like a foreigner in his own countries (Texas or Mexico). Vallejo would not be satisfied with Bancroft's history of California and wrote his own "verdadera historia" (true story) of the history of his people in the state. The historical role of both these men, however, would not be forgotten, for two cities are named after them: Seguin, Texas, and Vallejo, California.

11. The City of Los Angeles justified their actions based on a plan to build a public housing project. This, however, never materialized due to the interest of council

members to entice a professional baseball team to Los Angeles. Dodger Stadium, the current home of the Los Angeles Dodgers, was built on Chavez Ravine. Local residents were coerced to sell their property and soon heavy machinery completely flattened their land to make way for the stadium. As of this writing, it is a bit incongruous that the most ardent fans of the Dodgers are descendants of the 1950s Chavez Ravine residents who, if they wish to see a game, are forced to revisit the site of barrio's destruction. Ultimately, it seems that barrios and their citizens are meant to either disappear altogether or somehow continue to exist by ironically nourishing themselves with the *migajas* (crumbs) of assumed social progress.

12. The infamous Zoot Suit Riots of the 1940s are also mentioned.

13. These include the Crusade for Justice founded in Colorado and La Raza Unida Party in Texas. See Carlos Muñoz Jr. (1989).

14. This barrio, Geraghty Loma, is considered one of the oldest in Los Angeles. It is also associated with the predominantly Hispanic street gang located in the area of East Los Angeles.

15. *Caras viejas y vino nuevo* comes to mind.

16. With the disarmament of the gangs, drugs were simultaneously eliminated. Each time that the Federación took over a gang house, it also took or destroyed drugs. The economic value of the narcotics that the Federación annihilated runs into the millions of dollars. Without drugs and weapons, the barrio woke up from its nightmares. (Note: All translations of *Pequeña nación* in this article are mine.)

17. In writing about the Chicanas' work within the nationalistic Chicano Movement, Sonia Saldívar-Hull (2000) writes that "for countless isolated Chicanas, in both rural and urban terrains of the borderlands, economic limitations, undereducation, and entrenchment within a masculinist family structure impeded participation in organizations that were considered radical and dangerous" (129). The aggressive and dangerous undertaking of the Federación Mujeres de las Tijeras defied these limitations. Looking at the bigger picture, they accepted the tragic consequences that these confrontations might bring.

18. This is reminiscent of several of the cultural nationalist goals of the Crusade for Justice, including the founding of Escuela Tlatelolco, a private school that introduced Mexican and Chicano culture to its students.

19. "With time, the public forgot about the victims of the massacre" (135).

20. An example of the controversies Chicanas have faced in terms of their representation of la Virgen de Guadalupe is the art of Alma López and her controversial Guadalupe paintings; see also the various interpretations of la Virgen by Chicanas, as expressed in Castillo (1996).

21. In scene 12 of *Luce de Bohemia*, in the dialogue between Max Estrella and his friend don Latino, Max makes the following comment regarding the esperpento: "Los

ultraistas son unos farsantes. El esperpentismo lo ha inventado Goya. Los héroes clásicos han ido a pasearse en el callejón del Gato . . . Los héroes clásicos reflejados en los espejos cóncavos dan el *Esperpento*. El sentido trágico de la vida española sólo puede darse con una estética sistemáticamente deformada . . . Las imágenes más bellas en un espejo cóncavo son absurdas" (The ultraists are a deceitful bunch. Goya invented the esperpento. The classic heroes have gone for a walk to the Gato alley . . . The classic heroes that are reflected on the concave mirrors produce the Esperpento. The tragic meaning of Spanish life can only present itself using a systematically deformed aesthetic . . . The most beautiful images on a concave mirror are absurd) (106, my translation).

22. La Virgen and sexuality are also present in Sandra Cisneros' short essay "Guadalupe the Sex Goddess." Cisneros writes: "When I look at la Virgen de Guadalupe now, she is not the Lupe of my childhood, no longer the one in my grandparents' house in Tepeyac . . . She is Guadalupe the sex goddess, a goddess who makes me feel good about my sexual power, my sexual energy" (1996, 49).

23. "Do you love me, dear Virgin? Mother of Jesus, your son, another wretched son, a sacrificed one, that could not fornicate with women who he desired and whom they kept waiting to be secretly screwed by him on a given night."

24. His carnal and spiritual hunger was directed at the Virgin who appeared in the canvas to then allow him to love her and create new images of her and her world, virtuous results of divine love and his insatiable hunger for her. He desired more and more of her precious body.

25. I slept in the living room, below the painting of the Virgen de Guadalupe to which I had never paid much attention. For the first time, I discovered the fine quality of the work. I approached it to enjoy the sublime face of the Sacred Mother, and I realized that the small angel below had her feet, her face, and her body full of horns, and on the forehead, the name "La Penca" written over it.

26. "The most beautiful images on a concave mirror are absurd. / And where is the mirror? / At the bottom of the glass" (my translation).

27. "Spain is a grotesque deformation of European civilization." In our interpretation, Spain = *El chicano*; European civilization = *Anglo American society*.

28. Descriptives taken from the title of Marc García-Martínez' book, *The Flesh-and-Blood Aesthetics of Alejandro Morales: Disease, Sex, and Figuration* (2014).

WORKS CITED

Castillo, Ana, ed. 1996. *Goddess of the Americas: Writings on the Virgin of Guadalupe*. New York: Riverhead Books.

Cisneros, Sandra. 1996. "Guadalupe the Sex Goddess." In Castillo, *Goddess of the Americas*, 46–50.

García-Martínez, Marc. 2014. *The Flesh-and-Blood Aesthetics of Alejandro Morales: Disease, Sex, and Figuration*. San Diego: San Diego State University Press.

Lomelí, Francisco A. 1998. "Hard-Core Barrio Revisited: Violence, Sex, Drugs, and Videotape through a Chicano Glass Darkly." Introduction to Alejandro Morales, *Barrio on the Edge / Caras viejas y vino nuevo*, translated by Francisco Lomelí, 1–21. Tempe, AZ: Bilingual Press / Editorial Bilingüe.

McWilliams, Carey. 1948. *North from Mexico: The Spanish Speaking People of the United States*. New York: Greenwood Press.

Morales, Alejandro. 1996. "Dynamic Identities in Heterotopia." In *Alejandro Morales: Fiction Past, Present, Future Perfect*, edited by José Antonio Gurpegui, 14–27. Tempe, AZ: Bilingual Press / Editorial Bilingüe.

———. 2005. *Pequeña nación*. Turlock, CA: Orbis.

Muñoz, Carlos, Jr. 1989. *Youth Identity, Power: The Chicano Movement*. New York: Verso.

Saldívar-Hull, Sonia. 2000. *Feminism on the Border: Chicana Gender Politics and Literature*. Berkeley: University of California Press.

Soja, Edward W. 2010. *Seeking Spatial Justice*. Minneapolis: University of Minnesota Press.

Valle-Inclán, Ramón del. 1978. *Luces de Bohemia*. Madrid: Austral.

Villa, Raúl Homero. 2000. *Barrio Logos: Space and Place in Urban Chicano Literature and Culture*. Austin: University of Texas Press.

SIX / Heterotopia and the Emergence of the Modern *Ilusa* in *Waiting to Happen* / MARGARITA LÓPEZ LÓPEZ

> We are in the presence of a phenomenon . . . This woman is a heteroclite. Let her speak, for she is possessed not by evil but by overwhelming knowledge . . . The women . . . took her to their dwellings, their homes, which existed between the walls of two large, magnificent homes in Coyoacán . . . like thousands more, lived in the uncalculated, unexpected, and unseen cracks, in the spaces that the middle and upper classes unknowingly created behind and against the walls of houses, apartments, office buildings, and skyscrapers. —Alejandro Morales, *Waiting to Happen*, 2001

Alejandro Morales' remarkable, even visionary, narratives contribute to that distinctive class of literature that gives voice to the oppressed, the marginalized, the conquered, and the silenced. Much of his work unfolds in populated and colonized heterotopic spaces—intense and ever-transforming spaces that appear contradictory and almost ephemeral. In "Dynamic Identities in Heterotopia," Morales characterizes these spaces as "not quite attainable or explainable, and perceptible only by change" (1996, 22). In short, such spaces are both other yet another, both harmonious yet irreconcilable. In this regard, heterotopia virtually always associates with an acute sociopolitical quality that is found within many of Morales' works in general and definitely within his novel *Waiting to Happen* (2001) in particular. In this work there functions a particular space, flexing through temporal and spatial rifts, crossing the geopolitical borders of the United States and Mexico, and ultimately centering on the megalopolis of Mexico City.

According to Aguilar Camín (1975), by the end of the 1960s this megalopolis was a transformative space, wherein massive protests were led not only by the constantly oppressed *obreros* but also by the urban middle class that had emerged as a result of Mexican capitalism, which brought with it the growth of cities, an increase in services, vibrant consumerism, and better access to education. After the 1980s the middle class gained economic and political power, while the government imposed new taxes and proposed new global economic policies. These economic reforms widened the gap between those with power and those without, thereby expanding the disparity between social, ethnic, and gender groups. Such a situation created an atmosphere that Raymond L. Williams (1995) refers to as a crisis of the concepts of "trust" and "truth" at every level of personal and institutional life in Mexico. Dreams of grandeur ended abruptly and Mexicans once again found themselves poor and colonized (a reality portrayed in much of the literature of the day). Educators, physicians, students, and intellectuals all joined in the streets to face this crisis caused by the government's repression of its own people. The intellectuals focused on the country's history and current reality, its social relations, culture, economy, and relation with imperialism, and a large number of publications criticized the horrors perpetrated by the government. It was, in short, a moment in Mexican history that engendered a subversive discourse to reexamine and question official accounts, while the concepts of "nationalism" and "national identity" were reformulated to become an integral part of political critique.

In spite of the characteristic heterogeneity of Alejandro Morales' novels, they all share a tendency to shed light on the artificial construction of history and identity through remarkable superimpositions of fact and fiction. The complex reality represented in *Waiting to Happen* reveals a world that is both factual and fictional, symbolic and real, magical and fantastic—a world, in short, of real big problems and serious concerns. The novel interweaves factual and fictionalized spaces to present multiple Mexican and American perspectives, all stitched together through the rather remarkable transcultural, liminal protagonist J. I. Cruz. It is through this protagonist that a longing for a nation lost is articulated; that backward and suffocating cultural institutions afflicting the nation and the individual are demystified; that the marginalized groups who are silenced and disregarded are given voice. In exploring the mistrust, isolation, rejection, and doubt toward Mexico's political system experienced by its people, *Waiting to Happen* also subverts the patriarchal discourse of official history by including not only multiple histories and voices but a powerful female identity that embraces heterogeneity while at the same time rewriting history. As a result, Morales' remarkable novel constitutes a strategy of retrospection, resistance, and rebellion that implicitly offers its reader a glimpse of hope toward a better world.

In "Feminist Postmodernities," Jean Franco states that "we are entering into a (postmodern) period of the end of the master narratives—the global and totalizing theories that were always based on the exclusion of the heterogeneous" (1995, 111). It is thus from these gaps or exclusions that Morales' innovative and thought-provoking novel seeks to undermine official historical truth and explore alternate ways of establishing new levels of reality concerning historical pasts and presents. As mentioned, *Waiting to Happen* presents the dynamic protagonist J. I. Cruz, an *ilusa* (mystical dreamer or divine illusionary) who embodies a voice seeking justice and speaking for the disenfranchised in contemporary Mexican society. By focusing on this ilusa, the analysis in this essay considers the discourse of interstitial geocultural spaces and textual heterotopia in an effort to propose alternate and diverse possibilities in relation to identity formation. It further explores heterotopia in the historical representation of restrictive and oppressive Mexican society, with women as agents of social change. David Harvey's, Kevin Hetherington's, and Michel Foucault's concepts of heterotopia are taken into consideration, juxtaposed with notions of the border and history as conceptualized by Morales himself. In the process, this analysis complements Morales' intensely personal and creative aim to enrich Mexican American and Chicana/o/x literature, history, and identity conceptualization.

When embarking on a journey through Morales' narrative, the reader finds histories, experiences, characters, and views that surround the author's life. In his interview with José Antonio Gurpegui, Morales asserts the following about his earlier writings:

> In one way or another [they] reflect that, my particular experience or somebody that I knew; so there is the interjection of autobiographical elements, of biographical elements, of history, of community history, family history, state history, national history. So there is that element in all my work. (1996, 10)

Waiting to Happen is no exception to this disclosure. However, the novel extends its history to presenting a world connecting contemporary Mexico City and Southern California. This is a world in which the characters find themselves constantly dealing with borders while seeking a better life, a utopian dream—a setting its author characterizes as "a time and space in which borders, both literal and figurative, exist everywhere." Besides, Morales, a native of Montebello in East

L.A. who resides in Orange County, writes from that heterotopian perspective described as "an idea that attempts to bring order and understanding to a space accommodating a wealth of displacement of different entities" (Morales 1996, 23). Consequently, the author associates this concept with the daily reality lived as part of California's contemporary migration experience: "The image of people desperately running, crossing the border, heading north, journeying to utopia, but discovering heterotopia" (23). He further explains that while seeking utopia,

> To confront a border and, more so, to cross a border presumes great risk.... People will not leave their safe zone, will not venture into what they consider an unsafe zone. People cling to the dream of utopia and fail to recognize that they create and live in heterotopia. (23)

In *Waiting to Happen*, readers are faced with characters who embody this contrasting idea of crossing borders, trying to reach a utopian ideal of a better place only to find that they have inadvertently integrated themselves into heterotopia. Such is the case with J. I. Cruz: even though she makes the trip to Southern California (which according to Morales, represents a future urban world), she is unable to establish herself there and sooner or later will have to make another trip, but not without first being subject to an environment where fantasy and reality blur. In "Dynamic Identities in Heterotopia," Morales addresses this blur, claiming that "the heterotopian ambience of Southern California, the ceaseless creation of fantasy, mythology, and mythography ... Hollywood, Disneyland, and the border ... produce the fantasy and the dreams that urban heteroclites live out vicariously" (24). The protagonist of the novel, therefore, moves to Mexico City for what seems like a great employment opportunity that would also allow her to live near her parents. Her relocation to the megalopolis, however, leads to a series of events that will situate her in a constant state of displacement.

The novel portrays characters and events in that globalized Aztec capital Mexico City, all of which surround J. I. Cruz, a heteroclite woman who does not follow common rules, and, in general, what is normal. By doing so, the text opens and positions itself within historiographical narratives of the Other. Specifically, the novel is based on work chronicled by the journalist Cassandra Arenal Coe, another female character living in the interstice of urban experience. Coe's chronicles, which are meant to establish a sense of credibility within the novel as intertextual writings, stem from the author's conscientious effort to both examine the abuse suffered by women and children in Mexico and to establish a critical account of the nation's political crimes and the collapse of its democratic system. This narrative tactic of Morales' manifests itself into what Ian Chambers defines as

> neither fixed nor stable, but one that is open to the prospect of a continual return to events, to their re-elaboration and revision. This retelling, re-citing and re-siting of what passes for historical and cultural knowledge depend upon the recalling and re-membering of earlier fragments and traces that flare up and flash in our present. . . . These fragments that remain as fragments: splinters of light that illuminate our journey while simultaneously casting questioning shadows along the path. (1994, 3)

Morales represents this interstitial world through the use of alternate stories to emphasize the distortion of reality that Francisco Lomelí identifies as "future shock" (*Waiting to Happen* back matter) to accentuate the state of distress and disorientation in Mexico during the crisis of the 1980s. The historical representations in *Waiting to Happen* serve to undermine the official bureaucratic history of the antidrug campaign during the terms of Presidents Carlos Salinas de Gortari and George H. W. Bush.

Hence, the juxtaposition of official and alternate histories throughout *Waiting to Happen* further blurs the distinction between history, fiction, and reality due to the ambivalence of the relationship between the events and their respective documentation by the characters themselves. The protagonist's conclusion about these histories, that "Cassandra had written a story closer to the truth than reality" (117), is supported by Cassandra's and J. I. Cruz's individual and collective experiences in Mexico. They both had access to privileged information of the events and an understanding of what is presented as Mexico's official history. By the same token, a manuscript by another female character, Vanessa Morfaz, describing the corruption in which she is involved with the Anti-Narcotic Brigade, is categorized as "fiction" by a reporter unaware of such activity and who, as a result, states that the "'accusations and scenarios she described were ludicrous and unbelievable; nothing that absurd could happen in Mexico or anywhere else'" (163). The reporter utterly refutes the facts, as well as the many versions presented as logical explanations for one major scenario involving the disappearance, abduction, torture, and death of Southern California professor Kim and his wife:

> What happened to the Kims was simply another misfortune in the random chaos of Southern California's constant movement and stillness; tension

and tranquility; danger and safety; fear and bravery; hate and love; sorrow and joy; future and past; history and fiction; and a multitude of borders, places and misplaces, and languages and language existing in a familiar and cajoling space of strangeness that keeps open the void for symbolic fiction to nurturing common life. (89)

All the while Vanessa, her bodyguard Endriago, and the others directly involved in this couple's demise sarcastically celebrate the inaccurate historical accounts by the American media—the presumed experts in discovering and reporting the truth but who, in reality, could not conceive the existence of the secret Mexican narcotics operation. In this way, the novel brings to light much more than a simple acknowledgement that history is written by those in power. What seems to be put into question are the facts themselves.

In *Waiting to Happen*, Morales presents a fragmented narrative, open to alternate modalities of articulation, of heteroclite voices—personal, subversive, shocking, and unpredictable. He presents a work that deconstructs and breaks with traditional teleological linearity, a work that explores the space of the oppressed to include their voices and to establish a new horizon for the writing of history. Morales' fragmented narrative follows a desire to challenge the homogeneity of historical narratives. He does not reconstruct the past but instead attempts to fill in its gaps and limitations. The fragmented structure of the novel consequently emphasizes the impossibility of fully and accurately verifying any interpretation of official history with respect to the concept of national identity and marginalization of the Other. The postmodern style of *Waiting to Happen* is well exemplified by the narrator's description of Cassandra's chronicles as "a mixture of fact and fiction, of the real and the imagined, and of the normal and the paranormal . . . a version that offered . . . an option, a way to go" (114). Kevin Hetherington, in *Badlands of Modernity: Heterotopia & Social Ordering* (1997), also associates this type of fact-fiction postmodern discourse with heterotopia, which he describes as "spaces of *alternate ordering*, an ordering based on a number of utopics that come to being in relation to a tension that exists within modern societies between *ideas of freedom* and ideas of control or discipline" (x, my emphasis).

Hetherington's analysis of Foucault's definition of heterotopia as "sites . . . textual . . . as much as geographical ones . . . whose existence sets up unsettling juxtapositions of incommensurate 'objects' which *challenge the way we think*" (42, my emphasis) further identifies the discourse of social change as one stemming from heterotopia. Foucault's (1986) concept of heterotopia refers to the coming together of incompatible spaces into a single space. These places of Otherness, then, defy the way thinking is ordered. Furthermore, David Harvey (1990) also characterizes heterotopias as "incommensurable spaces that are juxtaposed or superimposed upon each other" (48) in a way that allows for such incommensurability to form sites of contention or resistance. As a result, the inclusion of heterotopia in this historiographical novel helps reaffirm the place of the marginalized within the present time, as well as to propose possibilities for a utopian future. Thus, *Waiting to Happen* represents a postmodern textual space that critiques historical consciousness. The interstices or gaps where the marginalized characters exist are therefore reevaluated as places of possibility in terms of questioning, resistance, protest, and transgression. It is here where the novel stresses the significance of women's voices, not only through Cassandra's writings but also through J. I. Cruz and other female characters. They appear as the agents of change in the novel. Through their efforts, the repressed gain a voice in society. It must be emphasized here that their quest for change in the story is directly related to Morales' selection of Salinas de Gortari's presidential term as the setting for the novel, as it allows for a plethora of possible alternate histories in the overall narrative. For instance, regarding Mexico's political climate, Cassandra expresses her pressing desire to make a change, while reaffirming her alliance with an assassinated Mexican journalist who wrote on the freedom of expression against abuse. Cassandra states that "We Mexicans have become accustomed to the abuses of authority . . . Abuse is a fact of life in Mexico. It's an accepted part of our daily existence; and I, Cassandra Arenal Coe, like Manuel Buendía, *want to change that*" (100, my emphasis).

In the same manner, the first of two epigraphs in the novel, an excerpt from an article by Carlos Monsiváis published in the *Boston Globe* in September 1996, not only illustrates the meaning of the book and its title but also presents a depiction of that critical period in Mexico:

> The *gravest moment* in Mexico. . . . *The government doesn't have any credibility*, nor do the political parties. The economy is in disarray. Dependence on the United states is extraordinary. There is guerrilla violence in several states. There is discouragement; there is fear. It is the worst public security situation that we've ever seen . . . much despair . . . It is not the fear of a catastrophe: it's *not knowing what could happen* next. The catastrophe that has occurred is the daily uncertainty, the fear of the next surprise. (1, my emphasis)

During this time, Mexico's insecurity and crisis intensify; the division between the rich and the poor widens; the economy, the state, and their political and traditional institutions all suffer unbelievable setbacks, as does the nationalistic discourse. Consequently, the many levels of this political and economic crisis contribute to a moment of diminished nationalism in which everything is questioned.

Nonetheless, while the heteroclite voices in *Waiting to Happen* put authority to question, the novel also puts forward an effort to try to understand the violence committed by Mexicans against their own brothers and sisters. The danger and mistrust in everything and everyone places heteroclite J. I. Cruz in the role of a medium for the nation's self-analysis. Explicitly so, the narrative voice bears out Monsiváis' quote by stating that Mexicans find themselves "living insecurely, a common place" (108) and further describes the condition-state-place of difference surrounding the protagonist:

> The violence returned when México contended with a terrible economic crisis. Thousands of small businesses closed, unemployment soared, and foreclosures and unpayable debts skyrocketed. People took to the streets to peddle labor, gum, fruit, and, at night, their bodies. Many were young people who had come from outside the city to search for jobs and found frustration and starvation. The context of their lives was violence and poverty while the rich proved the cliché that the wealthy get wealthier. The politicians, like the President and his family, his camarillas, the bankers, and big business, "los meros," were off in Europe and the United States vacationing and enjoying themselves. They were revealing to the world, "Qué los mexicanos son más que chusma, más que una bola de pelados, más que unos indios sucios, más que unos simplones frijoleros del rancho." Back home life became macabre, and the violence escalated. (97–98)

As a result, the sense of mistrust in the elitist Mexican government conveyed within the plot enables a potential questioning of patriarchy and Western imperialism. Subsequently, J. I. Cruz, a supreme feminine incarnation of what is prohibited within the exclusively masculine national setting, appears as a figure who, like Cassandra and the iconic Frida, lives in "the interstice of experience" (172). This entails the heterotrophic space of rich and poor, souls and humans, voice and silence, upper and popular culture, traditions and transgressions, homosexuality and heterosexuality, life and death, mothers and daughters, patriarchy and feminism, educated and uneducated, violators and violated, imperialists and anti-imperialists, etc. From this liminal position, J. I. Cruz affirms an anti-authoritarian discourse against the government, stating, "Todos los presidentes quienes hayan abusado de su poder and who have become millionaires at the expense of the Mexican people should be imprisoned. If they're living a luxurious exile, they should be found and eliminated!" (183). This alludes clearly to Salinas de Gortari, who was exiled from Mexico in 1995 because of his involvement in Mexico's economic crisis as well as his controversial connection to several murders, including that of the late presidential candidate Luis Donaldo Colosio.[1]

These efforts to widen the readers' collective historical memory with the histories of the conquered imply a number of presumptions and conclusions. The first is that the various versions of history are not only relevant to the past but also influence the present and the future. The second posits that historical discourse describes history only implicitly, as an objective process of progression and purpose. This further suggests that all forms of the status quo are the inevitable result of a development with its own right to exist within the present and into the future. From such a perspective, the progress of history is shown as a tragic loss, not only of human lives but of options and opportunities in general, since only one possibility takes place, thereby suppressing alternate histories.

Nonetheless, it is these alternate (or other) histories in *Waiting to Happen* that focus on recovering some of these losses by disputing the monopoly of the possibilities taking place in the "land of reality." One can take as an example the American and Mexican news media which, as the narrator declares,

> have become monolithic information companies capable of moving great amounts of fact and fiction; capable of moving amounts of narcotic fact or fiction all over the world; and capable of creating history, wars, image, and icon makers that make or break the political messiahs. (50)

Morales here turns to Mexican journalistic writings, first, as textual means for the articulation and distribution of alternate histories and, second, as another far-reaching channel to criticize oppression. A protest article written by Cassandra in *El Nacional* declares, for instance, that representatives of both countries "created the drug paranoia and . . . went along with it to justify its policies against illegal immigration and its militarization of the border" (81). The novel also alludes to an article in the newspaper *El Excélsior* that severely condemns

> the Mexican government and especially President Salinas for permitting DEA agents to run roughshod over the state of Chiapas. . . . destroying Mexico's

natural resources and murdering its people ... Destroying thousands of acres of jungle in Chiapas or thousands of acres of pine forest in Michoacán will not save one addict in New York or Los Angeles. It will instead kill hundreds, perhaps thousands, of Indians in Mexico. The drug hysteria only detracts the public in the United States and Mexico from the real agenda that is led by a group of Mexican and United States investors interested in turning Mexico into a nuclear power and small-arms-producing country. This group imports drugs from other parts of the world to transport to the United States. (82–83)

Morales' novelistic criticism of Salinas and Bush's war on drugs is uncompromising and serves to uncover their false pretense to a public safety agenda and, more importantly, to condemn the impunity of those massacring Mexico's indigenous peoples and destroying its natural resources, all the while implying how investors make profit on the undisclosed arms business between the two countries.

From a postcolonial perspective, the focus on articulation for the purpose of recovering and rewriting the history of unseen and silenced social groups serves to present this text not only as what Charles Bernstein (1990) identifies as an alternative aesthetic convention but also as an alternative social formation. Even though the publication of this *El Excélsior* article causes the dismissal of some editors and even though the newspaper's official voice, along with Mexican and American news reporters, scientists, politicians, and historians reject such stories "as ridiculous, fatuous, probably written by some deranged writer of fiction" (82), one cannot ignore the subversive ideological impact of the article with respect to a panoramic approach toward power relations and the oral tradition of historical narratives.

Furthermore, the novel also confirms how the selective nature of historical archives supports the inseparable link between historical knowledge and political power. In *Waiting to Happen*, the process of rewriting history by government leaders manifests as a parody that assumes a complicity between the reader, key female characters, and the narrator; the latter easily condemns President Salinas, who "like other presidents, transformed by the populace into the political high priest, *manipulated the system* with impunity, encouraged solutions, and *revised history* for the betterment of the Mexican people" (123, my emphasis). Here, the past is reinterpreted with the understanding that leading government figures create a history in their own image by excluding subordinated people and producing, instead, historical documents that highlight powerful public figures. In this case, the narrator explicitly illustrates such rewriting of history:

The dictatorship of Porfirio Díaz was no longer interpreted as a period of exploitation of the Mexican people; as a time of pillaging Mexico's natural resources, exporting its wealth, and selling its land to foreign interests; as a moment of giving special, economic privileges to foreign companies; as a sanctuary for allowing the church to accumulate wealth and power; or as a haven for políticos, militares, and caudillos for raping and killing Mexican women, men, and children. Instead it was presented as a great economic growth and prosperity, of technical development, of mining advancements, and in railroad transportation networks ... a Francophile gaudy way of life for the rich, and misery for the poor, but dominated by peace and tranquility on the Mexican side of the border and by conflict and rage on the United States side of the border. (123)

Although these alternate discourses mock official history, they do not pretend to remedy its bias. This heteroclite plot of intertextuality and the historical in *Waiting to Happen*, together with biographical references, supports the legitimizing purpose of historical knowledge to remind us of the eventuality of history as a precondition to change the status quo. Thus, one of the novel's primary objectives is to open windows into the past and relive it to include the perspective of history's conquered and oppressed populations.

Even more, *Waiting to Happen* proposes what is to be a story of triumph. The second epigraph, a quote from Keneally's novel *Schindler's List*, declares that "this is the story of the pragmatic *triumph of good over evil.*" (1, my emphasis). With its heteroclite voices—voices outside the norm—Morales' novel presents a history of the masses, an inverted version in which the oppressed assume focal roles in the retelling of history. One instance is the detailed description Cassandra fashions of a sick game captured on a photograph she inherits in which soldiers are sadly and horrifically raping an Indigenous woman:

The game took three to play: two soldiers and one woman, preferably a young, Indian woman. The object of the game was to maintain calm while raping the woman and reaching orgasm. One soldier had to attain orgasm without moving the woman's body and thereby preventing her head from bobbing upon the razor-sharp blade. The second soldier had to steady the bayonet firmly under the woman's chin without cutting her, until his companion reached orgasm. To survive, the woman had to remain perfectly still, frozen, until both men took their turn and finished with her. Probably not many women survived this game called by the soldiers "congelar la polla." The women who violently resisted were raped and murdered. According to my sources, many women opted for death rather than to give any pleasure to the soldiers. (152)

Considering the literary refocus on the marginalized, conquered, and oppressed, one can understand how the horrific images of rape and violence committed by the police and the military against women, Indigenous people, and children are presented to the reader not just to indict the abusers but to emphasize and confirm what the victims have had to endure. It is the survivors' resilience that is ultimately emphasized.

J. I. Cruz thereby serves as a corroborating voice that confirms the unbelievable acts captured in the chronicles and in the series of photographs Cassandra inherits. After Cruz sees the last of these pictures, which "showed two soldiers ... holding the rifle and bayonet high, with the woman skewered through her anus and through the throat and head," the narrator reaffirms that "J. I. simply refused to believe what she beheld, but the photographs were real" (152). This confirmation in the novel, first by the chronicles and second by the protagonist, serves not only to emphasize the reality of violence and torture in Mexico's past and present but also to reaffirm literature's socio-aesthetic role in the building of a less violent, and much less depraved, new social order in the future.

All the observations and instances thus far examined substantiate how *Waiting to Happen* envisions women as main agents of a new history. Indeed, Morales' novel contextualizes the ilusa J. I. Cruz as a woman capable of returning to Aztlán for the purpose of "saving" her country, the women, and the marginalized from patriarchy and imperialism. Therefore, the novel's critique of men in power who have positioned women as conquered objects, incredulous and violated, and who have profited from doing so, is now contrasted with the rewriting of women as prophets, messengers, and agents of the future. J. I. Cruz, a modern woman with Frida's impulse and Sor Juana's devotion, lives within the schism between patriarchy and feminism, with the potential to deconstruct the safekeeping of patriarchal gender roles. Morales describes the ilusa, a woman violated and seduced, as a heteroclite, becoming in the process a "being living and actively participating in a space of multiple dimensions, languages, perspectives, logics that are constantly struggling to become comfortable, living in a place of differences, a place of otherness" (169).

Accordingly, Morales imbues into the novel's female iconography a modern saint, La Santa Ilusa de las Grietas (The divine saint of the crevices, or the holy saint of those who dwell within the crevices), a woman who inherits strength from souls and voices of survival and who is "possessed by the energy of enchanted, powerful women of the past who loved Christ in and through her" (218). As an ilusa, J. I. Cruz is an individual not only capable of dreaming of a utopic future but also one acquiring supernatural powers conducive to protest, resistance, and miracles, one whose voice must be heard because, just as the other *heteróclitas de las grietas*, she "is possessed not by evil but by overwhelming knowledge" (167). As such, she will lead her faithful followers, the "población de las grietas," in a series of transforming events, first doing so at a city-wide protest that causes "los días del alto" (a shutdown) in Mexico City:

> Thousands of vehicles had a part taken from their mechanical system that made the motor inoperable. J. I.'s people had understood the metaphor and executed her instructions swiftly and convincingly. The heart of the internal combustion engine and gasoline-transportation systems had been damaged so that the vehicles were brought to a halt.... The television newscasters described this new group of people who had shut down Mexico City as systematic, spontaneous, and religious. (208)

The well-known fact that this megalopolis has one of the highest automobile pollution levels in the world is contrasted by the force J. I. Cruz and her people show in making change possible. Later in the novel, a second significant event in which the air pollution completely disappears occurs when the followers of La Santa Ilusa de las Grietas dismantle ten of the city's subway trains.

Waiting to Happen explores heterotopia in the historical representation of globalized Mexican society, with women as agents of social change. The novel examines a praxis of decolonization in Mexico City through the inclusion of hybrid individuals, an alternate possibility of identity conceptualization. From the interstitial spaces and based on the premise of an implicit apprehension by the controlling systems in society—and their binary ideologies of restriction and oppression—the protagonist's identity is reaffirmed as the heteroclite ilusa who emerges to become the leader of "women, children, old folks, the poor, the homeless, the hungry, the disenfranchised, the marginalized, the faithful, all of J. I.'s people" (217). While confined in the convent at Amecameca, she hears the voice of Father Cristóbal, whose words paint a detailed picture for J. I. Cruz of the time and space that surround her, highlighting her important role in rewriting history as it pertains to her and Mexico's immediate present:

Maybe the environment, the streets you've walked, the houses you've inhabited, the ancient earth you've touched, the situations you've lived—maybe the environment has somehow stored information and energy from beings who lived and from events that occurred here in the Valley of Mexico and remain housed in the space of Mexico City and its surroundings. Maybe there are times in history when under the proper circumstances, the information and the energy will be reconstructed so that you and other people can feel, see, hear, smell, and speak to those people and relive those events of the past existing and influencing the present. (203)

In this garden of history, "the modern city of Mexico, where past, present, and future are the playground of wealth, poverty, omnipresent religion, miracles, violence, passion, love, and continuous surprises" (180), the protagonist searches for utopia between an unplanned labyrinth of coffee houses, restaurants, bars, taco stands, discotheques, plazas, museums, schools, universities, stadiums, bullrings, hotels, churches, pyramids, temples, synagogues, squares, theatres, palaces, high-risers, monuments, cemeteries, convents, brothels, and mansions. The narrator describes how, in her search around Mexico City, J. I. Cruz "discovered a megalopolis where millions lived in marginalized conditions, where poverty and hunger were the rewards for super-exploitation. Her people were proud of surviving the abuses they suffered . . . They had lived" (189). She finds heterotopia, a world with gaps and breaches in which she and her people learn to live and to create new survival strategies, a world that demands not only a different way of thinking but one in which "history is harvested and collected, to be assembled, made to speak, re-membered, re-read and rewritten" (Chambers 1994, 3). Thus, Morales' heterotopia of Mexico City and Southern California offers a more heterogeneous complexion that reflects the intricacies of reality. *Waiting to Happen* is both formed and informed by a narrative mechanism of time and space—from the past to the present and into the future—including historical figures whose voices do not have a place in official history but whose resistance is now part of the marginalized characters as they bring change for the future.

In her quest to discover the multiple aspects that make up her identity as an *ilusa* with feminine, fantastic, and real dimensions, the protagonist enters this heterotopic expanse and saves her sanity through writing. Furthermore, J. I.'s residency in and contact with a Mexican heterotopia allows her to see memory (or history) as a necessary clue for her self-awareness and for taking her through a process of understanding, as the narrator states: "The house is an impossible dwelling to possess and to make a home; too many souls claim time and space in it" (19) . . . "survival didn't have to be in this house" (232). It is here, in what Morales refers to as the heterotopic space inhabited but not quite attainable or explainable, and perceptible only by change, where the otherwise cynical and dark novel opens itself to other possibilities or new spaces. As a consequence, women reinvent themselves, and we get a glimpse of a window to a utopian future. The heteroclite J. I. Cruz personifies the novel's concerns *against* (the prevailing attitude of) suppressing the past, yet *for* (the sorely needed) acts of rebellion that could help bring about an improved and ideal state of things. *Waiting to Happen*, then, exemplifies a call for what Erna Pfeiffer refers to as the impossible utopia, in which "la ficción, híbrida y cambiante, se llega a una fijación, aunque precaria y efímera, de los relampagueantes fuegos fatuos de los residuos históricos" (1999, 118). It is the novel itself, as an historiographical text of alterity and aperture, that becomes ephemerally a utopia, a habitable space that saves its inhabitants from dissolution. Through Cassandra's rewriting of history—her chronicle on diaspora and the continuous oppression, the nexus between Mexican and Mexican American identities—transgresses borders, reaffirming that "consciousness, culture, and a definite personal expression transcended any place" (232) and that the mythical Aztlán can then be established as a utopia.

Morales' novel engages in a dialogue of ideas about history—not to repeat it, but to open it to other possible interpretations and modes of writing, reading, creating, and perceiving. This work develops as a rich dialogue and testimony to the importance of communication to avoid repeating mistakes committed in the past. It represents a dialogue bridging between past and future—the rewriting of history. Morales' sociopolitical message and literary stylistics are key to his exploration of heterotopia in a world characterized by cruelty and violence, which escalated under the Salinas presidency. The novel paradoxically seeks to propose another truth, one beyond the rational. The persecutions, disappearances, and murders exemplified in its plot are all deeply rooted in the Mexican nation's political system. The author's stylistic employment of texts outside official history, such as manuscripts, newspaper articles, photographs, and chronicles by and in favor of the Other, as well as his references to historical figures symbolic of an indisputable resistance, is a direct questioning of these practices against the marginalized—particularly against women. This is where Morales' ilusa serves to rewrite history in Mexico:

Women waited, loving, nursing, caring for their children, waiting for a sign to make their lives bearable and meaningful. A woman with a thousand wrinkles on her face of the Madonna . . . a woman with ninety-nine years on her shoulders leaned on a cane and moved slowly . . . a pregnant girl with a radiant smile, thick, black hair, and a broad nose . . . professional female reporters, photographers, writers, anthropologists, artists, and filmmakers . . . came to get the story, the image, and the sounds; or to listen to testimonies of faith; to see the shrines to the *Santa Ilusa de las Grietas*; and to attempt to record the spectacle. (215)

The author's political statement is clear in the novel's polyphonic discourses—popular, political, ecclesiastical—all highlighting the importance of women and his concern for a world in which the characters undergo an identity crisis. Morales' work disputes the concept of identity as predetermined by those wielding power and enjoying the monopoly of representation in official history, in contrast posing a utopian view of giving voice to the voiceless.

NOTE

1. See the PBS documentary *Murder, Money, & Mexico*.

WORKS CITED

Aguilar Camín, Héctor. 1975. "La cultura mexicana de los setentas." *La Cultura de México*, suplemento Siempre!, August 27.
Bernstein, Charles. 1990. "Comedy and the Poetics of Political Form." In *The Politics of Poetic Form: Poetry and Public Policy*, edited by C. Bernstein, 235–44. New York: Roof Books.
Chambers, Iain. 1994. *Migrancy, Culture, Identity*. London: Routledge.
Foucault, Michel. 1986. "Of Other Spaces." Translated by Jay Miskowiec. *Diacritics* 16, no. 1 (Spring): 22–27.
Franco, Jean. 1995. "Feminist Postmodernities." In *The Postmodern Novel in Latin America: Politics, Culture, and the Crisis of Truth*, edited by Raymond L. Williams, 111. New York: St. Martin's Press.
Gurpegui, J. A. 1996. "Interview with Alejandro Morales." In *Alejandro Morales: Fiction Past, Present, Future Perfect*, edited by José Antonio Gurpegui, 5–13. Tempe, AZ: Press / Editorial Bilingüe.

Harvey, David. 1990. *The Condition of Postmodernity: An Enquiry into the Origins of Cultural Change*. Oxford: Blackwell.

Hetherington, Kevin. 1997. *The Badlands of Modernity: Heterotopia and Social Ordering*. London: Routledge.

Morales, Alejandro. 1996. "Dynamic Identities in Heterotopia." In Gurpegui, *Alejandro Morales: Fiction Past, Present, Future Perfect*, 14–27.

———. 2001. *Waiting to Happen*. Sunnyvale, CA: Chusma House..

PBS. 2017. *Murder, Money & Mexico: The Rise and Fall of the Salinas Brothers*. Documentary. Accessed September 15, 2018. https://www.pbs.org/wgbh/pages/frontline/shows/mexico/.

Pfeiffer, Erna. 1999. "Nadar en los intersticios del discurso: La escritura histórico-utópica de Carmen Boullosa." In *Acercamientos a Carmen Boullosa: Actas del Simposio "Conjugarse en Infinitivo, La escritora Carmen Boullosa,"* edited by Barbara Dröscher and Carlos Rincón, 107–19. Berlin: Edition Tranvía.

Williams, Raymond L. 1995. "Mexican Postmodernities." In *The Postmodern Novel in Latin America: Politics, Culture and the Crisis of Truth*, 21–42. New York: St. Martin's Press.

SEVEN / City History and Space Politics / Los Angeles in Morales' *River of Angels* / BAOJIE LI

Alejandro Morales stands out in contemporary Chicano literature due to his emphasis on historical novels.[1] He has a predilection for rediscovering the past and re-representing it through narrative, especially the past of Mexican migrations and the ongoing acclimatization of Mexican Americans. Born in a family of Mexican immigrants in Montebello, east of the City of Los Angeles, Morales grew up in the community of the Simons Brickyard no. 3, where his father worked. Spending most of his time within the Los Angeles area, he forged a natural attachment to the place and has thus far been devoted to situating his stories in and around that region. It is therefore justifiable to call him a native writer of Los Angeles, as is exemplified in his 2014 novel *River of Angels*. This epic story chronicles two families of different ethnic backgrounds, all within the framework of the temporal changes not only of Los Angeles but of the venerable river itself. The evolution of this river and the transformation of the city parallel a linear continuity of family as well as the merging of Anglo-American and Mexican American blood. As the fluctuation of people's lives coincide with the ever-changing borders of their L.A. living spaces in the novel, this study outlines how Morales' narrative chronicle of Los Angeles is inextricably linked with the community of Mexican Americans, and how space functions in combination with ethnicity to divide people in the process of urbanization and modernization. Additionally, the study explores how the (con)textualization of the history of the city aesthetically transcends the historical narrative.[2]

River of Angels exemplifies the writing techniques and motivations characteristic of Morales' historical fiction. Taking Los Angeles as the background, the novel describes the development of the city and the changes in people's lives over the span of more than a century. City history works as the background and framework, and the story unfolds parallel to the geographical changes of the city. The reproduction of physical space embodies the power relation between characters, and the historical narration outlines the urbanization of Los Angeles. Within this narration, the author interweaves realist and magical realist elements to illustrate differing layers of sociohistorical reality.

The name "River of Angels" literally refers to the Los Angeles River. The novel therefore establishes a chronological trajectory of Los Angeles through foregrounding the river and its important role in the development of the city:

> Were it not for the Los Angeles River, the city that shares its name would not be where it is today ... The Los Angeles River has always been at the heart of whichever human community is in the basin ... It has supplied the residents of the city and basin with water to drink and spread amidst their grapes, oranges, and other crops. It has been an instrument by which people could locate themselves on the landscape. It has been a critical dividing line, not only between east and west, north and south, but between races, classes, neighborhoods. (Deverell 2004, 93)

According to Morales, in writing the novel he sought to provide an outline of the city and trace how each of its parts developed.[3] In the narrative, the vicissitudes of the Los Angeles River match the main storyline of the developing metropolis, leaving the reader to imagine the bygone, powerful nature of the waterway (in comparison to modern times, where it has virtually become a trickling creek in most places). In the beginning of the novel, the prologue narrator comes across a wall of past photographs of the river, which triggers a deep curiosity about the history of the river, its bridges, and the city as a whole. The novel eventually proves that the river's influence is not just geographical but economic, psychological and cultural, and still being felt, especially as the demarcation between the West and the East sides of Los Angeles. The pages of the story present the ever-changing relationship between people and the waterway, exemplified by the flooding of the river, the erection of bridges, and the division between communities, among other historical events. More notably, from the portrayal of the temporal urbanization and spatial compartmentalization of this self-styled "City of Angels," we see that ideological factors dominate the layout of the city.

Moreover, we also come to see that the contextualization of city history in the novel helps foreground the power relations involved in the reproduction of urban space.

Henri Lefebvre theorizes, in this regard, the (re)production of space and the conceptualization of "the space of spaces" (2); he also emphasizes the political implication of space in general, especially the so-called "mental space," which implies both the social and the physical kinds. He stresses the ideological implication of mental space, arguing that "a powerful ideological tendency, one much attached to its own would-be scientific credentials, is expressing, in an admirably unconscious manner, those dominant ideas which are perforce the ideas of the dominant class. To some degree, perhaps, these ideas are deformed or diverted in the process, but the net result is that a particular "theoretical practice" produces a mental space which is apparently, but only apparently, extra-ideological" (1991, 6). In sociological terms, ideology itself contains such factors as demographic composition (in the axes of race and gender, for instance) and economic situation (in the axes of class, vocation, and social status). When reflected in the reproduction of urban space, these factors may be represented in the relationship between space and polity, physically manifested through urban development and city history, with the latter referring to the verbal and nonverbal records of a city in its formation, transition, and development. The completion of city history mainly involves two aspects, geographical and humanistic. The first manifests as the city's geographical changes, such as size, location, landmarks, street layouts, and functional zoning; the second involves factors like population and its composition, popular lifestyle and customs, value system, artistic architecture, and cultural symbolism. Surely, these factors often work together to constitute a unique urban landscape. They constitute in turn some sense of attachment, or in David Lowenthal's words, they are "selective nostalgia about particular times and places" (1975, 3); for Li Fan et al., they represent "psychological identification based on collective memory" (2010, 65). In addition, the literal meaning of "city history" also refers to the actual process of historiography, the textualization of historical materials, namely, the encoding, storage, and extraction of these historical records, which can be used to reflect the geographical and cultural features of the city. In the history of urban development and the process of geospatial planning, ideological elements, power relations, and the distribution of benefits are likely to play a key role in deciding the city's positioning and functioning. Edward Said thus connotes geography "as a socially constructed and maintained sense of place" (2000, 180). From the history of a city, the mapping of production relations can be perceived.

That is the case in *River of Angels*, which reflects the power relation between ethnic elements and urbanization. Based on the history of Los Angeles, the novel unfolds in a linear narrative, with the main storyline framed by shifts in the ownership of land, the symbiosis and hybridity of races, and the collision and negotiation of different cultures. It describes the early eighteenth-century origin of the city as a settlement of Spanish and Mexican colonizers. As the story unfolds in the mid-nineteenth century, Los Angeles is still part of Mexico and the US-Mexico War is still brewing. The indigenous people in the novel at this time seem to follow their traditional way of life, maintaining a harmonious relationship with the river. The story initially revolves around the family of Abelardo Ríos, whose very name indicates a symbolic connection with the river. The shift of sovereignty over the land, the discovery of gold and the consequent Gold Rush, and the steady inflow of immigrants of various origins frame the changes in the physical and generational surroundings of the Ríos family. The growth of the city of Los Angeles is perceived and measured from the perspective of the changes to the river that flows near their home.

In the novel, Mexican Indian culture is stressed as something natural—particularly for the Ríos family, who have been living on the riverbank for years. Abelardo Ríos "inherited his ranch from his father, who had received his land from his father. It was Abelardo's father who had named the parcel El Rancho el Cachito de la Porciúncula. In reality, his ranch was a small portion of land, *un cachito*, surrounded by holdings taken over by Anglos who had recently come into the area" (4). The Ríoses are Mexican Indians, and their intimacy with the river is typical of Native American cultural ecology. They are spiritually connected with the river, to the point that Abelardo named his sons "Sol" and "Otchoo," meaning "the sun" and "trees," respectively, to represent the spirits of heaven and earth. This natural connection represents harmony between human beings and nature in Native American culture. Abelardo is familiar with the cycles of the river and respects the power of its water: "It was an ever-growing force on earth. It came from beneath the earth, and it sustained the strength of our flesh and bones.... a person must humbly learn how to approach, to be near, to walk, to swim, to release, to drink, to bathe, to irrigate, to boil, to capture, to protect and to cross water" (52). Abelardo's approach to existence and survival involves following the mood of nature. He listens to nature's rhythms, knowing how to live peacefully with the river and where to build houses so that people can be safe from the disturbance of its annual flooding. Moreover, his wisdom helps Anglo immigrants settle down in the pueblo, often saving many from the rage of the river, including the Plummers, whose refusal to take Abelardo's advice endangers their own lives and that of Sol. Morales, then, characterizes the relationship between man and nature as dialectical: water is the source of life, and it can be dangerous enough to devour life; while knowledge from and with nature is beneficial, it can also be dangerous. Indeed, "Toypurina had often warned her husband that his profitable knowledge was not only beneficial—but also hazardous" (53). The sudden fluctuations both of the river and of the fortunes of the Ríos family sadly proves her correct, as Sol gets swept away on the stormy night when he risks his life to save Mrs. Plummer, only to be rescued by the lizard people. Sol's acquisition of the ability to live like an amphibian enables him to traverse the border between the land and the waters. In Sol, Morales creates a character who understands the language of animals and befriends both the weak and nature; at the same time, his uniqueness allows the novel's principal antagonist, Philip Keller, to judge him as backward and crazy. In all, the Ríos family's change in fortune also benefits from their knowledge of the river. Their patch of land is close to the water, which is considered potentially dangerous and is not craved by speculators, as a result of which they are able to keep the land. The father and sons transport travelers across the river, launching their own ferry business. Nevertheless, the prosperity and growth of the village eventually disturb its old peace and harmonious amity and balance, bringing about irreversible changes to both the land and its people. This development epitomizes the Mexican Indian concept of ecology—characterized by harmonious human coexistence with nature—while also demonstrating what occurs when this harmony and balance is compromised.

In *River of Angels*, the steady arrival of Anglo settlers sparks the initial urbanization of Los Angeles, diluting the mentioned Native American ecological concepts and beliefs. In the process, the relationship between man and nature loses its naturalness; it instead begins to assume ideological qualities. Because of changes to both the ownership of land and the relation of production, social ecology begins to replace natural ecology. Morales writes of people of different skin colors and ethnicities pouring into Los Angeles as it begins to assume the initial features of a modern city. The transformation in the social identity of the Ríoses from farmers to business owners heralds the transition of Los Angeles from a relatively agricultural community to an industrial society. The Ríoses keep upgrading their business, which begins as the Ríos and Sons and Cyland River Barge Transport Company and eventually becomes the Sun Construction Company. They also move upward from the riverbank to the hard land, free from the confinement of the river but exposed to the less-predictable tides of the time.

Their old ferry service takes on the characteristics of modern business to become part of American commercialization. Otchoo Ríos' assumption of the new name of "Oakley Rivers" signifies a second baptism, ceremoniously compromising his Mexican Indian identity to assume a considerably more Anglo-American one. This transition bears double symbolism: in addition to Otchoo's new social status as a businessman, it implies the commercialization of the relationship between people and the river, the transformation from the previous peaceful coexistence to an interest-orientated commercialization of the land. As the city continues to expand, Oakley's company begins to undertake the construction of bridges across the Los Angeles River, eventually becoming one of L.A.'s most trusted builders. The relationship between man and river evolves into a more lucrative enterprise, with the river being objectified, harnessed, altered, and transformed. This change manifests the characteristics of urbanization, such as "the adaptation of urban lifestyles by rural residents as reflected in population growth, the expansion of the areas with urban architectures, and the formation of urban landscapes and gradual completion of the cycle of urban lifestyles" (Yao Shi-mou et al. 2008, 93). On the societal level, the protagonists' social relationships also undergo change, with established social orders encountering particular challenges. Oakley's marriage to Agatha Banac, the daughter of a prosperous bank lawyer, for example, symbolizes his movement into the originally exclusive European American community: "Oakley handled all the legal and financial negotiations, keeping the company on firm ground. He could account for every penny coming in and going out" (29). All this time, the physical function of the river to provide water resources drastically decreases, signifying in the novel the disintegration of natural ecology, of natural resources exploited to the point of exhaustion. The connection between man and nature, then, starts to become more commercialized, legalized, and correspondingly corporatized.

In addition to these changes, Morales in *River of Angels* represents the process of urbanization in a spatial dimension, in the form of the compartmentalization of space. The diachronic transformation of the city is twice complicated by synchronic city planning, enabling each of the urban communities to be culturally unique and reflect different relations of production. The novel typifies spatial compartmentalization as cultural negotiations and conflicts of interest between ethnic groups, especially the Mexican/Indian and Anglo-American. Urban districts function as demarcations for socioethnic relations. Racial elements prove decisive in the zoning and functional orientation. The city eventually gets separated into East and West Los Angeles, with the former becoming a community representatively "Mexican," "Latino," and "Black." The geographical separation of ethnic groups in city space reflects what Lefebvre (1991) conceptualizes as the influence of hegemony. He theorizes the social space with "the advent of capitalism" as a triple interweaving relationship:

> The advent of capitalism, and more particularly "modern" neocapitalism, has rendered this state of affairs considerably more complex. Here three interrelated levels must be taken into account: (1) biological reproduction (the family); (2) the reproduction of labour power (the working class per se); and (3) the reproduction of the social relations of production—that is, of those relations which are constitutive of capitalism and which are increasingly (and increasingly effectively) sought and imposed as such. The role of space in this tripartite ordering of things will need to be examined in its specificity. (32)

Throughout the narrative, the core images of "river" and "bridge" reflect the changes in the relations of (re)production of space. Hegemonic power as decision-maker has accumulated capital and information, facilitating the ambition to isolate, and in turn to discriminate against, the marginalized group confined to a specific location as a result of the hegemonic manipulations of social space. The small villages present at the beginning of *River of Angels* get replaced by modern buildings; people of diverse ethnicities and economic status are distributed into different communities (rich or poor, white or ethnic, etc.). The socially empowered claim and hold the land being commodified, that is, the most fertile or the most expensive at the center of the city. Thus, power affects the welfare of both physical and social spaces. Dominant groups with access to political and economic power occupy the metropolitan core business districts and live in the most expensive neighborhoods, isolating laborers and the overwhelming majority of ethnic minorities. The zoning of the city reflects the intermingling of capital and ethnic hegemony:

> to the north and west [were] the affluent homes of Hancock Park, Hollywood, Brentwood, Beverly Hills. Builders invested in middle-class residential ventures for Anglo-American families. Along the river and across the greater Eastside, the city council had zoned the area for industrial development and for working-class Anglo families. Mexican housing was torn down or pushed to the edges of the newly developed sections. The Mexicans pushed against the river banks and railroads yards, lived in abandoned farm

worker camps, segregated company towns, in areas that had not been designated for them in this city envisioned as Anglos only. (103)

This vision appears fairly vague when perceived from Albert Rivers' point of view when he begins to gain consciousness about ethnic differences. The segregation between the Anglos and Mexican Americans becomes more and more clarified as the story progresses, and Albert begins to experience its impact personally as it concerns his relationship with an Anglo girl, Louise Keller.

However, the establishment of the border has already betokened border-crossing, suggesting the possibility of exceptions to the rule. The Riverses, empowered by economic success, can afford property in the most expensive community in the city, ensuring their children access to good education and the prospect of being initiated into the upper strata of the society. Nonetheless, they are disempowered because of their ethnicity, so that they are accepted hesitantly by the prosperous neighbors in the affluent neighborhood. This contradiction manifests most notably in the characterization of Philip Keller, who is representative of the Anglo exclusionists in his capacity as a member of the elite Aryan Club. These privileged members of Southern Californian society believe firmly that Los Angeles should be home to the Aryan master race. As such Keller takes on the historical task of safeguarding the purity of Aryan blood and naturally becomes outraged at the foreboding inflow of immigrants:

> The country had to segregate the low ape-like Negroes, descendants of slaves. But the new immigrants entering the country today were the most disgusting and dangerous half-breeds. The brown- and the yellow-skinned people were the worst. They seem to come in hoards and disappear into their communities. These were the Chinese, Japanese and Mexicans. And even worse were the filthy, syphilitic drunks—the so-called "American Indians." (182)

In contrast to the clear border between races, struggles for space never stop at a clear-cut line. Even when the dominant successfully manage to segregate the dominated beyond the color line, they are always alert against daring transgressions, for example, the presence of trespassers such as the Rivers family, who are seen as devaluing the property of their upscale communities. The prospect of interracial marriages is even more disastrous because of its potential to stain the pure Aryan blood. When the challenge is more clearly felt, the white community becomes increasingly desperate to expel colored people from their center.

In Morales' novel, the bridges represent border crossings, with a dual function: to facilitate communication between spaces and simultaneously subdivide space. The bridges built by contractors like Oakley Rivers connect the west and east sides of the river, integrating the city's geographical spaces; they also help segregate the city and reinforce the separation between social, physical, and psychological spaces. More than a dozen bridges across the Los Angeles River separate East Los Angeles from its mirror equivalent on the west side of the bank. Mexican workers work during the day in factories and shops in West Los Angeles, help clean the Anglos' homes, mow their lawns, or take care of their children. They return at night to the eastern part of the city because the Anglos do not want them close by. The effects of segregation appear well embedded and consonant with the city's character and daily movement. As seen in the novel, the construction of these bridges makes it easier for the laborers to retreat into their space because "the rich didn't want Mexicans living with them or anywhere near them, so that East side, known as 'East LA,' was developed for Mexican workers to inhabit" (xi–xii). East Los Angeles therefore represents an alternative side of the metropolis: poor, colored, chaotic, and dirty. Both in Morales' novel and historically speaking, Mexican labor functions as the main workforce in the process of urbanization and urban construction. However, Mexicans are deprived of the right to enjoy the welfare of urbanization and modernization, instead being segregated into ethnically designated and clearly confined urban spaces. This division of labor and the exchange between capital and work dissimulate the hegemonic nature of social space, justifying the separation and, in essence, the exploitation of Mexican labor. This mechanism conforms to what Lefebvre conceptualizes as the "language of things and products": "They use their own language, the language of things and products, to tout the satisfaction they can supply and the needs they can meet; they use it too to lie, to dissimulate not only the amount of social labour that they contain, not only the productive labour that they embody, but also the social relationships of exploitation and domination on which they are founded" (1991, 80–81).

In Morales' story, in which the Los Angeles River plays a central role, the narrative of city history is retrospective. In other words, whatever the narrative strategy, the ultimate significance of the discourse lies in its inspiration for a (re)production of the present, as Dean Franco remarks, "Contemporary cultural production often means turning to an overlooked or misunderstood usable past; in the process, modern cultural efforts produce a cultural archive as much as they are produced by it. The modern demands of memory, including the demand for a history and the need for narrative that coherently establishes a meaningful present, make cultural archiving selective, value-laden, and political: it produces the past while producing the present" (2005, 377). In combination with the attempt to use historical fiction to rediscover the ignored and/or the forgotten, the significance of retrospection in the novel becomes clearer. The work focuses on people's intercultural experiences and mutual acculturation, highlighting the sociopolitical implication of specific acts, such as bridge construction. Business endeavors are presented as "value-laden," archiving the excavation of the past. Morales also uses Native American cultural elements to enhance the sense of retrospection, such as the lizard people, *curanderismo*, the ageless *curandera* Mother River, Porciúncula, Toypurina' s disturbed ghost, and Sol's rebirth and his miraculous faculty with nature's language. Moreover, these factors, fantastic embodiments of the indigenous concept of "animism" and "equality of all lives" in Indian natural ecology, help achieve an effect of cultural insight that non-Mexican readers might struggle with because it may seem foreign to them. For instance, the lizard people living deep underground signify a Native American belief in the transformation between forms of life and the cycling of life between levels of existence: "The lizard people come up to save the defenseless who are drowning or have drowned in the river and take them to their home deep underground. Few have seen them, because, when lizard people are changing from human to lizard or from lizard to human, their appearance is terrifying" (36).

Indeed, in this Chicano novel the narrator subtly shifts between positions of cultural identification, thereby underscoring not only differences between Native American and European American cultures but, more importantly, a resultant confusion with or rejection of an unfamiliar or "alien" culture. People with "terrifying appearance" echo European American aesthetics and their sense of estrangement from "alien" faces, for instance, Mexicans with dark skin, Chinese with long pigtails, and Japanese with slanted eyes, etc. Instances of this sort are abundant in the novel, despite the contributions and sacrifices of ethnic groups for the development of Los Angeles. For example, a vase retrieved by Sol and Albert from the riverbed serves as a tangible representative of a forced ethnic compromise, namely the Declaration of Public Inclusion of the Chinese Property. In this dispute over land transfer, the state dealt in a particular (and subtly malevolent) way with Chinese American families who refused to abandon their homes and surrender their land to the city council :

> Then, about twenty police officers surrounded several blocks in Chinatown. The medical people broke into three teams escorted by five policemen. Each team had the city council's authority to enter every house and apartment in the four-bock area.... The Chinese family members were lined up in front of a table, where the nurses registered them, and then they were forced to board the buses. (72)

As these people are condemned as alleged patients of tuberculosis—the accused "homo sacer" in Giorgio Agamben's words (1995, 162)—it is justifiable to lock them in hospitals and sanatoriums for the safety of the overall population. In a way, the Aryan Club members employ the same malevolent rationale when they propose the forced termination of reproduction of what they sickeningly see as the "lower races":

> These subhuman races, Uncle Philip believed, had to be stopped from breeding, which justified sterilization of men and most definitely women, who, being of a lower race, tended to mate with any man available. The sterilization procedure could be involuntary, done without their knowledge until a law was passed to require this necessary procedure. A program of elimination had to be planned and followed to maintain America as a country of racial purity. (182)

These two excerpts from *River of Angels* illustrate not only how government and politics exist within any dimension of physical and social space but also how ideological supremacy impedes and manipulates the survival of the socially disadvantaged.

This dynamic is even more thoroughly manifested in the heartbreaking love affair between Albert and Louise, exemplifying the confluence of racial dominance, economic supremacy, and the aforementioned ideological politicization of space. The Rivers as a prosperous new middle class of ethnic origin, and the Kellers as the (mostly) liberal middle class of Aryan origin, represent the emerging power to redraw the city space. The Riverses relocate to the exclusive residential community of Hancock Park, a move that would provide access to one of the best schools in the city: "[Agatha] had enrolled Albert into the Thomas Mat Academic Center, which she considered the best private school in the area" (55–56). On the other hand, for Philip Keller and his exclusive Aryan Club, white supremacy and racial advantage must be protected. These privileged men are representative of the upper class that has benefited the most from political and economic hegemony and has had access to the superior resources of the country:

> The Members all of white northern European stock, wanted to make Los Angeles a new-world Aryan fatherland. Most of the members were wealthy professionals involved in government, banking, publishing, real estate, science and education. They had attended universities either in the East or in the old country. They believed in God and were convinced that they had a sacred duty to establish and maintain Southern California as an Aryan-led community. (85)

They are not ready to compromise their privileges, becoming desperate to defend against the upward movement of the "mongrel races" (85). The professionals among the upper class have concocted a whole system of knowledge to theorize the inferiority of the colored: "According to the experts—Darwinists, university professors, members of the Aryan Club of Southern California—Indians, particularly of the California tribes, were inherently inferior, prone to drunkenness and infested with disease like tuberculosis and syphilis" (85–86). Through this reasoning, Aryans and Anglos justify their distribution of social wealth and fortifying their economic base. From an alternative perspective, their desperation can be interpreted as a sense of danger in the face of an impending threat to their world order. Indeed, the urbanization and various architecture projects it involved, such as bridge construction, helped establish a new class of entrepreneurs as represented by the Kellers and the Rivers, who are gaining economic power and technological maturity. Their upward movement may disturb the former monopoly over knowledge by the upper class, which causes the radical nationalists in the Aryan Club to become desperate to guard against physical, biological, and psychological "impingements" into their space by nonwhites. Philip Keller's final decision to murder Sol and Albert underscores this sense of danger when his preaching of eugenics, specifically involuntary sterilization to terminate the reproduction of the purported subhuman races, falls on his nephew and grandniece's deaf ears.

The novel highlights the absurdity of the studies commissioned by the American Eugenics Association in the first half of the twentieth century. The tragic love of Albert and Louise reflects both spatial and ideological politics, in which dominant forces attempt to keep at bay ethnic intrusions into their realm. The hegemonic power impinges the survival and reproduction of underprivileged groups through "scientific" means. In this way, it controls the distribution of urban space and space production, keeping the "inferior" race in its own place. Surely, the outcome of the story echoes the warning of the Rivers' matriarch, reinforcing the political expression of knowledge. Thus, hegemonic power, aided by capital, knowledge, and space, maintains its dominance and exerts its influence in various aspects of social life.

When interpreted in this regard, it can be seen that the tragedy is not unique to the Riverses, and that historical trauma reaches the victimizers as well, those who have imposed suffering in the name of love. Everyone involved in the process gets boomeranged. The propaganda of racist eugenics has deprived Philip of rationality and humanity. Race becomes the only standard to judge a person, and his prejudice against people of color obscures his reasoning. Philip rejects Albert Rivers despite his middle-class background, academic excellence, and perfection in personality. In his eyes, Albert's birth defects could never be amended, and his racial disadvantage weighs more than everything else put together. In his paranoiac murders of Sol and Albert, Philip commits a crime more serious than homicide—a horrific reverse avunculicide as Albert is one of his own family members. Philip escapes legal punishment with the aid of police: "Keller had acted in self-defense.... The police officers, who had written the initial reports and who were sympathetic to the ideology of the Southern California Aryan Club, suggested to Philip Keller that, this being his second reprieve, he should consider going away on vacation" (241). In spite of the escape, this serves as the last straw in the vulnerable relationship between Philip and Ernest Keller's family, leading to their consequent estrangement, which weighs more than any legal punishment. Thus, by rejecting and murdering Albert, Philip negates his own social relationships and his status as a social being, for his nephew's family is actually his only family. Being obsessed with people's biological origins while ignoring the sociological, Philip takes an antihuman and antisocial position. In standing guard over Aryan advantages, he is preyed upon by his worship of eugenics, leading him to alienate his only family and even his own nature as a man: "[his] dedication and faith in his dream that the Aryan master race would rise to power and rule the world had cost him his relationship with his loving family" (249). He is victimized when inflicting harm unto his family, which explains his twenty years' devotion in a remote Benedictine monastery to redeem his crime. At this point, family tragedy and the love story bear the weight of history that appears to transcend the fate of the individual characters.

In addition to the hardships, sufferings, and transformations of Los Angeles and its people, *River of Angels* expresses hope for the future, represented by the three children of Albert and Louise and by Philip Keller's ultimate redemption. The narrator in the prologue may represent Morales' alter ego. He sounds like a cultural liberal who celebrates cultural pluralism in his criticism of hegemonic discourses (characterized by neonativism and eugenics). As the narrator indicates, neonativists, concerned by the ever-increasing Latino population, have called for the closure of the border between the United States and Mexico. In relation to this background, the narrative proposes a counterdiscourse, claiming that

> borders cannot be controlled—shut down by the military or by a great wall or technical devices—simply because inherent human migration cannot be stopped, detained, held back by artificial means. Attempts to control borders, to stop the movement of people, have and will cost lives and billions of dollars. Human migration is a natural phenomenon, as natural as the mass migration of birds, fish and butterflies. It will cease when there is no need to move. (ix)

Though the Los Angeles River separates the city into two halves, functioning as a kind of migratory boundary to geographically mark racial and class distinctions, its bridges still facilitate boundary crossings. Despite the attempt to pin down the boundary between ethnicity and culture, it shifts constantly and city space is thus continually remapped in the novel:

> prejudice, discrimination, racism ran through the Southern California streets, neighborhoods, towns and counties, but still some crossed the established social lines, broke the taboos, crossed the cultural and racial borders, and their life struggles became a little tougher. Nonetheless, the Mexicans, the Japanese, the Chinese, the blacks—many thousands of people—endured life at the margins of society. (79)

Though Philip Keller embodies such control, prejudice, discrimination, and racism, there is hope in his awakening and repentance, which ultimately implies that racism is futile and hybridity is unstoppable.

In view of contemporary Chicano literature and Alejandro Morales' writing, *River of Angels* represents a new height in the genre of historical novels, in which the author traces the Mexican American contribution to the urbanization and growth of the City of Angels. Moreover, the narrative deals with social negotiations in the context of urban space and the dubious nature of knowledge and technology. It is based on the construction of ethnic discourse with the evolution of East Los Angeles as the anchor, but it transcends the traditional motif of ethnic identity. This study has analyzed, from the perspective of the history of the city, the occupation of geographical and social spaces by Mexican Americans, and their spiral movement along or across the borders between these spaces. In conformity with the coexistence of cultural groups in the international metropolis of Los Angeles, division of space represents the tensions, negotiations, and reconciliations between Mexican Americans and those of Anglo origin. Morales restores the ignored stories of Mexican American bridge-builders to chronicle Los Angeles' history and in doing so he echoes what A. S. Byatt (2000) terms the "political desire" of "foreign" writers to write. As it presents the history of bridge construction and urban planning, this novel maps out power relations, reflecting Morales' own (political) desire to focus on a silenced marginal group. Alejandro Morales' historical fiction thus signifies a remarkable representation of crucial sociopolitical and geocultural themes in Chicano literature.

NOTES

1. This is an expanded, revised, and translated version of a paper first published in 2017 in *Shandong Foreign Language Teaching and Research* and which was also included in *Foreign Literature Studies* 3 (2018), published by the Information Center of Renmin University, China.
2. The term is used as interchangeable with "city history" in this essay for simplicity of expression.
3. Morales made this statement in one of his classes at UC Irvine.

WORKS CITED

Agamben, Giorgio. 1995. *Idea of Prose*. Albany: State University of New York Press.
Byatt, A. S. 2000. *On Histories and Stories: Selected Essays*. Cambridge, MA: Harvard University Press.
Deverell, William F. *Whitewashed Adobe: The Rise of Los Angeles and the Remaking of Its Mexican Past*. 2004. Berkeley: University of California Press.
Franco, Dean. 2005. "Working through the Archive: Trauma and History in Alejandro Morales's *The Rag Doll Plagues*." *PMLA* 120, no. 2 (March 2005): 375–87.
Lefebvre, Henri. 1991. *The Reproduction of Space*. Translated by Donald Nicholson-Smith. Cambridge, MA: Basil Blackwell.
Li, Baojie. 2017. "Urban History and Space Politics: Los Angeles in *River of Angels*." *Shandong Foreign Language Teaching and Research* 38, no. 5 (September): 58–64.
———. 2018. "Urban History and Space Politics: Los Angeles in *River of Angels*."

Foreign Language no. 3 (March): 85–88. Information Center for Social Sciences, Renmin University China.

Li, Fan, Zhu Hong, and Huang Wei. 2010. "A Geographical Study on the Collective Memory of Urban Historical Cultural Landscape." *Human Geography* 25, no. 4 (July): 60–66.

Lowenthal, David. 1975. "Past Time, Present Place: Landscape and Memory." *Geographical Review* 65, no. 1 (January): 1–36.

Morales, Alejandro. 2014. *River of Angels*. Houston: Arte Público Press.

Said, Edward W. 2000. "Invention, Memory, and Place." *Critical Inquiry* 26, no. 2 (Winter): 175–92.

Yao, Shi-mou, Wang Chen, Zhang Luo-cheng, Chen Zhen-guang, and Song Ping. 2008. "Urbanization and Its Coordination Relationship of Resources and Environment." *Progress in Geography* 27, no. 3(March): 93–101.

EIGHT / *Pequeña nación* / Big (Feminist) Revolution / **AMAIA IBARRARAN-BIGALONDO**

Since their emergence, Chicano/a literature and arts have addressed stories that manifest the individual and group-specific identity of a disadvantaged community. The situation of the community living in US barrios reflects this disadvantage, that of an unbalanced society in terms of the distribution of wealth, access to education, and in general, the inalienable right to a dignified life within a capitalist, materialist social pyramid. Michael Matsunaga, a member of the Los Angeles Chamber of Commerce, notes that today, those who live below the poverty threshold in the neighborhoods of L.A. are mostly people of Latino/a origin. Although he found that indicators of extreme poverty declined at the national level after the 1990s (1), in the case of the Los Angeles the data collected showed the opposite trend. Among the various reasons, Matsunaga points to changes in the labor market caused by the massive influx of immigrants, industrial restructuring, and a general change in the regional and global economy (3). Indeed, the arrival of immigrants from Central America and Latin America has altered the demographic configuration of the city and in the turn of the new century,

> the City of Los Angeles was approximately 47 percent Latino and 11 percent Black, while CPNs (Concentrated Poverty Neighborhoods) were 74 percent Latino and 17 percent Black. Latinos are 13 times more likely than Whites to live in an area of concentrated poverty, Blacks are 12 times more likely, and Asians are 4 times more likely. (5)

In this context, there are many young people who, lacking opportunities for economic, social, and personal development, sadly resort to membership in street gangs as a means of subsistence. Chicano sociologist James Diego Vigil has extensively studied the roots, causes, and consequences of the existence and proliferation of Chicano/Latino youth gangs. He emphasizes the complex and diverse origins of this phenomenon, pointing to the "multiple marginality" of those who engage in it. In his words, "there are ecological contrasts (visual and spatial distinctions), economic strains (underclass and secondary labor market), social dysfunctions (family stress and school failure), cultural discontinuities (hybrid mixture, syncretic cholo), and psychological ordeals (adolescent status crisis and group identity)" (2002, 57). These gangs, the *clicas*, have been studied by many sociologists and academics from different disciplines.[1] All of them have given an account of the socioeconomic situation of the barrios, of the emergence of street gangs, of the complex causes that drive young people into criminality. In these studies, the gang members are presented, and without obvious reasons, as victims of a depressed economic and sociocultural mechanism that leads them to seek life solutions in the gang structure and, in some way, in the social refuge that the gangs provide them, both economically and socially, and even emotionally.

Chicano/a literature and the arts, as a means of representation of the community from which they arise, have reflected the existence of gangs in such works as *Always Running* (1993) by Luis Rodríguez and *Locas* (1998) by Yxta Maya Murray. Chicano cinema has also reflected the phenomenon tangentially and/or directly in *Boulevard Nights* (Michael Pressman, 1979), *Stand and Deliver* (1988), *Blood In, Blood Out* (Taylor Hackford, 1993), *American Me* (Edward James Olmos, 1992), and *Mi Vida Loca* (Allison Anders, 1993).

Similarly, all of this is portrayed in "Pequeña nación," one of the three novellas by Alejandro Morales that comprise the eponymous collection. This novella is, in my opinion, essential for understanding (if possible) the phenomenon of the existence of urban gangs in its most global aspect. Morales, in a proof of narrative skill and human coherence, takes a different tack from that of all the previously mentioned works (and even his own work, *Caras viejas y vino nuevo*) and exposes the reality of these gangs from the point of view of the direct victims of their extreme violence: that of the inhabitants of the barrios in which they operate. More specifically, he focuses on the plight of the barrio women, the mothers and neighbors of the gang members. On the one hand, the novella follows other works in this genre by presenting the gangsters as victims of an unbalanced socioeconomic and cultural system. On the other, Morales describes them as perpetrators of the fear, insecurity, and violence with which the barrio residents must live. His characters, both victims and gang members, know the harshness of barrio life. According to Juan Antonio Sánchez, Morales' novel *Caras viejas y vino nuevo* reflects the "Chicano experience" by focusing on the plight of the youth trapped in urban neighborhoods: "Characteristic of Alejandro Morales' commitment to his people is the denunciation of the imposed suffocating circumstances that do not let them develop naturally as individuals, as a people, and as a collectivity" (41). "Pequeña nación" parallels the ambiance of the hard-core barrio life found in *Caras viejas y vino nuevo*, showing how and why these young people join gang life and "la vida loca." We come to see such gang members as desperate young people, impoverished and ill-prepared educationally, victims of a ruthless and cruel society that in turn makes them ruthless and cruel. And it is here that the originality and relevance of "Pequeña nación" lies. It assumes the inevitability of the existence of gangs because of the "multiple marginality" they are victims of (Vigil 2002; 2007). Yet, Morales goes a step further and presents the impact of the gangs on people, specifically women, who also suffer from an evident marginality, to which they must add the violence and insecurity created by the gangs. He addresses the collective response of the women to their untenable situation, turning the novella into a symbol of feminist, collective, self-managed revolution.

Morales moves away from the self-referentiality that sometimes characterizes the work of diverse Chicano/a authors, as well as from the mere denunciation of the external agents disadvantaging the community. These, without a doubt, are multiple and reflect the evident social hierarchy through which American society is organized, originating from a structural racism and class division. He, on the contrary, is

> a writer who cares about the fate of his people. In his work, he tries to offer a "totalizing" panorama of a Chicano social reality in a country with complex multicultural characteristics. Morales tries to offer a more specific representation of the Chicano, with their positive and negative sides. Through his works he tries to explain and make us understand, the past of his people to connect it with the present and to, thus, discover its place in this world, with the purpose of living a future in line with the existential ambitions of any other human being. In this sense he is a writer who is highly committed to his society. (Rosales May 1995, 3)[2]

Morales demonstrates an obvious social honesty, and therefore, literary honesty, by reflecting in his work, as Rosales May affirms, a negative phenomenon that he denounces and to which he provides a powerful solution. It is my intention, in the following pages, to expose the relevance of Morales' work as a document of high social denunciation, of female empowerment, and of direct action. In short, "Pequeña nación" is the moving story of a pequeña, big (feminist) *revolución*. In it, the residents of the barrio brutalized by the gangs choose to take direct action against them, led by the women. Significantly, Morales places women in the center of his narration and constructs them as the (only) ones capable of challenging the gang's violence directly and efficiently. These women, mothers, family, and neighbors of the gang members, led by the protagonists of the novella, organize themselves and encourage the rest of the barrio residents to join in the fight against those who, for various socioeconomic structural reasons, turn their anger against the supposedly defenseless population of their neighborhood. The women's uprising against the gangs, thus, symbolizes the direct challenging of the multiple layers of marginality, discrimination, and institutional violence that they endure. The protagonists develop a strong political consciousness as women and as part of a community. Moreover, and in a more conceptual reading of their struggle, their fight challenges directly the very essence of patriarchy and male domination of and within the ideological state apparatuses (the press, the church, the police, among others), as defined by Louis Althusser (1970). All of them create ideologies of control and domination and are essentially patriarchal, and in the particular case of the novella, subjugate the inhabitants of the barrio. The gangs, similarly, are essentially hierarchical and patriarchal. The fight of these women is, thus, feminist and antipatriarchal, communal and anticapitalist. It is a pequeña, big, revolución.

The novella opens with two quotes. The first from an anonymous *cholo* from Ontario who justifies the use of violence as the only way to survive in the neighborhoods and defends the existence of what he calls his "little nation," which in his own words they control, dominate, and through which they find their sense of belonging and brotherhood:

> The only thing we can do is build our own little nation. We know that we have complete control in our community. It's like we're making our stand and we're able to express ourselves this way. We're all brothers and nobody fucks with us. We take pride in our own little nation and if any intruders enter, we get panicked because we feel our community is being threatened. The only way is with violence. (55)[3]

In it, a human convergence emerges, reminiscent of the concept of "imaginary community" defined by Benedict R. Anderson (1991), whose members will defend until the end a shared and common good; in this specific case, they will do so through extreme violence, including death if necessary and, in any case, through their own social death. Next, Morales offers a reflection by Luis J. Rodríguez, exposing the inevitability of the practice of criminality among young people crammed into American prisons, which he defines as "criminals of want," victims of the obvious hierarchization of democracy and of the granting of life opportunities according to one's social class. Rodríguez's words, in some way, "legitimize" the violence advocated by the cholo of Ontario and define crime as a consequence of the violence of the nation-state toward those who are not situated in its most favored strata. He says,

> Criminality in this country is a class issue. Many of those warehoused in overcrowded prisons can be properly called "criminals of want, those who've been deprived of the basic necessities of life and therefore forced into so-called criminal acts to survive. Many of them just don't have the means to buy their "justice" (89).

"Pequeña nación," on the contrary, proposes a different solution. Making use of his deep knowledge of the history of the Chicano/a community in the United States, Morales opens and closes the novella in a circular way, inserting the situation of Montebello (the neighborhood where the events occur) into a broader sociohistorical context, the creation of the city of Our Lady Queen of Los Angeles in the year 1871. Thus, it shows that the marginality and disadvantage of this neighborhood in particular and of others are multiple and complex (here I echo Vigil's notion of multiple marginality, extending it to a previous sociohistorical moment), emerging from the very conception of the Southwest of the United States in general, and California and Los Angeles and its neighborhoods in particular. The creation of these geographic, sociopolitical, and cultural spaces, in short, is part of an act of territorial and cultural domination and the consequent subjugation of its inhabitants, which Morales represents and denounces through the history of a cemetery, a symbol of the spiritual and sociodemographic roots of a town. The opening words narrate the lives of the founders of the city, who created their "little nation" in the lands that the Mexican government had granted, and

> There, in the Town of Our Lady of Los Angeles, they worked, they met with women and had children. There, in the Town of Our Lady of Los Angeles they lived, died, and were buried. From each loved one buried in the earth grew roots through which the fields, the corn fields, the animals, the hearts

were irrigated and the food that sustained the living was produced. Love and labor gave them the right to declare that this land was theirs, and through it they were willing to die defending it. They never abandoned or fled from the lands that made up the town of Our Lady of Los Angeles. (56)

The connection between the earth, death, and life is evident in these words, as is the relevance of the defense of the community and the "small nation" built through work, love, tradition, and death. However, after establishing this concept of belonging, territoriality, and defense of the land (the turf, in the case of the gang members) as understood by the founders of the city of Los Angeles, Morales goes further back in time and tells the story of an Indian against whom "the whites and the Mexicans had burned the bodies of his family and had thrown away the bones and ashes" (57). He recalls "the case of an Indian who refused to leave the lands surrounding the camphor tree. The Indian, after his wife and five children were killed for resisting the authorities, after they burned the house, killed the animals and trampled the cornfield, went to the camphor tree and there, sheltered by the branches of the tree, sat down to look at what he had loved so much and worked to improve" (57). These words, are, in my opinion, an evident exposition of the arbitrariness of the concept of nation, territoriality, and frontier. Unlike the human community created through lived experience and through the connection to the land created by the living and the dead (as in the case of the Indian, the founders, and even the gang members), the institutional community—the nation—establishes circles of power and domination that marginalize those not included in them. The human community, on the contrary, is formed by individuals of diverse origins who share powerful bonds. As will be clearly explained by the author, this bond occurs specially after death, when the inhabitants of the land come back to it and become one with it.

In this context, the narration of the history of the cemetery of the founders becomes relevant for understanding the concept of the "pequeña nación." As explicated in the text, the cemetery had its origins in the cemetery of the Misión de San Gabriel. After exceeding its capacity to house the deceased, and in an attempt to stop the spread of random burial sites, the cemetery was moved to another area of the city on the proposal of Bishop Mora. Following pressure (and financial aid) from the powerful American Protective Association (APA), he proposed to move it to the outskirts of the city, away from the luxurious mansions of the most powerful in Boyle Heights. The opening and end of the novella occur at the cemetery, as does the beginning of the construction of what later on will be defined as "clementine theory" (the ideological roots of the revolution to come, articulated by Micaela Clemencia). Thus, the cemetery is presented, on the one hand, as the sacred space where the living and the dead join the land and thus grow their roots, creating and unbreakable link between the physical and human space that the barrio represents. The move of the cemetery to another area, encouraged by the APA, anti-Catholic and anti-immigrant in its conception, becomes a metaphor for the dishonesty of the Church (personified by Bishop Mora) and its moral defeat in the face of fierce capitalism. When the events narrated in the novella occur, the cemetery represents the decay of the communal spirit in a barrio whose residents are killing each other in the name of the defense of an "imaginary" territory they consider their own. It is thus fitting that Micaela Clemencia, the story's protagonist, is first presented in this symbolic place. She is a respected woman in the neighborhood, a teacher, known to everyone, since

> everyone recognized her for her activities, her efforts to organize the neighborhood against the plan to take one hundred and fifty acres located in the heart of East Los Angeles to build a new stadium for two teams: one for football and one for soccer. "The Los Angeles Latino population loves soccer. They'll be willing to sell their land," the mayor of Los Angeles had publicly declared, accompanied by two Latino county supervisors. This was not the first time that the county or city had taken the properties and houses of the Mexicans and declared them uninhabitable using the right of "Eminent Domain" to build a stadium. The case of Chávez Ravine is still in the memories of Mexicans. (60)

The opening of the novella marks, without a doubt, its tone. Like other works by Morales, "Pequeña nación" is a tale of obvious social denunciation, and I would dare to say it is one that clearly and in detail lists all those layers of marginality and oppression denominated by Vigil as "multiple marginality." Moreover, the work openly condemns the abuses committed by institutions such as the police, the press, and/or the authorities in general, which add to the great damage that the gang members exert on the inhabitants who are not linked to their microcommunities. The novella describes said layers as interrelated and interdependent, but the violence meted out by street gangs appears from the beginning of the narrative as the one most directly affecting the lives of the inhabitants of the neighborhood. The writer's complaint goes beyond the mere presentation and rejection of this violence, clearly expressing that the gangs operate in complicity with a police force that looks the other way and with a press that feeds on the violence as a means of criminalizing and "ghettoizing" the neighborhoods, justifying and hiding, in a way, the lack of socioeconomic resources that affect them. Thus, after the presentation of the history of the cemetery, which evidences the abuse of the authorities over the people in the barrio, who are ignored and, in some way, belittled by the city, Morales connects with the contemporary history of the neighborhood. Micaela, while at the cemetery, thinks:

> People were upset, fed up with the killings in the streets, the innocent victims who died daily because of the bullets that appeared suddenly from one second to another to end a life. People were disillusioned, angry, furious with the police, who seemed to do nothing after the murder of a child, a young man, a Mexican. The neighbors felt that there was no police protection, that they did not make the effort to apprehend the murderers, to bring them to justice and make them pay with life imprisonment or with the death penalty. Micaela thought that the police, the Los Angeles County Sheriffs, were there to see that Latinos did not leave the area, to ensure the entry and free circulation of alcohol and drugs, to maintain a high number of criminal activities to justify their positions, their jobs as investigators, patrollers, and guards in the prisons of Los Angeles County. It was known that the police and security guards' union had hired the largest agency of opinion specialists to protect their interests in state and national government. The police and other anti-criminal bodies were maintained and justified by the growth of crime. This situation was not exclusive to the Latin colonies, because the same clementine theory applied to all Asian and African-American neighborhoods.[4] (59–60)

These words are indispensable, on the one hand, for the thematic development of the novella, but above all, as the axis of the evident and forceful denunciation that they express. Through them, like in the abundant studies that clearly demonstrate that people of racial profiles, such as Latin or African American, and in particular, men, are victims of indiscriminate and arbitrary police persecution, the author denounces the fact that the police favor the existence of crime, drugs, and insecurity in the barrios. Sabrina Hill, referring to a study by renowned sociologist Robert Staples, concurs that

> Staples (2011) posits that over the last many years, Latinos and blacks in the U.S. continue to endure stigma associated with racial profiling. Majority

of the whites view a predominantly white police force as their frontier of defense in keeping crime confined to Latino neighborhoods and black ghettos. Consequently, the police force is regarded by many scholars as the best source of racial tension in the U.S. A considerable number of police officers are brought to trial for harassing or murdering Latino or black citizens. Correspondingly, the few who are brought to trial are in most cases not convicted. (13)

In this situation, and in particular, in the face of the violence perpetrated by the gangs, the neighbors of these communities live in a continuous state of fear, provoked by what sociologists Bursik and Grasmick call "social disorganization" (1993). Studies have shown that often it is women and the elderly who experience this state of fear and are prone to expressing the sentiment that the neighborhood has changed and the level of security has declined (Hill 2013). However, Morales' novella is proof of the opposite, becoming a symbol of feminine empowerment in particular, and of a community, in general.

The women in Morales' work, and in particular Micaela, understand, on the contrary, that the fear of the people of the neighborhood comes, in effect, from the violence of the gangs. Above all, it stems from the fact that the police do not act to pursue the gangs or control their actions. This leads Micaela to confront the police directly:

> What are you good for? You know who they are and you let them free to kill again. Letting them free, you try to control the community with fear. You do not protect us, you just want to keep us cornered, sunk in fear. You are policemen who produce and control with fear. You know who these thugs are, but you choose not to do anything. But when one of your own, a policeman, dies, you always find the killer. If the victim is a poor Mexican, Asian, black, homosexual, you only write it down in your statistics books as proof of the uncontrollable gang presence in the neighborhoods of the scared poor, Micaela had told them as she left the station. (71)

Micaela's words, in some way, confirm Hill's study and corroborate the existence of a sense of fear among the population of the neighborhoods where the gangs operate. Although she defines the gangs as directly responsible for the distress of the neighborhood's inhabitants, she protests that this responsibility is shared with the police, who, in some ways, favor and encourage it. In this untenable situation, Micaela, an orphan raised by Benedictine nuns, decides to act. She follows the example of her mentor, Sister Caterina Triger, "a nun who professed the theology of liberation" and who taught her the importance of "Seeing," "Analyzing," and finally "Acting" (61). The sister followed the example of Louise Michel (1830–1905), an anarchist and feminist educator and writer, who, during the Paris Commune (1871), promoted the creation of soup kitchens for children, as well as day care centers, orphanages, and other social services. Micaela, like Sister Caterina Triger, Louise Michel, and the anarchist movement in general—which promulgates the existence of free individuals who, in a self-managed way, directly respond to concrete problems—opts to put direct action into practice.

She does so together with two widows from the neighborhood, Felícitas and Paca, who, after the death of their husbands (one of them a filmmaker and the other an engineer), decide to study and become the "archive of the neighborhood" through their photographic reports and recordings of neighborhood life. In their connected, twin houses, the symbol of sisterhood and community, the two women collect photographs and diverse histories of community life, becoming symbols of the "neighborhood experience press." Their work contrasts the sensationalism of the official press, which supports the apathy of the police with its reports. Thus, another example of Micaela's "clementine theory" explains that

> the police and the journalists are getting ready to emphasize the scandal and the criminal element that, according to them, saturates the *barrios* of Los Angeles. They create a growing distrust between the people of the neighborhood and the police and they also increase the constant tension between the Latino communities, the police authorities, and the outsiders. The people of the *barrios* distrust public institutions more and more. (67)

After the "gratuitous" rape and murder of a young girl from the barrio by gang members, and once it is confirmed that her identity had been confused with that of another girl whose relatives were members of a rival gang, the three women decide to act. They set fire to the car of Celicio, one of the gang members who perpetrated the horrible crime. The next morning, "when she entered the classroom, Micaela felt that the children were looking at her in a different way. But she did not have any remorse. She smiled and started with the first lesson of the day" (75). In this step toward the "achievement of power," the three women, who gradually gain the trust of other women from the neighborhood and the broader community, have among their primary objectives the control of gang members and the police, obvious culprits for the violence, fear, and the feeling of insecurity in the neighborhood.

Beginning in a quasi-spontaneous way, the women of the neighborhood, led by Micaela, Paca, and Felícitas, bring communal justice against Celicio, the most violent gang member and murderer of the young woman and of others. Once apprehended by the group of women, and after resisting, "Celicio stopped fighting and lay still on his back looking at the faces and female hands ready to give him another beating with domestic tools. The group had grown to more than thirty women who kept Celicio, the gangster terrorist, rapist, and murderer, prostrated and surrounded. They knew who he was, they knew about his rapes and about the fact that he had tried to kill Micaela or some of the others, or all of them, or anyone who was in that house that night" (76). The women, armed with domestic tools, thus, become a symbol of the barrio's voice and of the voice of its women in particular, who had left their private domestic spaces and taken to the streets. Equally symbolic is the fact that they strip the gang member of his clothes, which identify him as a member of a specific group and, in some way, provide him with a group identity. Without his gang uniform, Celicio is devoid of his identity, his sense of belonging, and consequently, his authority. The point of depriving someone of their clothes, according to sociologist Kate Soper (2001),

> is to put him or her "out on the heath," to snatch away the clutched straw of human dignity. As all prison camp guards and torturers have been aware, to force the victim to initiate the process of dehumanization, to signal contempt for personal identity by playing with mocking the aspiration to preserve it. The power of denuding the other in these contexts is also the power to depersonalize the other's clothing or adornment. (21)

The justice exercised by the women over the gang member has to do, in this sense, with the fact of unmasking and dis-identifying him from the symbol of his power, of that which identifies him with his gang, and consequently, with his absolute power and his control over the barrio and the lives of its inhabitants. Based on the certainty that the police share responsibility for the situation of violence in the neighborhood, the women try to control (and consequently, punish) the police for their tolerance of the street gangs and related injustices. Thus, after an incident in which two police officers beat a Mexican boy in the street, the women "disarmed them, then undressed them; they did not take care of them nor did they give them a bath, but they sent them walking naked, to the East of Los Angeles" (81).

After this episode, another group of detectives comes to the neighborhood to investigate the event; the people of the neighborhood corner them, and Micaela pronounces the following words:

> You should know that we women, grandmothers, wives, mothers, daughters, girlfriends, and girls have taken control of our *barrio*. And anyone who harms us will have to deal with us. We, the women of the Geraghty *barrio*, address *cholos* and *cholas*, any gang member who causes us suffering, who harms us with violence, who terrifies us, anyone who comes with a gun to threaten us, to kill our beloved children. We warn addicts, those who sell drugs, not to do so in this *barrio*, because if we find them we will take everything they own and throw them out and, if they sell drugs again, it will cost them dearly. (83)

These words function as a political and social manifesto and point to each of the agents responsible for the degradation of the neighborhood. In another sense, they represent the relevance of direct action and the power of the people against the institutions that look the other way from the problems of the most disadvantaged, or, as the work decries through its characters and its plot, that favor and encourage these problems to protect the welfare of those in power:

> "We also warn the police not to come and help us, because we do not need their help, not to come to harm us, not to come to search our houses, not to come to arrest our children, not to come to take pictures of us. We do not want them in our *barrio*, because from here on we announce that the neighborhood is ours and that we are going to protect our families and property and we will be the ones who will decide the punishment of the violators of peace in our lives. We do this with love, with the love of God and with the love that we share among us. We are not afraid of anyone or anything because our weapon against criminals and violence is love, and with love we will win," Micaela unabashedly proclaimed. (83)

In the same way, the novella excoriates, through its protagonists, the manipulation and lack of scruples exhibited by the press when dealing with the problems of the barrios, and in particular, the favoring of the inaction of the police and the institutional abandonment of these socially and economically depressed areas. After the episode in which the women strip the two policemen of their clothes,

> the journalists tried to interview the neighbors, but none cooperated with them and sent them out of the neighborhood, frustrated. The next day, the

pictures of the cops getting into the car appeared on the front page of the *Herald Examiner*. The journalists named the streets and described in detail the neighborhood where "some of Los Angeles County's best community servants" had been attacked and dishonored. On the television, reports of the *barrio* gangs were broadcast, where the sheriffs had been shamed. "Is it not enough that the sheriffs and the L.A. Police are there to protect and serve them?" And in another report the announcer declared: "And the thanks they got was they were attacked and stripped of their clothing and weapons." (84–85)

This first subtle and then obviously denigrating and accusatory campaign against the women's actions will reach its climax at the end of the narrative, when numerous women will be killed with the connivance, justification, and "logistical" support of the press.

In the temporal development of the novella, and before its dramatic end, the evolution of the work and the actions of the group of women appears as the narration of a feminist revolution. In an assembly, they decide to be constituted as La Federación de las Mujeres de las Tijeras (Federation of the Women with Scissors), "dedicated to the salvation of the children and women victims of the influence, abuses and attacks of the gangs, the police and the mass media of society" (107). In addition to the already described "gang cleaning" of the barrio, these women devote all their effort and work to promote the education of children in the neighborhood, a fact they understand to be indispensable to redefine its future and the lives of each of its members. The women, in short, create their own "pequeña nación" and establish actions of direct action to recover the course of barrio life. In this sense,

> Naturally, the women were happy with the results of their efforts to destroy the most active and dangerous gangs and their arsenals. This effort, according to Micaela and the group's plan, was to stabilize the *barrio*, to eliminate fear, and to sit in its front yards and walk freely through its streets. After achieving these objectives, they would dedicate themselves to changing the economic and sociological conditions of the neighborhood, which were the main contributing factors for the generation and existence of gangs. (123)

Having acknowledged the importance and meaning of the fact that the women have taken direct responsibility for the barrio and, in some way, for the ridicule and public exposure of the institutions, these institutions—with the support of a press that publishes news claiming the women are witches and murderers who develop witchcraft rites and "strip their victims and also store weapons to form a female army, a military legion of women dedicated to justice" (119)—decide to send the army to the neighborhood and provoke a massacre in which many of the women are killed. The novella closes in a circular way, explaining that the parcels of land belonging to the houses that were burned in the attack (Felícita and Paca's twin houses, among others) were sold again, flowers and life grew in them, and "the public forgot the victims of the massacre, the women of the Federation. Its members contemplated, from the heights of Rose Hills, East of Los Angeles and El Calvario, the cemetery where they were never buried" (135). Just as the founders and the Indian and his family, the women return to their land and become one with it, with their "pequeña nación," in a highly symbolic way. This hopeless end, which highlights the difficulty and indeed impossibility of improving the lives of those in the barrio, is the culmination of a utopia of anarchist and feminist inspiration that proposes a better world wherein its protagonists, individuals who are devoted to their lives and those of their peers, struggle in harmony for the common good. It was nice while it lasted. Moreover, the novella rejects the unjust reality of the barrios and the situation in which their inhabitants live and proposes a possible solution that, even if fictitious, could be a reality if those who have direct responsibility (governments, police, and press, among others) would take direct and committed responsibility.

While being a feminist fiction, the novella is also a sociopolitical study of the life of the barrio, the reasons for the existence of gangs, the direct responsibility of the police and the press in their proliferation. It employs a narrative style, characters, and a specific time and space to insert reflections such as the following:

> Young people who are in the gangs are young people who cannot be easily saved. Many of them have already tasted the glory of prison. Many of them are institutionalized beings. They have no fear of the system, that is, the police, the prison. The worst thing they can do is to kill them, and they are not afraid to die. From their youth, they consider the penal system as a school, a home, because in it, they have everything they need. They are turned into dependent-on-the-penal-system beings by the criminal authorities. This process of institutionalizing *barrio* youth guarantees thousands, if not millions, of jobs and trillions of dollars. Jobs and dollars which are all related in one way and another with the production and maintenance of the crime

culture and the culture of the criminal. Being imprisoned gives them prestige among their peers, and they enjoy the publicity they receive from the mass media of newspapers, radio and television, which satisfies their hunger to be recognized, to have an identity. (107)

This and other reflections that condemn institutions such as the press (as for example, "You hope for more killings to keep your eye-witness, action news, first impact fucking job. . . . you and the police are as parasitic as the gang bangers and all of you are the problem. You with your cameras, microphones, and helicopters descend on us. . . . You're not here to protect us but to expose us, to keep us here, keep us corralled in our neighborhoods. You justify the police action against us and warn the outside world not to come in so that the police can have free rein" [92]), make the novella a powerful and explosive political manifesto that attacks directly what psychological studies such as those cited above expose. And unlike the previously mentioned novels and studies, it puts the focus on the real victims, that is, on the people directly affected by the criminal action of the gangs. These, in addition to being victims of the "multiple marginality" to which Vigil refers, live in fear (Hill), and their lives are conditioned by the macroviolence of the institutions and the "micro-violence" of the gang. In conclusion, giving voice to the most disadvantaged and fictionalizing a forceful political manifesto of clear social accusation, Alejandro Morales has managed in "Pequeña nación" to tell the story of a "small, big, *revolución*." Moreover, it is the story of a feminist revolution that, regardless of the fact that it was written in the nineties, is exemplary of the feminist revolution that is taking place at the end of the second decade of the twenty-first century. Its women organize among themselves under a strong drive of self-defense and a deep sense of sorority, becoming the agents of their revolution and the perpetuators of direct action against all things that mark their existence as disadvantaged. The Federación de las Mujeres de las Tijeras, under the leadership of Micaela, Paca, and Felícitas, thus, becomes the forerunner of movements such as the contemporary "Me Too," which is today bringing issues of female discrimination to the public scene. "Pequeña nación" is accordingly the story of those who have always been considered small and minor but who are essential for the functioning of society: women. "Pequeña nación" calls for the importance of the "small" people and "small" communities, which, in communion, can make big things happen.

NOTES

1. Among them, we should include the names of the aforementioned James Diego Vigil (1988; 2002; 2007; 2010; and others), Joan W. Moore (1991) and idem. and Robert García (1978), and Lisa C. Dietrich (1998).

2. In Spanish originally. My own translation.

3. Some quotes from the novel, or parts of them, are translated from Spanish (my translation).

WORKS CITED

Althusser, Louis. (1970) 2014. *On the Reproduction of Capitalism: Ideology and Ideological State Apparatuses.* Translated by G. M. Gosgharian. London: Verso.

Anders, Allison, dir. 1993. *Mi Vida Loca.* Channel Four Films.

Anderson, Benedict R. 1991. *Imagined Communities: Reflections on the Origin and Spread of Nationalism.* London: Verso.

Bursik, R. J., Jr., and H. G. Grasmick. 1993. *Neighborhoods and Crime: The Dimensions of Effective Community Control.* Lanham, MD: Lexington Books.

Dietrich, Lisa C. 1998. *Chicana Adolescents: Bitches, Ho's, and Schoolgirls.* Prager.

Hackford, Taylor, dir. 1993. *Blood In, Blood Out.* Hollywood Pictures.

Hill, Sabrina. 2013. "A Meta-Analysis of the Extant Literature on Racial Profiling by U.S. Police Departments." Master's thesis, California State University at Monterey Bay.

Matsunaga, Michael. "Concentrated Poverty Neighborhoods in Los Angeles." Working paper. Accessed March 28, 2021. http://www.lachamber.com/clientuploads/LUCH _committee/052610_ConcentratedPoverty.pdf.

Menéndez, Ramón, dir. 1988. *Stand and Deliver.* American Playhouse.

Morales, Alejandro. 1998. *Barrio on the Edge / Caras viejas y vino nuevo.* Translated by Francisco A. Lomelí. Tempe, AZ: Bilingual Press / Editorial Bilingüe.

———. 2005. *Pequeña nación. Tres novelas cortas.* Phoenix: Orbis Press.

Moore, Joan W. 1991. *Going Down to the Barrio: Homeboys and Homegirls in Change.* Philadelphia: Temple University Press.

Moore, Joan W., and Robert García. 1978. *Homeboys: Gangs, Drugs, and the Prison in the Barrios of Los Angeles.* Philadelphia: Temple University Press.

Olmos, Edward James, dir. 1992. *American Me.* Olmos Productions.

Pressman, Michael, dir. 1979. *Boulevard Nights.* Warner Bros.

Rodríguez, Luis J. 1993. *Always Running: La Vida Loca Gang Days in L.A.* Willimantic, CT: Curbstone Press.

Rosales May, Jesús. 1995. "La narrativa de Alejandro Morales: Encuentro, historia y compromiso social." PhD diss., Stanford University, 1995.

Sánchez, Juan Antonio. 1999. *The Portrayal of the Chicano Experience in the Novels of Alejandro Morales*. PhD diss., Michigan State University, 1999.

Soper, Kate. 2001. "Dress Needs: Reflections on the Clothed Body, Selfhood and Consumption." In *Body Dressing*, edited by Joanne Entwistle and Elizabeth Wilson, 13-32. New York: Berg.

Vigil, James Diego. 1988. *Barrio Gangs: Street Life and Identification in Southern California*. Austin: University of Texas Press.

——. 2002. *A Rainbow of Gangs. Street Cultures in the Mega-City*. Austin: University of Texas Press, 2002.

——. 2007. *The Projects: Gang and Non-Gang Families in East Los Angeles*. Austin: University of Texas Press.

——. 2010. *Gang Redux: A Balanced Anti-Gang Strategy*. Long Grove, IL: Waveland Press.

This original article is part of a project financed by the Spanish Ministry of Economy and Competitiveness (code: FFI2014-52738-P), the European Regional Fund (ERDF). It was also completed under the auspices of the research group REWEST funded by the Basque Government (Grupo Consolidado IT1206-16).

NINE / Bodies in Motion in *The Place of the White Heron*, Volume Two of the Heterotopian Trilogy / A Glance through the Panopticon / ADAM SPIRES

In the forthcoming *The Place of the White Heron*, volume 2 of his trilogy, Alejandro Morales continues his penchant for voicing the essence of Aztlán, a space of both cultural possibility and cultural tension, which he characterizes as a "heterotopia." This heterotopic space in the novel could potentially augur a progressive future, but as it is Morales' tendency to expose human fear and ignorance while shedding light on the shadows of the in-between worlds that Aztlán and heterotopia embody, the potential for harmony is oftentimes corroded. In this space governed by the eternal laws of power and profit, any such notion of a progressive future or harmony is instead distorted to rationalize the age-old ambitions of WASP hegemony. In short, *The Place of the White Heron* reads as an allegory of the violence, racism, and international friction that characterize the relationship between the United States and Mexico, in which powerful, denigrating, and long-lasting attitudes are displayed on both sides of the border. Indeed, Morales presents a familiar battle zone in which the ideology that divides "us" from "them" becomes the default standard.

Themes in this, his latest novel, will be familiar to the Morales reader: the Chicano struggle against injustice and antiquated religious norms; the instability of identity, epitomized by "border chameleons" (118); crime and the unexpected violence that lives next door; and a synchronicity between upheavals south of the border and the ongoing miracle work of the protagonist J. I. Cruz, the somewhat reluctant and less-than-sublime saint who is as surprised by her strange abilities as those who witness her miracles.[1] For instance, J. I. witnesses the Acteal Massacre (Chiapas), the awakening of Popocatépetl (Mexico City), and the border underworld of the maquiladora belt. She subsequently returns from Mexico in this second installment and commences life anew in Southern California, where she reengages with miracle work. Befriending a retiree and her Mayan workers, J. I. spends time on their ranch, protecting them from land seizure by the state. Her yuppy neighbors, meanwhile, are involved in dangerous criminal activities. The novel follows multiple intriguing plots, with J. I. involved in each one—the most conspicuous of which involves a continuing correspondence with Endriago, the monster central character in the novel's forerunner *Waiting to Happen* (2001).

As the second installment of Morales' trilogy, *The Place of the White Heron* captures the inexorable coalescence of the two countries. In the first volume, we concluded that "Mexico is eternally tied to the United States and the United States is eternally tied to Mexico" (136). In its sequel, we read that these ties are so close that the two countries actually experience role reversals: "We are Latin America and they are the United States. They are here and we are there. That's what makes the United States squirm, especially here in California" (93). On this point, the action may shift north, but the problem of violent crime, too often motivated by primitive attitudes of hatred and racism, ignores national boundaries, as is noted at the conclusion of *Waiting to Happen*:

> Nazi eliminationist ideology eventually dominated the thinking of millions of Germans, who became practitioners of its policies. In the United States eliminationist ideology against Mexicans had become a focal point of political activity, creating a hysteria, a neo-nativism, a neo-xenophobia, an anti-Mexican collective consciousness that made common folks willing participants in a policy tantamount to Nazi eliminationist activity against the Jews. (135)

It is the same hatred and racism that lie beneath a judicial system that encloses the Mexican community into the barrio under conditions of optimum growth for criminality, legitimizing its own "millions and millions of business dollars" (132), and the same hatred and racism that fuel media sensationalism, perpetuating lopsided stereotypes. But the attention here is not on the barrio, the gangster, or community retaliation as we have read before in works like *Little Nation* (2014). It is, rather, the most idyllic of California oases that harbor violence and corruption, perpetrated by the least expected, seemingly model citizens. *The Place of the*

White Heron, the Náhuatl meaning of "Aztlán," is a bona fide heterotopia, a space that combines many and often incongruous elements that unavoidably intersect and collide, in turn producing a measure of distortion and unpredictability. It is in this bizarre realm of Aztlán where J. I. lands, continuing where the story left off in *Waiting to Happen* by crossing the border to seek refuge from the dangers in her Mexican homeland, only to rush into new ones.

BORN ON THE FREEWAY

In *The Style of Gestures* (2012), Guillemette Bolens studies "kinesic intelligence and kinesthetic knowledge" (5)—specifically, the dynamics in which a reader is provoked by expressive emotions, shifts, and movement within a text—as important factors in reader cognition and sensitivity to a text. Bolens explores readers' cognitive ability—their "kinesic intelligence"—to comprehend and even relate to these motions, shifts, and movements in their interpretation of literature. Given the sprawling, moving freeways that structure and characterize Southern California and, accordingly, crisscross the geography of Morales' novel, it is unsurprising that constant movement figures prominently as a central motif. As such, our cognition ("kinesic intelligence"), the metropolitan context of perpetual motion, and Morales' signature writing style combine to shape our interpretation. Beyond a mere feeling of flight, highway transit, border crossings, and runaways, the often-uncertain fluidity of motion in the novel produces something more akin to chaos, presenting a space of instability that challenges otherwise stable concepts like identity, nation, religion, and utopia. The protagonist J. I. Cruz embodies this unpredictable instability. She was conceived on the border, carried to full term in Mexico, and born north of the border on a freeway in Orange County, where she was delivered by migrant workers. In effect, she was born a body in motion, with instincts for navigation and an allegiance to workers on the move. So much the better in Aztlán, where constant movement renders the crossing of cultural borders an inevitable practice. A defining characteristic of Morales' heterotopia—"movement, the leitmotif of Southern California" (40)—bodies in motion emerge as one of the novel's most fundamental narrative tropes: "I was a nomad, a migrant journeying across a constantly changing territory too great to belong to me, but which had consumed me, had involved me thoroughly, making me cross a wealth of borders, making me live, develop skills of resistance, of survival" (136). There is, however, a trade-off insofar as any sense of rootedness and belonging is compromised, striking at one of the core tenets of the Chicano

Movement. Consequently, the only consistency in "the fast evolving world of Orange County" (256) is movement and change. No matter one's background, the outcome is the same: bodies in motion. Whether the brown tide of migrant workers, or the ensuing white flight to the "planburbs" (54), Morales' heterotopia is a space of continuous shifting that disrupts any sense of self, at times overwhelming J. I., who laments, "There was no peace of mind here, only constant mental movement" (198).

To amplify the effects of heterotopia's dizzying activity, Morales inserts an anachronism into his narrative, a contrastive sanctuary, an enclave of bygone ranch life where connections to the land and to one another have yet to be eroded by the modern world. At Dougherty's Twist, slow food and lasting dinner conversations are the norm, coupled with a healthy regimen of outdoor chores. The location offers a contemporary view into a precolonial utopia before the mad rush of the nineteenth century. As a pastoral oasis, Dougherty's Twist serves J. I. as a stopping ground within heterotopia's rat race, calling attention by way of juxtaposition to what is lost in the drone of the modern economic machine accelerating California's already hurried pace. But what would happen were the machine to stop, as conceptualized in E. M. Forster's (1909) pioneering dystopia? In a quasi-somnambulant state, J. I. conjures up such a question, addresses it, and exposes the perverse human nature that drives the dystopian machine of progress. Reading like a climax to the motif of perpetual motion, bridges are blown up in the novel, and freeways are blocked or destroyed—"causing a week-long traffic jam that ruined many a life, drove people to turn against their automobile neighbours and made some literally commit suicide or murder" (287)—laying bare the central premise that the economic model propelling the eternal movement of trade and commerce in Orange County ("the OC") is hostile to life itself. Dynamic as Morales' heterotopia may be, punctuated by cultural transfer, the array of bodies in motion remains driven by a single universal law: "Money is what keeps everybody in Orange County greased up. It's the fuel that keeps everything moving, and movement is the great archetype of Southern California" (15).

Spurred by economics, the buzz of movement is a clearly defined property of Morales' narrative heterotopia, which exacts an intensifying kinesthetic sensibility from the reader as the bodies in motion accumulate. Our resultant view of the OC is characterized by "millions of people working to achieve their individual utopias ... usually in a hurry, always busy" (246); "keep moving, keep working" (133) in a "never-able-to-catch-up culture" (142) for "speed counts in America"

(103), driving "the freeways to labor in an adjacent county and sustain their OC utopia" (53). Other tangents of bodies in motion include drive-by killings (38), running for fitness and mental health (120, 299), allusions to railway deportations (208), pilgrimages (241, 263), and even a dead *"alma en pena"* (roaming soul) (192) condemned to forever wander. At length, the totality of these images renders a narrative that captures unmistakably the volatility of a heterotopia, a spatial dynamic that requires navigational skills from reader and resident alike, for, as J. I. concludes plainly, "We are all migrants in Aztlandia" (119).

WHITE FLIGHT FROM HETEROTOPIA

Originally conceived by Michel Foucault in "Of Other Spaces" (1986), the human geography of heterotopia is meant to convey a space of otherness under nonhegemonic conditions, a concept that has proven especially germane to Morales' portrayal of Aztlán owing to the region's bourgeoning mosaic of cultural difference and, importantly, the ongoing struggles against WASP hegemony. Subtitled "the *heterotopian* trilogy," these are the novels where said geography is arguably at its most salient. Revisiting pioneer days, the narrator reminds us in *White Heron* that Southern California was founded by settlers of diverse ethnic backgrounds—Indigenous, Spanish, African, Mulatto, Mestizo, and Asian—"an appropriate prototype and metaphor for the future, for the twenty-first century" (141), and today's demographic evolution toward an ever-increasing ethnic majority bring this origin full circle. Even the wording of the foregoing, "ethnic majority," is outmoded as Latinos are no more ethnic in California than they are anywhere else in Latin America. This begs the long overdue question: when will the "waning Anglo hegemony" (34) fade altogether, abridged in the history books as a parenthesis of colonial injustice and illegal expansion derided as an ill-fated drive for power, influence, or homogeneity? Then again, just as the United States begins to make headway, however protracted, toward improved intercultural relations, the country is dragged back into a bygone era of collective oblivion. Notoriously, in his announcement of presidential candidacy on June 16, 2015, Donald Trump made his coveted headlines by targeting Mexicans with inflammatory accusations, blaming them for society's ills such as drugs, crime, and rape. Though the data proves that the reverse is true, that crime rates are lower among the immigrant and illegal immigrant demographics, Trump in repeated press releases makes no apologies for his false accusations.[2] Why would he? He owes his ascent to the presidency to having pandered to a political base that unabashedly prefers "alternative facts" to the "inconvenient truth."[3] The problem that his media spectacle created, however, is real. Such skewed remarks, no matter how asinine, did have and continue to have an impact on public perception that, in turn, drives immigration policy.

The second volume of Morales' trilogy could not come at a more relevant time. Just as the political pendulum swings to such extremes of prejudice, Morales shows us how the United States and Mexico, in fact, mirror each other in both their shortcomings and their approaches toward one another. Aztlán in these novels aptly represents a yet unresolved microcosm of backward thinking within the greater world of plurinational democracy, open borders, and transnational coalescence.

By the turn of the twentieth century, the population of white Europeans in Mexico had dwindled significantly while the Mestizo and Indian numbers swelled, triggering fear in the United States, where "some of the culturally hegemonic groups saw themselves in danger of political extinction, of being overrun by the masses from the Third World" (1). By the twenty-first century, this demographic trend had not only grown to engulf the region but had also become enriched with further complexity, as J. I. observes upon arrival at the John Wayne Airport in Santa Ana: "I thought I had landed in Japan" (17). The novel opens against the backdrop of this heterotopia's ethnic diversity and proceeds to develop a familiar conflict that is instigated by the aforementioned hegemonic groups who endeavour to "stabilize our borders, stabilize our language and stabilize our culture" (75) in a space where the only norm is instability.

The antagonist in the Chicano struggle has not changed but, to be clear, Morales provides a brief chronology (207–11) of its pivotal moments: military hostility (1846), a miscarried treaty (1848), persecution through taxes and lawyers, peon labor, repatriation, Zoot Suit profiling (1940s), congressional bills, the Bracero Program (1942–1964), Operation Wetback (1954), urban renewal ("Mexican barrio eradication"), eminent domain, English-only propositions, the Simpson-Mazzoli Bill (1982), the Rodino-Simpson Bill (1986), the so-called "Save Our State" Proposition 187 (1994), and now "the triple wall, the U.S./Mexican border wall like the ugly Berlin Wall" (222). All of this was brought about, according to the author, by "the great gringo fear that we were going to take over California" (209). It is this fear of "too many brown faces" (208) that spurs the white bodies in motion who take flight in search of the next peripheral outpost of a WASP utopia, only to be absorbed once again by heterotopia's inescapable reach. It bears asking an obvious question: what laborers will lay the foundation of this remote and exclusive WASP enclave built of Simons brick,[4] or what landscapers will manicure its green oasis? What is implied here in the novel is that it is only when the affluent WASPs bend their backs to scrub their own toilets, grow and pick their own food, and shingle their own roofs under the blistering California sun that they will fully safeguard their eugenic communes against heterotopian incursion. What is more, diversity increasingly transcends class, striking terror in their hearts "when they [WASPS] saw Mexicans sitting on the judge's bench, teaching in universities, gaining professional positions . . . taking over sections of cities once dominated by Anglo Americans" (211). The futility of white flight notwithstanding, driven by the illusory prospect of privilege and power, new suburbs crop up, requiring further high-speed networks for the (white) bodies in motion:

> New rapid toll roads went directly to the edge cities, modern paradises where mostly white affluent middle-class couples created their personal utopias. Daily, men and women drove the freeway and looked down at paradise lost to the new immigrants. They realized their parents had allowed themselves to be pushed out of paradise. Their parents had not stayed to protect their turf, their utopias; they had not stayed to work with the new neighbors. Instead, because of fear and ignorance, they ran to new developments in Orange County, a county they were currently losing to the new immigrants. (284–85)

It is not only a fear of losing their share of the American Dream to another, but specifically the fear of doing so "to a 'non-American,' a foreigner, an illegal, a minority" (255) that impels the last-ditch effort of white flight. In the extreme, such fear and ignorance always carries with it the potential to radicalize nativist groups—see allusions to "Neo-Nazis" (256–57) and the "Berlin Wall" (222)—which, given the political climate under Trump, bodes an ominous future. When the catalyst is the US president himself, intolerance becomes emboldened. The parallels are eerily unambiguous between the reproving ethos in *White Heron* that warns "a racism of slogans has become a racism of acts" (257) and the corollaries between a president's speech and the ensuing escalation of white nationalism.

The resonance of moving bodies, the mad rush of cars, the headlong dash from one safe harbor of sameness to the next, betrays a fear of heterotopic spaces, of "the in-between because it was the place of the uncanny" (175), running counter to the heterotopia envisioned by Foucault. By contrast, J. I. comes equipped with a worldview adapted for today's diverse landscape: "I acquired the habit of living between worlds, existing in a border zone, a frontier that was radically incongruous, a frontier that ran through my language, music, food, dress, architecture, life, everybody's life" (118). For J. I., between the troubles of her Mexican past in *Waiting to Happen* and her gringo predicament in this sequel, her identity remains mutable, fluctuating between two and oftentimes opposing worldviews. But she recognizes her own mobile identity, one without a solid foundation, as is the norm in heterotopia: "Southern California was an endless identity-crisis circus" (18). For the global citizen in general, and for life in bizarre Aztlandia in particular, the ability to cross borders—literal and figurative, national and linguistic, ethnic and ideological, etc.—benefits those who can rise above stagnation. Vital for our evolving world "where movement and change are infinite" (118), adaptation remains a survival skill. Heterotopians adapt, negotiate, harmonize, or simply blend in like a "border chameleon" (118), whereas among those who, because of whatever prejudice, find themselves unable to navigate a changing world, the reality of shifting diversity is liable to trigger a primordial fear and that rather primitive response of fight-or-(White) flight.

CHURCH IN STASIS

Conspicuous in Morales' novel is an early tangent best summarized as a "war on Catholicism" (39), a battle against an authoritarian institution that reduces the complexities of a dynamic world into an archaic system of binaries—light versus dark, good versus evil, angels versus demons, heaven versus hell, etc.—presupposing a simplistic division that practically renders two groups of Chicanos: either the "fearful faithful" kneeling in church (39) or the "drive-by killers" of street gangs (39). Though a convenient means to social order in medieval times, such binary beliefs and superstitions prove regressive in today's freer-thinking world. The wane of organized religion is attributable to a complexity of factors, to be sure, but in the heterotopia of Aztlán, what Morales decries explicitly is the latent discourse of colonial victimization that relegates working-class Mexican Catholics to "God's most innocent children" (39). Heads bowed and indoctrinated to believe that theirs is a fate of poverty and humility, they wait in vain for their many needs to be met by invoking the supernatural through prayer, whereas to take pride and action for oneself would be to challenge the authority of the Church and to question one's own preordained destiny. For J. I., advocating a healthier future for the Mexican working class begins with accepting that

"Catholicism has done more harm than good" (38). What is more, in contrast to its kinesthetic surroundings, Catholicism is portrayed in the novel as stagnant, timeworn, and immobile, and thus incongruous with the ever-changing movement within heterotopia. As J. I. in her role of straight-talking protagonist observes, "Mexicans deserve better than the humble, self-sacrificing, superstitious, emotional, icon-worshiping, phallus-centred, failure-oriented Catholicism that has tracked us for centuries" (55). In effect, it is the Church in stasis that appears destined to be passed by as the many bodies in motion make progress toward improving their busy lives.

It is not that the novel is bent on irreverence; rather, it conveys heterotopia's values in the more practical direction of the everyday hero. As in *Waiting to Happen*, the trilogy questions the supposed virtues of purity and holiness and develops a perhaps more relatable ethos—"the next savior of the world will not be a man, but a sinful woman, debauched" (8). Posited throughout the narrative are the influential women of Mexico's past, but they are neither replicated from the traditional blueprint atop a pedestal, nor immaculate. Instead, J. I. beholds them throughout the vulgarities of daily life on the freeway, in the bedroom, or sipping wine at receptions: La Llorona, Coatlicue, Malintzin, La Virgen de Guadalupe, Sor Juana Ines de la Cruz, and Frida Kahlo, roaming the streets of heterotopia. In line with a trend that characterizes the better part of Morales' latest fiction, the strong female galvanizes the central storyline. It is thus the everyday working woman on the move to make ends meet who is accorded a sacred status: "I worship nobody / I acknowledge the Mexican / or Central American working woman / sitting on the bus bench / at five in the morning / . . . / I praise the Mexican / or Central American woman / . . . / I offer respect to that woman / who survives low pay / dirty words / [etc.]" (165–66). Notably, the greatest obstacles to the working woman's mobility in heterotopia are the social hierarchy confining her to a humble class and the institutions that perpetuate it—in this case, the police, the politics, and the Church. Ultimately, these are the forces at work that bog down any space of a potentially kinesthetic, fluid nature. Even the nimble protagonist falters in her efforts to move through the quagmire of convention upheld by California's long-standing bureaucracies. She exclaims, "I had come to a standstill. My movements were constrained by political and disciplinary institutions" (323). This is a momentary halt to mark the climax of a storyline otherwise characterized by constant movement.

A WHITE HERON AT THE CONFLUENCE

As if to counter the legacy of colonial-based religion described in the foregoing, Morales evokes the gods of old: "Tetzlacuipocla, The Smoking Mirror, had entered the city and struck back at the Christian God who had ruled the city for hundreds of years" (272). This is the sort of departure that we might come to expect from "El Tlacuilo."[5] Indeed, just like the eponymous bird that stands guard over J. I.—"the white heron had come from far away, far away not only in distance but in time" (277) —so too do the ancient Aztec gods bring their forces to bear in the heterotopian space of Aztlán. It recalls the rightful place of the indigenous, yet another frontier to enrich the already complex mosaic. Moreover, it is the timeless indigenous legacy that unites the two countries in both the narrative and the ontological space. Aztlán and her peoples compose an a priori challenge to established norms as they transcend political borders and social order. They also unite the two otherwise disparate homelands internalized by J. I.'s consciousness insofar as indigeneity presents a natural interface within the matrix of heterotopia for reconciling the present and past conflicts between two nations. In this respect, Sarah Kavanaugh argues in her study of the dynamics of indigenous space that "Foucault's heterotopia and the frontier both exist as abstracted spaces of interaction not only between the normative and the deviant, but also between the past and present" (2011, 169). For J. I., the indigenous past is a channeling link to the interactions between the normative and deviant, between the discourse of power and the sacred Other, between present and past—in short, a simultaneity of place and experience best observed through a heterotopic lens. The sequel's storyline takes place north of the border, but Mexico looms large in J. I.'s reality and, on a transcendental level, the indigenous forces of old bring her present-day relationship with both countries to a critical confluence.

This simultaneity of place and experience surfaces in Orange County through events that originate in Chiapas, where Mayans endure one neocolonial incursion after the next, all in the name of Mexican progress. For instance, in an independent OC bookstore Morales explores a subplot of criminal intrigue, with one struggling entrepreneur likening his crusade against image-driven media progress to the Mayan struggle for independence. Repeatedly, news of Chiapas make headlines here and then filters across the border into an evolving worldview. More concretely, a family of Mayans are detained by INS agents who mistake them for Chinese immigrants living in the country illegally. They are, in fact, guest workers at Mrs. Dougherty's homestead, complete with Mexican passports and work visas. Serving a calculated purpose in the narrative of faulting both countries for the family's adversity, the Mayans expose the ignorance that lie behind aggressive attitudes toward indigeneity: "Of course they didn't understand Spanish or Chinese. They were Mayan Indians and spoke Mayan!" (89). Elsewhere, fear and prejudice at the sight of the Mayans trigger derision when someone asks, "Wonder where those Neanderthals came from?" (124). The fact that all races save African share varying degrees of Neanderthal DNA is a point clearly lost on the Mayans' aggressor, who fails to appreciate that "we were [all] a band of postmodern border-region Neanderthals, just like everybody else" (125). For the bigoted in general, and the nativist in particular, difference of any kind equates a threat. For this family of Mayans under Mrs. Dougherty's care, capricious attitudes and an arbitrary border are the least of their concerns compared to the urgency of escaping persecution by the Mexican army were they to be deported back to Chiapas. Lest the reader forget, Morales provides details of atrocities from the front lines of an excavation that are redolent of the Acteal Massacre (1997), developing the Chiapas story of injustice in concert with the thickening plot further north, but with an intriguing twist. Morales writes that "the Indian population battled to escape extinction from deliberate genocide practiced by the government and private interests, and from experimentation practiced by large pharmaceutical companies" (290), calling to mind parallels from his earlier novel, *The Captain of All These Men of Death* (2008). In a sense, the indigenous legacy reads like a signpost along the busy intersections of Aztlán's bodies in motion. Unwavering and foreboding, the indigenous concurrence in the misfortunes of Mexico and the United States serves notice that both countries are long overdue in putting to right their shared colonial relationship.

Further evocations of the two countries' shared destiny include the Ciudad Satélite suburban utopia of Mexico D.F. emerging in tandem with Orange County as planned communities of commuters seeking "a trouble-free, nonviolent, healthy lifestyle in modern housing" (53). This seems to demand in turn wider and faster freeways to thrust the upper-middle class into the respective neighboring megalopolis, Mexico City or Los Angeles. As one character says, "I zoomed by at seventy miles an hour. Shortly I would drive over and into the heart of LAMEXICO, LAMEXICANGLASIA, AZTLAN ANGLO ASIA" (102). These correlations between North and South, however, do not imply cultural cohesion so much as a common omen. Endriago reenters the tale at this point and unearths the hundreds of massacred Mayan Indians in Chiapas. This causes J. I. to reflect on how the earthquakes of Mexico City and the landslides of California can swallow people whole (32). Additionally, as Popocatepétl erupts and ignites fires across Mexico City, she encounters entire apartment blocks ablaze in Tustin, California (273), and, elsewhere, she contends with a raging fire fueled by winds that carry the ghosts of Chiapas. Morales writes that "a low wind brought voices, not happy voices but terror-stricken, unintelligible, screaming voices of ancient people, struggling, clawing their way out of the automatic weapons' fire" (294), making plain to the reader that the two worlds are, in effect, one. A crucial idea that one develops from reading this novel is that ancient Aztlán, while overlaid with modern heterotopia, still obeys the indigenous spirits that oversee "two worlds coming together, the existence of a profane and a sacred world coexisting and overlapping, forming spaces where they both communicated and affected one another" (276).

CRIME AND PANOPTICON

Foucault (1975) envisioned the panopticon as a metaphor for a disciplinarian society, more specifically for its inherent desire to observe and to normalize through a culture of surveillance, with the result of creating in the subject a consciousness of permanent visibility to the powers that be. Oppressive by design, the model of prison architecture, this figurative interpretation of the panopticon is equally threatening in its tyranny of power/knowledge relations. For instance, research into CCTV systems reveals that the level of intrusiveness, the specifics of targeting, and the precise aims of monitoring are all shaped by the prejudices of the observer, and as Kevin Haggerty (2011) points out, ethnic groups in particular receive a disproportionate amount of attention from the authoritative gaze (32–33). The dystopian Big Brother effect is unmistakable here. Add to this the thirty-foot monolith prototypes made to order at the San Diego-Tijuana border by the Trump administration, and it becomes painfully clear that within heterotopia an oppressive WASP panopticon is indeed at work and calibrated for racial profiling.

Though the future of the monolith border wall is uncertain, the implied incarceration coupled with excessive surveillance relegates the Mexican community to a pariah status within their own homeland. Bigotry, surveillance, and the psychological fallout from domineering governments inspire the Morales trilogy, to be sure, and though the term only appears in this latest novel in a passing reference—"The panopticon forces prohibited my faithful from assembling to worship, to wait for La Santa Ilusa de las Grietas to come outside" (310)—the gaze of the panopticon remains implicit throughout *White Heron*. J. I. endures relentless scrutiny by the authorities, by the media, and by her followers, but her woes over her lack of privacy are scarcely the issue. It is, rather, the misguided attitudes of preemptive justice inside the WASP panopticon that Morales continues to bring to the fore. Media stereotypes of Latinos, the calculated police harassment of Latino youth, the multimillion-dollar industry of crime and incarceration, and eminent domain over entire neighborhoods are some of the lowlights endured by a Mexican community harassed by a disciplinarian society, "not only by the INS but also by marauding, independent racist organizations that removed Mexicans from the streets" (309).

In this work, the lament of racial profiling comes intertwined with an additional story of crime and punishment, one that appears almost retaliatory against conventional stereotypes as it stems from the other side of the heterotopian spectrum and casts serious doubt on the misguided principles that underlie California's would-be paradise. This secondary storyline follows the criminal exploits of a yuppie couple in Newport Beach that embodies the ideals of modern-day utopia: beauty, health, education, and work ethic. Conspicuously, even their dog is a consummate utopian, a perfumed golden retriever: "hasta los perros son hedonistas" (even the dogs are hedonists) (11). As fitness gurus, the couple represents literally perfect bodies in motion "rushing toward an occurrence" (122), but said "occurrence" culminates with a SWAT team offensive to confiscate their arsenal of automatic weapons. The subplot comes to an end when the model front runner in the American Dream is "viciously blown out of her brain, out of paradise" (148). Here the heterotopia of deviation is turned on its head, incarcerating or liquidating those whom utopia is originally meant to privilege. It is an unambiguous collapse of the utopian social order, raising the question of utopian desire itself, which, as Morales has stated from the very beginning, "is unattainable in heterotopia" (1996, 25). A microcosm of multiple environments that affirm difference in spite of a punitive society that criminalizes diversity, the heterotopia of Southern California is too complex to command with any degree of certainty. It exceeds the limited gaze of the WASP panopticon. Hegemonic rule and surveillance culture thus break down at the point where cracks in the utopian foundation allow the beautifully deviant to slip through.

Fluid and ever changing, Aztlandia is where the life force of the ancient indigenous culture blends with the wayward values of the upwardly mobile, where internal borders proliferate (class, race, gender, worldview, etc.) to such an extent that they shift and merge, blurring the view of authoritarian rule and confounding the aims of disciplinarian society. Such is the human geography portrayed by Morales—"Southern California and Orange County fell back into the sphere of randomness, constant movement, ubiquitous change, pervasive surveillance, and capricious uncertainty, retreated into a domain where ancient spirits meander like rumors through modernity's heterotopia" (304). Just as Aztlandia ranges beyond political borders, so too does Morales' novel, spreading the intrigue of crime and panopticon beyond any single focal point, transcending race, class, creed, etc. The underworld present at both of Mexico's borders (in Chiapas and along the maquiladora belt) surfaces with open-ended plots of conspiracy, prefiguring the third and final installment of the trilogy. Endriago has taken refuge in Chiapas only to discover the horrors committed against the Mayan Indians by both paramilitary forces and the multinational pharmaceutical industry. Similarly, in the northern part of Mexico, where young women are victimized in the no-man's land of the maquiladora belt, defenseless against corrupt police and narcogangsters, the novel concludes with J. I. crossing the border back into Mexico. Meeting her father at his new assembly plant, "la Maquiladora de los Sueños de la Imagen" (329), she is greeted by a crime scene involving another dead girl, which Morales aesthetically equates as "a testimony to big profits" (333).

The Place of the White Heron is therefore a natural extension of the first book in the trilogy, with a seamless flow of narrative, a coherence of style and tone, and the protraction of familiar characters. It bears mentioning that there are themes here overlapping with a number of Morales' latest publications unrelated to the trilogy: *The Captain of All These Men of Death* (2008), *Little Nation* (2014a), and *River of Angels* (2014b). There are still other themes—gang life, land seizures, and the matriarch's struggle against both—that merit consideration as they constitute yet other signature motifs of injustice, crime, and panopticon. As noted, there are definite echoes of *Little Nation* at work in this novel, in the representation of how the state exploits and institutionalizes gang culture—"We need the criminals to keep and to justify our jobs" (132)—and in the segregation of the Mexican barrio ("Racism and economic prejudice was alive and well behind the Orange Curtain in Santa Ana, California" [179]). In addition, there is the government's unfortunate penchant for declaring eminent domain to supplant whole communities from their rightful lands: "In order to widen the freeway, *Mexicanos* of one of the oldest barrios in Santa Ana had lost their land and homes: another sacrifice, another contribution to the progress of Orange County and Southern California" (184).[6]

From the microcosm of thematic local land struggles to a global economy that perpetuates abusive power relations, *White Heron* posits the Chiapas case study, which, emblematic of any marginalized community, runs parallel to the discontents further north with the added challenge of fighting corruption in relative obscurity. Even though globalization paradoxically provides a platform for broadcasting the Zapatista uprising and its postmodern revolution to win international hearts and minds through the internet, the perverse gap between rich and poor fostered by global economics has not changed. What is more, with the better part of the EZLN hype having run its course, Chiapas remains as vulnerable and contentious as ever—both in reality and in Morales' work.

In sum, it is once again a similar future of Aztlán that awaits readers in the yet unwritten third and final installment of the heterotopian trilogy. Absorbed by the acceleration of science and technology, and by how they have an immediate impact on our daily lives, Alejandro Morales conjures a foray into speculative fiction to produce another futuristic view of the border with a LAMEX resonance.[7] To forecast what dangers await J. I. in the future, we need to look no further than today's scientific trends. Advances in virtual reality, self-driving cars, 3D printing, and artificial intelligence make repeated headlines, indicators of the mounting presence of technology in our homes and at work. Such is the nature of speculative fiction, which this novel may be classified under in some respects. But how are these rapid developments going to be counterbalanced by demographic trends, specifically the continuous growth of Mexican populations in urban centers on both sides? Given Morales' penchant for confronting social injustice, and his forewarnings of the WASP panopticon, would it not be surprising if, in the final volume of his heterotopian trilogy, ingenuity were to segue into stories of abuse and prejudice . . . an outlook that is distinctly *dys*topian?

NOTES

1. *The Place of the White Heron* is Morales' title for his manuscript, which is currently under review with various publishers. All page references are taken from the manuscript and, like the title itself, are subject to change. The manuscript is referenced in citations by this title.

2. Michelle Ye Hee Lee, "Donald Trump's False Comments Connecting Mexican Immigrants and Crime," *Washington Post*, July 8, 2015, www.washingtonpost.com/news /fact-checker/wp/2015/07/08/donald-trumps-false-comments-connecting-mexican -immigrants-and-crime/?utm_term=.50073a4c9a92.

3. The phrase "alternative facts" was coined by Republican counselor to the president

Kellyanne Conway, during a press conference on January 22, 2017, when she defended false statements by the White House Press Secretary Sean Spicer. The blatant political spin on provable falsehoods prompted immediate concerns over the parallels between the Trump administration and Orwell's dystopia, *Nineteen Eighty-Four*. In other respects, the Republican Party continues to dispute the inconvenient truth of our planet's climate change. See Gore (2006).

4. An allusion to the historic Simons Brickyard, the East Angeles corporate factory-turned-township where Morales' parents worked and the area where he grew up.

5. Publishing under the name "Alejandro Morales," the novelist adds the alias "El Tlacuilo," the Aztec artist, scribe and storyteller.

6. As the geography of the *Little Nation* and *River of Angels* titles imply, both works tell place-based stories. They voice a spirit of belonging to one's own land, of rootedness, and of honoring and preserving family lineage against the ghettoization of the barrio, or the segregation of Mexican labor along the shores of the Porciúncula (the original name of Los Angeles and its namesake river). In these works we witness the latest development in Morales' writing, in which the intrigue revolves around the matriarch and where the role of protagonist in the fight against injustice is assumed by a strong female lead. Heroic characters from *Little Nation*—Rebecca Carter, Micaela, and the Women's Scissor Federation—take supporting roles or, at the very least, are referenced in volume 2 (258). Similarly, like Toypurina (*River of Angels*), and Mama Concha and La Beaugival (*Little Nation*) before her, Mrs. Dougherty, well into her golden years, stands with shotgun in hand to protect her estate and her adopted Mayan family against land seizure. Finally, J. I. herself, the trilogy's heroine, is bolstered in her struggles throughout the novel by Mexico's honor roll of historic women: Coatlicue, La Llorona, La Virgen de Guadalupe, Sor Juana Inés de la Cruz (for whom J. I. is named), and Frida Kahlo. Indeed, personal connections to the space beneath one's feet are forged through family and, more often than not, the battle to protect land and family—and to fend off the WASP panopticon—is championed in the novel by a woman.

7. The title of part three of *The Rag Doll Plagues*, "LAMEX" is an acronym for the high-speed super corridor between L.A. and Mexico City, envisioned for the year 2027.

WORKS CITED

Bolens, Guillemette. 2012. *The Style of Gestures: Embodiment and Cognition in Literary Narrative*. Baltimore: John Hopkins University Press.

Forster, E. M. (1909) 1997. "The Machine Stops." In *The Machine Stops and Other Stories*, edited by Rod Mengham. London: André Deutsch.

Foucault, Michel. (1975) 1995. *Discipline and Punish: The Birth of the Prison*. Translated by Alan Sheridan. New York: Vintage.

———. 1986. "Of Other Spaces." *Diacritics* 16, no. 1 (Spring): 22–27.
Gore, Al. 2006. *An Inconvenient Truth: The Planetary Emerging of Global Warming and What We Can Do about It*. Emmaus, PA: Rodale Press.
Haggerty, Kevin D. 2011. "Tear Down the Walls: On Demolishing the Panopticon." In *Theorizing Surveillance: The Panopticon and Beyond*, edited by David Lyon, 23–45. London: Routledge.
Kavanaugh, Sarah Schneider. 2011. "Haunting Remains: Educating a New American Citizenry at Indian Hill Cemetery." In *Phantom Past, Indigenous Presence: Native Ghosts in North American Culture and History*, edited by Colleen E. Boyd and Coll Thrush, 151–79. Lincoln: University of Nebraska Press.
Morales, Alejandro. 1992. *The Rag Doll Plagues*. Houston: Arte Público Press.
———. 1996. "Dynamic Identities in Heterotopia." In *Alejandro Morales: Fiction Past, Present, Future Perfect*, edited by José Antonio Gurpegui, 14–27. Tempe, AZ: Bilingual Press / Editorial Bilingüe.
———. 2001. *Waiting to Happen: The Heterotopian Trilogy*. Vol. 1. San José: Chusma House.
———. 2008. *The Captain of All These Men of Death*. Tempe, AZ: Bilingual Press / Editorial Bilingüe.
———. 2014a. *Little Nation and Other Stories*. Translated by Adam Spires. Houston: Arte Público Press.
———. 2014b. *River of Angels*. Houston: Arte Público Press.
———. Forthcoming. *The Place of the White Heron: The Heterotopian Trilogy*. Vol. 2.
Orwell, George. (1949) 2008. *Nineteen Eighty-Four*. London: Viking.

TEN / Race, Space, and Magical Realism in *The Brick People* and *River of Angels* / ADINA CIUGUREANU

There has been substantial discussion in urban and cultural studies about the existence of a so-called third space that completes and compensates the two already recognized spaces: the lived-in and the imaginary. Intimating the concept of this "third space," Foucault first used the term *des éspaces autres* (the other spaces) to describe a combination of the real with the utopian-imaginary or a mixture between real and parallel spaces—to which he also applied the concept of "heterotopias" (Foucault 1986, 11–17). Influenced by Foucault, the geographer Edward Soja was fascinated by the concept of "other spaces," taking it further to propose the "Thirdspace," which he describes as not only connecting the real and the imaginary but also going beyond them to form a "trialectics" (Soja 1996, 61). In Soja's view, "trialectics" does not differ very much from Foucault's heterotopia. These concepts were articulated further by semioticians and cultural critics, such as Jean Baudrillard (1994), Edward Said (1978), and Homi Bhabha (1994), in whose work "other spaces" grow to be either hyperreal areas, creating the imaginary with no real model on which it could be based, or hybrid zones, mixing the real with the virtual or two types of different cultures.

Identifying the "third space" from a postcolonial perspective, Bhabha (1994) introduces the concept of the "hybrid zone," in which the individual is compelled to mix their native culture with that of the colonist, in whose world they have to live. Under the specific colonialist circumstances, the individual becomes a "decentered subject," because they are no longer the subject of their own world. Instead, they are doomed to occupy a third space, gaining a special identity in a labile cultural environment, subject to fluid temporality, which Bhabha calls "a borderline culture of hybridity" (225). Whether the individual remains in the (former) colonized space or leaves it, they will carry the "borderline culture of hybridity," the "third space," with them all their life.

In this line of thought, Gloria Anzaldúa's collection of essays and poems, entitled *Borderlands/La Frontera: The New Mestiza* (1987), presents the Mexican American border and its effects on persons inhabiting there. Anzaldúa looks at the frontier as a three-dimensional zone, in which the two sides of the border create a synthesis generating a third element she defines as "a new consciousness—a *mestiza* consciousness" (101–2). Described as "a source of intense pain" (102), this third space cannot be enclosed in the discourse of the border in a geographical sense because it extends to all kinds of margins that transgress the border and migrate inland. Like Bhabha's "borderline culture of hybridity," Anzaldúa's version of third space forms and grows with the person born on the border zone and is forever attached to the individual's consciousness. The mestiza consciousness rises from lived experience; therefore, it is a concept that exists within anybody who lives between two cultures. To the Chicana Anzaldúa, this third space, generated by the border dynamic, is always looked upon as a margin and, most probably because of this, as a source of constant resistance.

Thus, it is clear that the "third space" as conceptualized by all these critics and theorists is meant to both address and break binary systems. While Andalzúa represents it as a synthesis of a two-sided culture that results in mestiza consciousness, for Homi Bhabha it is a zone in which any individual born in the colonial world lives. He extends the cultural hybridity of the border to any kind of border, wherever it may be in the colonial world, irrespective of nationality. Though Bhabha looks at cultural hybridity from the perspective of the colonized forced to adapt to the colonizing culture, his concept applies to Chicano history and culture as an inverted hybridity—more specifically in the context of the Mexican immigrant struggle to preserve their cultural identity on a somewhat foreign land (which ironically belonged to their forefathers, centuries before). Similarly, while mestiza consciousness was initially intended to cover Mexican American bordered duality, it is a concept that also pertains to the effects of a two-sided culture in any space that undergoes, or has undergone, the practices of colonialism and conditions of occupied territory.

In what follows, I shall consider two of Alejandro Morales' Southern California novels, *The Brick People* (1988) and *River of Angels* (2014), from the perspective of the third space and/or mestiza consciousness. As these two novels take place in zones very close to the Mexican border, the questions arise: How do Mexican immigrants adapt in a culturally hybrid zone, and what are the effects of racism on their vulnerable consciousness? How is the "third space" created? How does it function, and how does it affect the immigrant and nonimmigrant communities in these two works? A comparison between an early work (*The Brick People*) and a recent one (*River of Angels*), both looking at the late nineteenth- and early twentieth-century Mexican migration to Los Angeles, should reveal both the formation and function of the aforementioned racial-spatial theoretical concepts.

HISTORIOGRAPHY, PALIMPSEST, AND MAGIC REALISM

Generally referred to as a combination of historiographic fiction and autobiography, Morales' *The Brick People* could be read as a novel in which an inverted "borderline culture of hybridity" is created in a heterotopic space, largely dominated by the relevance and enactment of mestiza consciousness. Most of the action of the novel takes place at Simons Brick Co. Yard no. 3, founded by the Englishman Walter Simons in 1904 in Montebello to compete with the brick factories his brothers had established in Los Angeles in the 1880s. While Simons Brickyard became, in a short while, the largest brick factory in the world, its owner created in it a heterotopic space for the Mexican laborers who came in large waves from Mexico to find work. By replacing Chinese workers with Mexicans, mostly as a result of the Chinese Exclusion Act of 1882 still in effect at the turn of the twentieth century, Simons created a first-generation Mexican labor population; indeed, he encouraged large families of Mexicans to cross the fluid US-Mexican border, which knew no check points at the time. He provided for this population a combination of workspace, campsite, home, and corporate space, possibly bringing to mind the Victorian workhouses of Dickens' London. In Simons' brickyard (which practically became a town in and of itself), the immigrants were worked to exhaustion, but as opposed to English policy in London, they were allowed to live with their families in houses rented from the owner, receive a fair wage for their work in comparison to what Mexican workers were generally paid at the time, and were awarded a five-dollar gold piece for each child born.[1]

The land in the novel on which the Simons brothers' brickyards sit is not just any conventional land. The piece of land on which Joseph Simons built his factory in nearby Pasadena, for example, was once owned by the fictional character doña Eulalia Perez de Guillén and her husband, who planted an oak that grew a new branch every time a son was born. Severed by the people who wanted her land after doña Eulalia's husband died and her sons were murdered, the tree and the pit near it became her grave. In time, it magically became the birthplace for millions of "indescribably large brown insects" (13). Like in a horror story, these insects overtake and virtually consume anyone who interferes with the land (13), to magically disappear and reappear at different times in the story with different people as a kind of symbolic blight. This is not the first time in Morales' fiction that the earth, the plants, and the animals—cockroaches in this case—develop a life of their own. In developing life, their intention seems to be to guard the earth and to essentially take revenge on those who ignore or misuse it. This little parable within the novel offers its own particular meaning: on the one hand, Morales creates the first layer of the palimpsestic space that he will populate with enduring characters; on the other, the story is meant to allude to that third space, and to remind readers that the land the Americans bought or snatched, sold or developed, had belonged to other peoples before. The appearance of millions of insects to attack and eventually consume each of the land-snatching Simons brothers when they approached death is testimony to an abominable curse that the Mexican immigrants attributed to doña Eulalia. Morales uses the strategy of magical realism to subvert the popular comparison of the Mexicans with cockroaches. He uses the words "brown insects" in the novel, which may indeed be read as the effect of doña Eulalia's curse for having been dispossessed of her family and land, while introducing the word "cockroaches" in relation to the Mexicans, when he presents the interview given by Walter Simons' second wife about her husband's accomplishments and deep care of the Mexican immigrants: "Mexicans, like cockroaches, are extremely adaptable. They will survive anything. Many might perish, but there will always be survivors to propagate the race. They're just like cockroaches" (134). So Morales distinguishes between the no-name "brown insects" that come out of the earth at crucial moments and invade the bodies of the owners of the factory and "cockroaches," the derogatory nickname given to Mexicans by others.[2]

In *River of Angels*, on the other hand, we find not cockroaches but lizards, who make their appearance before a character passes away and connects them to the lizard people myth. These are creatures who live underground, rescue people from drowning, cure them in an underwater world, and are willing to communicate only with naturally gifted people who are able to understand and talk to nature at large. According to legend, the indigenous natives who disappeared during the colonizing periods were not dead but taken to a better place by their ancestors, who in turn became the earth spirits, so powerful that they could move mountains and transfigure their bodies to trick the evil invaders. They could be as minute as the smallest particle, as big as the tallest human and as imposing as a mountain. The earth spirits transformed their physical human likeness into reptiles: the lizard people. (7)

The lizard people, together with the indigenous communities that have vanished from the face of the earth, or suffered tragic death, live in "clandestine communities" in "great underground cities near the Pacific," one of them located underneath Los Angeles (7–8). The lizard people's world is more than a parallel space: it becomes heterotopic when the lizards interfere with the humans, by saving them from drowning, taking them to their world, and returning them to their families after they are cured or saved from imminent death. It is also a hyperreal space for the humans who live in the lizards' world before they are sent back to the "real" above-ground world.

The connecting gate between the two worlds in Morales' novel is the Los Angeles River, famous for its unpredictable floods, unseen currents, and sudden change of beds in the nineteenth and early twentieth century before it was tamed by bridge and highway constructions. Interestingly, the more the humans industrialized the city, the more the magic power of the river and its surroundings decreased, until by the end of the novel it almost disappears. In striking contrast, at the beginning of the novel, the Ríos family, started by the Mexican Abelardo and the indigenous Toypurina, knew "the language of the river" and possessed its secrets, which protected the family for generations from the Spaniards, Anglo foreigners, Catholic priests, and other Indian groups (8). Like the brown insects of *The Brick People* who attacked the Anglo foreigners, the river was merciless with the Anglos unless they asked Abelardo for help and listened to his advice. It was Abelardo who could speak to the Great Spirit of the river and ask for protection.

Like the brown insects in *The Brick People* who appear at crucial moments in the novel when life meets death, the lizard people in *River of Angels* make themselves known when Abelardo's son, Sol, drowns. He is taken to their world to be revived, cured, and returned. The second time the lizards make their appearance is when Sol and his brother Otchoo are on the verge of transgressing the realm of the living to the realm of the dead. There, Sol has a vision with lizards and angels, while Otchoo sees three lizards on the threshold of his house before he goes into the garden where he passes away. Besides these two male characters who encounter lizards, there are the two women, Toypurina and the River Mother, who are also strongly connected to the Great Spirit of the river and to the lizard people. When Toypurina Ríos becomes old and frail, she vanishes, yet her spirit roams the river and her house, accepting or rejecting the people who try to live in it. The River Mother is an old woman of an unknown age whose role, besides curing people through magical means, is to collect various objects belonging to the river's many victims, which are constantly brought to her. Through this heterotopic magic realism, Morales manages to bring forth a very important message: the land, the river, and nature in general are not merely decorative components of gorgeous sceneries but are, together with the animals for whom they offer a habitat, living components of a space that could be both generous to its inhabitants and fierce, demanding justice when it is abused, violated, or merely ignored.

A different story found at the beginning of *The Brick People*, and connected to a morbid moment in the history of Los Angeles, becomes symbolic of the human sacrifice that lies at the base of the building boom of Los Angeles' urban development. While digging in the north section of Joseph Simons' brick factory in search of good clay, the Mexican workers discover a mass grave in which hundreds of Chinese men, women, and children are buried. They were the victims of the Chinese massacre of 1871. Wrapped in a moving "Romeo and Juliet" story of two young Chinese belonging to two inimical families, the discovery of the bodies buried in the most productive earth for the making bricks gives Morales the opportunity to place another layer (and another race, besides the indigenous and the Mexicans) on the palimpsestic space of the brickyards. It is their blood that apparently fertilized the red clay. Turning this "special" clay into millions of bricks used in the construction of the administrative buildings in Los Angeles is both metaphorical and symbolic. It not only speaks to racial-spatial dynamics but reveals that the blood of the Chinese immigrants and the sweat and blood of the Mexican workers lie under and within the Los Angeles city hall, its police station, and other government buildings—as well as in the numerous brick houses built for the rich classes.[3]

The imposing presence of these brick government buildings in Morales' novel is indebted to the tragic death of both the Chinese and doña Eulalia's family. When the brick buildings cracked or collapsed during the 1933 earthquake, their reconstruction ironically called for the use of even more bricks from the Simons brick factory. The blood sacrifice required in the preservation of the solidity of a building may also be read as another strategy used by Morales to highlight the magical realist properties of this historical-cultural space. Moreover, the red dust left behind during the brick-making process has tragic effects on the workers and their families, who get poisoned and die of respiratory disease. Therefore, brick also has a literal double effect: it builds walls and it kills the workers who inhale its dust. Morales manages to make a distinction between the strength and endurance of the Mexicans, who work for years before the red dust produces terminal effects on their lungs, and the Anglos living outside the brickyard, whose death comes after a few months of inhaling the red dust blown into their neighborhood. In the end, the brick and the dust both paradoxically stand for opportunity, survival, and death.

THIRDSPACE AND MESTIZA CONSCIOUSNESS

Rather than structuring his narrative as a story-within-a-story, Morales structures it as layers, one on top of the other. The common denominator is the land, constantly connected with the past along with the present space it occupies. Space in *The Brick People*, for instance, is divided between inside (the camp, the brick factory) and outside (Los Angeles, the neighboring towns, and communities), seen from the perspective of characters who reside in the camp, sheltered by the rented houses and the love of their own families, to whom the outside world means danger and insecurity. In advertising the camp as an ideal place for the Mexican workers when he started to develop it, Walter Simons demonstrated his understanding that in order to have a successful business he would have to provide not only houses for the Mexican families but also a school for the children, a Catholic church, a clinic, and a general store from which the residents could buy necessities. Thinking of ways to enlarge the community and raise production, Walter Simons realized the importance of keeping the workers under control by also controlling their children:

> Walter feared the children. He would give them a school, a church, a clinic, everything, and create a paradise in which his workers would depend totally on him, so much so that the rising unrest in Mexico would not affect him or his people. They would never leave, he thought. (70)

In his visionary mind, Walter Simons realized that high brick production depends on the containment and contentment of the workers who, having come from a politically and economically destabilized country, would place high value on shelter, a job, and a salary sufficient to feed their family. Therefore, Walter built a "golden cage" for his workers and their families, to keep them safe within the camp walls and under his total domination. This "golden cage" represents a "third space," as Bhabha and Anzaldua might envision it. It is an artificial space created for the Mexicans, who are given the impression that they live in a world of plenty and provided security. In reality, however, they have next to nothing in this world because the land, the houses, and the workforce itself ultimately belong to the owner. Their personal possessions, as limited as they are, could suddenly disappear in case of standard termination of employ, or of more tragic events such as earthquake or fire.

In *River of Angels*, Morales introduces the Ríos/Rivers family, whose members are endowed with the magic of spiritually owning the land and the ability of mastering the river's movements. With the coming of the Anglo immigrant and after the "toll" of lives and goods that the river itself claims, the Ríos/Rivers family members consider it their mission to protect the survivors, help them cross the river in barges, and get involved in the construction of bridges, accepting the newcomers without any prejudice. Eventually, the land is parceled and sold by L.A. city authorities, to be divided into spaces for Anglos on the West side of the river, and spaces for Mexicans on the East side. In between the two sides, very close to the east riverbank, there lies the Sun Construction Company, started as a joint venture by a young Mexican Indian man, Otchoo Ríos, and an Italian family, the Morretti brothers, with the purpose of building bridges and railroads across the river. Symbolically, the two families represent the joint effort of local Mexican Indians and immigrant Europeans to tame the fickle river and develop the city for everybody to live in it by connecting the two sides.

Because both the Morrettis and the Ríoses live in an Anglo space, when they are about to sign the documents to set up the construction company, the law firm considers that the name Otchoo Ríos is too complicated to use and will lead to misspellings. Therefore, the Mexican indigenous name, Otchoo Ríos, becomes the anglicized Oakley Rivers. Despite this name change, and Oakley's marriage to an Anglo woman, however, the brown color of his and his son's skin could not be so easily changed. This becomes a central theme, creating a conflict of miscegenation later in the novel. In spite of the name change, neither Otchoo/Oakley nor his son Albert manage to obliterate their roots completely. They are examples of the formation of mestiza consciousness as revealed in their attempts to adjust to the white culture and in their constant rejection as mixed-blood people, as Other. Yet it is the mixed-blood people (Indians and Mexicans) who understood and managed to master the spirits of the river and the natural force of the earth, who opened their arms to anybody who wanted to settle down, irrespective of race, beliefs, and color. The bridges built by the white people fall down. It is only the bridges built together by immigrant Europeans and the mixed-blood Mexicans that resist both time and nature's capriciousness.

In *River of Angels* Morales enlarges the meaning of mestiza consciousness by mixing two components essential in the process of its formation: language and landscape. Since any individual is born into a language and grows up in a particular landscape, that individual's consciousness carries these two components with it forever, constantly reverting back to them with any new acquisition of a language or any moving to a different landscape. Through magical realism, Morales reveals how, through a language of their own, the land and the river could befriend the people caring for them and turn against those who violate their space. Therefore, the land, perceived and understood by Mexicans through their own particular language, may be read as *lang*scape.[4] In Morales' novel, the river with its various "scapes" is known and understood only by the Ríos family and the River Mother, responding to specific words, sounds, and motions interlinked with the landscape. For example, Sol Ríos, the character who lived with the lizard people for a while, could communicate with the river, the river vegetation, and animals that would disclose hidden treasures to him or offer him food.

> "Don't be afraid to talk to the ugly objects that float [on the river]. Speak to them, because they will listen to you." Sol repeated this advice in stuttered sounds, phrases, sentences, as if each repetition had a different meaning. Albert listened, learned and remembered. Uncle and nephew explored the river by boat, on horseback and on foot. They invested hours searching the deep pools, shallow flats, muddy and sandy shores that gave up their entangled gifts. (68)

Collecting valuable things that the river took from the people who drowned in it was not an easy task. Sol and his nephew Albert talk to the river and show respect to its vegetation, "thick shrubs, bright flowers, green grasses, ferns and trees" (68) in order to extract the treasures. At one such moment, they meet "a large golden mountain lion with a rabbit in its mouth" (68), a fresh kill. The two do not run away; on the contrary, Sol stops and when the lion "crouched down low," slowly wagging its tail, Sol steps forward and addresses it:

> "Thank you, but we're not hungry. Go and eat. Watch over us!"
> The cat turned once, twice, as if he wanted to stay, and on the third turn

he fixed his gaze on Sol and gently made his way back into the brush leading up the hill. (68)

The use of *lang*scape not only enhances magical realism in the novel but also implicitly speaks to the dynamics of mestiza consciousness at work. It further creates an indestructible bond between the river with its landscapes and the local Mexicans and Indigenous people with deep roots in that particular space because they are the only ones capable of controlling the river, its vegetation, animals, and bottomless mud pools.

From a topopoetic perspective, the apprehension of space is made through the combination of land, language, and the senses. The inclusion of the senses in this land-language combination is covered in geocriticism by the concept of "*land*guage" (Tally 2011, 4). In *River of Angels* the land on the two sides of the river, the language used by the Mexicans and indigenous people, and the senses that are heightened when the characters approach the river and interpret its language fuse into a somatic consciousness that bridges land, language, and sensory perception. Amazed at Abelardo Ríos' "intimate knowledge of the river's ways" (6) and his capacity to speak to the river, the Anglos find out that this ability has been transmitted from generation to generation:

> The Indians listened to plenty of water, to plenty of trout, to plenty of animals, and to plenty of vegetation, and to plenty of wind and rain, to all that combined to understand the river's voice, to sing the river's cycles, to know the river's space and to sense the river's movement. . . . Abelardo learned how to detect the river's feelings by sitting for hours, sometimes for days, listening to the Indian elders, the wise men, the wise women, whose culture, stories and language had survived thousands of years. (6)

The dual terms, *lang*scape and *land*guage, are meant to foreground an extremely important feature in Morales' fiction: the unbreakable connection between the Mexicans and the land of their fathers and forefathers, which they claim as belonging to their collective consciousness. The blending of *language* and *land* creates a well-delineated consciousness of a particular space—Los Angeles—which, under the historic circumstances of colonization and the pressures created by the policies of eviction and relocation following the urban renewal plans of city development, is shaken, divided, lost, and regained in the very complex process of creating duality, of embracing ambiguity and contradiction. In Anzaldúa's view, "a consciousness of duality" (59) is a mestiza consciousness, used as a survival strategy "designed for preservation under a variety of conditions" (109). It is exactly what Morales describes in these two novels.

SPATIAL (RE)LOCATIONS AND MISCEGENATION

The Mexicans who toiled and helped turn Los Angeles into a metropolis at the beginning of the twentieth century first lived in *colonias* at La Placita, right in the heart of the city. That was the very place where, on September 4, 1781, the city was baptized as "El Pueblo de Nuestra Señora la Reina de los Angeles de Porciúncula" (The Town of Our Lady the Queen of the Angels of Porciúncula). Almost a century and a half later, based on the new development plans of the city, the Mexicans were evicted and relocated to the east of the Los Angeles River, only to be zoned out once more and sent further east. This push eastward is described by Morales in *River of Angels* as painful, resembling a colonizing eviction rather than a progressive urban renewal plan:

> Along the river and across the greater Eastside, the city council had zoned the area for industrial development and for working class Anglo families. Mexican housing was torn down or pushed to the edges of the newly developed sections. The Mexicans pushed against the river banks and railroad yards, lived in abandoned farm worker camps, segregated company towns, in areas that had not been designated for them in this city envisioned as Anglos-only. (103)

The relocation of the Mexican families "to the immigrant quarters of Los Angeles that were thought of as Mexican reservations" (104) in the 1920s is one of the moments in the history of Los Angeles when space was territorialized and reterritorialized, located and relocated, according to class distinction and race segregation. Additionally, the space occupied by the Mexican immigrants (and Chinese, for that matter) was generally seen as contaminated with filth and various diseases, such as "tuberculosis, typhoid, cholera, flu, venereal diseases and, the worst, plague" (104), which required immediate measures of cleansing and replacement. Instead of looking for health measures and helping cure the population, the authorities sped up the process of clearing the zone out, especially after unexpected fires burst out in the areas described as "unhealthy." The fire that bursts out at Simons' brick factory camp in *The Brick People*, for instance, is a revealing case in point in this respect.

In both novels, however, Morales describes the process of building and rebuilding the Mexican communities, usually at a different location, in the manner in which Raúl Homero Villa describes the process of "barrioization" in his 2000 volume *Barrio-Logos*. While according to Villa "barrioization" comes into play especially after World War II with the setting up of the workers' union and the organization of union's strikes, Simons' "golden cage" in *The Brick People* may be described as a successful attempt of "barrioization" as early as the 1920s. The economic Depression on the one hand and information technology on the other (the radio became largely popular at the time) formed the background against which the workers eventually began to organize themselves and demand their rights. Contrary to Simons' intention of helping the Mexican children integrate more easily into American society through the school he had opened, the youth developed a hyphenated identity and mestiza consciousness. Their struggle for survival in a hostile environment, once they left that "golden cage," was more intense than they had imagined it. They became aware of the derogatory attitude of the Anglos toward the Mexicans once they left the camp.

Bullied and hated because their skin color and accent, the young people were denied jobs and housing in the white neighborhoods. Moreover, the Zoot Suit riots of 1943, the consequence of young Mexican Americans' disinclination to adapt and their desire to stand out, making themselves visible in the society in which they lived, caused them to choose the label "pachuco" for themselves (connoting aggressive and dangerous behavior). Although the Mexican youth from Simons' Brickyard were not involved in the riot, because they were living at the sheltered camp and not in the open Mexican barrio, they also got the "pachuco" label attached to them. Shocked by the racist manifestations but eventually understanding the cause, the Mexicans tried hard to maintain their families and to continue the lifestyle they had been used to as "barriological" tactics of sociospatial existence, largely described by Villa in his study.

Seen from the inside, the world outside the brickyards in the novel was almost unknown and little explored by the residents, as the focus is on the life of Mexicans before and after their arrival at the camp. Glimpses of the outside world and space start with the moving out of Malaquías de León and his family, who had to quit the job and leave the house rented from the owner, Walter Simons, because the camp did not offer him the freedom of mind and action he was longing for:

> [He] refused to obey the understood Simons rule which demanded that workers buy groceries, clothes, shoes, and other living necessities at the company general store [. . . .] Malaquías demanded the right to spend his

salary when, where and on whatever he desired. He did his purchasing outside of Simons in the neighboring town. (105)

Expelled by the Mexican supervisor loyal to the owner, the de León family set up outside the walls of the camp, sharing the space with a small Japanese American community, known for their farming activity. Yet this shared space was once again invaded by the Anglos: immediately after the bombing of Pearl Harbor, the Japanese were identified as enemies, evacuated, and herded to internment camps.

The Mexicans who dared leave the camp for good could hardly integrate into the outside world. They refused to join the ill-famed Mexican barrio in Los Angeles, the place of the Zoot Suit crimes, and were not welcomed to live in the white neighborhoods. To them, the barriological process proved very strenuous; they needed much determination to surpass the difficulties encountered after leaving the golden cage. Eventually, they managed to purchase land, build homes, and start a new life on the East side of the Los Angeles River. Their successful endeavor may be read as an act of reconquering a tiny portion of territory from the vast land that once belonged to their forefathers.

The building of the bridges whose purpose was to secure a lived-in space shared by all races living in Los Angeles is suddenly subverted by a new wave of racial beliefs related to eugenics and miscegenation. Questions like "Are you a Mexican?" (105) or "Why does Luisita have pink skin like a little baby piggy?" (179) strengthen the feeling that there is a distinction between the whites and the browns that goes beyond skin color. Albert Rivers/Ríos, the son of Oakley Rivers/Otchoo Ríos, is represented as a bridge across three races—He is "Mexican, Indian and Anglo" (115) —which appears to be the answer to one of his questions about his identity. Clearly, he has more queries about this issue:

> "Why am I not as dark as the Mexicans who work for us? Why don't we speak more Spanish? Why does Tío Sol [Albert's uncle] speak Spanish fluently? Did my grandmother name you 'Oakley'? Why don't we have a Mexican last name?" (115)

Color difference in skin is seen as a mark of racial distinction and superiority, at the heart of the opposition of Aryanism to crossbreeding. Grounding this fictional story on historic facts, Morales introduces the name of the leaders of the eugenics movement, such as Harry H. Laughlin, the reputed New York scientist invited to give a talk at the Southern California Aryan Club, whose members include Philip Keller, one of the Anglo characters and the uncle of Albert's Anglo wife, Louise. Quickly adopting the Aryan ideas and the eugenics theory, Uncle Philip becomes convinced that his mission in life is to guard the purity of the white race, starting with his family, whose white skin and blue eyes makes him proudly announce that they all belong to the superior Aryan race. Therefore,

> [he] felt compelled to warn his family about the innate inferiority of dark-skinned people and the physical dangers and genetic risks of associating with unfit humans. Among the most contaminated by miscegenation were Italians, Russians, Spanish and Jews. . . . But the new immigrants entering the country today were the most disgusting and dangerous half-breeds. The brown and yellow-skinned people were the worst. . . . They were the Chinese, Japanese and Mexicans. (182)

Fascinated by the idea of keeping the Aryan race pure and eliminating from society the "unfit or inferior human examples" (181), Philip Keller believes that "these subhuman races . . . had to be stopped from breeding, which justified sterilization of men and, most definitely, women" (182). He starts working on a program intended to implement the sterilization procedure without the patients' knowledge, until a law concerning the elimination of the inferior races could be passed. Besides investing in eugenics research, contributing to the construction of a ranch in the Santa Monica mountains to accommodate an Aryan master race community, and constantly trying to talk his family into putting an end to the marriage of Albert Rivers to his niece Louise Keller on grounds of future miscegenated children, Uncle Philip spearheads the actual practice of eugenics. Disappointed by his family's lack of reaction to his diatribes and infuriated by the news that Albert and Louise are going to have their second child, Philip and a few Aryan supporters attack Albert, beat him up, and nearly castrate him. Albert recovers, yet after a while there is news of his having fathered a third child. When Uncle Philip finds out, he cold-bloodedly (ironically) murders Albert on the bridge built by the Kellers and the Riverses connecting the two sides of the city. Though the encounter on the bridge that ended in Albert's death could have created a breach in the mutual understanding and good cooperation between these two families, ultimately the connection between the Anglo and the Mexican families does not break. Nor does the bridge collapse, as previous bridges literally and figuratively did. With time and World War II approaching, the eugenics movement begins to disintegrate and the Aryan ranch in the mountains becomes an empty and isolated space.

In both *Brick People* and *River of Angels*, Morales builds his stories on facts (the Simons Brothers brickyards, the building of bridges across the Los Angeles River by the Mexican workers, and the eugenics movement in the 1920s, etc.). Both novels foreground the epic struggle of the Mexican immigrants who strive to build a better life for their families on a territorialized space that once belonged to their forefathers. Though barely accepted by the Anglo colonizers, they contributed to the rise of the Los Angeles metropolis by making the red bricks used in the construction of the city houses, including the governmental and administrative buildings, and by assembling the bridges that connect the two parts of the city. While the brickyard in *The Brick People* effectively stands for a palimpsestic space or "third space" producing hybrid cultures, the bridge in *River of Angels* conceivably stands for the endeavor of building the city as an ideal community, irrespective of race and ethnicity. However, the mestiza consciousness remains the constant denominator characterizing the Mexicans in both tales, the inescapable feature that seems to delineate and divide the races and the ethnic groups. Though set up in Los Angeles, the Simons Brickyard may be looked at as a microcosm border zone between Mexico and the United States, due to the fact that it is the space in which the Mexicans could live both as Mexicans and as Americans.

Indeed, their clinging to their Mexican identity proves unrealistic and their shifting to an American identity proves scary and painful. It is the hybrid identity that helps them survive in a space in which the scarred memories of their forced migration from Mexico makes them stronger and more resilient. On the other hand, the Los Angeles River and the bridges built across it do not prevent the Mexicans from becoming aware of their hybrid identity—the acts of name-changing or attending the best schools do not erase the mestiza consciousness of the Mexican characters. Endowed with the ability of communicating with the river and the land, and with the capacity of curing diseases that physicians find incurable, the Mexicans are even more strongly perceived as the Other, as aliens, as weird, crossbred creatures that should be either sent away or annihilated. All in all, both novels present a clash between the Anglos and Mexicans that is viewed as a rejection-acceptance process in which the Anglos' rejection meets the Mexicans' unceasing fight for acceptance. Yet in both stories it is notable that no Mexican character ever rejects an Anglo outright; they generally try to understand them. The same cannot be said for Anglo characters, who mostly reject the Mexicans in casual and systematic ways that sadly ensure the racial-ethnic daily struggle for acceptance that in many cases becomes an ultimate struggle for basic human survival.

NOTES

1. See the documentary *The Brick People*, OCShowbiz, 2012, for the historical details about the Mexican immigrants and their work at Simons Brickyard no. 3.

2. He may have also alluded to Oscar Zeta Acosta's semifictional novel *The Revolt of the Cockroach People* (1973), whose title, based on the famous Mexican song "La cucaracha," is a metaphoric reference to the Mexicans living in squalid housing, oppressed and easily dispossessed by the dominant power.

3. There is a famous legend in Romanian folklore about the builder of a church who did not manage to finish its construction because the northern wall constantly collapsed after being erected. The builder, Master-Mason Manole, had a dream in which he was told that the construction needed a human sacrifice in order to resist time—not any kind of sacrifice, but a special one, his wife's. He was to bury his wife in the falling wall and this would secure the existence of the church forever.

4. *Langscape* is a concept referring to the perception of a particular landscape through a particular language, attached only to that local landscape (Moslund 2014, 11).

WORKS CITED

Acosta, Oscar Zeta. 1973. *The Revolt of the Cockroach People*. San Francisco: Straight Arrow Books.

Anzaldúa, Gloria. 1999. *Borderlands/La Frontera: The New Mestiza*. San Francisco: Aunt Lute.

Baudrillard, Jean. 1994. *Simulacra and Simulation*. Ann Arbor: University of Michigan Press.

———. 2000. *The Vital Illusion*. New York: Columbia University Press.

Bhabha, Homi. 1994. *The Location of Culture*. London: Routledge.

Foucault, Michel. 1986. "Of Other Spaces: The Principle of Heterotopia." *Lotus International: Quarterly Architectural Review*, 11–17.

Kirsch, Michael, Alejandro Morales, Alessandra Morales-Gunz, and Art Kirsch, dirs. 2012. *The Brick People*, OCShowbiz.

Morales, Alejandro. 1988 *The Brick People*. Houston: Arte Público Press.

———. 2014. *River of Angels*. Houston: Arte Público.

Moslund, Sten Pultz. 2014. *Literature's Sensuous Geographies: Postcolonial Matters of Place*. New York: Palgrave Macmillan.

Said, Edward W. 1978. *Orientalism*. New York: Vintage.

Soja, Edward. 1996. *Thirdspace: Journeys to Los Angeles and Other Real-and-Imagined Places*. Oxford: Blackwell.

Tally, Robert T., Jr. 2011. "Introduction: On Geocriticism." In *Geocritical Explorations: Space, Place, and Mapping in Literary and Cultural Studies*, edited by Robert T. Tally Jr., 1–12. New York: Palgrave MacMillan.

Villa, Raúl Homero. 2000. *Barrio-Logos: Space and Place in Urban Chicano Literature and Culture*. Austin: University of Texas Press.

ELEVEN / Mestizaje, Cultural Identity,
and Environmental Degradation
in Alejandro Morales' *The Rag Doll Plagues* /

MANUEL M. MARTÍN-RODRÍGUEZ

As readers surely know, Chicano/a/x literature came of age during the second half of the twentieth century, and its present status as a thriving US ethnic literature is felt both at the national and international levels, with conferences celebrated in multiple countries. The term "Chicano,"[1] which presently designates US citizens and residents of Mexican origin, was historically often taken as a slur, reserved for newly arrived Mexican immigrants. As has been the case in many other contexts, Mexican Americans in the late 1960s embraced the pejorative term, turning it into the marker of a new identity (neither Mexican nor American, yet both) and into a symbol of ethnic pride. Earlier labels fell short of conveying the identarian complexity that "Chicano" now represented: both "Hispanic" and "Latino" seemed to neglect the indigenous component of the Chicano/a/x heritage; "Mexican American" (with or without the hyphen) reflected a quasi-schizophrenic split without the possibility of a synthesis. "Chicano," on the other hand, was seen as a sort of tabula rasa (or "*tabula raza*" as the common pun goes) that accounted for novel subjectivities while embracing the multiple roots of this people, first annexed to the United States by conquest in 1848 and then steadily made significantly larger by successive waves of immigration from Mexico.

In this context, the Chicano/a/x vindication of mestizaje comes as no surprise. For Chicano/a/xs and Mexicans, mestizaje came to designate the coming together of Spanish and indigenous peoples and cultures in the Americas, with further miscegenation occurring when African slaves were brought to New Spain. In this context, mestizaje first carried with it a kind of Atlantic (Spanish) European configuration.[2] Later, after the US annexation of Mexican territory and population, a further mestizaje gradually took place, as people of Mexican origin intermarried with Anglo-Americans. While this later mestizaje tends to appear in Chicano/a/x literature and folklore in a much less positive light, the first is celebrated as essential to Chicano/a/x culture (notwithstanding denunciations of the Spanish imperial project). In contrast, the second oftentimes connotes suspicions of betrayal and *agringamiento*, of selling out, in short, to the dominant powers.[3]

In this study I contend that an additional process of Chicano/a/x mestizaje is underway, and that even if its population figures may still be comparatively low, it is capturing the imagination of late twentieth-century and early twenty-first-century Chicano/a/x writers. Contrary to the previous two processes discussed above, the most recent mestizaje is a product not of the Atlantic but of the Pacific. In California—always a trendsetter as far as political, cultural, and demographic changes are concerned—the fastest-growing population groups (and the demographic majority) are those of Mexican and Asian origin. According to the 2010 census, Latino/a/xs in this state accounted for 38.2 percent of the population (compared to 16.9 percent nationwide), and residents of Asian origin reached the 13.9 percent threshold (but were only 5.1 percent in the nation as a whole).[4]

These figures confirm that, in the so-called Golden State, the descendants of Latino/a/x and Asian ancestors together constitute the majority of the population, a trend that has only increased since 2010, providing some Chicano/a/x and non-Chicano/a/x authors with an interesting new perspective from which to consider identity and mestizaje. In fact, mixed marriages between Asian and Latino/a/xs in the United States have been documented as a noteworthy tendency since the first decades of the twentieth century. The massive arrival of Punjabi immigrants (most of them single men) resulted in the birth of a Chicano/a/x-Punjabi community that has been studied by Karen Isaksen Leonard (1994), and the same can be said about marriages between Chicano/a/xs and Korean Americans or Filipino Americans.[5]

As the twenty-first century unfolds, the noted population trends in California can be confirmed by a number of parameters. To employ an example from of my own institution, the University of California Merced, student enrollments reveal a 20.5 percent Asian/Pacific Islander (with a vast Asian majority within that group) and 53.3 percent Latino/a/x (overwhelmingly of Mexican descent) matriculation, for a combined 73.8 percent of the entire student body.[6] Even this anecdotal piece of evidence serves as a hint of the dimensions that this new mestizaje may take in the coming decades.

Among the authors who have written about the evolution from past to future mestizajes, Alejandro Morales stands out for his sustained and rich envisioning of Asian-Chicano/a/x cultural and biological blendings. He is the author of nine books, published between 1975 and 2014.[7] His novels and short stories typically combine rather explicit passages on death, sex, and violence with a dystopian, lyrical vein that keeps the reader unsettled between the crudest kind of realism and an intangible—yet recurring—idealism. Morales' topics and settings range from a depiction of daily life in marginal(ized) neighborhoods in the Los Angeles area (e.g., *Caras viejas y vino nuevo* [1975]) to exploring foundational moments of Chicano/a/x history (as in *Reto en el paraíso* [1983] and *The Brick People* [1988]).

But the novel that best reflects his deep interrogation of cultural identity, mestizaje, the future, as well as environmental degradation, is *The Rag Doll Plagues*, published (perhaps not coincidentally) in 1992, the year of the significant and contested commemoration of the arrival of Christopher Columbus to the Americas five hundred years earlier. As if to further cement that connection, *The Rag Doll Plagues* is divided into three books, entitled "Mexico City," "Delhi," and "Lamex," which all take place between the geographical/urban referents of Los Angeles and Mexico City, though at different periods of time, from the colonial era to the late twenty-first century. The tripartite division, in this context, inevitably recalls Mexican novelist Carlos Fuentes' ambitious work *Terra Nostra*, which includes a variation of Julius Caesar's description of Gaul as an epigraph (*terra nostra divisa est in partes tres*—our land is divided into three parts). This connection seems especially appropriate since Morales also employed an epigraph from *Terra Nostra* in *The Brick People*, thus confirming his familiarity with Fuentes' novel.[8] As much as Fuentes' work can be described as a "collision between the Old World and the New" (Goytisolo, 224; my translation), Morales' *The Rag Doll Plagues* begins as a collision between those two worlds. It then proceeds to consider the twentieth-century coming together of (or additional collision between) Indigenous/Spanish America and Anglo America, to finally envision a future in which the Asian/Chicano/a/x mestizaje could take place—that is, with the exception of miscegenation with the African population of the Americas (which plays only a background role in the novel). *Rag Doll Plagues* can be read as a history of the successive waves of mestizaje that have shaped and transformed Chicano/a/x identity. The tripartite geographical division invoked by Fuentes becomes in Morales a temporal structuring device that permits chronicling the history of mestizaje in Lamex, a land stretching from Mexico City to Los Angeles.

The first part of the novel, "Mexico City," takes place in colonial New Spain as the eighteenth century is about to end. Viceroy Juan Vicente de Güemes, the second count of Revillagigedo, is in charge of the Spanish colony. Not without a certain degree of exaggeration, Morales subjects this historical figure to a rather harsh depiction, presenting him as a weak and inefficient leader. As a consequence, Mexico City languishes in the most abject kind of neglect and abandonment. Sanitary conditions are dire, which results in a widespread plague that turns its victims into virtual human rag dolls. No cure is known for the disease, prompting the court authorities to send Doctor Gregorio Revueltas directly from Spain, as newly appointed director of the *protomedicato*, to combat the epidemic. Revueltas is Morales' narrator in this first part of the novel, and he spares the reader no details on his racist views and loathing of mestizaje. Thus, standing for the first time in front of the vice regal palace, Revueltas contrasts the beauty of its art decorations with the ugliness of city dwellers:

> The cherub's golden wings shimmered in the afternoon sun, which passed over the center of the Main Plaza, and contrasted with the filthy central fountain where Indians, Mestizos, Negroes, Mulattoes and the other immoral racial mixtures of humanity drank and filled clay jugs with foul dark water while they socialized. (11)

Don Gregorio nonetheless ends up acclimating to this multiracial New Spain, which he later considers his adoptive country. His identity transformation is so profound that, at the end of this segment of the novel, he refuses to return to Spain to marry his Castilian fiancée, Renata. The utopian discourse associated with mestizaje is focused, then, on don Gregorio's newly found tolerance for miscegenation and, more precisely, on the character of Mónica Marisela, the daughter of Viceroy Juan Vicente de Güemes and an unidentified lover whose description, nonetheless, suggest an identity (at least partly) indigenous to New Spain. This first part closes with Revueltas' affirmation of his new identity and of the utopian hope that the young girl represents a product of the union of the old world and the new: "I kissed Mónica Marisela and I heard liberation in her innocent giggle, which offered a new century in my new country" (66). In referring to New Spain as "*my* new country" [emphasis mine], don Gregorio exemplifies what I have analyzed elsewhere as the liminal moment of transition or crossing from the space of the nation to a denationalized zone that permits the adoption of new, original identities (Martín-Rodríguez 1996, 89).

The plot of the second part of *Rag Doll Plagues*, called "Delhi," unfolds during the last decades of the twentieth century in the Los Angeles area. Its narrator/protagonist is another physician, named Gregory Revueltas, a descendant of don Gregorio. Gregory and his girlfriend (a Jewish woman named Sandra Spears) lose the child that Sandra was expecting. Just as don Gregorio, Sandra experiences a profound personal and cultural transformation toward the end of her life, and she ends up being considered (and revered) by the local Chicano/a/x population as one of them. Beyond Los Angeles, Sandra and Gregory travel to Mexico in search of a cure for a disease she suffers from. There, they discover deep personal connections with the pre-Hispanic past, as well as with don Gregorio's own feelings, as expressed in his personal diaries, which the couple reads during their Mexican sojourn. Unfortunately, Sandra dies of AIDS-related ailments later on in the novel.

At first, "Delhi" appears not to share in the utopian vision of mestizaje with which the first part of the book concludes. Gregory and Sandra are childless, and so apparently are their closest friends. None of the couples mentioned in this second book produces a twentieth-century Mónica Marisela who could represent a better future. A more careful reading, however, reveals Morales' strategic placing of the symbolic coming together of races in an almost oblique manner. The setting takes place at the wedding of one of Sandra's relatives. Don Gregorio's earlier intransigence and racism are echoed here in comments uttered by Sandra's father: "I just don't know about these mixed race marriages. He's the first one on your side of the family to . . ." (74). For the reader, the reference remains incomprehensible until Gregory adds more information: "[Sandra's] uncle came in from the side entrance and on his head was her brown very curly hair. Down the aisle marched a stunning Asian woman" (74).

Beyond whatever tinges of orientalism may contaminate Alejandro Morales' utopian vision,[9] his invitation to look at the Pacific area as the source of the next wave of mestizaje is confirmed in the third and final part of the novel, entitled "Lamex." The action takes place at the end of the twenty-first century, at a time in which Mexico, the United States, and Canada have merged politically. Lamex, then, refers to the territory between by Mexico City (where the first book of the novel takes place) and Los Angeles (the setting for the second). The older plagues of La Mona and AIDS are now replaced by devastating eco-epidemics brought about by tons of trash and toxic spillages that constantly threaten the inhabited areas of this borderless entity—in which, ironically, class divisions have sharpened.

The protagonist/narrator, also named Gregory Revueltas, is a physician like his ancestors. The world he inhabits is ruled by technological inventions (his partner and lover, Gabi Chung, has a robotic forearm, for instance), but Gregory refuses to abandon the humanistic values of the past, here represented by the printed books of his ancestors. As medical director of the Lamex health corridor, Gregory accidentally discovers a cure for one of the deadly plagues: those afflicted are cured when they receive blood transfusions from Mexicans born and raised in Mexico City (MCMs, in the terminology of the novel). Because of the sustained environmental degradation in that city, its residents have developed a mutation that drastically lowers their red blood cell levels.

Despite this apparent reterritorialization that seems to privilege Mexican-ness, the twenty-first-century world of *Rag Doll Plagues* is profoundly mestizo and deterritorialized. As the narrator explains in some detail, "Monterey Park/East Los Angeles was a center for Mexican/Asian culture. Chinese, Japanese, Koreans and Southeast Asians had migrated in great numbers at the turn of the century. The Chinese had become the dominant force in sheer numbers" (148). This explanation goes on to occupy the entire page, with additional details about the arrival of millions of Chinese nationals to the Los Angeles area. Once there, "in order to survive and coexist, the Mexicans and Asians united economically, politically, culturally and racially. The common cross-cultural, racial marriages were between Asians and Mexicans" (148). From that point forward, and in a much more developed manner than in books 1 and 2, the environment and mestizaje become conjoined in the novel, especially because the question of whether to produce biological offspring is partly predicated on calculations regarding the likelihood of survival in a world that has lost its ecological balance. This is clearly apparent in the predicament experienced by Ted Chen (a third-generation Chinese American) and his wife Amalia (a California-born Mexican) who, in principle, could provide the novel with the Mónica Marisela of the twenty-first century. But their reservations about environmental degradation and the ensuing plagues result in a deep hesitation about having children.

In this context, it is easy to see that the epidemics that Morales describes in his book are not to be understood just at face value, as a series of environmental/medical disasters. Their symbolic significance is also worth analyzing because, if the body is "a site of signification—the place for the inscription of stories—and itself a signifier, a prime agent in narrative plot and meaning" (Brooks 1993, 5–6), then it could be argued that the sick body in this novel is both a site of signification and a signifier of the transcultural encounter between hegemonic and subaltern subjectivities. It is both a symbol and a symptom of threats to the integrity of the dominant powers. It is only through contact with disease and epidemics that changes in identity and national affiliation come about in the three worlds inhabited by the successive Gregorio/Gregory Revueltas. Don Gregorio, as he combats La Mona, ceases to see himself as a Spaniard and sees in the mestiza Mónica Marisela the seeds of hope for an independent (and mestizo) Mexico. The first of the two Gregorys, while combating AIDS, travels to a Mexico that he can no longer consider home. Somewhat paradoxically, his disconnect from the land of his ancestors can only be remedied through the intervention of Sandra Spears. The ensuing double process of deterritorialization is best summarized in the following quote, in which we are told that Gregory fails to find his ancestral roots in Mexico. Instead, what he encounters are deeply transformed cultural roots that hybridize Mexican identity while destabilizing (to a certain extent) his own Chicano identity:

> Enchanted by the city, we eagerly allowed our minds to be invaded by a kind of a collective hypnosis. A reverie brought about by a continuous differentiation of the old and the new . . . and the faces of people who represented nomadic Mesoamerican, European, African and Asian cultures. These were the Mexicans, inheritors of the world's cultural tribes. (115)

The Mexicans that Gregory encounters there are not the descendants of the Aztecs or the Mayas, lineages that were venerated and embraced during the Chicano Movement, but immigrants from four continents.[10] At first, the reader may be tempted to think that Morales is invoking the influential Chicano Movement notion of the Cosmic Race, as coined by José Vasconcelos. Instead of the syncretism implied in Vasconcelos' (2017) concept on the fusion of all previous cultures and races into the Mexican race, what Morales emphasizes here is nomadism, not arrival; process, not product.[11]

As for the second Gregory, who lives during the late twenty-first century, his discovery of a cure for one of the powerful pandemics results in the fact that, for the first time in the history of the three amalgamated countries, the hegemonic group's survival literally depends on the blood of its subalterns. In light of the recent waves of massive deportations and of the limitations in access to medical and social services by immigrants, not without a good dose of irony, Morales' narrator delights in stating that all the rich families in Lamex fight for the opportunity to have a couple of Mexico City Mexicans at home. In this manner, *Rag Doll Plagues* subverts dominant perceptions of the foreign and/or the subaltern subject as a potential agent of disease that needs to be examined prior to admission into the res publica. Now the subaltern and the foreigner are objects of desire, precisely for their health benefits.

When we consider all three geographical/historical scenarios invoked in *Rag Doll Plagues* of colonial New Spain, California/Mexico in the twentieth century, and a twenty-first century that fuses spaces to create new geopolitical entities, it becomes quite possible to read Morales' novel as a rejection of millenarist anxieties that construe immigrants as both a physical and metaphysical danger to the nation. Instead, the novel appears to suggest that crossing borders and worlds has been the norm rather than the exception throughout history, and that migration and mestizaje benefit the nation and ensure the future of its population. Likewise, disease (especially that which results from ecological degradation) ceases here to be a problem associated with those underdeveloped areas of the planet from which modern migrants depart to become instead a product of the *First World*— a consequence of unrestrained production and unsustainable consumerism.

To that effect, the third book of the novel offers us the contrasting examples of Gabi Chung on the one hand and Ted and Amalia Chen on the other. Gabi is a firm believer in the positive value of technological advances, as well as in the new hierarchical relations that they bring about. Not surprisingly, in order to advance professionally, she volunteers to have a computerized arm implanted. Notwithstanding previous feminist conceptualizations of the cyborg, most notably Donna Haraway's "A Cyborg Manifesto" (1985), Gabi's decision is presented in the novel as a false mestizaje, a combination of human and machine that literally and metaphorically dehumanizes her.[12] As the novel advances, mechanical failures of the robotic arm result in the need for frequent charging, which in turn produces serious consequences for Gabi's body to the point that her arrival anywhere is said to be preceded by the distinct smell of burnt flesh. Mindful of the consistent and distressing failure of that mechanical hybridization, Gabi sadly commits suicide by fatally increasing the voltage of her robotic arm's charger.

On the other hand, Ted and Amalia opt for an alternate route that joins not only their respective ethnic origins but also the past and present. For them, the only sustainable future is one in which humanity ceases to produce tons of waste while learning to reuse and recycle materials. As the owners of a restaurant located on the first floor of their home, Ted and Alicia serve as mediators between the privileged world of Gregory and Gabi and that of the downtrodden of the twenty-first century, especially those who inhabit the gigantic neighborhood of the dumpster, a so-called Lower Life Existence Concentration known as El Mar de Villas. An abandoned freeway, whose construction must have resulted in the displacement of the inhabitants of an earlier neighborhood, serves as access to this barrio.[13] The road is punctuated by numerous crosses marking the deaths of victims of diseases provoked by toxic waste. The first time Gregory enters El Mar de Villas, accompanied by Ted and Amalia, he is taken aback by the chromatic objects and the people's ability to recycle discarded materials:

> I had never visited such a remarkable space. The practicality of the objects was simple. What struck me were the brilliant windows made from the glass of broken bottles. Ted and Amalia, who had never traveled this far into the Lower Life Existence concentration, had been mute since we began our ingress. (173)

The significance of this strategy of recycling, of converting the past into both present and future, may be better understood alongside the ideas presented by Chela Sandoval in her *Methodology of the Oppressed* (2000). According to Sandoval, as part of the development of an oppositional consciousness to negotiate cultural and financial globalization,

> people of color in the United States, familiar with historical, subjective, and political dislocation since the founding of the colonies, have created a set of inner and outer technologies to enable survival within the developing state apparatus, technologies that will be of great value during the cultural and economic changes to come. (79)

Unlike the brave new world represented by Gabi Chung and industrial technological advances, the survival strategies of the dwellers of El Mar de Villas point more toward the kind of technologies referenced by Sandoval, in the *Rasquache* tradition of making do with what one has. Theirs is a world in which, as Renato Rosaldo has also discussed in a different context (1989), the swap meet replaces the museum, a perfect image of the postcolonial momentum in which cultural artifacts circulate through unexpected sites and circuits while nothing remains sacred or immutable.

The ensuing effect of spiritual nourishment that Gregory experiences upon entering El Mar de Villas is complemented by actual food ingested at Ted and Amalia's restaurant. There, "Ted prepared a succulent meal of Mexican and Chinese cuisine. I had never tasted such exquisite flavors. I probably had not eaten for days. My body had adjusted to ingesting little food, but today I felt as if

I could never be satisfied" (175). Rather than utilizing traditional ethnic foods as a reterritorialization strategy, as it had been all too common in 1960s and 1970s Chicano/a/x literature, *Rag Doll Plagues* deterritorializes even food, which is now presented as a telling synthesis of Asian and Mexican cuisine.[14]

In contrast with the artificial mestizaje represented by Gabi, then, Ted and Amalia opt for a blending of cultures of past and present that strengthens ecological balance, rather than impacting it in a negative manner. Chapter 18, only two paragraphs long, is eloquent in this regard. The first paragraph recalls Gabi's suicide, while narrating the transformation of Gregory into one of the leaders of El Mar de Villas; the second announces Amalia's pregnancy. Gabi's death and the impossibility of living a life like hers is thus contrasted with Amalia's (and Ted's) respectful and responsible approach to procreation and life.

As the novel advances, the increasing political influence of the inhabitants of El Mar de Villas secures a position of power for Gregory. His workspace is now an old library full of printed volumes from the past. In it, he reflects on the future, represented by the Mexican-Asian mestizaje: "From up here, surrounded by thousands of books, I wonder when will I have time to love a woman and have children, like normal people did in the late twentieth century. I can only protect and enjoy Ted and Amalia's baby, for that child represents the hope for the new millennium" (199–200). The third book, therefore, closes in a similar manner to the ending of the first, that is, with an adult who represents the (now deterritorialized) old order considering the symbolism of the mestizo child as a symbol of the new order.[15] The main difference between the two books is that mestizaje has now taken a Pacific-Asian turn.

Morales' new and original understanding of Chicano/a/x mestizaje has attracted relatively little attention, even though the novel was published almost three decades ago, and even though I first alluded to this element twenty-two years ago in "The Global Border" (1996, 92). Only Stephen Hong Sohn has suggested the convenience of considering the triangle Mexico/USA/the Pacific from the perspective of what he terms "relational identity politics" (2012, 175) in order to begin exploring "the Asian Pacific American Borderlands" (174). But Sohn, who writes from the perspective of Queer Theory, is rather critical of the idea of a mestizaje based on heterosexual normative reproduction, as proposed by Morales.[16]

This apparent lack of critical interest is even more significant if we consider the way in which academic discourse has moved from discussing mestizaje in more or less biological terms to conceptualizing the so-called critical mestizaje. In his book on this topic, for instance, Rafael Pérez-Torres (2006) asserts:

Mestizaje occupies a valued position in Chicana critical discourse because, as a descriptive term and a cultural practice, it helps embody the idea of multiple subjectivities. Moreover, mestizaje signals the embodiedness of history. As such, it opens a world of possibilities in terms of forging new relational identities. (3)[17]

In turn, though he does not refer to Morales' transnational vision, Juan E. de Castro studies the uses of mestizaje for the creation of national identities, including the teleological process of nation-building (2002). On that latter aspect, Pérez-Torres astutely observes that, while in Mexico the process of nation-building entailed a rejection of the native in favor of the mestizo, Chicano/a/xs actually embraced the indigenous component of their identity in conceptualizing the nation of Aztlán (6). However, as suggested by Mary Pat Brady's (2002) study of nineteenth-century journalists, that search for the indigenous roots during the Chicano Movement was also fraught with issues of temporal amnesia. According to Brady, "the affirmation of mestizaje, of Aztec ancestors, depends on its deferral into the past, establishing a temporal shield of sorts through a denial of contemporary relations, of ongoing mestizaje" (36). This suggests that Pérez-Torres' analytical framework may be more useful for studying literature from the 1960s and 1970s, rather than more contemporary novels like *Rag Doll Plagues*. In fact, it could be argued that contemporary literary discourse on mestizaje (Morales' novel included) moves away from the rural environments up to that time associated with indigenous peoples to search for new mestizo positionalities in multicultural urban centers.

The multiple subjectivities to which Pérez-Torres alludes have expanded from an Atlantic-centered notion of mestizaje to one that is based on the Pacific as well, suggesting the strategy of developing a trans-Pacific Chicano/a/x literary criticism and theory. Even though this study concentrates on *Rag Doll Plagues*, other works could be closely examined in future contributions to trans-Pacific Chicano/a/x studies. These include works such as Rolando Hinojosa's *Korean Love Songs from Klail City Death Trip*, which considers the transculturation of Chicano soldiers as they dwell and even decide to remain in Asia; the experience of folklorist and author Américo Paredes who fought in World War II and considered remaining in Japan afterwards; the work of filmmaker Michael Arias, the son of Chicano novelist Ron Arias and director of *Tekkonkinkreet*, among others (himself the father of two Chicano-Japanese children); as well as other texts not yet brought to wider public attention, including the anthology *XicKorea: Poems,*

Rants, Words Together, featuring poems by San Francisco Bay Area authors Beth Ching, Arnoldo García, and Miriam Ching Yoon Louie.[18]

Literary texts like these, but most significantly *Rag Doll Plagues,* are exceptional examples of the new processes generated when we stop thinking about history in purely terrestrial ways and recenter our focus instead on Atlantic-Pacific oceanic notions as loci for unique cultural and identarian positionalities and transformations within a modernized sense of mestizaje. More precisely, they emblematize the present and future Pacific-based Chicano/a/x mestizaje. They scrutinize it from an ecocritical perspective that stresses the need for the kind of regeneration that immigration and mestizaje produce. At the same time, they decry the effects of environmental degradation, particularly as they result in issues of environmental justice that affect certain groups more than others. Perhaps for this very reason, Morales' *Rag Doll Plagues* and some of the other texts briefly alluded to here argue that mestizaje is not connected to territorial conquest and occupation; rather, it remains open to the maritime ebbs and flows that bring together remote—and formerly distant—shores to create bridged peoples.

NOTES

1. The term "Chicano" has undergone multiple transformations as a result of critical and popular challenges to its ability to truly represent the people it has come to designate. Chicanas first called attention to the fact that they did not see themselves represented in a term ending in the masculine "o." Alternative labels such as Chicana/o, Chican@, and other variations were adopted. More recently, additional endings have been recognized by some to account for alternative subjectivities and sexualities, with "Chicanx" currently becoming a widespread term. Gender and sexual inclusiveness, however, has resulted in additional issues, among them the fact that a term like "Chicanx" erases the Spanish language ending, thereby undoing decades of proud reclamation of that language by Chicanas and Chicanos. My preference is to employ the term "Chicano/a/x," which visually represents the successive terms and challenges, thus visually preserving the history of the term while maintaining visible its Spanish root. It is also worth keeping in mind that inclusiveness and disenfranchisement are sociohistorical (rather than just grammatical) processes, and that nongrammatically gendered terms like "American" or "Mexican" are not necessarily more inclusive than grammatically gendered ones.

2. Mestizaje has been a keystone of Mexican identity since, at least, independence from Spain. As Robert Young observes, "It is under [Porfirio] Díaz, then, that *mestizaje* achieves its apotheosis, and becomes the norm of both a hegemonic nationalization of

identity and a sovereign institutionalization of state" (1994, 88). It is worth noting that the centrality of mestizaje continued during the Mexican Revolution of 1910–1920, a period that exerted a strong influence on Chicano/a/xs.

3. See, for instance, José E. Limón's (1977) study on *agringado* jokes.

4. United States Census Bureau, "Quick Facts," http://quickfacts.census.gov/qfd/states/06000.html, accessed August 22, 2018.

5. See Williams-León and Nakashima (2001).

6. "Undergraduate Students by Ethnicity," University of California Merced, http://www.ucmerced.edu/fast-facts, accessed August 22, 2019.

7. Morales is writing a new novel, set in Japan (personal communication).

8. On the significance of that other epigraph, see Gutiérrez-Jones (1995, 82ff).

9. On this aspect, see Sohn (2012), in which the author criticizes gender and sexuality elements in the novel, which he finds marred by a heterosexist optic (167–69).

10. The poet Alurista and playwright Luis Valdez were among the first to popularize this indigenous quality in Chicano/a/x literature. They believed that the indigenous cultural root was part of the Chicano/a/x unconscious and that literature could be the means to bring that past to the fore. That, in turn, would generate a feeling of ethnic/cultural pride that would help Chicano/a/xs cope with oppressive conditions in the present (Martín-Rodríguez, 1993, 113–15).

11. Morales' views on culture are, therefore, similar to those that Paul Gilroy characterizes as "rhizomorphic, routed, diaspora cultures" in *The Black Atlantic* (1994, 28).

12. Marc Priewe suggests that, in this sense, Gabi serves as a dissuasory model for Gregory (2004, 406). Stephen Sohn, in turn, interprets this characterization as an example of the stereotype of the model minority (2012, 164–65). R. Garay, in turn, labels Gabi a "technological Malinche" (2012, 156), as she criticizes Morales' perpetuation of gender hierarchies inherited from the Chicano Movement period.

13. The displacement of Chicano/a/x communities by the construction of freeways or by other kinds of urban developments is a frequent theme in Chicano/a/x/ literature. Raúl Homero Villa's *Barrio-Logos* (2000) provides a detailed analysis.

14. Martín-Rodríguez (2000, 39–40).

15. In "The Politics of Blood," López-Lozano (2003) observes that none of the three Gregorys has children with the respective female protagonists of each book. For him, this results in "a conflictive and contradictory reading of *mestizaje* as an answer to the ills of a world that remains socially stratified" (41). Yet, as I hope to have demonstrated in this study, Morales exemplifies the respective mestizajes through other couples' unions, reserving for the three doctors the more distant role of observers/historians.

16. In addition, perhaps as the result of an all-too-quick reading of the existing scholarship, Sohn fails to give credit to or engage with some earlier critical contributions that had considered Morales' Pacific-oriented thematics.

17. In his book, Pérez-Torres uses "Chicano" and "Chicana" indistinctly, as non-marked gender terms.

18. For an analysis of *XicKorea*, see Martín-Rodríguez (2015, 435–37).

WORKS CITED

Arias, Michael, dir. 2006. *Tekkonkinkreet*. Studio 4oC.

Brady, Mary Pat. 2002. *Extinct Lands, Temporal Geographies: Chicana Literature and the Urgency of Space*. Durham, NC: Duke University Press.

Brooks, Peter. 1993. *Body Work: Objects of Desire in Modern Narrative*. Cambridge, MA: Harvard University Press.

Castro, Juan E. de. 2002. *Mestizo Nations: Culture, Race, and Conformity in Latin American Literature*. Tucson: University of Arizona Press.

Ching, Beth, Arnoldo García, and Miriam Ching Yoon. 2002. *XicKorea: Poems, Rants, Words Together*. Oakland, CA: Xingao Productions.

Fuentes, Carlos. 2003. *Terra Nostra*. United Kingdom: Dalkey Archive Press.

Garay, R., and Z. L. Joyce. 2013. "Reading Alejandro Morales's The Rag Doll Plagues through Its Women: Gender, Sexuality, and Nationalistic Complexity." *Bilingual Review / Revista Bilingüe* 31, no. 2 (May 2012–August 2013): 141–65.

Gilroy, Paul. 1994. *The Black Atlantic: Modernity and Double Consciousness*. Cambridge, MA: Harvard University Press.

Goytisolo, Juan. 2013. *Disidencias*. Pamplona: Leer-e.

Gutiérrez-Jones, Carl Scott. 1995. *Rethinking the Borderlands: Between Chicano Culture and Legal Discourse*. Berkeley: University of California Press.

Haraway, Donna. 1985. "A Manifesto for Cyborgs: Science, Technology, and Socialist Feminism in the 1980s." *Socialist Review* 80:65–108.

Hinojosa, Rolando. 1980. *Korean Love Songs: From Klail City Death Trip*. Berkeley, CA: Justa.

Leonard, Karen Isaksen. 1994. *Making Ethnic Choices: California's Punjabi Mexican Americans*. Philadelphia: Temple University Press.

Limón, José E. 1977. "Agringado Joking in Texas Mexican Society: Folklore and Differential Identity." *New Scholar* 6:33–50.

López-Lozano, Miguel. "The Politics of Blood: Miscegenation and Phobias of Contagion in Alejandro Morales's *The Rag Doll Plagues*." *Aztlán: A Journal of Chicano Studies* 28, no. 1 (Spring 2003): 39–73.

Martín-Rodríguez, Manuel M. 1993. "Aesthetic Concepts of Hispanics in the United States." In *Handbook of Hispanic Cultures in the United States: Literature and Art*, edited by Francisco A. Lomelí, 109–33. Houston: Arte Público Press.

———. 1996. "The Global Border: Transnationalism and Cultural Hybridism in

Alejandro Morales's *The Rag Doll Plagues*." *Bilingual Review / Revista Bilingüe* 20, no. 3 (September–December): 86–98.

———. 2000. "The Raw and Who Cooked It: Food, Identity, and Culture in U.S. Latino/a Literature." In *U.S. Latino Literatures and Cultures: Transnational Perspectives*, edited by Francisco A. Lomelí and Karen Ikas, 37–51. Heidelberg: Universitätsverlag C. Winter.

———. 2015. "El Pacífico que viene: Futuro, identidad cultural y ecocrítica en la literatura chicana de fin de siglo." In *Conocer el Pacífico: Exploraciones, imágenes y formación de sociedades oceánicas*, edited by Salvador Bernabéu Albert, Carmen Mena García, and Emilio José Luque Azcona, 423–38. Seville: Editorial Universidad de Sevilla.

Morales, Alejandro. 1975. *Caras viejas y vino nuevo*. Mexico City: Joaquín Mortiz.

———. 1983. *Reto en el paraíso*. Ypsilanti, MI: Bilingual Press / Editorial Bilingüe.

———. 1988. *The Brick People*. Houston: Arte Público Press.

———. 1992. *The Rag Doll Plagues*. Houston: Arte Público Press.

Pérez-Torres, Rafael. 2006. *Mestizaje: Critical Uses of Race in Chicano Culture*. Minneapolis: University of Minnesota Press.

Priewe, Marc. 2004. "Bio-Politics and the ContamiNation of the Body in Alejandro Morales' *The Rag Doll Plagues*." *MELUS* 29, nos. 3–4 (Autumn–Winter): 397–412.

Rosaldo, Renato. 1989. *Culture and Truth: The Remaking of Social Analysis*. Boston: Beacon.

Sandoval, Chela. 2000. *Methodology of the Oppressed*. Minneapolis: University of Minnesota Press.

Sohn, Stephen Hong. 2012. "Minor Character, Minority Orientalisms, and the Borderlands of Asian America." *Cultural Critique* 82 (Fall): 151–85.

Vasconcelos, José. 2017. *La Raza Cósmica*. Mexico City: Porrúa.

Villa, Raúl Homero. 2000. *Barrio-Logos: Space and Place in Urban Chicano Literature and Culture*. Austin: University of Texas Press.

Williams-León, Teresa, and Cynthia L. Nakashima, eds. 2001. *The Sum of Our Parts: Mixed Heritage Asian Americans*. Philadelphia: Temple University Press.

Young, Robert. 1994. *Colonial Desire: Hybridity in Theory, Culture, and Race*. New York: Routledge.

TWELVE / Translation as Rewriting and Resituating / The Two English Versions of *Caras viejas y vino nuevo* by Alejandro Morales / ELENA ERRICO

INTRODUCTION

This article compares the two existing translations into English of *Caras viejas y vino nuevo* (1975, henceforth ST), Alejandro Morales' first novel.[1] The text, a recent rare example of Chicano literature written entirely in Spanish, is regarded as a pioneering work because, quite apart from the literary production connected to El Movimiento, it depicts a sordid and disturbing image of Latinos, in sharp contrast with the edifying identity discourse that had previously dominated the Chicano literary scene (Lomelí 1996; Morales 1995). In Morales' words, *Caras* is "one of the first barrio gang novels" (1995, 17), in which extreme violence and marginalization in the barrio are explicitly narrated, often dwelling on sexual and scatological details. Initially, *Caras* was not received favorably, so much so that the author could not find any publisher in the United States willing to accept the book and ended up publishing it in Mexico. Probably the obstacle was as much its extreme stylistic experimentalism as the theme it dealt with. Francisco Lomelí, who produced the latest translation (henceforth TT2), points out that "the Chicano reading public was simply not prepared to receive such striking depictions of the hard-core barrio, with its crude, graphic details imbedded in a language that resisted itself" (Lomelí 1998, 5).

The plot of *Caras* starts with the death of Julián, one of the two main characters, in a car crash. His life on the edge, prey to addictions, gets worse as a result of his mother's death, due to his sense of guilt for making her suffer and the rejection of the new relationship his father started, which causes Julián to confront him with the help of his friends, the Buenasuerte brothers, who are usually on drugs. While these are circumstances that cause the car crash, the rest of the novel is basically a flashback exploring the factors that led to this tragic outcome.

Morales describes his novel as "written in a convoluted Spanish that offered a vision de un mundo torcido" (1995, 17). His narrative and stylistic experimentalism can be identified at various discursive levels, such as a syntactic fragmentation with a prevalence of short utterances that are often elliptical and merely juxtaposed with each other (Lomelí 1998), an extended use of synecdoche (body parts for individuals), the personalization of objects, and the overlapping of different voices and perspectives, which makes it difficult to identify who is speaking due to the absence of text markers signaling this information (Albaladejo Martínez 2007). In addition, the overuse of semicolons in short utterances seems to define a narrative rhythm that resembles more film technique than written texts (Lomelí 1998, 9).

Below we reproduce the start of the novel, in which Julián recalls his late mother with affection and commotion:

> Ella siempre ha sido alguien a quien podía correr para seguridad y ayuda. Es una mujer maravillosa, una gran mujer que ha criado muchachos que no son tan mal. Es inteligente; habla bien el idioma de estas partes y tiene amigas en todas las tiendas del pueblo. Viste bien y con su pelo que se le hace más y más canoso anda, habla y actúa como una reina.
>
>   La madre de Julián era todo esto y más para él. Pero todavía había algo en la vida o en ellos que les prohibía expresar libre y exteriormente un amor cariñoso. Su madre lo quería y su amor se manifestaba en todo lo que hacía para él y la familia. Como su esposo, ella también era muy gritona; les gritaba mucho a los dos muchachos. Esto era bueno; su esposo lo hacía para enderezar a los dos muchachos, para hacerles obedecer; por eso lo hacía. Era de filosofía moderna, para corregir a un niño era necesario amarlo; sin embargo, veía que Julián se estaba perdiendo y ella trataba de indicarle el camino de buena astilla; trató hasta la hora de la muerte, trató de ayudarle a su hijo. No hay nadie en el mundo que pueda describir los sentimientos de una madre, lo que siente una madre al perder un hijo.
>
>   Julián sabía; el vivía con esa pena de saber que había lastimado a su madre

muchísimo; yo tengo que proteger la memoria de mi madre. No quería que doña Matilde viviera en la misma casa con su padre. (ST, 25)

Syntactically the structure is quite simple: sentences are short and mainly joined by coordination, often without explicit connectives and separated by semicolons. According to the *Diccionario panhispánico de dudas* (*DPD*), the use of this punctuation mark in Spanish is the most highly dependent on subjectivity, since most of the time it can be replaced with other punctuation marks (full stop, colon, or comma). In general, however, if the semantic link between the two utterances is weak, the semicolon is preferred as opposed to the full stop.[2] The *DPD* description focuses on the fuzzy and ambiguous nature of this punctuation sign and in general on the idea of a certain continuity between utterances when it is employed. In this case the semicolon functions as a cohesion resource in combination with the extensive—even obsessive—use of different forms of repetition.[3] The semicolon is also preferred to introduce perspective changes, when one would expect at least a full stop: in "él vivía con esa pena de saber que había lastimado a su madre muchísimo; yo tengo que proteger la memoria de mi madre," the transition from the free indirect speech to the interior monologue takes place by mere juxtaposition and a weak pause marked by the semicolon. This voice overlapping and alternating between the narration in the past and in the present is expressed using the comma. In the given example, it is not clear if "era de filosofía moderna" is part of the narrator's description, if it is a fragment of Julián's free indirect speech, or if it is a fragment of his mother's free indirect speech, like the following utterance: "para corregir a un niño era necesario amarlo."

I have referred to the peculiar utilization of punctuation in the novel because it arises from a stylistic motivation similar to that of the extensive selection of *imperfecto narrativo*, a stylistically marked use of Spanish *imperfecto* in literary fiction. In his introduction to *Caras*, Lomelí argues that the presence of this verb form expresses the idea of time indeterminacy and adds a sense of chaos and absence of limits to the text (Lomelí 1996; 1998).[4] He incorporates the translation solutions he adopts into English, a language whose verb system lacks an equivalent form to render the imperfecto, linking it to a change of attitude toward Morales' writing that brought about a translation that retained as much as possible the harshness of the source text. The first translation, by Max Martínez (henceforth TT1), adopts a more didascalic approach, which according to Lomelí, "facilitated the accessibility of the work but fundamentally altered its effect" (1998, 19). In the TT1 fragments I analyze here, the *imperfecto* is translated almost solely as simple past, which does not convey the multiple aspect nuances of the Spanish original narrative form.

The authoritative translation decisions made by Lomelí in TT2 are illustrative of manipulation as conceptualized by the School of Manipulation in translation studies, that is, an active and deliberate intervention in the translation process, constrained in the first place by extratextual factors, namely power, ideology, and patronage (Lefevere 1992). According to Lefevere, translation is a form of rewriting and resituating that reflects a certain ideology and poetics. Ideology is defined as a set of habits, conventions, and worldviews that guide our actions, whereas poetics is as much an inventory of literary resources (genres, symbols, characters, prototypical situations, etc.) as an idea of what literature should be and what social role it should play (Lefevere 1982, 236). In the case studied, clearly TT2 was also the product of a change in these two factors, which brought about a more accurate and faithful treatment of Morales' novel. Patronage, according to Lefevere, is "the powers (persons, institutions) that can further or hinder the reading, writing, and rewriting of literature" (1992, 15). In this case Lomelí's proficiency in both languages assured the visibility of a translation at odds with the idea of fluency, intended as readability and normalization—the most popular approach in the editorial market (Venuti 2008).[5]

THE MARKED USE OF *PRETÉRITO IMPERFECTO* IN *CARAS*

It is crucial to identify textual evidence that confirms the different approaches adopted by the two translators, with a focus on the *imperfecto*. The prominent car crash episode at the beginning of the novel serves this purpose best.

The *pretérito imperfecto* tense occupies a peripheral position in the Spanish past tense system, as opposed to *pretérito indefinido*, which is considered the narrative tense par excellence given that it expresses the idea of action ended, of closure. This is because the habitual implication in a narration of past events is typically a concatenation of events taking place one after the end of the other. Imperfecto, on the contrary, expresses diverse nuances of meaning, including an incomplete perspective on states, actions, or processes (as indicated in the etymology from the Latin *imperfectus*, i.e., unfinished). One of the most telling examples of its expressive potential is found in the beginning of Gabriel García Márquez's *Crónica de una muerte anunciada* (1981). Here the coexistence of the backward movement of memory and the forward movement of announcement in the very title and the circular nature of the novel may be seen: "El día en que lo iban a matar, Santiago Nasar se levantó a las 5.30 de la mañana." The "ir a" construction conjugated in the imperfecto, unlike the other options ("mataron" or "matarían"), expresses a prediction in the past and thus helps retaining a sense of uncertainty and suspense until the end of the novel (which is already alluded to in its title).

Thanks to its aspects of openness and indeterminacy, imperfecto is used in a wide range of temporal references to add pragmatic connotations and as a grammatical metaphor even in contexts of present or future (Reyes 1990, 46). As Reyes affirms, "a past action, which is presented as being in progress, without including its start or end, is a 'suspended' action, prone to slide chronologically towards the present or the future, and also prone not to be an actual, real action" (47, my translation).[6]

In *Caras*, actions tend to be grammaticalized with the imperfecto, relying on the temporal ambiguity of this form. Actions are represented as limitless, closely connected to or even overlapping with prior or subsequent ones. As an example, notice this portion of the narrative just moments before the car crash:

> El pie estaba contra el hierro de abajo; ya no podía más, y la carcancha charenga llegó hasta cincuenta y cinco; el Turco no sentía el pie; apenas veía. ¡Venga sesenta! ¡Venga sesenta! ¡Chaaaahiii! ¡Qué curada! ¡Qué locura, qué enfermos, qué felicidad!
>
> Pero los gritos del Román no se distinguían de los gargatones y carcajadas de los otros. Miedo, terror tronaron. ¡Mamá! ¡Maamáa! ¡Ma . . . ma . . . máaaaa!
>
> Se hundió más el Turco en el espacio que ocupaba física y mentalmente; la cabeza y las manos que *conducían* el auto ya no lo *hacían*. (ST, 31; my emphasis)

At the end of the fragment there is a semantic inconsistency in that the copresence of two imperfectos narrativos would suggest that the two actions are simultaneous. However, they contradict each other: the conventional implication of "ya no" is that the action of the verb stops taking place, which clashes with the previous imperfecto, indicating the very same action. This anomaly triggers a nonliteral reading: As el Turco kept sitting on the driver's seat, he was probably still holding the steering wheel, but he did not really have control over his own actions, or he had simply stopped driving. The sense of chaos and indeterminacy is also accentuated by the alternation—abrupt and without any transition—between past narrative, direct speech, and interior monologue. Löbus (2015), who applied the categories identified by Brés (2005) for French to Spanish, classifies this as a cohesion resource, that is, a discursive means of emphasizing the connection between different actions. In *Caras*, cohesion is hardly ever achieved by means of complex syntax; rather, Morales arrives at it by an alternative means, such as the aforementioned semicolon, repetition, and imperfecto narrativo, whose aspect semantics also facilitates the coexistence of multiple voices belonging to different chronological moments with more "natural" transitions in terms of sequence of tenses between the present indicative of interior monologues and the narrative pasts (cf. the beginning of the novel).

Löbus also investigates the case when imperfectos designating actions coexist with canonical imperfectos, as happens in the aforementioned *Caras* fragment, where "estaba," "podía," "sentía," and "veía" describe states or dynamic events without delimitation and contextualize the main action. This is the core idea of the "discourse hypothesis" (Bardovi-Harlig 2002) that, on the basis of the notion of grounding, studies the language resources used by narrators to focus the target reader's attention on the major elements of the narrative. As a result, two strategies are established: the main action develops chronologically in the foreground, while secondary elements (the time and place of the action and the speaker's evaluation), which add extra information, remain in the background (Hopper 1982). According to this hypothesis, the perfectivity/imperfectivity contrast arises from the need to distinguish between foreground and background. The consistency between the idea of perfectivity and that of foreground lies in that a narrative usually develops according to a time sequence (i.e., an event starts after the previous has finished) and is thus more easily associated to telic verbs and perfective forms.[7] The background, on the contrary, is structured according to events whose end is not necessarily a prerequisite for the next to occur; hence they are usually in combination with stative and atelic situations. In marked uses, as it applies to *Caras*, the extensive use of imperfecto narrativo tends to merge the narrative plan (the foreground) with the background (context), "creating the impression that characters' actions belong there and are part of the space, they are no longer personified subjects" (Löbus 2015, 5). After all, depersonalization of human beings is a recurring element throughout the novel.

Imperfecto indeterminacy is all the more evident under a contrastive perspective, namely, when it comes to translating it into English. Spanish and English do not organize the perfective/imperfective aspect contrast in the same way and in English there is no equivalent for the pretérito imperfecto. However, there are various forms expressing categories of imperfectivity: the progressive aspect is grammaticalized with the past progressive (habitually with the forms "used to"/"would") and continuatively with the simple past. Moreover, in English the aspect distinction is neutralized for states. In *Caras*, this difference in verb systems poses a translation challenge, which is tackled in different ways in TT1 and TT2, as I argue later in this essay.

PRETÉRITO IMPERFECTO TRANSLATED IN *CARAS*

Lomelí points out that stylistic experimentation is a defining feature of *Caras* and thus he comments on his own translation strategies "to capture the author's original sense of experimentation as well as his Daedalian and, at times, deranged and disjointed virtuosity . . . and to recreate the explosive nature of the barrio—which is much like a time bomb—and its marginal condition, together with the author's unclear geographical allusions with an ambiguous construct of references" (Lomelí 1998). He intentionally interprets the choice of imperfecto in the ST as a resource aimed at giving a sense of urgency of a perpetual present, "an uncountable past that is approaching the present" (11). Consider these two translated versions of the fragment describing the moments just before the accident, where in TT2 source text peculiarities and ambiguities are all present:

| Se hundió más el Turco en el espacio que ocupaba física y mentalmente; la cabeza y las manos que conducían el auto ya no lo hacían. (ST, 31) | El Turco sank deeper into the space he occupied physically and mentally. The head and hands no longer steered the car. (TT1, 12) | El Turco sank even further physically and mentally into the space he occupied; the head and hands that drove the car no longer did so. (TT2, 32) |

Martínez deletes the contradictory utterance, whereas Lomelí preserves it, thus producing an equivalent effect despite the use of the past tense.

Moreover, note the following translation, where multiple voices overlap revealing the different solutions adopted to render imperfecto, which Lomelí translates with a past progressive:

| Manejaban su charenga muy felices. ¡Echa a la vieja fuera de casa! ¡Es una puta! (ST, 27) | They drove the heap happily. Kick the hag out of the house! ¡Es una puta! (TT1, 8) | They were happily driving their old clunker. Throw that ol' lady outta the house! She's a whore! (TT2, 26) |

Chapter Twelve **219**

Martínez's text sustains word-for-word the Spanish language expression ("¡Es una puta!"), which is possibly an attempt to exoticize and make more dynamic a target text that is overall very conventional.[8] In TT2 the translator does not utilize any bilingual resources, but rather uses an equivalent register in English, even emphasizing graphically nonstandard pronunciations (e.g., "Throw that ol' lady outta the house").[9]

In the following example, conversely, aspect dynamics in TT2 are expressed through a grammatical resource, the auxiliary *would*, which stresses the obsession of Julián's hatred:

| La mente de Julián se torcía de locura al oír los chismes y mentiras que decían los Buenasuerte. (ST, 25) | Julián's mind churned in fury upon hearing the rumors and lies the Buenasuertes told him. (TT1, 8) | Julián's mind would wrench with rage upon hearing the gossip and lies the Buenasuerte brothers told him. (TT2, 24) |

Below two verbs appear, "saber" and "vivir," whose semantics are inherently durative (referring to a state rather than an action):

| Julián knew. He lived with that pain. (TT1, 7) | Julián sabía; él vivía con esa pena. (ST, 24) | Julián knew it all along; he used to live with that grief. (TT2, 25) |

However, once again Lomelí conveys aspect traits, this time relying on syntax. Here he does so by means of a compensation in the first phrase, adding "all along," which makes more accurate the meaning of the past tense, and in the second "used to," which also emphasizes the idea of state that continues in the past (although in this case it seems to me fairly redundant).

In the following example, Max Martínez opts for a simpler solution, the literal translation ("to look" at for *mirar*). This impoverishes the utterance of the original imperfecto stylistic effect:[10]

| El muchacho miraba a doña Matilde.(ST, 29) | The young man looked at doña Matilde. (TT1, 10) | The young man glared at doña Matilde. (TT2, 28) |

In contrast, Lomelí comes up with a more sophisticated solution: while he retains the past tense, he selects a verb from the same semantic field as "mirar," which contains a semantic trait compatible with imperfectivity. "Glare" means "to look directly and continuously at someone or something in an angry way" (my emphasis)[11]. While the sema of rage is an addition, it makes sense if we think of the hatred Julián felt toward his stepmother.

The same semantic compensation mechanism exists with the following:

| Sin embargo, veía que Julián se estaba perdiendo y ella trataba de indicarle el camino de buena astilla (ST, 25) | Nevertheless she saw Julián was becoming lost and she tried to show him the right path. (TT1, 7) | However, she saw that Julián was going astray and she tried over and over again to show him the right path. (TT2, 24) |

In TT2 the simple past is enriched with the additional nuance of repeated effort provided by the adverbial phrase "over and over again," whereas in TT1 the verb aspect is not defined.

The following utterance describes Julián's aggression against his father, using solely *imperfecto narrativo*:

| Los nudillos de Julián sangraban y la sangre se mezclaba con la de su padre todavía gritándole y culpándolo; el mundo también lloraba. Las sirenas mecánicas impregnadas de odio y miedo se acercaban. (ST, 28) | Julián's knuckles bled and his blood mixed with his father's who still shouted at him and accused him. The world cried, too. The mechanical sirens swollen with fear and hatred came closer. (TT1, 10) | Julián's knuckles were bleeding, and his blood mixed with his father's who continued screaming at him and blaming him. The world also wept. The mechanical sirens brimming with fear and hatred were fast approaching. (TT2, 27) |

Once again, TT1 fails to convey marked imperfectivity, whereas TT2 adopts two different means: a grammatical one, the past continuous, and a lexical-semantic one, the periphrasis "continue" plus gerund.

The last example is extracted from the description of the injured passengers after the car accident:

| Goteaban en la misma ambulancia los hermanos, donde Román vio la sangre de Julián llenar el piso y las sábanas; el ayudante no pudo detener el derrame; Román no pudo llorar. (ST, 33) | The two brothers bled in the same ambulance. Román saw Julián's blood spill on the floor and on the sheets. The attendant could not stem the flow. Román could not cry. | The brothers were dripping blood in the same ambulance, where Román saw Julián's blood saturate the floor and the sheets; the assistant could not stop the flow of blood; Román was unable to cry. (TT2, 32) |

In this example, Lomelí again introduces a nuance that conveys the imperfecto metaphoric value. In addition, "to drip blood" is semantically more accurate than "to bleed" and translates the verb "gotear" literally, which calls the reader's attention on the inexorable agony Julián is suffering.

CONCLUDING OBSERVATIONS

Relying on a selection of patterns of imperfecto narrativo translation solutions, I have endeavored to explore how Francisco Lomelí's alternative translation (TT2) functions in comparison to Max Martínez's (TT1). While TT1 almost exclusively selects unmarked simple past forms and thus inadvertently mitigates the indeterminate and destabilizing effect expressed by the imperfective aspect, Lomelí manages to inventively reconstruct these traits in English using compensatory resources on the grammatical, semantic, and lexical-syntactic planes in order to make up for the absence of a one-to-one equivalent in the target language.

A possible explanation of the two contrasting translations employed could be a change in the sociohistorical context in which they were published. TT2 could afford retaining the nonconventional and harsh character of the text as a result of enhanced understanding and recognition of Morales' narrative nuances. TT1 was an admirable, yet cautious early attempt to disseminate the work of an author still not fully understood and recognized, and perhaps that is why Martínez wanted to narrate the Chicanos from the barrio in a somewhat normalized, or more accessible, way. Ironically, despite his declared intention to be faithful to Morales' narrative style, Lomelí opts for an alternate, perhaps more metaphorical translation of the title: *Caras viejas y vino nuevo* is correctly literalized as *Old Faces and New Wine* in TT1, but it is renamed as *Barrio on the Edge / Caras viejas y vino nuevo* in Lomelí's version. Martínez chooses to translate the title literally and retains the intertextual link with the book's epigraph, a quote from "To What Green Altar" by the US writer, poet, and painter Prescott Chaplin (1897–1968), which incidentally appears in English even in the ST: "Old faces and new wine . . . I followed the sun West." In this verse the reference to wine is ambivalent—both a Christian sacred element and a frequent cause of death in the barrio at the time.[12] Additionally, it is as a result of alcoholism (among other forms of substance abuse) that many barrio inhabitants become old not by age but because they are worn out by the excesses they indulged in throughout their lives.[13]

All in all, TT1 straightforwardly relates Chaplin's original verse, whereas TT2 contains a more discursive creation, which Lomelí (1998) justifies as a reference to barrio explosiveness. Despite this, TT2 compensates by adding the original title next to the translated one.[14] The decision in TT1 appears to be coherent with the adoption of nonadapted source elements in the text (e.g., lexical elements in Spanish, although these are basically formulaic items that do not affect the narrative texture in a deep way). At first sight, both these TT1 translation decisions could be categorized as source-oriented strategies (which complicate reader interpretation since they add an intertextual reference of difficult interpretation and potentially opaque lexical elements, respectively). However, I would argue in conclusion that TT1's fidelity is somewhat naïvely verbatim, since it tends to be equated with literality or nonintegrated borrowings and as such is limited to form. It fails to problematize the equivalence relationship between source and target text at a higher level, that of discourse, where (as I tried to show for imperfectivity) the TT1 dominant macrostrategy is simplification without compensation—overall ending up weakening the equivalence link between the two texts. Conversely, TT2 seeks discursive equivalence, which involves eclectic translational decisions and even overtranslations on the micro level of the translation technique.[15] While TT1 inadvertently tends to strip the text of its complexities and deconstructs Morales' implicit meanings and ambiguities, TT2 actively reinstills them with temporal nuances that engage the reader on a whole new, authentic, level. TT1 rewrites the ST in order to make it fit the Chicano literature "mainstream" of that time and in so doing ends up modifying the purpose of the ST. TT2 retains a closer link with the original, and precisely due to—not in spite of—its declared fidelity to the ST, it can be characterized as a virtual rewriting in the sense meant by André Lefevere: it is a creative response to a change of sociocultural circumstances that is meant to be transformative, so long as it aims at giving voice to a cultural expression of Chicano identity without suppressing the content of its hardcore reality.

NOTES

1. This is a revised and translated version of an article in Spanish, "La traducción como re-escritura: Las dos versiones en inglés de *Caras viejas y vino nuevo* de Alejandro Morales," forthcoming in *Rivista Internazionale di Tecnica della Traduzione* 20.

2. *Diccionario panhispánico de dudas*, s.v. "?", accessed October 31, 2018, http://buscon.rae.es/dpd/srv/search?id=XAD3nkRJmD6NjdyDQ0, accessed October 31, 2018.

3. If we look at the few lines of the above-mentioned excerpt, we shall find the following instances of repetition: "una mujer maravillosa / una gran mujer"; "lo hacía

[...]; / por eso lo hacía"; "una madre [...] / lo que siente una madre"; "esa pena, /esa pena de [...]." The very same text also contains lexical items that are repeated in their different morphological or derivational variants ("trataba/trató" in the former case, "gritona / gritaba" and "sentimientos/siente" in the latter).

4. This is basically due to the aspect dynamic which characterizes the use of pretérito imperfecto in Spanish. Aspect is defined as the temporal internal structure of a situation (Comrie 1976, 3) according to the speaker's perspective. If the activity is seen from the outside as having a start and an end, that is, if the focus lies on its time boundaries, we refer to the perfective aspect; if the activity is seen from the inside, without specifying its time boundaries, it is referred to as imperfective (Gili Gaya 1961, 148–49).

5. Lomelí was born in Mexico in 1947, emigrating to the United States at the age of seven where he first learned English (personal interview). English was, naturally, the imposed language. This is an increasingly frequent situation in countries like the United States, which forces non-native speakers to problematize such labels as "mother tongue" or "native language." Yet now it is no less "his own" language than Spanish, considering his mastery in doing justice to Morales' narrative style. Unfortunately, besides being from Texas and specializing in American literature, not much biographical information regarding TT1 translator Max Martínez is known.

6. Cf. *imperfecto de fantasía*, which is used by children when they play roles in their games.

7. A telic verb is a verb describing an action that has an end.

8. The ST, however, hardly contains any code-switching, calques, or borrowings from the other language.

9. In TT2 this graphical means tends to introduce changes of perspective, such as transitions to direct speech (which are usually not preceded by verbs of expression and perception) or, along with the present indicative, to refer to Julián's interior monologue fragments (cf. "I gotta protect the memory of my mother" (TT2, 24), or "he could hold back from shooting up, knowing he was doing the right thing. He knew it. *Admit it, I'm right. Say so Buenasuerte. Ain't that so, Turco?*" (TT2, 26, my emphasis). This strategy may have a mimetic motivation (to represent colloquial speech), or it may be meant to compensate the (inevitable) absence of dialect features in English, or help readers disentangle the chaos of the overlapping voices that accumulate as the narrative progresses.

10. The lexical level would be worth a more in-depth analysis to validate my general impression that in TT1 only the denotative component tends to be retained, or the more general or more popular meaning of a word is usually selected. For example, "pena" (ST, 25) is rendered as *pain* (TT1, 7), while in TM2 we have *grief* (TM2, 24). Here the reference is psychological pain, which is the core meaning of "grief" (*Mer-*

riam-Webster, s.v. "grief (n.)," accessed October 31, 2018, https://www.merriam-webster.com/dictionary/grief), as opposed to *pain*, which is more general and polysemic.

11. https://dictionary.cambridge.org/it/dizionario/inglese/glared, sub voce. Accessed October 31, 2018.

12. Cf. Albaladejo Martínez 2007, 378–79.

13. For this interpretation I am indebted to Lomelí.

14. The publishing choice to add the source parallel text to the translation is also significant in this respect because it gives literal and not merely metaphoric visibility to Morales' original work.

15. In the sense intended by Molina and Hurtado Albir, as a "result obtained that can be used to classify different types of translation solutions" (2002, 507).

WORKS CITED

Albaladejo Martínez, Manuel. 2007. *Hacia una cartografía de Los Ángeles a través de la literatura chicana*. Ph.D. thesis, Universidad de Alicante. http://www.cervantesvirtual.com/obra/hacia-una-cartografia-de-los-angeles-a-traves-de-la-literatura-chicana—0.

Bardovi-Harlig, Kathleen. 2002. "Analyzing aspect". In *Tense-aspect morphology in L2 acquisition*, edited by Rafael Salaberry and Yasuhiro Shirai, 129–54. Amsterdam: John Benjamins.

Bres, Jaques. 2005. *L'imparfait narratif*. Paris: CNRS-Editions.

Comrie, Bernard. 1976. *Aspect*. New York: Cambridge University Press.

García Márquez, Gabriel. 1981. *Crónica de una muerte anunciada*. Madrid: Debolsillo.

Gili Gaya, Samuel. 1961. *Curso superior de sintaxis española*. Barcelona: Vox.

Hopper, Paul 1982. "Aspect between Discourse and Grammar." In *Tense and Aspect: Between Semantics and Pragmatics*, vol. 1, 3–18. Amsterdam: John Benjamins.

Lefevere, Andrè. (1982) 2000. "Mother Courage's Cucumbers: Text, System and Refraction in a Theory of Literature." In *The Translation Studies Reader*, edited by Lawrence Venuti, 233–49. London: Routledge.

———. 1992. *Translation, Rewriting, and the Manipulation of the Literary Fame*. London: Routledge.

Löbus, Triin. 2015. "El imperfecto narrativo como recurso estilístico y técnica narrativa." *Proceedings of ACTES/ACTAS/ATTI, XIXème Congrès des romanistes scandinaves*, Reykjavík, August 12–15, 2014, 1–12. Reykjavik: Sigrún Á. Eiríksdóttir. https://conference.hi.is/rom14/rom-lectures/.

Lomelí, Francisco A. 1996. "Rereading Alejandro Morales' *Caras viejas y vino nuevo*: Violence, Sex, Drugs, and Videotape in a Chicano Glass Darkly." In "Alejandro Morales: Fiction Past, Present, Future Perfect," edited by José Antonio Gurpegui, special issue, *Bilingual Review / Revista Bilingüe* 20, no. 3 (September–December 1995): 52–60.

———. 1998. "Hard-Core Barrio Revisited: Violence, Sex, Drugs, and Videotape through a Chicano Glass Darkly." Introduction to Morales, *Barrio on the Edge*, 1–21.

Molina, Lucía, and Amparo Hurtado Albir. 2002. "Translation Techniques Revisited: A Dynamic and Functionalist Approach." *Meta* 47, no. 4 (December): 498–512.

Morales, Alejandro. 1981. *Old Faces and New Wine*. Translated by Max Martínez. San Diego: Maize Press.

———. 1995. "Dynamic Identities in Heterotopia." In "Alejandro Morales: Fiction Past, Present, Future Perfect," edited by José Antonio Gurpegui, special issue, *Bilingual Review / Revista Bilingüe* 20, no. 3 (September–December): 14–27.

———. 1998. *Barrio on the Edge / Caras viejas y vino nuevo*. Translated by Francisco A. Lomelí, with parallel source text. Tempe: Bilingual Press / Editorial Bilingüe.

Reyes, Graciela. 1990. "Valores estilísticos del imperfecto." *Revista de filología española* 1, no. 2:17–55.

Venuti, Lawrence. 2008. *The Translator's Invisibility: A History of Translation*. 2nd ed. Abingdon, UK: Routledge.

THIRTEEN / History and
Fiction in Alejandro Morales'
Narratives / LUIS LEAL

In his fiction, Alejandro Morales has with great skill managed to redress the history of California from a Chicano perspective.[1] Given that the depicted geographical space in his novels is rarely removed from his native region (metropolitan Los Angeles), that region metaphorically becomes the mirror of the history of Southern California, and by extension, of the territories ceded to the United States by Mexico upon signing the Treaty of Guadalupe Hidalgo on February 2, 1848. The only novels in which part of the action occurs in spaces outside of his native region are *La verdad sin voz* (1979),[2] a chapter in *Reto en el paraíso* (1983), which takes place in Mexico, and parts of the last novel, *The Rag Doll Plagues* (1992).[3] In *La verdad*, the spaces bifurcate between the historical and fictitious, either in California, Texas, or Mexico. In *Reto*, one of his protagonists, Dennis, takes a trip to Mexico and describes some cities of the interior, and in *Plagues* we find the Novohispanic colonial ambience, the cities of Mexico City and Morelia during the eighteenth century, as well as California and northern Mexico. In this study we propose to analyze the relationship between the historical and fictitious elements used by Morales in his novels.

While aware that the dividing line between history and fiction is blurry and that all history contains fictitious elements and all fiction has historical elements, a new genre was created, the historical novel, where Morales' works might fit, even though in them fiction dominates over history. It would be best to say that they are representative of the so-called new historical novel, which is characterized not so much by reproducing historical facts as they occurred but by its revisionist function. This new historical novel, according to Morales, "gives another point of view of history, one that's absolutely necessary."[4] In Chicano fiction, Morales' novels, along with Nash Candelaria's, are perhaps the ones that best give us that other point of view, even if they're not necessarily the first to do so. Both authors have their antecedents in works from the nineteenth century, such as the novel *The Squatter and the Don* (1885) by María Amparo Ruiz de Burton. However, in this study it is not our objective to trace the trajectory of the new Chicano historical novel, but instead to analyze those by Alejandro Morales from that perspective. Neither do we pretend to point out the connections his novels have with Latin American fiction where one of the new trends that currently prevails is the new historical novel.[5] But, we propose that much like the Latin Americans writers (Carlos Fuentes, Gabriel García Márquez, Eugenio Aguirre, etc.), Morales has utilized the paradigm of his precursors by combining two apparently antagonistic discourses, that of the historical and the fictional. Nonetheless, he never goes to the extreme of the testimonial novel, even if his fiction intertwines autobiographical elements and real surroundings, as he himself has admitted.

FIRST SIGNS

In his first novel, *Caras viejas y vino Nuevo* (or *Barrio on the Edge*), we find realistic environments, such as the barrio, where Chicano characters live, which seems "parece que jamás cambiará" (1975, 34) without being linked to that space. Besides, the historical references are vague and generalized. For the elders of the Revolución, "era un tema predilecto, describían en detalle a los generales y sus personalidades, batallas y pueblos que habían ganado. Se discutía también la política actual y se criticaba al señor presidente y a su administración" (43). Two compadres talk about the death of Doctor Nagol (Logan, the protagonist of the novel *Verdad*, written backwards) without being precise where it happened, although the reader assumes it was in the barrio where the action unfolds. That character, who appears and disappears, becomes the protagonist in the second novel by Morales, *La verdad sin voz*, in which Logan's death takes place in a town in Texas.

At the end of the first novel, *Caras*, a note is inserted which, even without the reader's knowledge, is historic because it recounts an event that transpired in the suburb where the author was born. It has to do with the sale and collapse of the brick factory that employed most of the people from the anonymous barrio. That segment, as brief as it may be, transforms the fictitious discourse of the novel into a historical narration. But for the reader to be able to capture that metamorphosis, it is necessary to read the subsequent novel by Morales, *The Brick People*, not published until 1988, in which the same fictitious setting from *Caras* becomes the geographical place of the barrio in East Angeles, known as Montebello, where Alejandro Morales was born on October 14, 1944. Nevertheless, the illusion created by the author regarding the fictitious nature of the characters and the setting is confirmed by the anonymous author in the publicity note included in the back cover of the first edition, which says, "The life of the Barrio—a Latin American barrio in some city of the United States—will give the reader the elements of conscience on a reality and a silent and bitter struggle for the survival and identity that the stars and stripes don't want to allow."

FROM THE JOURNALISTIC NEWS ITEM TO THE NOVEL: *LA VERDAD SIN VOZ*

Before dedicating a whole work that recreated the life of inhabitants from the barrio of Montebello that had developed around a brick factory, Morales publishes two other important works, *La verdad sin voz* (or *Death of an Anglo*) in 1979 and *Reto en el paraíso* in 1983. The former begins with an epigraph taken from José Revueltas' novel *El luto humano* (1943), where we find the phrase that gives the novel its title: "Entonces la verdad sin voz, sin actitudes, sin gestos, nos es revelada amargamente" (Morales 1979, 8). According to the introduction that Judith Ginsberg prefaced in her translation of this novel, under the title *Death of an Anglo* (1988b), Morales told her he had read the story about Michael Logan in *Time Magazine*.[6] If we have no knowledge of that biographical news item, we assume that it deals with a historical character whose name Morales changed in *Caras* to conceal its historical origin, even though a synthesis of his life and cause of death are already provided (1975, 94–95). Logan's life is developed in *La verdad sin voz* while adding fictitious elements to it as well as his relations with two other characters, Profe Morenito, who moves within an American academic ambience, and Casimiro, a Mexican revolutionary who confronts the federal soldiers—not under the rule of don Porfirio (Díaz) but rather of a typical president from the PRI party from the decade of the 1950s. Fiction prevails in Logan's story and his milieu, considering that this narrative strand unfolds in a Texan town that exists in real space, Mathis, about thirty-five miles northwest of Corpus Christi on Highway 37. The author once again includes the customary disclaimer that the work "es un libro de ficción, sin embargo, algunos de los acontecimientos que se presentan son reales," and that "todos los personajes son imaginados y cualquier semejanza a personas vivas o muertas es pura coincidencia" (1979, 8). Since he had already told us that he had read Logan's story in a magazine, the warning about the other characters is undoubtedly necessary, given that the smart reader could find similarities among them and some well-known professors in an American university setting.

The historical element in this second novel is much more important than in *Caras*, but fiction still prevails. He inserts scenes from the history of Mexico, although without integrating them completely into Logan's life story; instead, he juxtaposes them structurally onto the central anecdote without connecting narrative links. However, it is in these scenes that we see the influence of the Latin American novel, above all those works in which the protagonist is a dictator. The president celebrates "el acto sagrado, el reto iniciado y mitificado desde 1910" (47). There are references to concrete historical events, such as "lo que pasó en Guerrero [Lucio Cabaña's rebellion] y en la Universidad" (60), and to the discovery of new petroleum deposits (101), as well as criticism of the government. A drunk man says, "vivo en la época del Porfiriato; ésa es la herencia de la revolución, un nuevo porfiriato" (101). Done in satirical terms, the criticism here is less direct than the one directed at the professors in North American universities. More than characters, they are simple stereotypes with names such as the "Ultimate Marxist," "Theoretical Roman," etc. Only Profe Moreno (meaning brown) stands out as the Chicano who sympathizes with Logan and whose colleagues want to fire him. Regarding this aspect in the novel, Morales wrote, "Yo había creado una series de personajes caricaturescos en un departamento de español at Corpus Christi University. Parece que ciertas personas de este departamento se empezaron a reconocer en los personajes y se enojaron conmigo."[7] On the other hand, other fictitious characters as well as incidents turned out to be true. When he wrote the novel, Morales did not know the town where the action took place. He admits that "when Mortiz held the book in the final stages of publishing it, I was invited to a conference in Corpus Christi. . . . Once I had finished the obligation of presenting my paper, I rented a car early Saturday morning and I went to become acquainted with Mathis, Texas" (1990, 7). His objective "was to see if in reality I could compare the fictional world of *La verdad sin voz* with the real world of Mathis" (6). Having conversed with various folks from the town, he realized that those persons I had invented and called "Margarita" or Mr. so-and-so were persons who actually existed. I found myself speaking with them and that I knew them. In the novel I had invented a certain Margarita who really existed. I invented various incidents and they all had happened as if they were real. It was an incredible experience, one comparable to the "Twilight Zone." (1990, 7)

The trip to Mathis was greatly beneficial to Morales, since it revealed to him that "literature and the creative process come to create certain truths, even though that might not be the intention of the author. Literature appeals to certain truths, be they poetic truths or of some other kind." (1990, 7).

FROM HISTORY TO THE HISTORICAL NOVEL: *RETO EN EL PARAÍSO*

With his next novel, *Reto en el paraíso* (1983), Morales begins the history of a region in California which extended, according to the map placed in front of the first chapter of the novel, into the large land holdings that had occupied the ranches of Lomas de Santiago and Rancho San Joaquín, the latter in front of the Pacific Ocean in the region where Irvine is located. Morales observes, "For this novel I started with various students carrying out research into the history of Rancho Irvine . . . *Reto en el paraíso* is the history of the James Irvine family. I wrote the entire novel thanks to a great deal of research that I did at the Bancroft Library, at the Huntington [Library] and in other libraries like the one at Irvine that contains texts, photographs and documentation that I present in the manuscript on Dennis Berreyessa Coronel's family" (1990, 8). From the extensive list of proper names collected in the preliminary "acknowledgments," one can find various historical characters, among them the name of Antonio Francisco Coronel stands out to whom is attributed a manuscript titled "Reto en el paraíso," the *fictitious* source of the *historical* background of the novel. Morales says in his acknowledgments that, accompanied by Father Felisberto Imondi Bianca—who had discovered the manuscript in the rectory of the Monte de Carmela church in Simons, California— he had the opportunity to read it: "Father Felisberto and I—Morales notes—read the manuscript in the rectory of the Saint Cecilia Church." According to the good father, the manuscript is not a book of memoirs but a novel. "You are reading—he tells Morales—probably the 'most important' novel, of the many written, by the

Mexicans who lost California." In other words, the history of California is fiction, and the best fiction is the one by Coronel. Given that we do not have any indication of any prior novel to the one written by Ruiz de Burton, published in 1885, we can deduce that the various histories of California that exist are novels. And in truth, the history of California begins in the pages of a novel, *Las sergas de Esplandián* (1510) by Garcí Ordóñez de Montalvo. Be that as it may, Morales put to good use the apparent manuscript by Coronel, from which the narrator cites frequently. This ingenious invention of an unknown novel written by a historical character is what renders *Reto en el paraíso*'s originality.

In the sixth "configuration" (the name the author gives his chapters)[8] we find the section "Coronel's Mansion" (1993, 198–200) written as a monologue by Coronel in which he exposes the decadence of the Californios. Among other things he says:

> Refugio . . . came to live here. He never returned to his house. The squatters took it. Then they stole Manuel Damián's land.[9] They have even stolen our history. They never paid for my report. . . . Reality does not exist for us. Only their world counts. I'm too old to fight. I can no longer do it. But I will never give them my writings. Never will I give them *Reto* nor the chronicles. Truthfully, never. Have them live in fictions, in their own fictions. (199)

Years after what was just mentioned, "Don Antonio was editing the last chapters of his work *Reto en el paraíso*, a manuscrito that got lost but which seventy years later would be discovered in a wooden box in a wardrobe of the Monte de Carmela church south of Montebello, California" (208). The motive for the unknown manuscript discovered by the author is a common narrative technique that has been in use (from Cervantes to Borges) to give credibility to the fictitious events.

In the same configuration the party is mentioned—here fiction prevails—that Coronel offered to celebrate having finished *Reto*, whose manuscript he showed to the guests. The novelist informs us that the manuscript "was one thousand two-hundred thirty-three pages long, written long hand, an impressive book" (265). In another satirical reference to the avatars of the manuscript, the incident is mentioned when

> Father Saúl offered don Antonio to read the manuscript or to give him an objective opinion based, according to the priest, on his years of study of philosophy and literature. Don Antonio accepted the offer from his friend with a slight suspicious doubt from literary criticism, which he relegated to

another mental level—different from and implicitly inferior to a creative and artistic mentality. Thus, don Antonio's manuscript passed on to a red, swollen, dipsomaniac priest. (266)

The section "Literature Is Fire" (269–71) is of interest because notes are further added concerning the existence of supposedly pre-Chicano novels. First, some biographical data are quoted regarding don Antonio, apparently taken from the obituary notice that appears, as we suspect, in some uncited newspaper, containing information that is perhaps also fictitious. Without using quotation marks, the section starts with these words in the present: "Today in his home on Olvera Street one of the outstanding citizens of the illustrious race of Californios, Don Antonio Francisco Coronel, died.... He arrived in California with his father Don Ignacio Coronel in 1834" (269). After providing other biographical but supposedly historical data, the fictitious note is then inserted, transporting the reader through time to the date of the great Californio's death, leading to putting words in the mouth of a newspaper salesman: "—Read all about it, the last of the Spanish dons dies!" (269).

The section continues with the description of the ceremony in honor of the dead man, during which various speakers delivered their funeral speeches, some in English, others in Spanish. One of the participants gives a criticism (better yet, a hyperbolic eulogy) of don Antonio as a writer:

> Don Antonio Coronel was one of the leaders of the main social gatherings of Los Angeles. Don Antonio was the leading voice in the area of prose. Just as Manuel Gutiérrez Nájera did, he recognized that the artistic world is not divided into literary camps; in Mexico of North America there isn't anything else but conservatives and the righteous. The conservative believes God gave him an innate stake to grammar. He is a writer endowed with divine correctness/right.... Don Antonio marked time with his works; our literary association became inspired in his novel *Reto en el paraíso*.... He taught us that literature is fire and a combat weapon. (270)

The omniscient narrator continues making a metacriticism, observing how criticism is exaggerated, presupposing the existence of numerous works by Mexican authors like Coronel, whose novel was among the last two remaining copies that no one reads, and of the author of two novels, *Frente la tranquilidad la locura* and *La hija de la ataraxia*, the disguised titles of two well-known novels from New Mexico.

The *historical* sources on Coronel are not abundant. Antonio Blanco S., in *La lengua española en la historia de California*,[10] reproduces "some pages of the manuscript [found at the Bancroft Library] *Cosas de California* (1877) in reference to the mining region of Antonio Franco Coronel" (600–616).[11] In *The Decline of the Californios*,[12] Leonard Pitt cites him frequently, making references to some bibliographical facts. He says, for example, that "from being "a struggling Mexican school teacher" he became "a prominent landowner, viticulturist, and community leader" (50) due to the gold that he managed to obtain during the gold rush. Pitt repeats that "the Mexican-born school teacher transformed by Sierra gold into a wealthy Californio, became the city's [Los Angeles] superintendent of schools in 1852 and its mayor in 1853. His father, Ignacio, was elected county assessor in 1853" (134).[13] Pitt also mentions that Coronel helped to translate the laws of California into Spanish, and that Helen Hunt Jackson, the author of the Indianist novel *Ramona* (1884), used to consult with him about the culture of the indigenous peoples of California, and it was he who told her the anecdote about the young woman who became the protagonist of her famous novel:

> A visit to nearby Camulus gave her a specific visual picture of a rancho. These impressions and experiences began to churn in her head as the beginnings of a novel, particularly when she mused on the tale Coronel told her of the hardships of the girl born to Hugo Reids' Indian wife. Mrs. Jackson envisaged the girl as the child of two cultures and made her the heroin of *Ramona*. (287)

In the case of this novel, it is not an easy task to separate fiction from history. How well the two elements are connected is difficult to unravel. This is what critic Marvin A. Lewis thinks:

> Morales in his acknowledgments gives credit to Father Felisberto Imondi Bianca, who gave him permission to read the manuscript "Reto en el paraíso" which was penned by Antonio Francisco Coronel and discovered by Bianca in Monte Carmela church in Simons, California. The novelist is supposedly told by the priest that he is reading probably the most important novel of the many written by the Mexicans who lost California. Whether or not such a manuscript exists, it becomes apparent that there are elements of the historical novel incorporated in the work to the extent that it places the multiple characters in a clearly defined historical framework and interprets their reactions to a concrete set of circumstances. *Reto en el paraíso* interprets the

impact of the transition from landowners to the landless upon the descendants of Don Ignacio and Doña Francisca Coronel: Antonio Francisco Coronel, Manuel Damián Coronel, and Refugio Coronel.[14]

There are quotes in Morales' novel supposedly taken from the manuscript; those in quotation marks gives them verisimilitude. Here is one example: "Singing," don Antonio writes in his manuscript titled *Reto en el paraíso*, "is my favorite pastime and I truly enjoy the melodies that I compose" (186). We also find references to the history of California that historian Bancroft wrote, based on the manuscripts of various Californios that were collected by his agent Savage. In Morales' novel, Coronel says: "I share a narration with Mr. Savage. I tell him what he wants to hear. . . . We and our culture disappear. They will know about us in history books: Bancroft's and ours. . . . Here in these manuscripts Don Antonio Francisco Coronel has written the true history of what happened to us in our California" (187).

It is of interest to compare the methodologies of the historian and that of the novelist in the episode of the deaths of don José de los Reyes Berreyesa and his two nephews, Franco and Ramón de Haro, who were assassinated by Frémont's soldiers in July 1846 upon landing their fishing boat along the coast. In the section "The Fishermen" (from Configuration II), Morales dramatizes the episode, but without referring to any source; the novelist places the narration in the mouth of another historical character, Juan Padilla. The information on that unworthy action from the history of the conquest of California by Frémont is told by Antonio Berreyesa in the "Account of His Recollections" (1877).[15] We do not know—the novelist does not have to, better yet, he shouldn't have to document—if the "Account" by Berreyesa served Morales as his source. The historian, on the other hand, sees himself obligated to document the origin of his information. Leonard Pitt, who also includes the episode in his history, tells us (30, footnote) that he took it from Berreyesa's "Account . . . ," which is found on pages 8–11 of the existing manuscript in the Bancroft Library. Not satisfied with the allusion to that atrocity incident, he comes to retell it, this time basing himself on news items taken from newspapers of the era. He adds, something Morales does not do, some news items by Californios that excuse Frémont:

> The third and most telling accusations against Frémont came from Don José de los Santos Berreyesa, who asserted that the conqueror had personally directed the "cruel and unsoldierly" killing of the de Haro twins and their aged uncle Berreyesa. The atrocity story had leaped from mouth to ear in

every old house and had gained added color because of the beating that the Berreyesas later took from squatters and lynchers. Another Berreyesa came to Frémont's rescue, however, and recalled that Kit Carson, not Frémont, had been the officer in charge of the fateful day. (200)

As sources of information for the aforementioned accusation and Frémont's defense, Pitt provides the titles and dates of two newspapers from Los Angeles, one a Californio publication, *El Clamor Público*, and the other Anglo, *Los Angeles Star* (200, note 13).

We will point out one more episode—of interest because in it figures a Berreyesa—which appears in the histories of California as well as in Morales' novel ("Encarnación Berreyesa," 126–37). This deals with the little-known rebellion of Juan Flores, who, after his escape from San Quentín in 1857, organized a gang with the help of Andrés Fontes, Encarnación Berreyesa, and other Californios. In Morales' novel these rebels are truly heroes, while in Pitt and other historians, they appear as bandits. In the chapter titled "Cow County Bandidos, 1856–1859," Leonard Pitt, referring to Los Angeles, says

> Into a town already steaming with resentment about lack of civil order and civil rights, in 1857 came one more explosive ingredient: bandits—not phantom bandits, but real and brazen ones. . . . The trouble began when the twenty-one-year-old Mexican Juan Flores broke out of San Quentín, where he was serving a term for horse stealing in Los Angeles. . . . A man of personal magnetism, Flores and his lieutenant, Pancho Daniel, assembled the largest bandit aggregation ever seen in California; more than fifty Spanish Americans from the territory between San Luis Obispo and San Juan Capistrano joined the ring. (167)

This organization of "outlaws" had a short life. Soon a group of rangers captured the main leaders. Pitt again points out:

> No less than 119 rangers and Indians converged on the outlaws. . . . El Monte rangers captured Flores and his lieutenant, Pancho Daniel. . . . To avoid further escapes, the El Monte men encamped at Los Nietos, simply hung their next nine captives—José Santos, Diego Navarro, Pedro López, Juan Valenzuela, Jesús Espinosa, Encarnación Berreyessa, and three others whose names they failed to note. (169)

Morales dramatizes the death of Encarnación Berreyesa in one of the most moving scenes of the novel. The encounter between Encarnación, Flores, and his companions—his "military," not "bandits"—is depicted with these words:

> Outside, under millions of stars, Encarnación embraced his cousin Plutarco [Lemus] and met Juan Flores, whom he immediately liked, plus Pedro Daniel and Andrés Fontes, about whom he had heard various accounts of his adventures. He greeted the other men and made his way to young Juan Flores. "Where is this army going?" "To San Juan Capistrano." (128)

In the previous section, "In a Scene of Fire" (Configuration VI), the novelist had already introduced the theme of Flores' rebellion, dramatizing doña Gracía's reaction upon discovering the death of her son Encarnación, as told by Coronel: "Encarnación was a victim of racism from the xenophobia that permeates all Anglos. Doña Gracía, they kill us, and they lynch us with whatever pretext. Encarnación's destiny is tied to that of Juan Flores and Pancho Daniel. Flores escaped San Quentín and joined Pancho Daniel in Santa Barbara" (126).

Other historical characters that appear and disappear in *Reto* are Andrés Sepúlveda, Pío Pico, the Yorba brothers, and others whose lives and adventures are seen less linked to those of Coronel and Berreyesa. The unity between these two important families, the Coronels and the Berreyesas, which provides added material to the author in order to interweave future novels, is begun with the marriage of Nicolás Berreyesa with Refugio Coronel, sister of Antonio Francisco (161). His brother Manuel Damián marries Rafaela Contreras, a marriage that separates the two brothers. Nicolás and Refugio have a son, Antoñito, and Manuel Damián and Rafaela a girl, Beatriz, characters who will reappear in future novels. In order to document the life of the descendants of the cacique Lifford, the author reproduces news items taken from the newspapers with precise biographical data: *Santa Ana Scribner*, Monday, January 12, 1959; *Los Angeles Times*, Tuesday, January 13, 1959; the *Popular Voice*, Tuesday, January 13, 1959 (290–93).

In Alejandro Morales' novel *Reto en el paraíso* there is a descendant who is not any less important than don Antonio Francisco Coronel, namely Dennis Berreyesa Coronel, son of Antonio Berreyesa III and grandson of Beatriz Coronel. Dennis, whose first name is fictitious, is the character with whom the first configuration opens. The lives of Dennis and the Lifford family constitute the fictitious part of the novel vis-à-vis the historical, that of the Coronel family, set in the remote past. In Dennis' world the history of the conflicts between Mexicans and Anglos repeats itself that had occurred from the beginning of the conquest of California by John C. Frémont. The two narrative discourses, however, are connected, given that the past serves to mirror the present; both eras are seen from the perspective of the vanquished. If Antonio Francisco Coronel is the representative of the decadent Californio, Dennis is that of the contemporary Chicano. The author states:

> I chose the name Dennis because it is an Anglo-American name and Dennis Berreyesa Coronel because this name represents one of the descendants of a family that encompasses the long history of California.... [Dennis] represents many of us. The academic process of Dennis'—I believe he graduated from UCLA—is the same process that many [Chicano] students experience, whether they are students that attend Harvard, Yale, Princeton or Berkeley. Although they may not want to admit it, that academic experience often changes them and they become different from their parents. (1990, 9)

And, above all, we could add, it changes Chicanas, portrayed in the novel by Rosario, who has influence over Dennis, in whom she awakens the consciousness of being a Chicano. She, according to Morales, is the "person who inspires and motivates him to search for that past.... She is a very militant woman. She is a woman who deeply believes in their Chicanismo. She feels much pride for her past" (1990, 9).

In the section "Grandmother" (57), we find the source of information that will serve the novelist to create his work. Beatriz, Dennis' grandmother, tells him that her father "worked in a brick factory, Simons Brick Factory, where we lived until his death" (57). The story "The Ballot Box" narrates the death of Dennis' father, Antonio Beyerresa, (59–60), crushed by a machine at the American Foundry. It is inferred that his death was due to the machinations of one of the Anglo workers, who was jealous for not having received the position of foreman which had been given to Dennis' father.

One of the methods used to link the two stories is that of photography. This method of connecting, also used by Arturo Islas in the novel *The Rain God* (1984), is introduced by the narrator through the advice that the grandmother gives her grandson Dennis, that is, that he should study the history of his ancestors, consequently handing him two photographs and telling him, "But, look, speaking of roots [Dennis goes to Mexico in search of them], these I found in some old papers, they are two photographs of your great-grand uncle Don Antonio Francisco Coronel. This is your history, young man, you should know it.

Handle the artifacts available to you and penetrate them with intelligence until you comprehend the true essence of the facts" (307).

In the plane, Dennis studies the photographs, but he reaches the opposite conclusion: the photographic images falsify reality. "The world is replacing reality through photography" (308). And, also, "It is a fucking photographic fabrication, a misrepresentation that distorts our history. In effect, Don Antonio is rendered a senile clown who likes to play the guitar to pretty women and who lives in the past. He's not at all a danger to the dominant society" (308). It is perhaps here where we find the motivation to write the novel as expressed by Dennis and captured by the narrator through the free indirect discourse: "He decided to invoke the positive history [a true history?], the one about the greatness of his people, Los Angeles' great Spanish heritage" (308). The attempt to deconstruct the photograph can be attributed to the desire to warn the reader of its falsehood, given that the same photo can be found in Pitt's book, who gives it the date, circa 1886, and he identifies the woman to whom don Antonio is singing as doña Mariana, his wife. According to *Reto*, in 1884 don Antonio married doña Marina (not Mariana) Rodilla y Herrero, a "woman thirty years young" (264).

The fictitious part of *Reto* is enriched by the alternative use of two languages, Spanish for the Hispanic characters and English for the Anglos; by the internal monologues; the intercalated short stories, the elements and at times those fantastic characters, such the monster of seven heads (191) and the flying horses (239); at times by the magical real, for example, Rafaela, "a witch wrapped in clothing" (206), and Coronel's trip into the magical forest; and by the presence of folkloric characters, such as Viejo Vilmas, an author of ten octosyllabic verses, some of which are reproduced in the text (36–39). Among the short stories, the ones that stand out, among others, are "The HIPITECA White Girl," which deals with the adventures of Debbie in Mexico. Who killed her? This serves to characterize Dennis Coronel Berreyesa (14–18); and "Well Paid," an anecdote of a character who hits his chauffeur because he left the car door open (99–101). The reminiscent elements of the novel by Gabriel García Márquez, *One Hundred Years of Solitude*, are similar; we will mention the case of incest between the cousins Antonio and Beatriz (Dennis' future grandmother), presented under the ironic title of "Innocent Amusement" (255–60).

While conversing with his friend Rosario Cecilia Revueltas, Dennis expresses a popular idea among historians and, to a certain point prophetic in Morales, that is, that history is about to reach its end:

I have heard that democracy in Latin America doesn't work because people are backward culturally. They are not sufficiently sophisticated for that kind of government to work. In our country democracy neither does it work well either, plus Communism will fail, and any other kind of government of the moment will also fail. The problem with us is that we are too sophisticated, too advanced technologically. We are at the point that we have to search for and invent a form of government because the ones that now exist are condemned. (112)

Reto en el paraíso ends in the decade of the 1930s. Some historical events are mentioned, such as the construction of the freeway from Los Angeles to San Diego (inaugurated in 1929), the film *All Quiet on the Western Front*, filmed in 1930, and the repatriation of thousands of Mexicans due to the Great Depression. In order to find work, the Berreyesa Coronel family permanently moves to Simons, the "miraculous city where I can find get work, where there is a bit of everything, where we can live in peace, from where we will never be thrown out. Let's go to Simons" (379). The last section now unfolds in Simons. It starts with a description (apparently taken from a newspaper) of the brickyard in Montebello where "the Simons Brick Company erected a walled, wholly Mexican company town" (380).

FROM HISTORY TO MEMOIRS: *THE BRICK PEOPLE*

Antonio Francisco Coronel (and also the author of *The Brick People*?) discovered

> that writing memoirs, true histories or works of fictions is to remain in our own personal solitude because the writer comes to feel abandoned, becoming highly fond of solitude. He recreates in it the events of the past while imagining an interpretation of life. In that way, the artist creates and original and authentic vision of the world. (Morales 1983, 191).

The solitude and desire to write the authentic history (in effect, achieved through novels, thereby considered as fictional) of a Los Angeles barrio that otherwise would remain forgotten, undoubtedly is begun in *Reto*, but it is in *The Brick People* where the memoirs prevail—not those of the grandparents like Coronel but rather his parents. Morales says: "His parents [Dennis's and the youth of his generation], who work in fields or in brickyards, as well as in *The Brick People*, do not develop an economic and political ability like the one available to his sons" (1990, 9).

In *The Brick People* history predominates over fiction. However, since it is essential, we read in the last page that "*The Brick People* is a work of fiction. Any similarity between the characters and people, living or dead, is coincidental." Without a doubt the warning is to protect the author from lawsuits, and not to suggest that historical characters are not present in the work, which opens in 1892 when the Indian Rosendo Guerrero arrives in Los Angeles and goes on to work at the Simons Brickyard in Pasadena as a foreman. The brickyard, under the direction of Joseph Simons, had then only forty workers, the majority of them from Guanajuato, the place of Rosendo's origins. Aspects of the history of the Chinese in Los Angeles are introduced in the first part, emphasizing extant hate toward them. Some scenes occur in front of the "Coronel building" on the Calle de los Negros (16–21).

The plot development is chronological: from 1892 we go to 1898, the year President Theodore Roosevelt and his Rough Riders rescue the battle of San Juan Hill in Puerto Rico. By then Rosendo is now don Rosendo and speaks English well. Contemporary Mexican history is also intertwined here, enumerating the favors don Porfirio granted to the Americans and the presence of William Randolph Hearst and other "robber barons" in Mexico (31–44). We also see the history of the United States, including Roosevelt's presidential campaign in l904 and the earthquake of San Francisco in 1906. Halley's Comet, which appeared in 1910, serves as the reason to join the two worlds, one represented by President Díaz of Mexico, who observes it from the National Palace in the Mexican capital, and the other by employee Melquíades de León, who sees it upon crossing the border en route to the brickyard in Simons in Alta California (68, 71).[16]

At the same time, the history of the Simons brickyard is recreated from the first day that they begin to build bricks. In 1990, Morales mentioned the precise years:

> Simons, a brick yard in East Los Angeles and also in Montebello, California, was founded in 1906 after the earthquake of San Francisco and lasted from 1952–53. By those years the owner, Walter B. Simons, was of advanced age and no one in his family wanted to continue with the administration of the business. Besides, brick was no longer accepted as an important material for construction. After the earthquake of Long Beach in 1933, the use of brick began to decline. (1990)

This part of the novel represents the socioeconomic background within which the lives of the workers are developed, on the one hand, who are almost all Mexicans, as well as those of the Anglo property owners of the brickyard. Of course it is the history of his family that matters to Morales, for obvious reasons: "For me, it was essential to salvage a completely lost and forgotten history by Anglo-American historians; a history that was never acknowledged. Everyone or 90 percent or more of the workers in Simons Brick Company from 1906 to 1952 were Mexicans who came from Irapuato and Abasolo, Guanajuato, in Mexico." And also: "*The Brick People* is a text of great importance to me because it deals with the history of my parents. You will notice that in the cover of the text is a photo of my father, Mr. Delfino Morales. In the work you will find the name of Nana, who is my mother; also, Mr. Revueltas, who is photographed with my father" (1990, 12). The history of his family, of course, was reconstructed in its own context. The novelist continues on to say, "In order to obtain the necessary information to write the text, what I did was to organize a group of students to identify persons who were living or had lived in Simons" (12). In this part of the novel oral history predominates. Morales continues, "Based on the multiple interviews that we conducted [I discovered that] people of 75, 80 or older . . . had very good recollections of what Simons had been" (12–13). The novel ends precisely with an interview with his father. "In that dialogue of the novel it is the voice of my father speaking" (13).

FROM THE PAST TO THE FUTURE: *THE RAG DOLL PLAGUES*

In 1990, when Alejandro Morales spoke at Stanford University on his works of fiction, he had just finished writing the novel *The Rag Doll Plagues*, but he had not published it. The work would not be published until two years later. If, in fact, the origins of *La verdad sin voz* was a newspaper item, that of *Reto* the chronicles of the Californios, and that of *The Brick People* the memoirs of his family, the origin of *Plagues* was the history of the examining board of physicians in Spain, a work that a Duke University historian gave to Morales:

> I began to read the book and it fascinated me so much that I began to create the first part. I knew I had to continue forward to write the second and third parts, and again I resorted to the role of researcher. I did considerable research regarding AIDS and the future. I had to take into account the demographic changes in California . . . in order to try to create the world that I portray at the end of the colonial period in Mexico. (1990, 15)

The title of the work was going to be *The Ancient Tear / La vieja lágrima*, later abandoned for the one it has.

The novel, divided into three parts, takes place in three spaces, two historical and one fictitious (Mexico, Delhi, LAMEX), and in three distinct periods (eighteenth century, the present, and the year 2089). Two techniques, one structural and the other thematic, join the three parts, which otherwise could be considered as three short distinct novels. However, in the three we find the duplication of characters (the presence of Doctor Gregorio Revueltas, for example) and the motif of a great plague. What is highly original is the theme of saving humanity thanks to the blood of Mexicans, which is similar to the first part in the recreation of the colonial environment in Mexico.

APPROXIMATE CONCLUSION

In general, we find that in his narrative works Morales tries to reconstruct the history of the Chicano while his perspective focuses on a microcosm, a reduced space in the southern part of California. From his first novels, which develop in a barrio of the metropolitan area of Los Angeles, California, he goes on to recreate the history of the Chicano people in the immediate past, and it is not until 1992 that he presents a panoramic vision of the Far West, subsequently launching his imagination into Mexico's remote past and into the future in a science-fiction space.

Morales' novels do not constitute a series of novels in the same way as the work of Pérez Galdós (in his *Episodios nacionales*) or Salado Alvarez in Mexico, the author of other *Episodios nacionales*.[17] Morales works are, first and foremost, fictional, in which the reader can encounter historical facts (or pseudo-historical ones) intertwined with fictional ones, making the latter prevail. But let us not think that these historical data are found organized in chronological order; to the contrary, they are historical references at the margins, but necessary in order to recreate the environment in which the characters—most of whom are fictitious—move.

The technique of history/fiction culminates in *Rag Doll Plagues*, which is not an amalgamation of history and fiction, but rather, better yet, as the author tells us in the unnumbered preliminary page, "a creation of fiction and poetry . . . of history and the imagination." And in truth, all of the narrative works by Morales partake in that fundamental characteristic common in all of works of fiction.

NOTES

1. The article appeared originally in a special volume of *Bilingual Review / Revista Bilingüe*, edited by José Antonio Gurpegui, 20, no. 3 (September–December 1995): 31–42. It was reprinted in *Alejandro Morales: Fiction Past, Present, Future Perfect*, ed. José Antonio Gurpegui (Tempe, AZ: Bilingual Press / Editorial Bilingüe, 1996), 31–42. It was translated by Francisco A. Lomelí with assistance of Sonia Zúñiga-Lomelí and lightly copyedited for consistency with the other essays in this compendium.

2. I cite the following editions: *The Brick People* (Houston: Arte Público Press, 1988); *Caras viejas y vino nuevo* (Mexico City: Joaquín Mortiz, 1975); *La verdad sin voz* (Mexico City: Joaquín Mortiz, 1979); *Reto en el paraíso* (Ypsilanti, MI: Bilingual Press / Editorial Bilingüe, 1983); and *The Rag Doll Plagues* (Houston: Arte Público Press, 1992).

3. I understand that Morales is preparing another novel whose scenery is in Mexico, as is noted in the first part of *Plagues*. (Editors' note: The subsequent novel that partly took place in Mexico is *Waiting to Happen* from 2001, after this article by Leal was first published).

4. Bentley-Adler (1989, 7).

5. Regarding the new historical novel, consult Menton (1993).

6. Morales (1988b, 5). In a paper that Morales delivered at Stanford University on November 5, 1990, he stated, "The origin of this book resulted from an article that a friend of mine gave me in Rutgers. It was an article that appeared in the magazine *Time* or *Newsweek*; can't recall which. The article title was 'Death of an Anglo'. The article mentions a man named Frederick Logan from Mathis, Texas" (4).

7. Morales (1990, 8).

8. Morales says, "My idea was to create a series of configurations, that is, to take a character and through that character create a world, a configuration of images, happenings, and all that was part of Dennis Berreyesa Coronel's world" (1990, 9).

9. The last name Damián appears here but as a proper name in the following novel, *The Brick People*.

10. Sánchez (1971).

11. Franco is used instead of Francisco due perhaps to the common practice in manuscripts of abbreviating the name in that manner: Fran/co. The Bancroft Library possesses the following manuscript, which is difficult to read, that we have consulted: "Documentos para la historia de California, los cuales pertenecían al Archivo Particular de Don Antonio F. Coronel y fueron por él depositados en la Bancroft Library, 1878" (manuscript C-B 75).

12. Pitt ([1966] 1970).

13. The life of Coronel as a gold digger as well as his activities as a schoolteacher are

included by Morales in the first part of Configuration IV, whose action occurs in 1848 (62–76).

14. Lewis (1989, 1816).
15. "Relación de sus recuerdos" (1877). Manuscript in the Bancroft Library.
16. Regarding Halley's Comet in fiction, see López (1987).
17. See Jiménez (1974).

WORKS CITED

Bentley-Adler, Collen. 1989. "Crossing Cultures: Morales' Novels Reflect the Dilemma of Dual Ethnicities." *UCI Journal* (January–February): 7.

Jiménez, Francisco. 1974. *Los episodios nacionales de Victoriano Salado Alvarez*. Mexico City: Diana.

Lewis, Marvin A. 1989. "Alejandro Morales (14 October 1944)." In *Dictionary of Literary Biography: Chicano Writers*, edited by Francisco A. Lomelí and Carl R. Shirley, 1816. Detroit: Gale Research.

López, Ernesto J. Gil. 1987. "El cometa Halley en tres escritores latinoamericanos [Roa Bastos, García Márquez, Agustín Yáñez]," *Revista Interamericana de Bibliografía* 37, no. 2:l90–200.

Menton, Seymour. 1993. *Latin America's New Historical Novel*. Austin: University of Texas Press.

Morales, Alejandro D. 1975. *Caras viejas y vino nuevo*. Mexico City: Joaquín Mortiz.

———. 1979. *La verdad sin voz*. Mexico City: Joaquín Mortiz.

———. 1983. *Reto en el paraíso*. Ypsilanti, MI: Bilingual Press / Editorial Bilingüe.

———. 1998a. *The Brick People*. Houston: Arte Público Press,.

———. 1988b. *Death of an Anglo*. Translated by Judith Ginsberg. Tempe: Bilingual Press / Editorial Bilingüe.

———. 1990. "Alejandro Morales en Stanford University." Paper delivered by Alejandro Morales at Stanford University, Palo Alto, California, on November 5.

———. 1992. *The Rag Doll Plagues*. Houston: Arte Público Press.

Pitt, Leonard. (1966) 1970. *The Decline of the Californios*. Berkeley: University of California Press.

Sánchez, Antonio Blanco. 1971. *La lengua española en la historia de California*. Madrid: Ediciones Cultura Hispánica.

FOURTEEN / Epidemics, Epistemophilia,
and Racism / Ecological Literary
Criticism and *The Rag Doll Plagues* /

MARÍA HERRERA-SOBEK

Ecology: the body of knowledge concerning the economy of nature—
the investigation of the total relations of the animal both to its inorganic
and to its organic environment; including above all, its friendly and inimical
relations with those animals and plants with which it comes directly
or indirectly into contact—in a word, ecology is the study of all those
complex interrelations referred to by Darwin as the conditions of struggle
for existence.

 Ecological literary criticism, in fact, begins from the presupposition that
an essential characteristic of all significant literary works is their uniqueness,
not as autonomous artifacts, as the New Criticism regarded them, but
as dynamic participants in a constantly self-transforming historical
environment—a major component of which is the diverse interpretations to
which outstanding works are subjected.

—Karl Kroeber, *Ecological Literary Criticism*, 1994

The *Los Angeles Times* reported on May 11, 1995, on its front page that "a team of federal disease detectives was dispatched to Zaire on Wednesday to investigate a deadly outbreak of what health officials strongly suspect is viral hemorrhagic fever—a devastating illness that can cause death within days by dissolving the body's organs" (1).[1] The mysterious virus was reported to be Ebola, one of the deadliest viruses known to humanity. The same issue of the *Los Angeles Times* describes it in the following way:

> Ebola was considered the most deadly virus before the appearance of HIV, which causes AIDS. The Ebola virus belongs to a class of organisms called filoviruses, which destroy the linings of the capillaries and blood vessels, prompting fluids to drain out of the circulatory system. The virus's course is painful, and victims typically become deranged and manic before dying of shock. (11)

The mortality rate reported is 80 percent of those it infects.[2]

It should not surprise us that Alejandro Morales, an internationally recognized Chicano novelist, anticipated in his work *The Rag Doll Plagues* (1992) a horrific virus that resembles Ebola.[3] Although two early outbreaks of Ebola erupted in 1976 and 1979, little was written on it before the May 11, 1995, outbreak, and it is doubtful Morales was aware of its existence from news reports. This possible lack of knowledge coincides with the commonly held view among literary scholars that serious novelists often have the uncanny ability to predict events in the future through their literary works. Perhaps authors with their developed sensibility are able to foresee the future better than the average person. Morales' novel once again gives credence to the belief that reality often mimics fiction.

In this study I center my attention on Morales' epistemological and ecological concerns and posit that he is the first Chicano novelist to systematically sustain an ecological perspective throughout his novel *The Rag Doll Plagues*. I further underscore the interrelationship between ecological concerns and social and racial injustice found in the novel. These issues are intimately linked to each other and one sustains the other. Morales' work is not merely one concerned with ecological problematics but one in which the ecology of the planet intersects directly with issues of racism, oppression, discrimination, and dehumanization. In addition, I point out how interwoven in the novel is a search for knowledge or an epistemophilic project directly linked to the relationship men have established with nature: that nature is to be conquered, exploited, *known*. All of these political matters are interlaced in a narrative whose infrastructure is girded by cyclical time in which events such as the plagues repeat themselves and characters appear, disappear, and reappear (i.e., Papá Damián and Gregorio) throughout the story à la García Márquez.[4]

ECOLOGICAL CRITICISM

Ecological criticism examines literature from the perspective of ecology and ecological thinking. According to Karl Kroeber, one of its devoted practitioners,

> ecological thinking insists that we be steadily conscious of living in a real natural world with which we meaningfully interact and in which our actions have discernibly specific consequences. An ecological vision, then, is one that assumes that all human beings bear profound responsibilities toward others, not just other humans, but other life forms—along with their and our habitat. That we exist not in elitist isolation but interdependently is a conviction that imposes concrete and difficult ethical burdens.... (61)

Book One: Mexico City

Morales' concern with ecological issues runs throughout the three interrelated novellas constituting *The Rag Doll Plagues*. In book 1, titled "Mexico City," the reader is transported to the colonial era in which the main character, Doctor Gregorio Revueltas, contrasts the baroque opulence of the Spanish ruling class, as exemplified by the Spanish empire's representative, don Juan Vicente de Guemes Pacheco de Padilla (Count of Revilla Gigedo, Gentleman of the Royal Bed-Chamber, Knight of the Holy Order of Alcántara, Captain of the Regal Guard, and Viceroy of New Spain) with the filth and abject poverty and oppression of the Indians, mestizos, Negroes, mulattoes, and other racial mixtures belonging to the lower strata of colonial society.[5] Doctor Revueltas, recently appointed director of the Royal Protomedicato, has just arrived Mexico and is quickly apprised of the horrible devastating plague that has ravaged the countryside and is now invading the city. The year is 1788 and the plague is commonly known as La Mona for the crippling effects it has on the body's extremities (the arms and legs of its victims lose their muscular support and become flaccid, resembling those of rag dolls).

The theme of an unhealthy environment produced through thoughtless human behavior, neglect, and ignorance is underscored throughout book 1. As Don Gregorio, the narrator, describes his trip from Veracruz to Mexico City, ecological disasters are encountered along the perilous journey. The Spanish physician begins to catch a glimpse of what is to come as he travels along a road near a river, The river, however, holds more than water, for it is full of decaying cadavers.

He is later informed that the floods and the plague, rampant in the countryside and threatening Mexico City, have decimated the population. Father Jude, the priest in charge of acquainting don Gregorio with his new duties and surroundings, informs him, "It begins like the pox [plague], but only in the extremities of the body. Then in a few days, it does horrendous damage to the internals" (22).

Ecological nightmares continue to assault don Gregorio's senses. His description of Mexico City's streets are horrific. "Only a block from my residence [convent of San Jerónimo] I was shocked by the bodies of hundreds of dead dogs in a pile covered with a blanket of flies that undulated like a black hair net on and above the decaying carcasses. Utterly filthy people argued over the freshest ones" (25).

However, if the physical environment is an ecological disaster, the social ecology of the colony is even worse. In particular, Morales zeroes in on the pervasive racism practiced against the Native American masses. A view of the economic inequality between the wealthy Spaniards, the rulers of the New World, and the vanquished Indians is provided through the descriptions of the elegant palaces or palace-like abodes of the Spaniards and Creoles and the wretched existence of the indigenous population.

At the personal level, the slave-like existence of the *indios* and the indifference of the ruling class are depicted at the very inception of the novel when don Gregorio is carried across the river on the shoulders of Native Americans.[6] The racist attitude of the newly arrived don Gregorio reflects the general low regard for the *indios* during the colonial period. The word *savages* and the belief that the Indian did not have a soul is explicitly articulated by the narrator (13). Morales has his protagonist express himself as a representative of the Spanish empire upon his arrival. His colonial discourse effectively conveys the racist character of the empire and carries with it all the negativity associated with the colonial enterprise. Don Gregorio's rhetorical mode of speaking identifies him with the colonial project, and the tropes he employs aid in the establishment, continuation, and affirmation of colonial authority. This rhetorical mode of speaking and thinking clearly delineates the relations of power between oppressor and oppressed. In particular, conceptualizations of the Indian in terms of an inferior (even nonhuman) being coincide with that form of colonial discourse described by David Spurr in his book *The Rhetoric of Empire: Colonial Discourse in Journalism, Travel Writing, and Imperial Administration* (1993). In this study Spurr subsumes under the rhetorical strategies of debasement those terms, phrases, descriptions, and so forth used to characterize the other as inferior.

Spurr perceives debasement as a form of negation since it "negates the value of the other" (Brooks, 4). The Indians at times rebelled against this oppressive status but as in the case of Pedro de Soria, an Indian chief from Pátzcuaro, Michoacán, these uprisings were brutally squashed (Morales, 36).

Two linkages are constructed in book 1 of *The Rag Doll Plagues*: one between ecological issues of human waste, filth, garbage, and improper hygiene and issues of racial and political oppression. When both environmental ecology and social ecology are addressed and action is taken to alleviate the stress on the population exerted by these two forces, a healthier climate, both medically and politically speaking, is produced.

Racial inequality in the colonies is addressed through the representation of the lower *castas* and their wretched living conditions. The following description associates in a subtle manner political/religious repression and environmental breakdown:

> As we passed the Palace of the *Inquisition* [italics are mine], men and women squatted facing each other and deposited excrement and urine into the canal that ran down the center of the street. As they met their human needs, they conversed with ease and cordiality. Upon finishing, they simply raised their garment and walked away. They had no paper nor cloth to practice anal hygiene. It was cleaner to defecate and stand than to employ your hand to wipe away the clinging or watery excess. Nonetheless, many adults and children did use their hands. The windows of the houses along this street were tightly closed in a desperate attempt to keep out of the gases of decaying animal and human waste.
>
> Immediately before the carriage, a window suddenly opened. Without warning, a pail of excrement and urine was tossed out. At many points, the drainage ditch running down the middle of the street was clogged with the manure and urine from animals and human beings. Puddles formed in which to my absolute consternation I observed children playing happily. When a cart would roll through the puddles its wheels stirred up and intolerable rankness. (Morales 26).

Sexual perversions are rampant. The narrator describes scenes where women perform fellatio acts on the streets in broad daylight at the entrance of bordellos and young boys are sodomized as others wait their turn (28). The protagonist himself is approached by children who "demonstrated how they would masturbate me. Some opened their mouths and knelt before me" (28). Meanwhile, the inhabitants of this perverted city merely looked on and laughed, demonstrating a crass indifference to the diseased, the prostitutes, the lepers, the demented, the homeless children, and the filthiness of the city (29).

Nevertheless, toward the end of the book 1 and through the efforts of don Gregorio (the good doctor from Spain who comes to love the New World and New Spain as time passes and he befriends the inhabitants), the disease, La Mona, begins to subside. The environment is improved through public works that reform sewage and garbage collection throughout the city. The change in the political climate is tied to this more optimistic and cleaner view of life. As the protagonist narrator states:

> I sensed a new attitude toward life grow within the people. University professors and students conversed about freedom and equality, about rationalism and liberalism. Intellectuals declared that human beings should no longer be oppressed by the trinity of the king, the priest and the landed aristocrat. They proclaimed that governments should be based on the consent of the people, that religion should be a private matter, that society should no longer be divided into hereditary classes, that a person should rise as high as talent would carry him. (61)

Book Two: Delhi

Two parallel themes once again permeate the story line in book 2, titled "Delhi." Here the plot takes place in the present and the twin issues of a plague and racism are intertwined in the narrative. The main protagonist likewise is named Gregory (English for Gregorio), and again he is a physician, this time practicing in Orange County, California.

Ecological concerns are expressed from the inception of the narrative in book 2. The storyline begins with the description of a "heroic green-blue cypress," which has managed to survive for several generations. "The behemoth tree was like pure delicate crystal: forever danger being broken, cut down by men and women concerned more with industrial profit than the preservation of natural life" (69). The narrator takes great delight in the moments of solitude he manages to steal from his busy schedule. Communion with nature is one of his great joys (the other is books and the pursuit of knowledge). This desire for solitude, however, is often broken by the hustle and bustle of the city, which intrudes on the protagonist's quiet reveries. There is a strong communicative bond between

Gregory and the cypress, and it is the cypress that encourages him to seek Sandra, who will become his lover. Sandra and nature will fuse in Gregory's mind; she will become an Anglo Coatlicue. Coatlicue in Aztec mythology is the Goddess of Life and Death, and her abstract attributes are concretized by means of a huge sculpture made of stone. On one side is the image of a woman with fangs; a skirt made of serpents surrounds her waist. Sculpted on the reverse side is the figure of a human skeleton. Gregory perceives Sandra, his lover, as the Great Mother: "I saw the world, the sea, the mountains in her legs, her arms, her face. The cosmos became her body" (69). Thus nature and Sandra are conceptualized as one, and she will incorporate within her body both life and death because, although she is young and full of beauty and life, her body is ravaged by hemophilia. In addition, she will be "contaminated" with the Acquired Immune Deficiency Syndrome (AIDS) virus and will succumb from the effects of that "plague."

The narrator, Gregory, is explicit in his perception of Sandra as the Great Mother archetype. In chapter 4 of book 2, he describes her:

> I traveled easily through Sandra's womb, as I did through her dreams, and I found that her face had been transfigured into the face of a serpent made up of two great serpents. She dressed in odd clothes that I had never seen before. She wore a singing skirt of undulating fields of corn. Her skirt became crystal and water. Although I tried, I failed to drink. Her lips, hair and desperate eyes rained all night as I lay next to Sandra Spear. That was the first night that she opened my chest and exposed my heart to her pain. . . . That night as I fell asleep, I saw above Sandra the green-blue cypress with its dripping roots exposed. (77–78)

Sandra is frequently associated with the natural elements, particularly light, rain, and the jaguar. Oddly enough, although Anglo, she is linked with pre-Columbian motifs: pyramids, volcanoes, sun calendars, warriors, and animals. In chapter 7 (book 2), Gregory muses:

> Sandra had physically recovered, and I thought I had found in her face the reflection of a Jaguar roaming the spaces of night. Her green-blue eyes fixed perfectly into my own almond-shaped brown ones. In an instant she possessed all faces, time and places, none of which were familiar to me, yet I knew them all. I remembered the cypress filled with birds, the great star dancing above, chasing away the clouds of winter. She was a priestess and she drank a cup of blood and raised a sword to the sky and violently thrust it

through my soul. Her fingers had grown like roots, penetrated and entwined through my body and soul. (83)

Toward the end of book 2 before Sandra's death, she is transformed completely into Coatlicue. "Sandra danced like energy among them [Mexican Indians]. Serpents wreathed out from her punctured skin. Sandra was the god [sic] Coatlicue and I feared her" (126). Even her initials reiterate the serpent motif: S. S.

Postcolonial discourse is evident in Morales' juxtaposition of the various racial groups in book 2. Racial identity defines class. In book 1 the class structure of the colonial period is conceptualized as a pyramid: the peninsular Spaniards occupy the apex, the *criollos* or Spaniards born in America form the second tier, while the mestizos form the third. The bottom of the pyramid, that is, its wide base, encompassed the bulk of the Indians, mulattos, and African Americans.

Book 2, on the other hand, juxtaposes the Chicano and the Anglo-American populations. The barrio in book 2 is an important character within the narrative structure, and the various barrio inhabitants are significant structural elements, both in the development of the plot and the message encoded in the novel. The barrio is located in Santa Ana, in the heat of politically conservative and reactionary Orange County, California. The narrator privileges the barrio and its people as the native race, founders of the area (71). The Indian heritage of the Chicano population is underscored, and barrio youth are identified via the military component of the Aztec class system as warriors. These "warriors" are juxtaposed to the effete and elite "narcissistic, health-conscious Orange County" (72).

Likewise, the barrio inhabitants are juxtaposed to Sandra Spear's wealthy family, particularly the doting, extravagant father who is able to afford high-priced toys—such as a twelve-cylinder Jaguar automobile, for his daughter. The class conflict and distance between rich and poor and white and brown are played out throughout book 2. It is only the love between the two star-crossed lovers, Gregory and Sandra, that is an attempt to overcome these distances. Nevertheless, the coming together of the two races is never achieved because the fruit of this love is lost in a miscarriage and soon after Sandra dies of AIDS. Book 2 follows previous US cinematic models, in which mixed-race marriages between Latinos and Anglos end in the tragic death of the Mexicana/Chicana/Latina. Miscegenation in the movie industry and as rendered in films has always been punished by death.[7] Here Sandra, an Anglo woman, meets an untimely and tragic death, and an ending featuring a Mexican American and Anglo living together "happily ever after" is thwarted.

At the personal level, racism is expressed by Sandra's father toward "Others" and particularly toward Gregory via his displeasure at Gregory's and Sandra's love. Institutional racism, on the other hand, is expressed through various sources in book 2. Hospital personnel display their stereotypical views of Mexican Americans through their classification of Sandra as a "homegirl" believed to have been stabbed (when she was actually bleeding due to her hemophiliac condition) and their refusal to provide her emergency service because they assumed she had no medical insurance. The police joined in the hospital personnel's racist policies by supporting and carrying out these policies as representatives of the law. Furthermore, their belief that Sandra's car, a new Jaguar, is stolen property and could not possibly belong to her (because they mistook her for a homegirl) underscores their racist attitudes toward the Chicano community—attitudes that have dire consequences when the issue at stake is emergency medical attention. Institutional racism is further displayed in the art and journalism world through the refusal of the Orange County Theater to mount a Hispanic play by the Spanish writer Federico García Lorca. Later, when the play is finally approved and becomes a great success due to Hispanic attendance, it is pulled out. The newspapers, likewise, display their own brand of racism through their critical reporting of the barrio homeboys' attending the play.

The political powers that be in Orange County used their clout to discourage Hispanics from further attending theatrical performances. The narrator-protagonist informs us:

> However, the anti-Latino political forces in Orange County, ever fearful of being overrun and of losing their cultural spaces to the Mexicans, covertly convinced the theater administration that it was dangerous to allow such a large amount of barrio homeboys to gather in one place, and that the homeboys presence scared away the patrons. (92)

Bigotry, however, is not limited to race and class in book 2 but extends to discrimination against those carrying the AIDS virus. When it is discovered that Sandra has AIDS, she is blackballed from obtaining roles at the Orange County Theater. When she confronts the director of the OCT, he shamelessly informs her, "Forgive me for being blunt. But many people believe you have AIDS and will not work with you" (109). People even refuse to be near Sandra: "They considered Sandra a human scourge, a Pandora's box filled with disease capable of destroying humanity" (112).

Book Three: LAMEX

Book 3 of the trilogy, titled "LAMEX," offers a more complicated and more creative view of racial relations as well as ecological perspectives. Both strands, the racial and the ecological, are highlighted throughout the narrative and brilliantly project the issues into a fictionalized world of a future that is only too real in its depiction of world pollution.

Book 3 catapults the reader into a future approximately one hundred years from now, or the 2090s. In this science fiction future, international borders are erased, and a geopolitical entity called the Lamex Coastal Region of the Triple Alliance, which extends from the center of Mexico to the Pacific coast, is created. In this "brave new world" freeways have been computerized, and geographic regions, where racial and class segregations are in effect, have been formed. The names of the various geopolitical regions convey the racial and class differences of the various population groupings: the Higher Life Existence is located in the city of Temecula, California (situated east of San Diego), while the Lower Life Existence neighborhood is located in the city of Chula Vista (situated south of San Diego). Lower Life Existence individuals come from the prisons, the lumpen, the criminals and "dregs of society" (137): "People found guilty of antisocial behavior that required separation from society were condemned to one of the nation's LLEs" (137).

It was in this Southern California region that an unknown contaminant killed five hundred people in a few hours (135). Doctor Gregory Revueltas, medical director of the Lamex Health Corridor of the Triple Alliance and his assistant and lover, Gabriela (Gabi) Chung, are directed to investigate.

The virus, which caused excessive swelling of the extremities and death, was believed to have been a

> spontaneous plague.... Produced by humanity's harvest of waste, they traveled through the air, land and sea and penetrated populated areas, sometimes killing thousands. Scientists throughout the world had identified thousands of those living cancers of the earth. They were of all sizes, colors and smells. Some were invisible. From our pollution we had created energy masses that destroyed or deformed everything in their path. (138–39)

The present plague was thought to have emerged from the ocean from one of three energy masses composed of filth floating along the coast of the Pacific Ocean.

The interesting and in fact clever twist given to the finding of a cure for the new plague is directly related to racial concerns, as the cure found serves as an allegory for the racism against the Mexican population living in the United States. Oddly enough the cure is found in the blood of those Mexican individuals who have been exposed to such high levels of environ mental contamination that they develop high levels of white blood cells. This "energized" or "immunized" blood is then capable of resisting the deadly plagues periodically infecting the mostly Anglo population. As is wont to happen in capitalist societies, the blood becomes a commodity; and following a historical path once tread before by Mexican nationals, this population becomes commodified and objectified. Mexicans are such desired objects by the Anglo middle and upper class that they are transformed into status symbols to be flaunted by the Anglo families who "own" their Mexican couples—the producers and "breeders" of future producers of the precious life-saving liquid. In the words of the narrator:

> The urgent need to possess Mexican blood reached the point of absurdity. The newspapers carried ridiculous articles about families fighting over one Mexican, or a family if Mexicans who refused to be separated. Euroanglos always wanted to be photographed with their Mexican at their side. People took their Mexicans everywhere, fearing that friends or relatives would steal them. Millions of MCMs [Mexico City Mexicans] signed contracts of blood enslavement. Here again, the Mexican population became the backbone of the LAMEX corridor. (195)

Mexican blood used as an antidote or as a vaccine to ward off the latest plague or other unexpected viruses that surface serves as an allegory for the Mexican blood shed from time immemorial. In the pre-Columbian period Mexican blood was offered by the Aztec priests to appease their god. Later, blood was spilled in the various wars and armed conflicts the Mexican nation has engaged in: the Spanish conquest, the Wars of Independence (1810–1921), the Mexican Revolution (1910–1920).

A critique of capitalism and the exploitation of the Mexican in the United States is intertwined with the ecological concerns related to pollutants, environmental contamination, and virulent epidemics. The Mexican is perceived as the savior who saves the United States from national catastrophes, just as Mexicans had saved the crops during the Bracero Program in 1942. Mexican "blood" or labor continued to the used in the agricultural fields and sweat shops of the US Southwest, thus making it possible for the Anglo middle class to enjoy an incomparable standard of living unequaled in the world.

The irony of the book 3 lies in the structuring of a fact of life—the Anglo world needs Mexican blood in the form of labor to survive in the style it has become accustomed to—into a fictionalized world where Mexican blood is the "vaccine" necessary for survival. The hated Mexicans become the beloved Mexicans because they are the only means of survival. Morales makes an effective, forceful, and at the same time humorous, use of allegory in encoding his message.

Morales' novel falls within the purview of cultural and political resistance literature. *The Rag Doll Plagues* serves as a response to the cultural and political colonization the mestizo has endured in the past centuries and will continue to endure in the centuries to come. In that sense, the novel offers a pessimistic view of racial relations and charts out a gloomy prediction of social relations between Anglos, Mexicans, and Mexican Americans in US society. In Morales's novel the binary construct of colonizer and colonized is clearly separated by race and class. One could accuse Morales of essentializing Mexicanness (symbolized by Mexican blood), that is, by positing the superiority of Mexican blood in the struggle for survival. However, this would be a superficial reading of the work because, as I previously pointed out, Mexican blood as antidote or vaccine is used as an element, albeit a most important one, in constructing the overall allegory of Mexican indispensability in the agricultural and textile industries and in a service-oriented economy.

Of particular interest is Morales' use of blood, disease, and the body as part of an "epistemophilic" project. (Epistemophilic as defined by Freud is the urge to know.) In Morales' novel it is the body in its diseased acceptation that impels the protagonist in his search for knowledge, in his drive to know. Because psychologists, such as Freud and Melanie Klein, have linked the search for knowledge to a primal sexual desire of the mother in the Oedipal romance, Morales' protagonists' (the three Gregorys') intense desire to know, to investigate is linked to the female protagonists in books 1 and 2, and the body of a woman is of central concern in book 3. Interestingly enough, the three female protagonists in the three sections die at an early age, at the conclusion of each narrative. As such the body becomes, as Peter Brooks frames it, "a site of signification—the place for the inscription of stories—and itself a signifier, a prime agent in narrative plot and meaning" (1993, 5–6).

An underlying theme of the novel is the various protagonists' epistemophilic desire. All three male protagonists explicitly state their love for books, for reading. This search for knowledge will be inextricably linked with ecological issues and in books 1 and 2, with the female protagonists, for it is through the diseased bodies of

Marisela, Laurinda, and Sandra Spear that the desire to know, to conquer nature demonstrating its most lethal face that is of paramount importance to the first two Gregorys. The desire to know will be equally intense in the third Gregory. Books will serve as a constant leitmotif throughout the three sections of the novel.

The diseased body in the novel will function as a linguistic signifier for the ecological disruptions and the abuses of nature by mankind. The plague will inscribe the body with a narrative, a narrative that will tell the story of nature gone awry due to pollution, contamination, and disregard for ecologically sound policies. The body will literally scream out the story of human neglect and abuse for all to see and hear.

Peter Brooks perceives a change in the conceptualization of the body in modern narrative, particularly within the erotic tradition, and its significance as the agent and object of desire. In his study *Body Work: Object of Desire in Modern Narrative* (1993), Brooks focuses on "bodies emblazon[ed] with meaning within the field of desire, desire that is originally and always, with whatever sublimations, sexual, but also by extension the desire to know: the body as an 'epistemophilic' project" (5). Thus as Brooks proposes and as is evident in Morales' novel, the body becomes "a site of signification—the place for the inscription of stories—and itself a signifier, a prime agent in narrative plot and meaning" (5–6).

Nowhere is this most glaringly explicit than in book 3, in which Gabi Chung, Gregory's assistant, has made the ultimate sacrifice and relinquished her own healthy arm for a computerized robotic one. The narrator describes it as

> just one of the inconveniences of severing an arm and hand from the elbow and replacing it with a computerized knowledge bank whose fingertips were laser surgical instruments and knowledge cylinders. . . . The competition to accumulate knowledge into one brain and one body for immediate access had escalated for fifty years, since the world had turned against humanity. (136)

Gregory had postponed severing his own arm for a robotic one, but the pressure was increasing from the board of directors, his bosses, to have it done. The computerized robotic arm, however, will eventually begin malfunctioning. There was an increasing smell of burnt flesh as Gabi was forced to recharge her arm more and more frequently; however, it would eventually fail her:

> Gabi's flesh had begun to reveal the damage of her life style, of the pressures of the job, of her arm that required more frequent recharging, and of

the constant odor of an elbow that refused to heal and now probably had become a malignant infection. Her body rejected the synthetic adapters between the electronic arm and her human flesh and bone. (196)

The failure thwarted Gabi's ambition to succeed and she committed suicide by electrocuting herself by pulling the voltage lever of the electrical charge unit to its maximum capacity while she was plugged to it. The demise of Gabi leads Gregory to leave the position of medical director of the Lamex Health Corridor of the Triple Alliance and devote his life to the care of the Mexican people of the El Mar de Villas and to devote his time to the reading of books.

Morales' protagonists' search for knowledge and the urge to know has its negative consequences if it is for personal ambition and is not in the service of humanity. The Gabi Chung allegory presents us with the perils of giving up one's humanity (even a part—in her case an arm) to fulfill personal ambition. A "purer" and more innocent search for knowledge, such as the reading of books or a search for knowledge in the service of humanity, is seen as proper and desirable.

The novel, *The Rag Doll Plagues*, affirms an ecologically balanced environment. It flings a strong indictment at those in power who consciously or unconsciously ignore the social and environmental ecology of our planet. It is one of the first and possibly the only Chicano novel to seriously address the issue of environmental responsibility without neglecting the social issues of racism and social injustice.

NOTES

1. This article was published originally in *Alejandro Morales in the Past, Present and Future Perfect*, edited by José Antonio Gurpegui (Tempe: Bilingual Press / Editorial Bilingüe, 1996), 99–108.

2. See also the coverage on the Ebola epidemic published in *Newsweek*, "Killer Virus: Beyond the Ebola Scare: What Else Is Out There?" May 22, 1995, 48–54.

3. All quotes will be taken from Alejandro Morales' *The Rag Doll Plagues* (1992).

4. See for example Gabriel García Márquez's *Cien años de soledad* (1967).

5. See Esteva-Fabregat (1995).

6. The "white man's burden" is literally the reverse since black and brown peoples were required to carry their masters on their backs as explicitly exemplified by the photograph that serves as a cover for Mary Louise Pratt's book *Imperial Eyes: Travel Writing and Transculturation* (1992).

7. See Cortés (1985).

WORKS CITED

Brooks, Peter. 1993. *Body Work: Objects of Desire in Modern Narrative*. Cambridge, MA: Harvard University Press.

Cortés, Carlos E. 1985. "Chicanas in Film: History of an Image." In *Chicano Cinema: Research, Reviews, and Resources*, edited by Gary Keller. New York: Bilingual Review.

Esteva-Fabregat, Claudio. 1995. *Mestizaje in Ibero-America*. Tucson: University of Arizona Press.

Kroeber, Karl. 1994. *Ecological Literary Criticism: Romantic Imagining and the Biology of Mind*. New York: Columbia University Press.

Márquez, Gabriel García. 1967. *Cien años de soledad*. Buenos Aires: Editorial Sudamericana.

Morales, Alejandro. 1992. *The Rag Doll Plagues*. Houston: Arte Público Press.

Pratt, Mary Louise. 1992. *Imperial Eyes: Travel Writing and Transculturation*. New York: Routledge.

Spurr, David. 1993. *The Rhetoric of Empire: Colonial Discourse in Journalism, Travel Writing, and Imperial Administration*. Durham, NC: Duke University Press.

Williams, Patrick, and Laura Chrisman. 1994. *Colonial Discourse and Post-Colonial Theory: A Reader*. New York: Columbia University Press.

FIFTEEN / A Dialogue with the Writer
Alejandro Morales / FRANCISCO LOMELÍ,
MARC GARCÍA-MARTÍNEZ, AND DANIEL OLIVAS

(MG-M) *What is your specific artistic or creative process, Alejandro? Is that process something that you can readily describe for us?*

(AM) Well, no, I don't really have a process, per se. I'm not sure how to answer that because the creative process is always a bit different. I can say that I have become more cognizant and therefore more aware of and sensitive to the process of writing. I'm a self-taught writer. I always thought that if I had attended a writing school or a program in creative writing that I would be a better writer. However, as I wrote and started to publish I realized that there were readers interested in the worlds that I created. To write my first novel, I assembled a variety of daily life scenes that I wrote down in notes, short descriptions of human emotions stemming from conflict, loss, joy, love, struggle, disappointment, etc. I searched and found these scenes in my home, neighborhood, and the community outside my safe zone. I knew fully well most of the characters in *Caras viejas y vino nuevo*. They were my friends, neighbors, family recreated as fictitious characters. Now at this stage of my writing process when I have an idea, event, incident, etc. that I want to develop into a story or novel, I usually create a biography of each character who will populate the narrative. Those who know me know that I'm a big believer in reading history, of peering into old photographs, listening to those who lived a certain experience. I'm always listening. Always reading and thinking about the past, and I regularly delve into mythology, philosophy, and even my family's own personal stories. When I write, or plan to write, I am inspired by all of it. The future as well. Once I have an idea in mind, the actual writing process begins by searching for any amount of material that I can find in notes, conversations, scholarly or nonscholarly books, magazine or newspaper articles, even through letters from friends and colleagues around the world. That's where [the] real lives and therefore real art can be found.

(DO) *What are some insights you have gained throughout the trajectory of your writing?*

(AM) I learned that we must write about the expansive Chicana/o/Latina/o experience because if we don't, nobody will . . . or non-Chicana/o/Latina/o writers will. It's imperative that we become a strong voice for our community but at the same time a voice that is directed to all readers, not just Chicanas/os/Latinas/os. I personally want my stories and novels to have something to say to people worldwide, by this I mean that human beings experience the same stages of life, perhaps in different ways, but all belong to the human community. Therefore, a story about the human condition that is written well will be understood in whatever language it is translated. And this leads me to comment on the labels critics and readers brand on us. Most of the time when I attend a conference or [am] asked to speak about my books they introduce me as a Chicano writer and that's okay with me. I am probably one of the very few Chicano writers who accepts that label. Some Mexican American writers today don't always want to be strictly identified as a Chicano/a writer. It seems that many prefer the term "Latina/o" or most recently "Latinx" writer. Regardless of the label I'm given, the trajectory, the course, and goal of my writing is [to] tell a hell of a great story that dialogues with readers worldwide.

(FL) *So you have developed an apprehensiveness about identifying terms or labels?*

(AM) Let's say the writer's first book as a Chicana/o, Latina/o, Hispanic, or Latinx writer gets published and receives a successful literary debut, a second novel receives high praise from readers and critics who confirm the wonderful talents as the ethnic writer. Of course the agent and publisher want to build on this literary success. Consequently, they demand that the writer produce more of the same style and themes explored in the writer's first two books. They might even transform the writer into a literary fixed persona that embodies the people and issues explored in [the] writer's debut works. The public will always expect the appearance of this conjured character produced by sales—not the real author who produced the novel. With time the writer performs the prescribed literary persona for the agent, publisher, and readers who have placed the writer into an ethnic literary niche, a writing cubicle to produce only stories, novels, poetry.

Not long ago I was invited to write a speculative story for an anthology of Latino/a speculative short stories. I had a few stories that fit into this genre and I selected the one that was the most advanced in the writing stage. I submitted "The Integrals or Cartographers of Consciousness" to the selection committee, which explored Carl Jung's theory of the collective unconscious and Jean Gebser's theory of the structures of consciousness and highly advanced nanotechnology by a team of four scientists from diverse specializations who attempt to capture images from the past by penetrating parts of the human brain that house memory. In the end, they are successful, yet their achievement meant that in mining the brain for images of ancient times it presented the possibility of radically changing human history.

The editors of that anthology sent me an email message informing me that after long consideration they decided not use the story in the anthology. The next day I called the editor who had invited me to submit a story. What was wrong with my story? There was a long pause all the way from the East Coast. The voice answered, "The committee felt that your story was not Chicano enough. There weren't any Chicano characters. None of the scientists had a Latino last name." They said that the story read like a scientific article. It just didn't have any Chicano/a/Latino/a characters, which confirmed to me that some editors still have stereotypical literary criteria. I guess they want to keep Chicano/a writers in controllable typecast literary cages. They wanted me to write only about my Chicano place and nowhere else.

(FL) *And yet your work has developed and evolved within and beyond such categories. How do you view your development and evolution as a writer from* Caras viejas y vino nuevo *to* River of Angels*?*

(AM) I don't follow traditional literary models or genres. I consider these too limiting. My novels are a conglomeration of characters, techniques, functions of time, space, place, and plot that together will hopefully tell a story that will have meaning to people worldwide—like the work of Jorge Luis Borges, Theodore Drieser, Alejo Carpentier, Julio Cortázar, Carlos Fuentes, Pablo Picasso, Pablo Neruda, John Rechy, Isabelle Allende, Gloria Anzaldúa, Elena Poniatowska, Cristina Rivera-Garza, Sandra Cisneros, Tino Villanueva, Ray González, Kazuo Ishiguro, Haruki Murukami, Reinaldo Arenas, Arturo Arias, Octavia Butler, Mary Wollstonecraft Shelley, Salman Rushdie, Toni Morrison, and Kathleen Winsor.

I like to think that my novels and stories have followed a neobaroque or neo-rasquachismo trajectory, as posited by Monika Kaup. I paraphrase Kaup, who argues that US Latino cultural production is a neobaroque decolonizing artistic expression that counters canonical norms, criteria, and standards. The neobaroque refuses to consider cultures as fixed self-contained systems, the property of distinct, segregated social, ethnic groups. The neobaroque brings together artists and writers who dare to break away from established artistic styles or writing norms. Kaup describes US Latino Neobaroque as an art of recycling, reusing or reworking the past through caricature, distortion, and perversion—even subversion. Kaup's theory of US Latino/a Neobaroque parallels Tomás Ybarra Frausto's theory "Rasquachismo, A Chicano Sensibility." My first three novels, *Caras viejas y vino nuevo*, *La verdad sin voz*, and *Reto en el paraíso*, typify this, and counter traditional novel-writing bound by genre.

As I said, I never had a formal education in writing, I just made do with what I learned from reading obtainable novels, short stories, poetry, and the stories shared by my family's elders. Since then I have combined a plethora of storytelling strategies, tropes, topics, use of time, place, and character development and an aggregation of historical events, local and regional superstitions, popular legends, beliefs, and traditions from different communities using different language expression from Spanish and English. This concentration of artistic elements in my novels can be compared to a baroque or neobaroque façade filled with details that literally, symbolically, and politically communicate meaning and stories.

(**DO**) *Another artistic element in your works is how harsh or, like you said, subversive they are.*

(**AM**) My novels are indeed subversive—that is, politically subversive, contra-Conquista, countercolonial—that challenge the status quo and propose the possibility of a new and better social order for humankind. In my books there are scenes that are shocking, yet reify the thinking, and the ugly, racist, social politics of the current administration in Washington, DC, as well as POTUS's eliminationist ideology specifically targeted and applied to the Mexican, Central American, Caribbean, and South American communities in the United States and abroad. As I said, my works [are] a product of the Chicano sensibility called rasquachismo and explained eloquently by Tomás Ybarra-Frausto in his article "Rasquachismo: A Chicano Sensibility." I take all those canonical literary genres and techniques, and appropriate them and then make them mine to deconstruct as I please to create my vision of life, the world, the cosmos, and all creation. This might sound a little crazy but that's the way I feel about the power of the imagination and of writing.

(MG-M) *With regard to this "Chicano sensibility," where do you see yourself in the Chicano/a literary cosmos? What's your current position in the expanding sphere of Chicano/a writers?*

(AM) I currently don't see myself in any specific location in the "expanding sphere" of Chicano/a, Latino/a writers. I don't want to be seen as being positioned in a particular place in some kind of singular literary realm. Some consider me a "pioneer" of Chicano/a literature, but this may be an uninformed statement. Chicano/a literature has a long history, it has antecedents, and some literary historians and critics claim that its roots are found at the start of the Spanish Colonial period in Mexico, and as we know that it has continued to produce up to contemporary times. The writers of the nineteenth and twentieth centuries could be considered the "fundadores" of modern and postmodern Chicano/a literature. The writers who inspired me were the Quinto Sol group of the 1970s, the canonical writers of the Chicano Movement like Tomás Rivera, Rudolfo Anaya, Rolando Hinojosa, and Estella Portillo Trambley. In addition, the modern and postmodern artists and authors from the United States, Europe, and Latin America influenced the way I saw the world, and I also claim North, Central, and South Native American oral and literary traditions and mythologies as part of my literary heritage.

So I am not really restricted to a particular sensibility or positioned squarely in the "Chicano/a literary cosmos." Writing is not being in one particular place at one specific time. Writing is a vast site where I see myself traveling through the past, present, and future. I refuse to be limited to space, time, or topic. Writing should always be a site of complete and unconditional freedom. I have always been a maverick, nonconformist writer who prefers to work independently unencumbered by outside expectations. Currently, I am working on three projects at different stages of development; one takes place in Japan from the 1920s to the beginnings of WW II, a second deals with 1960s Mexico City and Los Angeles and sites in the near future, the third is a speculative work that challenges common scientific beliefs. So I can be *anywhere* in the expanding sphere of art and knowledge and, most importantly, of the imagination and creativity.

(MG-M) *Chicana/o literature is a ubiquitous form of art, and yet despite this, it can be misunderstood. It is often analyzed through a bracketed lens that constricts it. What do you think?*

(AM) You're making a generalization that implies that there is only a single way of understanding Chicano/a literature, which is absurd. The idea that people are reading incorrectly or incompletely is not for me to say because any effort to read a story and get something out of it is its own reward. It's the act that matters. If a reader gets something out of reading my books but what they get is not what I originally intended, then ¡vaya maldita cosa! Big damned deal, right? My fiction is not some bargain or contract that readers must adhere to. But I see what you are trying to get at because some people have come to expect a certain portrayal or product with Chicano/a literature or art. Like a formula they anticipate. You say that Chicano/a literature, unlike the past, is numerous and becoming worldwide. I foresee the audience for it getting broader. What bothers me as a writer and a reader is when the literature is sold as a narrow category or when it eventually becomes [so] oversaturated with pretense, themes, or symbols that those readers cannot help themselves from expecting those very themes and symbols. If there is any misunderstanding of the literature, it happens because there is such heavy and persistent cultural dramatizations throughout the pages that they become inflexible markers of Chicano/a identity, and publishers and readers alike will not see past it. These recurrent topics, symbols are stereotypes promoted by agents, editors, and publishers who want to address a specific reader who believes these stereotypes constitute the Chicano/a Latino/a communities as a whole in the United States. Today diversity, hybridity, coalescence is a dominant social and cultural force in Chicano/a Latino/a communities throughout the country. Even so, major publishing houses continue to publish and sell stereotype-filled novels. Take a look at their latest literary product, *American Dirt* by Jeanine Cummins—a book that reinforces the deleterious side of cultural appropriation.

(DO) *So do you see a way to avoid that? A way to prevent this oversaturation of typecast themes and symbols?*

(AM) What's good is that the literature is diversifying and continues to do so. It's not that every book by a Chicano/a or Latino/a author nowadays is all about exclusively Chicano/a or Latino/a subject matter. We are not some brand, and we are finally leaving the barrios, the borderlands, the sweatshops, the streets behind to tell ancient tales or tell stories of futures to be. We do so in ways that really hit on our humanity and not only on our ethnicity. As writers we bring compelling narratives and insights that will speak to all readers. Is it a concern that our books are represented in ways that do not always allow us to speak in this way? Yes, but authors and teachers, scholars, and even students can do a lot to help ensure the current and next generation of Chicano/a literature and art. Not only has the literature had ample and diverse opportunities to continue to reach wider audiences, but we can read and support those authors or artists who choose to create literature of ample and diverse subject matter, and of the kinds of themes that testify to our cosmic universality.

(MG-M) *Richard "Cheech" Marín characterized Chicano/a art as "sophisticated and primitive simultaneously." What is your take on this characterization? Does Chicano/a art, in all its verbal, visual, and aural forms maintain this duality?*

(AM) His characterization is somewhat rudimentary. Sound bite essentialist, even. I worry that classifications tend to minimize, stereotype, and put Chicano/a art in an artistic niche. As I stated previously, Chicano/a artistic expression is multifaceted and constructed or drawn from a vast array of artistic, social, political, historical, psychological, religious, mythological, technological, and scientific, etc., discourses to which the artist may be receptive. Chicano/a art is much more than simply "sophisticated and primitive simultaneously," but of course we've been addressing a lot about this idea already in this conversation.

(FL) *At a panel of writers at the University of California Santa Barbara in the fall of 2016 you sat on a panel with Lucha Corpi and Helena María Viramontes and claimed that "literature by ethnic writers tends to be very prophetic." What did you mean by this?*

(AM) In their work, ethnic writers are producing a new knowledge that is needed to negotiate life in the urban and rural communities of the country today. The fast-changing demographic landscape has resulted in certain population groups sensing and fearing that once-stable white or single ethnic neighborhoods are being overturned, taken over by diverse ethnic or racial groups. The novels, short stories, plays, poetry, memoirs, autobiographies, and personal essays produced by ethnic writers are more important today than ever before because these works offer personal and general information about these new ethnic and racial groups entering the country and settling in long-standing white neighborhoods in urban and rural areas. These writings offer insights about ethnic populations that for years have been pushed to the peripheries of the literary canon, yet have become useful tools to learn how to live in the heterotopia (a place of difference and of diversity) communities growing in our cities and small towns throughout the United States. In the fragmented, hybrid, polarized country in which we live today ethnic writing posits a therapeutic literary experience that benefits the ethnic and nonethnic communities and enlightens readers about groups seen as other, foreign, and dangerous. This literary experience may even relieve the fear, suspicion, distrust, and worry that stresses daily life in the United States.

Ethnic writing offers a window into the daily experience of the diverse ethnic, racial, and religious populations that have recently arrived or that have been residing in the United States for generations and, moreover, demonstrates the differences among us yet reveals the similarities that unites the country. Ethnic literary works advocate applicable values: historical, sociological, moral, psychological, therapeutic, inspirational, commitment, honesty, and above all, of relevance to life in today's—and tomorrow's—society. Residents should consider and practice these values to better understand their neighbors and life in heterotopia today as well as tomorrow. So by reading ethnic literature readers gain enlightenment about ethnic groups and [some] knowledge for the future.

(MG-M) *Would you agree that this is what ethnic literature ultimately ought to do? To transcend race, ethnicity, and sociology and glimpse into the future of the human soul?*

(AM) An ethnic writer or any writer can't control how the reader is going to understand a novel or what meaning the reader will deduce from a text. Ten individuals may read an ethnic text or any novel and come up with ten specific interpretations, meanings that are not at all similar. If a scholar establishes that my oeuvre transcends race or ethnicity and glimpses into the future, then that is one way of understanding my literature. Ethnic authors should not be held to transcending race or necessarily to look into the human soul. I don't think ethnic writers or a particular literature should be assigned any specific goal. No writer of a particular ethnic, racial, or religious background should write about specific topics or to achieve explicit goals. They can write about the ongoing present, the speculative future, or history if they wish too.

(DO) *What concept of history prevails in your work, or inspires you?*

(AM) I'm inspired by lost, ignored, whitewashed, hidden history and the history of ordinary people that Miguel de Unamuno recognized as the intrahistory of the contributions of individuals who are not recognized, who are *ninguneados*—the unseen, the uncelebrated, the denied. Their jobs are not recognized but demeaned because they don't garner big amounts of money or fame. Some examples of these laborers and skilled workers are the trash collector, the butcher, the tailor, the harvest picker, the mechanic, the artist's apprentice, the secretary, the army private, the waiter, and the court jester. Intrahistory is not the history of so-called great men or women but of the laborers who have supported them and contributed to the success of their endeavors and accumulation of wealth and social prominence. Their voices are rarely heard because they are habitually quashed or lost or ninguneados. There are some theories and ideas about the marvelous and uncanny in history that have encouraged me to combine these ideas with empirical events.

Hayden White's theory offered in *Metahistory: The Historical Imagination in Nineteenth-Century Europe* really resonates with me. He challenges the idea that historians base their works on empirical evidence and therefore always write the truth. White has exposed, or revealed, that some historians, when they lack empirical documentation to move from point "A" to "B," actually will employ narrative techniques, the strategies of fiction writers. Today that narrative strategy is called literary journalism, nonfiction writing. Michel Foucault talks about vertical and horizontal history and power: those who end up with power, and then the thousands, millions who end up dead or following and are not heard from until they rise again. I like the fact that some theorists have declared that if it is not written it is not history. Others are convinced that history is dead.

I think that history can be found in so many sites, such as orality—memorized and passed on to future generations and literacy—written artifacts of all kinds that in the past were not considered sources of relevant historical information, and ephemera, or memorabilia: photographs, paintings, sculpture, music, dance, films, architecture, furniture, quilts, statues, clothing, pottery, from all classes of people, etc. History may be presented in a chronological, circular, rhizome, reversing structure. History is the constant struggle against time, and time for me is the energy through which all things travel and are worn away. Also, history can be marvelous as proposed by Alejo Carpentier's theory of "Lo real maravilloso" when he said that "what is the history of Latin America but a chronicle of magical realism?" In other words, the history of Latin America is so strange as to appear fictional, even marvelous. Jorge Luis Borges found the history of everything past, present, and future in the Aleph, the idea that all epistemologies known and unknown, all material objects created since primordial existence, can be seen in and through the Aleph, a fantastic space. Tony Morrison's idea of rememory and Gloria Anzaldúa's "La facultad" are also kinds, or forms, of history.

(FL) *What is your motivation for frequently resorting to a historical backdrop in your work, such as in* Reto en el paraíso *and* The Brick People?

(AM) Both *Reto en el paraíso* and *The Brick People* are novels that deal with fictitious and real people, simultaneously. Also, both these novels are histories of specific geographical regions in Southern California. *Reto en el paraíso* takes place in Orange County, California, and *The Brick People* occurs in Los Angeles, California. In addition, these novels occur in specific time periods: *Reto en el paraíso* begins on a tennis court in Park West Apartments in the 1960s but moves back in time to the nineteenth century and moves forward and backward chronologically. *The Brick People* is similar in that it occurs predominantly in the county of Los Angeles during the first half of the twentieth century with narrative references to the nineteenth century. The characters in both novels are of immigrant families. The topics are the lives of the elite and working-class, the latter which I equate to ordinary people. Some of the individuals the reader meets in the books are real people and others are fictitious. To write about the previously mentioned aspects of the novel I had to research the history of the geographical regions, the particular time frames in which the actions transpire, and the main characters and the communities to which they belong. In other words, I had to research and construct the historical contexts of the regions, the times, and the peoples that constitute the story (or stories) both novels tell. History is the canvas, the backdrop, background, context, events, and discourses in the time of the characters' lives.

The motivation and inspiration to write these came from two different sources: *Reto en el paraíso* came from a suggestion given to me by the late professor Richard Barrutia, who walked into my campus office and told me that I should write about the history of the Irvine Ranch. *The Brick People* is a book based on my family that I wanted to write ever since the thought entered my mind that I could be a writer and might possibly have the skill to write stories. History was not initially the main motivation of these books, rather it was the place, time, and people that compelled me to find more about their contributions to the development of the regions and communities to which they belonged. History became the epistemological tool, the material into which I embedded the personal story of each member of my family. I discovered that history was the background material, my canvas where I paint my story or stories of where I grew up and lived, of the time periods I explored and of the people and community I love and respect. History compiles itself and becomes this vast canvas, a kind of hologram that surrounds us that is recorded by humankind's orality, literacy, and art—forms of data and information preservation that represent delicate ephemeral efforts to record our existence. And in one way or another all my books deal with history. I don't think that I could create characters or write about real people without placing them squarely in a historical context. *Reto en el paraíso* and *The Brick People* and *River of Angels* all deal predominately with Southern California. These novels are a reconsideration of history and of the diverse communities who populated California.

(DO) *What inspired you to focus your energies on a novel centered on the Los Angeles River and its history?*

(AM) After finishing *The Captain of All These Men of Death*, a novel that primarily takes place in Sylmar, California—at Olive View Sanatorium during the World War II years—I started looking for another subject, something that would jump out and seize my interest. At the time I did have other projects—short stories, novels that were in different stages of development—but I needed to find a person, an event, a structure that would reach out from history and call on me to write its story. A friend invited me to attend a reading at the downtown Los Angeles Public Library. It was crowded when we arrived. I escaped into a hallway and found a series of photographs of the crews that built the bridges that crossed into downtown. They posed before the bridge that they were building. I peered into the photos searching for a Mexican face among the men. From that time on, those photos registered in my memory and wouldn't let go—what I saw, heard, felt from them. I began searching for information about the river and the workers who built the bridges. I came across the word "porciúncula" (a small portion, a little place) that was part of the name of the City of Los Angeles and in the original name of the river of Los Angeles. I read "porciúncula" as a metaphor for Los Angeles, evolving from little places, sites along the river, and extending in all directions, where even today people invest time and work to improve and to keep their little porciúnculas. Environmental concerns factored into where the diverse populations of the city lived in relation to the river, but race and ethnicity were always considerations, always important to the residential organization of the city. In the 1900s and 1920s the pseudo-science of eugenics had influence on the decision-making of the political and cultural powers that governed the city. The ideology of eugenics is a primary mover of *River of Angels*' story, where two young people from different racial, ethnic, and class backgrounds fall in love and become targets of those afraid of the changing demographics of the time.

(DO) *It's obvious that a great deal of research went into the writing of this book. Can you talk a little bit about that process and any surprises or pitfalls you encountered?*

(AM) The research consisted of delving into as much information as possible about events, places, demographics, individuals, local mythology, construction, eugenics, etc. I found a large amount of material in scholarly books, articles, newspapers, magazines, and newsletters from historical societies, letters from friends in Italy, photographs, and conversations with local historians while visiting Los Angeles sites like East Los Angeles, Boyle Heights, La Plaza, Hancock Park, San Fernando Valley, Calvary Cemetery, Watts Towers, Los Angeles River, and Juan Matías Sánchez Adobe. Pitfalls? I still wish I had found payroll sheets or ledgers identifying the workers who built the Los Angeles bridges.

(DO) *What was the editing process like?*

(AM) Editing is the fun part of publishing a book. It usually takes me three years, more or less, including the research, to write a first draft. After the first draft is finished, I pass the manuscript over to Carol Penn. She suggests revisions, changes, additions, or more research. We meet once or twice every two weeks until we have a manuscript ready to send to the publisher. My last two books took about two years to edit. Editing, while fun, is nonetheless a demanding task for the publisher and the writer. There are times when the publisher suggests that certain sections need to be eliminated or revised or that more research is needed. For example, I like to use Spanish in my books, but the majority is usually taken out. These editing questions are resolved through the process of negotiation, as the publisher and writer do revisions that might take weeks or months. For example, the original manuscript of *River of Angels* was much longer until some scenes were deleted. Also, most of the Spanish dialogues were translated into English (though some Spanish was left in the book). I am never satisfied with a book, but after years of working on it I have to let it go. And even after it's published I find things that I would take out or change. As I heard somewhere, a work of art is never finished, only abandoned.

(MG-M) *Share with us a profound truth that you learned or realized from composing* River of Angels—*not a historical fact or static tidbit of knowledge, but a significant truth.*

(AM) I really can't answer this question because I'm not convinced that "one profound truth" exists anywhere. I've never attempted to find or identify a "significant truth." Truths or facts are concepts that I question in my works. Monolithic historical truth is another concept that I suspect. I can nevertheless tell you what I have realized in writing previous books, yet experienced more intensely in writing *River of Angels*: There are stories of the present, past, and future swarm[ing] ubiquitously in the world, continuously reaching out to be seen, heard, smelled, tasted, and touched or felt, endeavoring to be recognized and to be told. Daily I hope for an epiphany, an insight of an entity that compels me to write a story. Inspiration can come from a place, church, sound, statement, aroma, object, photograph, mosque, painting, music, event, name, food, synagogue, book, film, temple, memory, cemetery, person, etc. When I sense this uncanny or marvelous moment, I immediately start to write several sentences, short sentences in my mind, on a notebook whatever I can grab at that moment. At that instant, something odd occurs: my heart races; the hair on the back of my neck stands up; I feel an icy breeze when I shouldn't; a person appears in an impossible place and quickly vanishes. As I expressed earlier, Anzaldúa calls this experience "La Facultad . . . the capacity to see in surface phenomena the meaning of deeper realities, to see the deep structure below the surface. It is an instant 'sensing,' a quick perception arrived at without conscious reasoning."

As I also alluded to, Morrison labels this uncanny or marvelous encounter a re-memory, an energy that remains at the place or near where a powerful, overwhelming event has happened to one or several individuals. It is an independent energy that does not depend on human consciousness to exist. A re-memory can survive indefinitely and has the power to directly affect the life of human beings who sense its presence. Just read the prologue, the epilogue, and the author's note of *River of Angels*, and you will learn how the story jumped out from a photo in a frame in a library and for years possessed me and made me listen to all the voices and places and troubles of its story.

(**MG-M**) *Speaking of photographs, "looking" at compelling old photographs seems to be a strategy of yours to link history and narration. We see it in* Reto en el paraíso, *in* Waiting to Happen, *and in* River of Angels. *You don't just incorporate photographs to layer meaning in these three works, but you employ them to effect character and plot. For example, in those respective novels Daniel, Cassandra, and Mark examine old photographs [and] their act of "looking" at these visual-historical texts not only develops their own character point of view but advances plot lines. Why are you so fascinated with photographs, and how have you come to rely on them as a narrative device?*

(**AM**) Like other personal or community ephemera, photos record history. They provide details of an individual, family, community, mob, protest march, nature, labor space, events, and objects of all kinds. Photographs are points of departure. The main inspiration of *River of Angels* was a series of photographs of the crews who built the downtown bridges that crossed the Los Angeles River to connect the West side and the East side. I ran into these photographs at a reading at the downtown Los Angeles Library on a summer day. Rows of historical photographs of Los Angeles circa 1931 ran the entire length of the walls. To my left, to my right and before me the photographs multiplied and drew me to them. I began to stare deep into each one searching for a Mexican face. I traveled back in time and space assuring myself that Mexicans were part of these crews that constructed these beautiful bridges built during the 1920s and 1930s. I couldn't distinguish between Mexicans, Anglos, Asians and blacks, as they all smiled at me. Finally, I spot a small crew with Mexicans, several sporting a big Zapata mustache. In another photograph, the men smile under their hats and lean on shovels; they resembled my uncles, my father. I concentrated on their faces waiting for a sign, a sound, and as I walked back toward the Mark Taper Auditorium I actually found myself starting to plot their life story.

[In] the case of Cassandra Coe, the journalist in *Waiting to Happen*, possession of photographs is tantamount to a death certificate. Cassandra obtained photographs of horrendous acts done to indigenous women carried out by the military and federal police in southern Mexico. But it's not only photographs that I use to find details, to create scenes, characters; I also find valuable information in paintings, music, songs, poems, novels, magazines, histories, biographies, etc. I research, read legal documents, birth certificates, marriage licenses, death certificates, official letters, financial statements, personal letters, yes several of my novels are based on the lives of real individuals, ordinary people. I have written several biographical novels and novels about ordinary people whose lives I have found rewarding and worthy of telling their story.

At present, I am writing *A Rainbow of Colors*, a biographical novel about Stewart Josiah Teaze and Helen Rohde Teaze, my in-laws who lived and worked in Japan as expats for about twenty-five years. Stewart was there longer than Helen. They lived an exciting and challenging life in Tokyo-Yokohama. I have inherited hundreds of documents, letters and essays and several books about life in Japan and Japanese culture and art that Stewart Teaze wrote. And of course albums of photos of people, places, and events taken at the Teaze home in Yokohama and a house in Lake Nojiri. In addition, I have a collection of many vacation travel photos. I like to visit the places where my stories take place. For this novel I traveled to Tokyo for a one-month research trip, and I plan to make a second trip. My personal writing method depends on many objects, materials, sources from which I glean information about the people, characters, and the worlds in which they live. And of course, [it] depends on having photos, of which I have many, of Stewart and Helen's life in Japan. Each photo works as a prompt that offers a vast amount of information of place, time, social status, economics, emotions, attitudes, and relationships of people and objects in the photo. To collect information from a photograph, I break down the photograph into sections by placing a paper with at least ten cutout windows over the photo. Depending [on] the size of the photograph you might have to cut twenty windows on large size paper windows. Then I look at each window carefully to describe and record what I see. You will be amazed how much information you will withdraw from one photo. The process will help you create more detailed, in-depth physical and psychological descriptions of the people or characters and the places in your novel. In my case, using this method I have excavated much more detail and narrative information for *A Rainbow of Colors*, a biographical novel.

Of course, one thing a writer must keep in mind is that photographic images can always be tampered with to offer a contradictory story about the subject. A photographer can ask a subject to pose to create an expression, a posture that communicates a radically different impression, a story than what the individual in the photo is living. A photo tech can make your clothes look raggedy like a poor homeless person. Oh, I think photographs can be deceptive and make subjects appear radically different from their original reality. For example, they can be changed to alter one's facial expressions, color of skin, hair, eyes—change someone older into someone younger looking, change something lovely into something monstrous looking.

(FL) Speaking of which, in the second half of your production there has been an emphasis or focus on some figures who come close to being "monstrous" or figures of monstrosity. How does that relate to Chicano realities? Do these figures highlight or magnify or do they in some form detract from a novelistic realism?

(AM) There are several "monstrous" figures in my novels and stories. Some who stand above others are Father Jude described as a monk from whose face the nose and upper lip had been sliced away to reveal long, deep, opened nostrils and upper gums and teeth. Father Jude is the protagonist's guide in the first book of *The Rag Doll Plagues*. There is also Endriago, a man born horribly deformed yet who becomes the powerful protector of J. I. Cruz the Ilusa and protagonist (who arguably could be identified as monstrous) in *Waiting to Happen*. Then there is, in *Little Nation / Pequeña nación* a tale about an adolescent nicknamed Prickles who suffers with a rare, rather repulsive physical abnormality that he never overcomes, but through his artistic talents he becomes famous, wealthy, and notorious. In addition to these, [there is] Philip Keller, the antagonist whose believes in eugenics and in the superiority of the Aryan race and social racism that compel him to commit horrible tragic crimes in *River of Angels*.

These are physically and psychologically powerful monster characters who break the social norm and are considered abnormal—though they are all redeemable. These characters in one way or another are fearless and act with impunity. They tend to abuse their power, ignoring the social and moral standards of their time and place. They develop a political agenda that allows them to rise above their social circumstances to act beyond morality. Certain characteristics of each one if brought together as a whole would constitute one powerful political, amoral, irredeemable monster who is present in today's society. Of course, the political beast is the most dangerous monster who rules by disqualifying the laws of the society to which the despot belongs in order to promote personal interests, political and economic power. These figures are very real and the human good and bad attributes they personify are relevant to us in the divided, volatile social order in which we live.

(DO) *In mentioning* Little Nation / Pequeña nación, *one of my favorite stories in the collection is also one of the most disturbing ("Prickles") concerning an artist with a physical deformity who becomes famous from his paintings of the Virgin of Guadalupe—but so much more happens between the artist and his paintings. Could you talk about this story and what inspired you to write it?*

(AM) The story is about a woman who lives with an abusive man. After years of being together they have a baby. They name the boy David. She is a talented quilter and embroiderer who makes beautiful quilts and embroidered pillows, tablecloths, and tapestries. She teaches her son her talents and as he gets older [he] begins to produce magnificent works of art. Her husband makes a lot of money selling all that his wife and son produce. Finally she throws him out and he never comes back. When David is about twelve years old he develops a disease that causes tumors to protrude from his bones. The tumors grow out in different parts of the body, including the face and eventually cause painful deformities. At school during a time when David's face was covered with tumors, a bully taunted and knocked him down calling him La Penca, Cara de Penca or "Cactus Face," or "Prickles."

Notwithstanding his physical condition, David became a brilliant and famous painter. I believe his inspiration were two women: Melissa, a girl he met at college whom he loved but could never have as a lover, and the Virgin of Guadalupe, whom in his loneliness and yearning he learned to love and paint in the traditional way. However there came a night, when unintentionally he painted the Virgin in a unique and controversial manner. In the morning David was marveled by the painting but kept the process of his creation a secret. From that moment on, he signed all his paintings with the nickname of "La Penca" that the schoolyard bully gave him years ago. These paintings became the most popular and the most expensive in his gallery. David believed that the Virgin guided him in how to paint her. To David, the Virgin meant unconditional love. David's relations with the Virgin was inspired by Yolanda López's images of the Virgin of Guadalupe and in particular the controversial digital print of "Our Lady" by Alma López.

(DO) *This collection was first published in Spanish ten years ago and was translated into English by Professor Adam Spires. Was this a difficult process?*

(AM) A point of clarification, the first story "Quetzali" was originally written in English. The other four were originally written and published in Spanish. I have never translated any of my books or stories. If I were to translate my work I would probably rewrite the novel or short story. Translation is an art form. I prefer someone else to translate. Little Nation was translated by Professor Adam Spires who has written articles and comparative studies about my writing. He writes and speaks fluently in English, Spanish, and French. When Professor Spires agreed to translate Little Nation, I was very pleased and confident that he would produce a superb translation. The process went smoothly. Professor Spires wrote the first draft and sent it to me. I read the manuscript and sent it to my personal editor, Carol Penn. We went back and forth making suggestions until finally we felt the translation was ready to send to Dr. Nicolás Kanellos, director of Arte Público Press, who read the manuscript and accepted the collection for publication. The book then went to the press's editor who made a few changes and at last we had the final manuscript for publication. Professor Spires wrote a superb introduction that I insisted be included in the publication. I am quite happy with the translation and the way the book finally came out. The book motivated me to write more short stories and I plan to have another collection of stories soon.

(FL) *Expanding on this idea of technique and process, many of your works, like* Reto en el paraíso, *are what might be termed "novelas totalizadoras" by the inclusion of various stories (parallel or not) to form a network of narrativities. How does this technique allow you to be more comprehensive in presenting a wider net of stories that interrelate or come together in a neobaroque format where multiplicity in storytelling reigns?*

(AM) As a graduate student I read Latin American novels, including those that critics consider "novelas totalizadoras." Carlos Fuentes's *Where the Air Is Clear*, *The Death of Artemio Cruz*; Gabriel García Marquez's *One Hundred Years of Solitude*, and others. These novels explored the experiences of an individual, a representative family, and an emblematic city, and attempted to reveal multiple aspects of their lives, and in the case of the city showed the kinds of people who resided in it and the many physical places that composed the physical body of it. The novel aspires to accumulate an abundance of information about characters and places constructing a kind of ethnographic view of character and place. The worlds that surround the characters and the detailed descriptions of sites in the city are a microcosm of meanings. The novels fuse the biographies of characters with the history of where they live and died.

Another important aspect of "novelas totalizadoras" is the inclusion of the mythologies (legends, myths, religious beliefs, superstitions, etc.) of the individuals, their communities, and of the country. For example, *The Death of Artemio Cruz* is the story of the life of Artemio Cruz and the history of twentieth century Mexico. *One Hundred Years of Solitude* tells the story about the Buendía family that allegorically represents the history of nineteenth century Colombia—and by extension, Lain America. *Where the Air Is Clear* narrates the story of Mexico City and its history as communicated by the different people who reside in it. The novels are interwoven with magical real, fantastic events and the lives of the characters are seemingly fantastic as to how they arrived to where their story ends. The novels explore the past and present of the authors' countries. *Rayuela*, an experimental novel by Julio Cortázar, is also considered a "novela totalizadora" that has 155 chapters that can be read by following the author's instructions or by selecting different chapters out of sequence. The novel could be read many times selecting different chapters for each reading. The idea of a novel containing the most important moments in a man's life and the history of a country is found in Borges' short story "The Aleph," a site where all things, all epistemologies, places, people, past, present, and future can be simultaneously experienced. Borges' "The Aleph" es un sitio totalizador.

I would suggest that most of my works can be considered "novelas totalizadoras" because they are constructed with many of the narrative strategies previously described and appropriated to facilitate writing in my rasquache or neobaroque novels.

(MG-M) *You speak of novels that fuse biographies of characters with the history of where they live and died, and I think of* Death of an Anglo, *which does precisely that. Given the current political and social climate in this nation, what role do you see* Death of an Anglo *in influencing attitudes, or even the consciousnesses, of today's readers—how relevant and instructive do you believe this 1979 novel could be in our 2020 society of complex hatreds, conflicting cultural identities, fragmentation, and an overall resentment for Mexican Americans and Latinas/os?*

(AM) So, in 1966, Dr. Michael Logan arrives in Mathis, Texas, [and] enters an atmosphere charged with ethnic, racial prejudice and hatred leveled at Mexicans. Even so, he opens his medical office in the poor Mexican neighborhood. Dr. Logan was well aware of the social, economic, and educational inequality Mexicans have endured for decades, especially in southern Texas. His understanding and willingness to serve soon wins the hearts of local Mexican families and others beyond Mathis. What he did in Mathis contested the ignorant prejudices of Anglo men and women who wanted him and the Mexican people they loathed gone, for they saw these people as socially unworthy to belong in their American white society. In considering *Death of an Anglo* an ethnic novel marginal to the American literary canonical criteria for excellence (if we can agree on what that is), we must understand that ethnic works can offer alternative values considered along with canonical criteria by which they may be deemed as high-quality narrative works. Values in ethnic writings often are allegorical to the beliefs practiced by the protagonist and secondary characters, whether they are Anglo or Chicano. *Death of an Anglo* demonstrates how Dr. Michael Logan's life story embodies positive values such as historical, sociological, moral, psychological, therapeutic, community, commitment, honesty, and most important, relevance. Dr. Logan lived by these values. For ethnic, racial, religious communities that are a target for POTUS's racially based immigration policies, recognizing and applying these values in daily life will build pride and strength to stand up and resist whatever psychological and physical attack this administration launches at us.

(MG-M) *In this novel you interrogate—at least place the spotlight on—the research university professor and the medical physician who choose lucrative safe* careers and thus ignore the needs of the Mexican American community. These are men of ego and self-interest, but then you create the "Anglo" healer Michael Logan, who commits himself personally, professionally, and politically to serving that community. What should readers take from such an irony? Should we learn from this character who dies a martyr's death for his commitment to the struggle for justice while the others turn their backs?

(AM) The central story of *Death of Anglo* is constructed on the life of Dr. Logan, who after graduation from medical school in Guadalajara, Mexico, refused to join his father's successful medical practice in Corpus Christi, Texas. Instead, after leaving his wife and two children in Corpus Christi, he went to Mathis, a Texas farm town with a large population of Mexican farmworkers to set up his office in an abandoned store on the Mexican side of town. The last doctor who treated Mexicans was kicked out of town by local Mathis Anglos. Yet this incident did not deter Logan. On the first day, he treated about fifteen patients. From that day on his patient load grew exponentially, and in a year he was able to gather enough money for the construction of a new clinic that served some sixty patients, mostly farmworkers, per day. The success of the clinic attracted patients, predominantly Mexicans, from miles away and anger and frustration of Mathis Anglos who didn't want more Mexicans in town. Dr. Logan's efficacious clinic served people who had limited or no access to medical treatment whether they could pay or not. Approximately after two years, the Texas Department of Health, Education, and Welfare came in with $167,000 for a migrant workers clinic in the area and after Anglo medical groups nearby turned the offer down, they approached Dr. Logan who accepted. His story ends in his abrupt death.

What compelled this young man to refuse to join his father's medical practice in Corpus Christi? Why would he go to Mathis, Texas, to set up his office on the Mexican side of town to treat mostly poor Mexican patients despite the racial situation? He knew that this would be highly risky. Consequently, he settled his wife and children in Corpus Christi for their safety. His behavior of dressing in a pinstripe suit to attend Mexican fiestas, *bautismos, quinceañeras, bodas, cumpleaños* didn't amuse the powerful anti-Mexican Anglo population. In addition, his riding into town on his motorcycle wearing country bib-overalls, going shirtless, wearing straw hats. and cowboy boots infuriated Mathis whites and created tension between him, the city politicians, and the Mexican haters. As an outsider, his political attitude, and relationship with the Mexican population, and his work as a doctor in a successful clinic threatened the long-established Anglo political rule in Mathis.

You know, the 1960s was a time of accelerated Chicano civil rights social activism nationally and in the Southwest: César Chávez and Dolores Huerta organizing California farmworkers; Reies López Tijerina founded the Alianza Federal de Mercedes to restore New Mexican land grants to the descendants of the Spanish and Mexican owners; in Colorado Rodolfo "Corky" Gonzalez helped establish the Crusade for Justice that focused on social, political, and economic justice for Chicanos; José Angel Gutiérrez in Texas was a founding member of the Mexican American Youth Organization in San Antonio in 1967, and help found the Raza Unida Party, a Mexican American third party movement that supported candidates for local elective office. Moreover, in early 1966 Martin Luther King and the Southern Christian Leadership Conference (SCLC) announced plans for the Chicago Freedom Movement, a campaign that marked the expansion of civil rights activities from the South to northern cities.

Concurrent to these civil rights endeavors, Doctor Logan also had concerns about the inequality of access to public health, the race discrimination, and the abusive unchanging poverty of Mexicans in south Texas. His actions were informed by the social demands made by the Chicano Movement and Martin Luther King's civil rights movement expanding throughout the country. Unlike "the research university professor and the medical physician who choose lucrative safe careers and thus ignore the needs of the Mexican American community," Dr. Logan ironically became an unexpected activist in the long struggle in Texas for Mexican civil rights. This made him a leader in the Mexican community and thus a dangerous force for change in the dominant Anglo social order. How could I not write about a man destined to become an unforeseen, significant yet unrecognized hero of the Chicano Movement?

(MG-M) *Sandra Cisneros defined a story as something that "makes people shut-up and listen" . . . something that "meets some need that you have in your life." As a concluding question to our* charla *here, what do you want your readers to listen to? Do you have unmet needs as a Chicano writer?*

(AM) Readers of my works, I hope, will find relevant meaning(s) that will help them negotiate life in today's complex and fast-changing world. I want my novels and stories to have something to say to everyone who reads them. I hope that in the many characters I created, their life stories, the places they inhabit, and the struggles that they experience, will lead readers to find in my work something to touch their hearts and minds. Hopefully, they will read my work, and hear my work, and want to become better people who will go out in the world and do good things for themselves, their neighbors, and fellow human beings. In the current atmosphere of demagoguery thrusted upon us by the political abnormal, Chicano/a stories have become even more crucial as methods of resistance to the false truths about the Chicano/a communities in the United States. Chicano/a literary production stands to disprove the repulsive, vitriolic images shouted and repeated to spur hatred of ethnic populations. The continuous reiteration of words and phrases such as "criminals," "rapists," "murderers," "drug smugglers," "illegals," "gang members," "the wall," "build the wall," "deportation," "send them back," produces a false truth and gnawing fear of a particular ethnic group, a stereotyping of all Latinos, a profile of a target to condemn. This is the first step of eliminationist ideology practiced by the current political monster and his faithful zealots, and literature can help stanch it.

So, yeah, literature can be a form of permanent insurrection. Its mission is to arouse, to disturb, to alarm, and to keep the readers, men and women wherever they reside in a constant state of dissatisfaction with themselves and the world. But as I have expressed so many times before, I ultimately hope my work really reifies Mario Vargas Llosa's idea of "La literature es fuego"—literature is fire. Fire can alter shapes, forms, and appearances. It changes things, and literature can do that as well. But to address your other question, I really don't have any unmet needs as a Chicano writer. I'm a relatively healthy and happy guy writing my way through life.

BIBLIOGRAPHY / DONALDO W. URIOSTE

Books by Alejandro Morales

NOVELS

Morales, Alejandro. *The Brick People*. Houston: Arte Público Press, 1988.
———. *The Captain of All These Men of Death*. Tempe: Bilingual Press / Editorial Bilingüe, 2008.
———. *Caras viejas y vino nuevo*. Mexico City: Joaquín Mortiz, 1975.
———. *The Place of the White Heron, Volume Two—The Heterotopian Trilogy*. (Forthcoming)
———. *The Rag Doll Plagues*. Houston: Arte Público, 1992.
———. *Reto en el paraíso*. Ypsilanti, MI: Bilingual Press / Editorial Bilingüe, 1983.
———. *River of Angels*. Houston: Arte Público Press, 2014.
———. *La verdad sin voz*. Mexico City: Joaquín Mortiz, 1979.
———. *Waiting to Happen, Volume One—The Heterotopian Trilogy*. San José, CA: Chusma House, 2001.

SHORT FICTION

Morales, Alejandro. *Pequeña nación*. Turlock, CA: Orbis, 2008. First published 2005 by Editorial Orbis Press (Phoenix, AZ).

POETRY

Morales, Alejandro. *Zapote Tree*. Pasadena, CA: Golden Foothills Press, 2021.

Novel Excerpts, Individual Short Stories, and Poems

NOVEL EXCERPTS

Morales, Alejandro. "*Barrio on the Edge*, excerpt." In *Latinos in Lotusland: An Anthology of Contemporary Southern California Literature*, edited by Daniel A. Olivas, 242–46. Tempe: Bilingual Press / Editorial Bilingüe, 2008.

———. "*The Brick People*, excerpt." In *Under the Fifth Sun Latino Literature from California*, edited by Rick Heide, 222–28. Santa Clara, CA: Santa Clara University, 2002.

———. "*Caras viejas y vino nuevo*, and *Reto en el paraíso*, excerpts." "La Comunidad," Sunday supplement of *La Opinión*, January 11, 1981, 3–5, 7.

———. "*Caras viejas y vino nuevo*, excerpt." In *Antología de la literatura chicana*, edited by María Eugenia Gaona, 160–64. Mexico City: Centro de Enseñanza Para Extranjeros, UNAM, 1986.

———. "*Caras viejas y vino nuevo*, excerpt." In *Chicanos: Antología histórica y literaria*, edited by Tino Villanueva, 402–13. Mexico City: Fondo de Cultura Económica, 1980.

———. "*Caras viejas y vino nuevo*, excerpt." In *La voz urgente: Antología de la literatura chicana en español*, edited by Manuel M. Martín-Rodríguez, 311–21. Madrid: Editorial Fundamentos, 1995.

———. "*Caras viejas y vino nuevo*, excerpt." In *Sighs and Songs of Aztlán: A New Anthology of Chicano Literature*, edited by F. E. Albi and Jesús G. Nieto, 151–60. Bakersfield, CA: Universal Press, 1975.

———. "*Death of an Anglo*, excerpt." In "Mestizo: Anthology of Chicano Literature," special issue, *De Colores: Journal of Chicano Expression and Thought* 4, nos. 1–2 (1978): 136–42.

———. "*Reto en el paraíso*, excerpt." In *De Nueva España a Aztlán: La literatura chicana en sus textos*, edited by Armando Miguélez, Marco Antonio Jerez, and María Sandoval, 87–95. Hermosillo: Instituto Sonorense de Cultura, 1992.

———. "*Reto en el paraíso*, excerpt." In "Prosa chicana: Primer acercamiento," Cultural Supplement, *La Opinión*, December 14, 1980, 11–12, 15, 136–42.

SHORT STORIES

Morales, Alejandro. "Cara de caballo." *Americas Review* 14, no. 1 (Spring 1986): 19–22. Reprinted in *Decade II: A 20th Anniversary Anthology*, edited by Julián Olivares and Evangelina Vigil-Piñón, 29–32. Houston: Arte Público Press, 1993. Reprinted in *The Floating Borderlands: Twenty-Five Years of U.S. Hispanic Literature*, edited by Lauro Flores, 34–37. Seattle: University of Washington Press, 1988; also in *Short Fiction by Hispanic Writers of the United States*, edited by Nicolás Kanellos, 149–54. Houston: Arte Público Press, 1993.

———. "El compadrito." In *Cien años de lealtad: En honor a Luis Leal / One Hundred Years of Loyalty: In Honor of Luis Leal*, edited by Sara Poot Herrera, María Herrera-Sobek, and Francisco A. Lomelí, 14–17. Santa Barbara: University of California, Santa Barbara, 2007.

———. "Concepción." *Camino Real: Estudios de las Hispanidades Norteamericanas* 3, no. 5 (2011): 189–99.

———. "The Curing Woman." *Americas Review* 14, no. 1 (Spring 1986): 23–27. Reprinted in *Short Fiction by Hispanic Writers of the United States*, edited by Nicolás Kanellos, 155–60. Houston: Arte Público Press, 1993.

———. "Energúmenos, the Possessed." *Ventana Abierta: Revista Latina de Literatura, Arte y Cultura* 13–14, nos. 39–41 (Fall 2015 and 2016; Spring 2016 and 2017): 59–64.

———. "I giardini di Versailles." In *En la frontera: I migliori racconti della narrativa chicana*, edited by Fernando Clemont and Klaus Zilles, 20–32. Milan: Gran Via Edizione, 2008.

———. "Integrals, Cartographers of Memory." *AlternaCtive PublicaCtions*, University of California Merced, 2019. Edited by Manuel M. Martín-Rodríguez. http://alternativepublications.ucmerced.edu/?p=526.

———. "Los jardines de Versalles." *Confluencia: Revista Hispánica de Cultura y Literatura*, 13, no. 1 (Fall 1997): 257–65.

———. "Jimena." In *Perspectivas transatlánticas en la literatura Chicana: Ensayos y creatividad*, edited by María Herrera-Sobek, Francisco A. Lomelí, and Juan Antonio Perles Rochel, 25–42. Málaga: Universidad de Málaga, 2004.

———. "La parábola de Quetzali." In *Actas de séptimo congreso internacional de culturas latinos en Estados Unidos*, edited by Axel Ramírez, 53–60. Mexico City: Universidad Nacional Autónoma de México, l997.

———. "La penca." *Ventana Abierta: Revista Latina de Literatura, Arte y Cultura* 2, no. 5 (Fall 1998): 54–58.

———. "Salió de la casa por la puerta de atrás." In *Literatura fronteriza: Antología del primer festival San Diego-Tijuana, mayo 1981*, edited by Herberto Espinoza, 110–13. San Diego, CA: Maize Press, 1982.

POETRY

Morales, Alejandro. "Gray Tears." In *California Fire and Water: A Climate Crisis Anthology*, edited by Molly Fisk, 123. Nevada City, CA: Story Press, 2020.

———. "In the Name of Self Defense." In *¡Ban c/s This!: The BSP Anthology of Xican@ Literature*, edited by Santino J. Rivera, 228–35. Saint Augustine, FL: Broken Sword Publications, 2012.

———. "'Make America Great Again'—A Man Made Disaster." In *When the Virus*

Came Calling: COVID-19 Strikes America, edited by Thelma T. Reyna, 184–85. Pasadena, CA: Golden Foothills Press, 2020.

———. "Matanzas Creek." In ¡Ban c/s This! The BSP Anthology of Xican@ Literature, edited by Santino J. Rivera, 222–23. Saint Augustine, FL: Broken Sword Publications, 2012.

———. "Morena Survivor on Andalusian Sand," Revista Canaria de Estudios Ingleses 81 (November 2020): 290–91.

———. "On an Island." In ¡Ban c/s This! The BSP Anthology of Xican@ Literature, edited by Santino J. Rivera, 224–28. Saint Augustine, FL: Broken Sword Publications, 2012.

———. "The Woman in a Box." In Camino Real: Estudios de las Hispanidades Norteamericanas, no. 1 (2009): 53–69.

TRANSLATED WORKS

Morales, Alejandro. La bambola di pezza. Italian translation of The Rag Doll Plagues, by Michele Bottalico and Angelinda Griseta. Salerno: Oèdipus, 2002.

———. Barrio in fiamme. Italian translation of Caras viejas y vino nuevo, by Rosa Giordano. Naples: Ad Est dell'Equatore, 2012.

———. Barrio on the Edge. English translation of Caras viejas y vino nuevo, by Francisco A. Lomelí. Tempe: Bilingual Press / Editorial Bilingüe, 1998.

———. Death of an Anglo. English translation of La verdad sin voz, by Judith Ginsberg, Tempe, AZ: Bilingual Press / Editorial Bilingüe, 1988.

———. Hombres de ladrillo. Spanish translation of The Brick People, by Isabel Díaz Sánchez. Houston: Arte Público Press, 2010.

———. "Integrales, cartógrafos de la memoria. " Spanish translation of "Integrals, Cartographers of Memory," by Margarita López. AlternaCtive PublicaCtions, University of California Merced, 2019. Edited by Manuel M. Martín-Rodríguez. http://alternativepublications.ucmerced.edu/?p=530.

———. Little Nation and Other Stories. English translation of Pequeña nación, by Adam Spires. Houston: Arte Público Press, 2014.

———. Old Faces and New Wine. English translation of Caras viejas y vino nuevo, by Max Martínez. Edited by José Monleón and Alurista. San Diego: Maize Press, 1981.

———. El olvidado pueblo de Simons. Spanish translation of The Brick People, by Isabel Díaz Sánchez. Alcalá de Henares, Spain: Instituto Franklin, Universidad de Alcalá, 2009.

———. Plager. Danish translation of The Rag Doll Plagues, by Tom Bernbom Jørgensen. Århus: Forlaget Klim, 1993.

———. Reto en el paraíso. English translation by Alicia Smithers. Mexico City: Grijalbo, 1992.

ESSAYS

Morales, Alejandro. "Dynamic Identities in Heterotopia." In "Alejandro Morales: Fiction Past, Present, Future Perfect," edited by José Antonio Gurpegui, special issue, *Bilingual Review / Revista Bilingüe* 20, no. 3 (September–December 1995): 14–27.

———. "Mariposas and Colibríes." In *September 11: West Coast Writers Approach Ground Zero*, edited by Jeff Meyers, 341–44. Portland, OR: Hawthorne Books and Literary Arts, 2002. Reprinted in *One Wound for Another / Una Herida por Otra: Testimonios de Latin@s in the U.S. through Cyberspace*, edited by Claire Joysmith and Clara Lomas, 217–18. Mexico City: Universidad Nacional Autónoma de México, 2005.

BOOK CHAPTERS / JOURNAL ARTICLES

Morales, Alejandro. "Ampliar el significado del cine chicano: *Yo soy chicano, Raíces de sangre, Seguín*." In *Cine chicano*, edited by Gary D. Keller, 155–75. Mexico City: Cineteca Nacional, 1988.

———. "Aztlán, Borderlands, Heterotopia." In *Evolving Origins, Transplanting Cultures: Literary Legacies of the New Americans*, edited by Laura P. Alonso Gallo and Antonia Domínguez Miguela, 237–48. Huelva, Spain: Universidad de Huelva, 2002.

———. "Cielos de la tierra por Carmen Boullosa: Escribiendo la utopía mexicana a través del eterno apocalipsis mexicano." In *Acercamientos a Carmen Boullosa: Actas del simposio "Conjugarse en infinitivo la escritora Carmen Boullosa,"* edited by Barbara Dröscher and Carlos Rincón, 193–201. Berlin: Tranvía-Walter Frey, 1999.

———. "The Conquest and the Colony in *The House of Forgetting* by Benjamín Alire Sáenz." In *Culture a Contatto Nelle Americhe*, edited by Michele Bottalico and Rosa María Grillo, 99–111. Salerno: Oèdipus, 2003.

———. "The Deterritorialization of Esperanza Cordero: A Paraesthetic Inquiry." In *Gender, Self, and Society: Proceedings of the IV International Conference on the Hispanic Cultures of the United States*, edited by Renate von Bardeleben, 227–35. Frankfurt: Peter Lang, 1993.

———. "En este lugar sagrado de Poli Délano: Las manifestaciones del exilio." *Confluencia: Revista Hispánica de Cultura y Literatura* 4, no. 1 (Fall 1988): 69–82.

———. "Expanding the Meaning of Chicano Cinema: *Yo soy chicano, Raíces de sangre, Seguín*." In "Chicano Cinema: Research, Reviews and Resources," edited by Gary D. Keller, special issue, *Bilingual Review / Revista Bilingüe* 10, nos. 2–3 (May–December 1983): 121–37.

———. "Imágenes de México y España en *Memories of the Alhambra* de Nash Candelaria." In *Las relaciones literarias entre España e Iberoamérica*, 797–809. Madrid:

Instituto de Cooperación Iberoamericana, Facultad de Filología, Universidad Complutense de Madrid, 1987.

———. "The Klail City Death Trip Series: A *Trovador's* Eternal Space for an Enduring Transitory World." In *Rolando Hinojosa's Klail City Death Trip Series: A Retrospective, New Directions*, edited by Stephen Miller and José Pablo Villalobos, 92–110. Houston: Arte Público Press, 2013.

———. "Notes from Southern California: South Coast Repertory's 1987 Hispanic Playwrights Project." *GESTOS: Revista de Teoría y Práctica de Teatro Hispánico* 3, no 5 (1988): 125–28.

———. "Los orígenes de la cultura chicana." In *El México olvidado: La historia del pueblo chicano*, edited by David Maciel, 269–317. Ciudad Juárez, Mexico: Universidad Autónoma de Ciudad Juárez, 1996.

———. "The Parable of Quetzali." In *El mito de lo umbilical, los Latinos en América del Norte: Actas del Séptimo Congreso Internacional de Culturas Latinas en Estados Unidos*, edited by Axel Ramírez and Patricia Casasa, 53–60. Mexico City: Universidad Nacional Autónoma de México, 1997.

———. "Terra Mater and the Emergence of Myth in Poems by Alma Villanueva." *Bilingual Review / Revista Bilingüe* 7, no. 2 (May–August 1980): 123–42.

———. "'. . . Y No Se lo Tragó la Tierra:' Orality as Structure in Postmodern Culture." *Discurso: Revista de Estudios Iberoamericanos* 7, no. 1 (1990): 67–79.

———. "'. . . Y no se lo tragó la tierra:' La tradición oral como estructura en la cultura postmoderna." *Nuevo Texto Crítico* 3, no. 5 (Fall 1990): 153–58.

———. "'. . . Y no se lo tragó la tierra:' Palabra y estructura en una cultura postmoderna." In *Culturas hispanas en los Estados Unidos de América*, edited by María Jesús Buxó Rey and Tomás Calvo Buezas, 494–500. Madrid: Ediciones de Cultura Hispánica,1990.

BOOK AND FILM REVIEWS

Morales, Alejandro. "Blues for a Lost Childhood by Antonio Torres." *Los Angeles Times*, January 21, 1990.

———. "*Chicano Park*, a Film by Marilyn Mulford and Mario Barrera." *UC MEXUS News*, no. 27 (Fall 1990): 21–22.

———. "*Cinema and Social Change in Latin America: Conversations with Filmmakers*, edited by Julianne Burton." *UC MEXUS News*, nos. 21/22 (Fall 1987/Winter 1988): 14–15.

———. "A Cuban Baroque Symphony, *The Chase* by Alejo Carpentier." *Los Angeles Times*, January 7, 1990.

———. "Home Boy Goes to Harvard, *Skin Deep* by Guy García." *Los Angeles Times*, February 19, 1989.

———. "Last Stop for Dreamers, *Mile Zero* by Thomas Sánchez." *Los Angeles Times*, September 17, 1989.

———. "Mexican Messiahs, *Man-Gods in the Mexican Highlands: Indian Power and Colonial Society, 1520–1800* by Serge Gruzinski." *Los Angeles Times*, July 16, 1989.

———. "Mexico and Her Late Father, *The False Years* by Josefina Vicens." *Los Angeles Times*, January 28, 1990.

———. "*The Promise: The Puerto Rican / Nuyorican Postmodern Condition* by José Rivera." *Hispanic Playwrights Project Bulletin*, Costa Mesa, CA: South Coast Repertory, 1987, n.p.

———. "Review of *The Fifth Horseman* by José Antonio Villarreal." *Mester: Revista de Literatura, Creación, Teoría, Interpretación* 5, no. 2 (April 1975): 135–36.

———. "*The Road to Tamazunchale* by Ron Arias and *Claros varones de Belken / Fair Gentlemen of Belken County* by Rolando Hinojosa Smith." *Los Angeles Times*, April 12, 1987.

———. "Through a Lens, with Ambiguity, *The Adventures of a Photographer in La Plata* by Adolfo Bioy Casares." *Los Angeles Times*, December 31, 1989.

———. "A Wedding of the Grotesque, *The Wedding* by Mary Helen Ponce." *Los Angeles Times*, November 19, 1989.

Critical Works about Alejandro Morales

BOOKS

García-Martínez, Marc. *The Flesh-and-Blood Aesthetics of Alejandro Morales: Disease, Sex, and Figuration*. San Diego: San Diego State University Press, 2014.

Gurpegui, José Antonio, ed. *Alejandro Morales: Fiction Past, Present, Future Perfect*. Tempe: Bilingual Press / Editorial Bilingüe. (Reprint of special issue in *Bilingual Review / Revista Bilingüe*, vol. 20, no. 3 (September–December 1995).

Rosales, Jesús. *La narrativa de Alejandro Morales: Encuentro, historia y compromiso social*. New York: Peter Lang, 1999.

ARTICLES AND BOOK CHAPTERS

Akers, John C. "Fragmentation in the Chicano Novel: Literary Technique and Cultural Identity." *Revista Chicano-Riqueña* 13, nos. 3–4 (Fall–Winter 1985): 121–27.

Alarcón, Francisco X. "Califas en una novela: El arte narrativo de Alejandro Morales. Parte 1." *La Opinión*, June 5, 1983, 6–7.

———. "Califas en una novela: El arte narrativo de Alejandro Morales. Parte 2." *La Opinión*, June 12, 1983, 6–7.

Aubrey, Bryan. "Critical Essay on 'The Curing Woman.'" In *Short Stories for Students*, edited by Ira Mark Milne, vol. 19. Detroit: Cengage Gale, 2004.

Ayala, Roberto. "The Space of Disease in Alejandro Morales's *The Captain of All These Men of Death*." In *Landscapes of Writing in Chicano Literature*, edited by Imelda Martín-Junquera, 151–60. New York: Palgrave Macmillan, 2013.

Benavides, Ricardo F. "Estirpe y estigma en una novela chicana." *Chasqui: Revista de Literatura Latinoamericana* 6, no. 1 (November 1976): 84–93.

Bentley-Adler, Colleen. "Crossing Cultures: Morales' Novels Reflect the Dilemma of Dual Ethnicities." *UCI Journal* 8, no. 3 (January 1989): 7.

Bottalico, Michele. "Illness in Alejandro Morales's *The Rag Doll Plagues*." *Cuadernos de la Literatura Inglesa y Norteamericana* vol. 5, nos. 1–2 (November 2002): 64–73.

Bottalico, Michele, and Angelinda Griesta. "Introduzione." In Alejandro Morales, *La bambola di pezza*, 7–13. Salerno: Oèdipus, 2002.

Bustamante, Nuria. "Permanencia y cambio en *Caras viejas y vino nuevo*." *Confluencia: Revista Hispánica de Cultura y Literatura* 1, no. 2 (Spring 1986): 61–65.

Carroll, Victoria. "Deforming and Transforming: Towards a Theory of 'Viral Mestizaje' in Chicano Literature." *Journal of Literary & Cultural Disability Studies* vol. 10, no. 3 (October 2016): 323–40.

Durán, Javier. "Alejandro Morales (1944-)." In *Latino and Latina Writers, Vol. I: Introductory Essays, Chicano and Chicana Authors*, edited by Alan West-Durán, María Herrera-Sobek and César A. Salgado, 383–404. New York: Charles Scribner's Sons, 2004. Available at http://go.galegroup.com/ps/i.do?id=GALE%7CCX1385800010&v=2.1&u=ivytech29&it=r&p=GVRL&sw=w&asid=126180412b1b2b87fa9c0e10534cda69#Q.

Elías, Eduardo. "La evolución narrativa de Alejandro Morales a través de sus textos." *Explicación de Textos Literarios* 15, no. 2 (1986–1987): 92–102.

Emmanouilidou, Sophia. "Temporal Dynamics and Spatial Horizons in Alejandro Morales's Novel *The Rag Doll Plagues*." In *Time, Space, and Mobility*, edited by Konstantinos D. Karatzas, 133–41. Warsaw: IRF Press, 2018.

Franco, Dean. "Working through the Archive: Trauma and History in Alejandro Morales's *The Rag Doll Plagues*." *PMLA: Publications of the Modern Language Association of America* 120, no. 2 (March 2005): 375–87. Reprinted as "Working through the Archive," in *Ethnic American Literature: Comparing Chicano, Jewish, and African American Writings*, 55–72. Charlottesville: University of Virginia Press, 2006.

Franco, Dean, and Adrianne Pilón. "Alejandro Morales: Mexican American Novelist and Short-Story Writer." In *Notable Latino Writers*, vol. 2, edited by Salem Press Editors, 467–71. Pasadena, CA: Salem Press, 2006.

Gamber, John Blair. "Toxic Metropolis: Alejandro Morales's *The Rag Doll Plagues*." In *Positive Pollutions and Cultural Toxins: Waste and Contamination in Contemporary U.S. Ethnic Literatures*, 57–90. Lincoln: University of Nebraska Press, 2012.

Garay, R. Joyce Z. L. "Reading Alejandro Morales's *The Rag Doll Plagues* through Its

Women: Gender, Sexuality, and Nationalistic Complexity." *Bilingual Review / Revista Bilingüe* 31, no. 2 (May–August 2012–2013): 141–65.

García, Mario T. "History, Literature, and the Chicano Working-Class Novel: A Critical Review of Alejandro Morales' *The Brick People*." *Crítica: A Journal of Critical Essays* 2, no. 2 (Fall 1990): 188–201.

Georgi, Sonja. "Past-Present-Future Loops." In *Bodies and/as Technology: Counter-Discourses on Ethnicity and Globalization in the Works of Alejandro Morales, Larissa Lai, and Nalo Hopkinson*, 197–245. Heidelberg: Universitätsverlag, 2011.

Ginsberg, Judith. "*La Verdad Sin Voz*: Elegy and Reparation." *Americas Review: A Review of Hispanic Literature and Art of the USA* 14, no. 2 (Summer 1986): 78–83.

Gonzales-Berry, Erlinda. "*Caras Viejas y Vino Nuevo*: Journey through a Disintegrating Barrio." *Latin American Literary Review* 7, no. 14 (Spring 1979): 62–72.

———. "Morales, Alejandro (1944–)." *Chicano Literature: A Reference Guide*, edited by Julio A. Martínez and Francisco A. Lomelí, 299–305. Westport, CT: Greenwood Press, 1985.

González, María. "*Caras viejas y vino nuevo*: Análisis temático y estructural." *Tinta* 1, no. 1 (May 1981): 15–18.

Grandjeat, Yves-Charles. "Jeux et enjeux du je dans la littérature Chicano." *Annales du Centre de Recherches sur l'Amérique anglophone* 17 (1992): 11–23, 265.

———. "L'Ici est l'ailleurs: *Reto en el paraíso*, d'Alejandro Morales." In *Multilinguisme et multiculturalisme en Amérique du Nord*, edited by Elyette Andouard-Labarthe and Jean Béranger, 203–15. Bordeaux: Presses de l'Université de Bordeaux, 1991.

Gurpegui, José Antonio. "Implicaciones existenciales del uso del español en las novelas de Alejandro Morales." In "Alejandro Morales: Fiction Past, Present, Future Perfect," edited by José Antonio Gurpegui, special issue, *Bilingual Review / Revista Bilingüe* 20, no. 3 (September–December 1995): 43–51.

———. "*Tortilla Flat* de Steinbeck y *Caras viejas y vino nuevo* de Morales: Dos perspectivas de una misma realidad." *REDEN: Revista Española de Estudios Norteamericanos* 3 (Spring 1990): 73–84.

Gurpegui, José Antonio, and Karen S. Van Hooft. "Bibliography of Works by and about Alejandro Morales." In "Alejandro Morales: Fiction Past, Present, Future Perfect," edited by José Antonio Gurpegui, special issue, *Bilingual Review / Revista Bilingüe* 20, no. 3 (September–December 1995): 109–14.

Gutiérrez-Jones, Carl. "'Rancho Mexicana, USA' Under Siege." In *Rethinking the Borderlands: Between Chicano Culture and Legal Discourse*, 80–89. Berkeley: University of California Press, 1995. Available at http://ark.cdlib.org/ark:/13030/ft5779p07b/.

———. "Resisting Cultural Dependency: The Manipulation of Surveillance and Paranoia in Alejandro Morales' *The Brick People*." *Americas Review: A Review of Hispanic Literature and Art of the USA* 22, nos. 1–2 (Spring–Summer 1994): 230–43.

Herrera-Sobek, María. "Epidemics, Epistemophilia, and Racism: Ecological Literary Criticism and *The Rag Doll Plagues*." In "Alejandro Morales: Fiction Past, Present, Future Perfect," edited by José Antonio Gurpegui, special issue, *Bilingual Review / Revista Bilingüe* 20, no. 3 (September–December 1995): 99–108.

———. "The Monstrous Imagination: Cyclope Representation in Art and Literature-Díaz Oliva and Alejandro Morales." *Perspectivas transatlánticas en la literatura chicana: Ensayos y creatividad*, edited by María Herrera-Sobek, Francisco A. Lomelí, and Juan Antonio Perles Rochel, 161–66. Málaga: Universidad de Málaga, 2004.

Jirón-King, Shimberlee. "Epic Linearity and Cyclical Narrative: Moving Beyond Colonizing Discourse in Alejandro Morales' *The Brick People*." *Hipertexto* 6 (Summer 2007): 25–36.

———. "Illness, Observation, and Contradiction: Intertext and Intrahistory in Alejandro Morales's *The Captain of All These Men of Death*." *Bilingual Review / Revista Bilingüe* vol. 29, no. 1 (January – April 2008): 3–13.

Kanellos, Nicolás. "Alejandro Morales (1944–)." *The Hispanic American Almanac: A Reference Work on Hispanics in the United States*, edited by Nicolás Kanellos, 454–55. Detroit: Gale Research, 1993. Reprinted in *The Hispanic Almanac: From Columbus to Corporate America*, edited by Nicolás Kanellos, 432–33. Washington, DC: Invisible Ink Press, 1994.

Kaup, Monika. "From Hacienda to Brick Factory: The Architecture of the Machine and Chicano Collective Memory in Alejandro Morales's *The Brick People*." *U.S. Latino Literatures and Cultures: Transnational Perspectives*, edited by Francisco A. Lomelí and Karin Ikas, 159–70. Heidelberg: Universitätsverlag C. Winter, 2000.

Lamb, Jeffrey N. "Lost in the Barrio: *Caras Viejas y Vino Nuevo*." *Cuadernos de ALDEEU* 16, no. 1 (Winter 2000): 191–99.

Lanslots, Inge, and An Van Hecke. "Bridging the Gaps in Southern California: Multicultural Spaces throughout the Works of Alejandro Morales." In *Literary Transnationalism(s)*, edited by Dagmar Vandebosch and Theo D'haen, 192–204. Leiden: Brill, 2018.

———. "Building Stories on *The Brick People*: Mapping Alejandro Morales's Otherness in Documentary and Fiction." *Journal of Internationalization and Localization* 3, no. 2 (January 2016): 182–95.

Leal, Luis. "Historia y ficción en la narrativa de Alejandro Morales." In "Alejandro Morales: Fiction Past, Present, Future Perfect," edited by José Antonio Gurpegui, special issue, *Bilingual Review / Revista Bilingüe* 20, no. 3 (September–December 1995): 31–42.

Lee, James Kyung-Jin. "Fictionalizing Workers in the Barrio." In *Urban Triage: Race and Fictions of Multiculturalism*, 30–63. Minneapolis: University of Minnesota Press, 2004.

———. "Fictionalizing Workers; Or, The Abuse of Fiction: Violence, Reading, and the Staging of Barrio-Space in Alejandro Morales's *The Brick People*." In *Re-Placing America: Conversations and Contestations: Selected Essays*, edited by Ruth Hsu, Cynthia Franklin, and Suzanne Kosanke, 5–30. Honolulu: University of Hawaii Press, 2000.

Lerat, Christian. "Esthétique de la 'reconstruction' du chaos et de la nostalgie de l'ordre dans *Caras viejas y vino nuevo* d'Alejandro Morales." *Annales du Centre de Recherches sur l'Amérique Anglophone* 19 (1994): 87–103.

Lewis, Marvin A. "Alejandro Morales (14 October 1944–)." *Dictionary of Literary Biography: Volume 82, Chicano Writers: First Series*, edited by Francisco A. Lomelí and Carl R. Shirley, 178–83. Detroit: Gale Research, 1989.

———. "*Caras viejas y vino nuevo* / La verdad sin voz." In *Introduction to the Chicano Novel*, 31–39. Milwaukee: Spanish Speaking Outreach Institute, University of Wisconsin-Milwaukee, 1982. Reprinted in *Introduction to the Chicano Novel*, 31–39. Houston: Arte Público Press, 1984.

Li, Baojie. "Urban History and Space Politics: Los Angeles in *River of Angels*." *Shandong Foreign Language Teaching and Research* 38, no. 5 (September 2017): 57–64.

Libretti, Tim. "Forgetting Identity, Recovering Politics: Rethinking Chicana/o Nationalism, Identity Politics, and Resistance to Racism in Alejandro Morales's *Death of an Anglo*." *Post Identity* 1, no. 1 (Fall 1997): 66–93. Available at http://hdl.handle.net/2027/spo.pid9999.0001.104.

Lomelí, Francisco A. "Alejandro Morales." In *Reference Guide to American Literature*, 3rd edition, edited by Jim Kamp, 619–21. Detroit: St. James Press, 1994.

———. "Hard-Core Barrio Revisited: Violence, Sex, Drugs, and Videotape through a Chicano Glass Darkly." Introduction to Alejandro Morales, *Barrio on the Edge / Caras viejas y vino nuevo*, translated by Francisco Lomelí, 1–21. Tempe: Bilingual Press / Editorial Bilingüe. Reprinted in *The Chican@ Literary Imagination: A Collection of Critical Studies by Francisco A. Lomelí*, edited by Julio Cañero and Juan F. Elices, 229–43. Alcalá de Henares, Spain: Instituto Franklin de Estudios Norteamericanos, Universidad de Alcalá, 2012.

———. "Morales, Alejandro (1944–)." In *Historical Dictionary of U.S. Latino Literature* by Donaldo W. Urioste, Francisco A. Lomelí, and María Joaquina Villaseñor, 208–11. Lanham, MD: Rowman and Littlefield, 2017.

———. "Rereading Alejandro Morales's *Caras Viejas y Vino Nuevo*: Violence, Sex, Drugs, and Videotape in a Chicano Glass Darkly." In "Alejandro Morales: Fiction Past, Present, Future Perfect," edited by José Antonio Gurpegui, special issue, *Bilingual Review / Revista Bilingüe* 20, no. 3 (September–December 1995): 52–60.

———. "State of Siege in Alejandro Morales' *Old Faces and New Wine*." In *Missions in Conflict: Essays on U.S.-Mexican Relations and Chicano Culture*, edited by Renate von Bardeleben, Dietrich Briesemeister, and Juan Bruce-Novoa, 185–94. Tubingen: Gunter Narr Verlag, 1986.

———. "La violencia como instrumento reivindicador en dos obras chicanas: *The Revolt of the Cockroach People* y *Pequeña nación*." *Revista Casa de las Américas* 299 (April–June 2020): 16–24.

López-Lozano, Miguel. "The Politics of Blood: Miscegenation and Phobias of Contagion in Alejandro Morales's *The Rag Doll Plagues*." *Aztlán: A Journal of Chicano Studies* 28, no. 1 (Spring 2003): 39–73.

Mariscal, George. "Alejandro Morales in Utopia." *Confluencia: Revista Hispánica de Cultura y Literatura* 2, no. 1 (Fall 1986): 78–83.

Márquez, Antonio C. "The Use and Abuse of History in Alejandro Morales's *The Brick People* and *The Rag Doll Plagues*." In "Alejandro Morales: Fiction Past, Present, Future Perfect," edited by José Antonio Gurpegui, special issue, *Bilingual Review / Revista Bilingüe* 20, no. 3 (September–December 1995): 76–85.

Martín-Junquera, Imelda. "*The Brick People* and the Struggle for Survival." In *Interpreting the New Milenio*, edited by José Antonio Gurpegui Palacios, 48–55. Newcastle, UK: Cambridge Scholars Publishing, 2008.

———. "Ecocrítica, racismo medioambiental y renacimiento chicano." In *Tendencias de la narrativa mexicana actual*, edited by José Carlos González Boixo, 229–43. Madrid: Iberoamericana, 2009.

Martín-Rodríguez, Manuel M. "Deterritorialization and Heterotopia: Chicano/a Literature in the Zone." In *Confrontations et Métissages*, edited by Elyette Benjamin-Labarthe, Yves-Charles Grandjeat, and Christian Lerat, 391–98. Bordeaux: Éditions de la Maison des Pays Ibériques, 1995.

———. "The Global Border: Transnationalism and Cultural Hybridism in Alejandro Morales's *The Rag Doll* Plagues." In "Alejandro Morales: Fiction Past, Present, Future Perfect," edited by José Antonio Gurpegui, special issue, *Bilingual Review / Revista Bilingüe* 20, no. 3 (September–December 1995): 86–98.

———. "El sentimiento de culpa en *Reto en el paraíso* de Alejandro Morales." *Americas Review: A Review of Hispanic Literature and Art of the USA* 15, no. 1 (Spring 1987): 89–97.

———. "El tema de la culpa en cuatro novelistas chicanos." *Hispanic Journal* 10, no. 1 (Fall 1988): 133–42.

Martínez, Danizete. "Dismemberment in the Chicana/o Body Politic: Fragmenting Nationness and Form in Oscar Zeta Acosta's *The Revolt of the Cockroach People* and Alejandro Morales's *The Rag Doll Plagues*." *DisClosure: A Journal of Social Theory* 21 (2012): 38–53. Reprinted in *Twentieth-Century Literary Criticism*, edited by Lawrence J. Trudeau, vol. 360. Farmington Hills, MI: Gale, 2018.

Martínez Wood, Jamie. "Morales, Alejandro (1944–): Novelist, Essayist, Short Story

Writer, Educator." In *Latino Writers and Journalists*, 153–55. New York: Facts on File, 2007.

McLellan, Dennis. "Building on Words: Family History Provides UC Irvine Professor Alejandro Morales the Material with Which to Lay the Foundation for Novels That Put Forth the Contributions of Mexican Americans." *Los Angeles Times*, February 12, 1995. Available at https://www.latimes.com/archives/la-xpm-1995-02-12-ls-31448-story.html.

———. "Latinos Have a Story to Tell: O. C. Writers Are Among Those Whose Works about the Hispanic Experience Have Found Wider Audience." *Los Angeles Times*, December 27, 1991. Available at https://www.latimes.com/archives/la-xpm-1991-12-27-vw-1084-story.html.

Milne, Ira Mark, ed. *Short Stories for Students: A Study Guide for Alejandro Morales's "The Curing Woman."* Vol. 19. Farmington Hills, MI: Gale, 2004.

Morales, Alejandro. "De cómo la mandala de *The Brick People* se inspiraba en una escena del poema de Villagrá." In "400 Years of Literature and History in the United States: Gaspar de Villagra's Historia de la Nueva Mexico (1610)," edited by Manuel M. Martín-Rodríguez, special issue of *Camino Real: Estudios de las Hispanidades Norteamericanas*, 4, no. 6 (2012): 101–11.

———. "The Evolution of a Chicano Writer: Four Novels by Alejandro Morales." In *Hispanorama*, edited by Renate von Bardeleben. Mainz, Germany: Johannus Guttemberg, Universitat Mainz, 1991.

Muñoz, Willy O. "*Caras viejas y vino nuevo*, la tragedia de los barrios." *Aztlán: A Journal of Chicano Studies* 15, no. 1 (September 1984): 163–76.

Padilla, Genaro M. "The Anti-Romantic City in Chicano Fiction." *Puerto del Sol* 23, no. 1 (Fall 1987): 159–69.

Pitman, Thea. "Mestizaje and Cyborgism on Either Side of the Line." In *The Cambridge Companion to Latina/o American Literature*, edited by John Morán González, 213–30. New York: Cambridge University Press, 2016.

Priewe, Marc. "Bio-Politics and the ContamiNation of the Body in Alejandro Morales' *The Rag Doll Plagues*." *MELUS: The Journal of the Society for the Study of the Multi-Ethnic Literature of the United States* 29, nos. 3–4 (Autumn–Winter 2004): 397–412.

Rodríguez del Pino, Salvador. "Capítulo III: Alejandro Morales y el compromiso a la juventud (*Caras viejas y vino nuevo*)." In *La novela chicana escrita en español: Cinco autores comprometidos*, 65–89. Ypsilanti, MI: Bilingual Press / Editorial Bilingüe, 1982.

———. "La novela chicana de los setenta comentada por sus escritores y críticos." *Bilingual Review / Revista Bilingüe* 4, no. 3 (September–December 1977): 240–44. Reprinted in *The Identification and Analysis of Chicano Literature*, edited by Francisco Jiménez, 153–60. New York: Bilingual Press / Editorial Bilingüe, 1979.

Rosales, Jesús. "El cronotopo del encuentro en *Reto en el paraíso* de Alejandro Morales." In "Alejandro Morales: Fiction Past, Present, Future Perfect," edited by José Antonio Gurpegui, special issue, *Bilingual Review / Revista Bilingüe* 20, no. 3 (September–December 1995): 61–75.

Ryan, Bryan, ed. "Morales, Alejandro 1944– ." In *Hispanic Writers: A Selection of Sketches from Contemporary Authors*, 319. Detroit: Gale Research, 1991.

Saldívar, Ramón. "History, Literature, and the Chicano Working-Class Novel: Critical Review of Alejandro Morales' *The Brick People*." *Crítica* 2, no. 2 (Fall 1990): 189–201.

Salvioni, Amanda. "Lo peor ya ocurrió—categorías del postapocalipsis hispanoamericano: Alejandro Morales y Marcelo Cohen." In "Altre Modernità: Rivista di Studi Letterari e Culturali," special issue, *Apocalypse* (June 2013): 304–16. Available at https://dialnet.unirioja.es/descarga/articulo/4962415.pdf.

Sánchez Benítez, Roberto. "Alejandro Morales y la fuga mística del caos / Alejandro Morales's Mystical Realism." *Nóesis: Revista de Ciencias Sociales y Humanidades*, 25, no. 49 (January – June 2016): 206–24.

Schedler, Christopher. "Bugs in the Capitalist Machine: The Schizo-Violence of Alejandro Morales's *The Brick People*." *MELUS: Multi-Ethnic Literature of the U.S.* 32, no. 1 (Spring 2007): 53–74.

Shirley, Carl R., and Paula W. Shirley. "Novel." In *Understanding Chicano Literature*, 117–21. Columbia: University of South Carolina Press, 1988.

Sohn, Stephen Hong. "Minor Character, Minority Orientalisms, and the Borderlands of Asian America." *Cultural Critique* 82 (2012): 151–85.

Somoza, Oscar U. "Choque e interacción en *La verdad sin voz* de Alejandro Morales." In *Contemporary Chicano Fiction: A Critical Survey*, edited by Vernon E. Lattin, 299–305. Binghamton, NY: Bilingual Press / Editorial Bilingüe, 1986.

Spires, Adam C. "Alejandro Morales: Writing Chicano Space." Introduction to *Little Nation and Other Stories* by Alejandro Morales, vii–xxvii. Houston: Arte Público Press, 2014.

———. "Brave New Aztlán: Toward a Chicano Dystopia in the Novels of Alejandro Morales." *Revista Canadiense de Estudios Hispánicos* 29, no. 2 (Winter 2005): 363–78.

———. "El lado grotesco de la pureza y el impulso distópico en *Waiting to Happen* de Alejandro Morales." In *Perspectivas transatlánticas en la literatura chicana: Ensayos y creatividad*, edited by María Herrera-Sobek, Francisco A. Lomelí, and Juan Antonio Perles Rochel, 287–99. Málaga: Universidad de Málaga, 2004.

———. "The Utopia/Dystopia of Latin America's Margins: Writing Identity in Acadia and Aztlán." *Canadian Journal of Latin American and Caribbean Studies / Revue Canadienne des Etudes Latino-Américaines et Caraïbes* 33, no. 65 (2008): 107–36.

Tatum, Charles M. "Contemporary Chicano Novel." In *Chicano Literature*, 126–28. Twayne's United States Authors Series. Boston: Twayne, 1982.

Tisdale, Ashely B. "Transfigured Women: Race, Gender, and Disability in Alejandro Morales's *The Rag Doll Plagues*." *Chiricú Journal: Latina/o Literatures, Arts, and Cultures* 3, no. 2 (Spring 2019): 94–113.

Toliou, Foteini. "Mestizaje and Intercultural Communication as the Analeptics to the Transhistorical Borderland Crises in Alejandro Morales's Novel *The Rag Doll Plagues* (1992)." *Revista Canaria de Estudios Ingleses* 8l (2020): 221–32.

Trejo-Fuentes, Ignacio. "Alejandro Morales: La rebelión por el lenguaje." In *De acá de este lado: Una aproximación a la novela chicana*, 201–14. Mexico City: Consejo Nacional para la Cultura y las Artes, 1989.

Van Hecke, An. "De vreemde wegen van een getuigenisroman. De Spaanse vertaling van *The Brick People*." In *Filter: Tijdschrift voor Vertalen en Vertaalwetenschap*. N.p. Nijmegan, Netherlands, 2018. Available at https://www.tijdschrift-filter.nl/webfilter/dossier/getuigenis-en-vertaling/2018-1/de-vreemde-wegen-van-een-vertaling/.

———. "Espacios heterotópicos y mágicos en *The Rag Doll Plagues* de Alejandro Morales." In *Convergencias e interferencias: Escribir desde los borde(r)s*, edited by Rita de Maeseneer, María Eugenia Ocampo y Vilas, and An Van Hecke, 179–94. Caracas: Editorial Cultura, 2001.

———. "Translation in Heterotopia: Alejandro Morales's Novel *Waiting to Happen*." In *La traduction dans les cultures plurilingues*, edited by Francis Mus and Karen Vandemeulebroucke, 211–22. Arras, France: Artois Presses Université, 2011.

Villalobos, José Pablo. "Border Real, Border Metaphor: Altering Boundaries in Miguel Méndez and Alejandro Morales." *Arizona Journal of Hispanic Cultural Studies*, no. 4 (2000): 131–40.

Waldron, John V. "Uncovering History in the 'Post Modern Condition': (Re)Writing the Past, (Re)Righting Ourselves in Alejandro Morales' *The Brick People*." *Confluencia: Revista Hispánica de Cultura y Literatura* 7, no. 2 (Spring 1992): 99–106.

Wang, Shouren. "The Combination of History and Imagination: Morales's English Novels." *Contemporary Foreign Literature*, no. 2 (2006): 44–51.

———. "*The Rag Doll Plagues*: A Book on Human Survival." *Literary Gazette* (Beijing) October 25, 2007.

INTERVIEWS

Aldama, Fredrick Luis. "Alejandro Morales." In *Spilling the Beans in Chicanolandia: Conversations with Writers & Artists*, 177–86. Austin: University of Texas Press, 2006.

Grandjeat, Yves-Charles, and Alfonso Rodríguez. "Interview with Chicano Writer Alejandro Morales." *Confluencia: Revista Hispánica de Cultura y Literatura* 7, no. 1 (Fall 1991): 109–14.

Gurpegui, José Antonio. "Interview with Alejandro Morales." In "Alejandro Morales:

Fiction Past, Present, Future Perfect," edited by José Antonio Gurpegui, special issue, *Bilingual Review / Revista Bilingüe* 20, no. 3 (September–December 1995): 5–13.

Lomelí, Francisco A. "Interview with Alejandro Morales." *Contacto Series*, October 17, 1984. Santa Barbara: Kerr Learning Resources Center, University of California Santa Barbara. Video recording.

López López, Margarita. "Conversations with Alejandro Morales, October 11, 2018–August 4, 2019." *AlternaCtive PublicaCtions*, University of California Merced, November 25, 2019. Edited by Manuel M. Martín-Rodríguez. http://alternativepublications.ucmerced.edu/?p=551.

———. "Conversaciones con Alejandro Morales, 11 de octubre, 2018–4 de agosto, 2019." *AlternaCtive PublicaCtions*, University of California Merced, November 25, 2019. Edited by Manuel M. Martín-Rodríguez. http://alternativepublications.ucmerced.edu/?p=932

Maciel, David. "La literatura chicana: Conversación con Alejandro Morales." *Revista Cambio* 6 (January–March 1977): viii–ix.

Monleón, José. "Entrevista con Alejandro Morales." *Maize: Notebooks of Xicano Art and Literature* 4, nos. 1–2 (Fall–Winter 1980–1982): 9–20.

Neff, Maja. "Approaches to a Hemispheric America in *The Rag Doll Plagues*: An Interview with Chicano Author Alejandro Morales." *Iberoamericana: América Latina-España-Portugal* 6, no. 22 (May 2006): 173–78.

Olivas, Daniel A. "An Interview with Alejandro Morales, Author of *Little Nation*." *La Bloga: The World's Longest-Established Chicana Chicano, Latina Latino Literary Blog*. January 4, 2016. https://labloga.blogspot.com/2016/01/an-interview-with-alejandro-morales.html.

———. "An Interview with Alejandro Morales Regarding His New Novel, *River of Angels*." *Los Angeles Review of Books*, December 10, 2014. https://lareviewofbooks.org/article/an-interview-with-alejandro-morales-regarding-his-new-novel-river-angels/#.

Rodríguez del Pino, Salvador. "Interview with Alejandro Morales." *Encuentro with Chicano Writers Series*. Santa Barbara: Center for Chicano Studies, University of California, Santa Barbara, 1977. Video recording.

Schreiner, Daniel. "The Once and Future Chicano: World Literatures between Intra-History and Utopian Vision: An Interview with Alejandro Morales." *Symbolism: An International Annual of Critical Aesthetics*, no. 17 (2017): 171–84.

BOOK REVIEWS

Anonymous. "Alejandro Morales, New Directions in Chicano Literature." *La Guardia*, May 8, 1978, 4.

———. "Libros recientes: El viejo barrio." *Excélsior: El Periódico de la Vida Nacional*, February 8, 1976.

———. "Nueva novela chicana escrita en español." *Defensa: Boletín de la Liga Nacional Defensora del Idioma Español*, nos. 4–5 (November 1976): 8–9.

———. "Review of *The Brick People*." *Publishers Weekly Reviews*, January 1, 1988. https://www.publishersweekly.com/978-0-934770-91-0.

———. "Review of *Caras viejas y vino nuevo*." *Booklist* 73, no. 21 (July 1977): 1640.

———. "Review of *Caras viejas y vino nuevo*." *Recent Books in Mexico: Bulletin of the Centro Mexicano de Escritores* 23, no. 3 (March–April 1976): 9.

———. "Review of *Caras viejas y vino nuevo*." *Revista Cambio*, no. 3 (April 1976): x.

———. "Review of *The Death of an Anglo*." *La Red / The Net* 2, no. 2 (1989): n.p.

———. "Review of *The Rag Doll Plagues*." *Kirkus Reviews*, October 15, 1991.

———. "Review of *The Rag Doll Plagues*." *Publishers Weekly Reviews*, January 1, 1991. https://www.publishersweekly.com/978-1-55885-036-1.

Avilés, Elena. "Heterotopia: Re-imagined Communities and Barrios Borderlands." *Confluencia: Revista Hispánica de Cultura y Literatura* 31, no. 2 (Spring 2016): 220–23.

Batiste, Víctor N. "A Kaleidoscope on Many Levels." *Revista Chicano-Riqueña* 13, no. 1 (Spring 1985): 91–94.

Benavides, Ricardo F. "Review of *Caras viejas y vino nuevo*." *Books Abroad* 50, no. 4 (Autumn 1976): 837–38.

Butler, Darren C. "*The Rag Doll Plagues*." *Magic Realism* 4, no. 3 (Spring 1994): 58.

Díez de Urdanivia, Fernando. "Alejandro Morales y la narrativa chicana: El escritor y su mundo." *El Gallo Ilustrado* (Sunday supplement of *El Día*), August 1, 1976, 15.

Dooley, Sally. "Review of *Death of an Anglo*." *Review of Texas Books* 4, no. 1 (Spring 1989): 2–3.

Escalante, Evodio. "Morales: Escrito en chicano." *La Cultura en México* 1188 (supplement to *Siempre!*), March 1976, ix.

Gonzales-Berry, Erlinda. "Doctor, Writer, Warrior Chief." *Bilingual Review / Revista Bilingüe* 9, no. 3 (September–December 1982): 276–79. Reprinted in *Contemporary Chicano Fiction: A Critical Survey*, edited by Vernon E. Lattin, 289–98. Binghamton, NY: Bilingual Press / Editorial Bilingüe, 1986.

Goodyear, Russell H. "Review of *Reto en el paraíso*." *Best Sellers* 43, no. 1 (October 1983): 239–40.

Hernández, Roberto E. "Review of *The Brick People*." *Vista* 4, no. 13 (November 1988): 27.

Herrera-Sobek, María. "Barrio Life in the Fifties and Sixties." In "Chicano Literature," special issue, *Latin American Literary Review* 5, no. 10 (Spring 1977): 148–50.

Jurgens, Jane. "Review of *The Rag Doll Plagues*." *Booklist*, December 1, 1991, 31.

JW. "Review of *The Rag Doll Plagues.*" *Books of the Southwest: Journal of Critical Articles and Reviews of Southwestern Americana since Los Angeles 1957*, no. 399 (February 1992).

Kaganoff, Penny. "Review of *The Brick People.*" *Publishers Weekly Reviews*, June 3, 1988, 79.

KM. "Review of *Reto en el paraíso.*" *Books of the Southwest: Journal*, no. 300 (November 1983): 11.

Lattin, Vernon. "Review of *Death of an Anglo.*" *Confluencia: Revista Hispánica de Cultura y Literatura* 4, no. 1 (Fall 1988): 163–65.

Lewis, Marvin A. "*Caras Viejas y Vino Nuevo*: Essence of the Barrio." *Bilingual Review / Revista Bilingüe* 4, nos. 1–2 (January–August 1977): 141–44.

———. "Review of *La verdad sin voz.*" *Revista Chicano-Riqueña* 8, no. 4 (Fall 1980): 83–84.

Lomelí, Francisco A. Blurb on book jacket of *Waiting to Happen* by Alejandro Morales. Sunnyvale, CA: Chusma House, 2001.

Lomelí, Francisco A., and Donaldo W. Urioste. "*Caras viejas y vino nuevo.*" In *Chicano Perspectives in Literature: A Critical and Annotated Bibliography*, 44. Albuquerque: Pajarito, 1976. Reprinted in *De Colores: Journal of Emerging Raza Philosophies* 3, no. 4 (1977): 80.

López López, Margarita. "Restoring History, Brick by Brick." *Latinx Talk*, March 24, 2020. https://latinxtalk.org/2020/03/24/restoring-history-brick-by-brick/#comments.

McLellan, Dennis. "In *Rag Doll*, the Plague's the Thing." *Los Angeles Times*, February 14, 1992.

Monleón, José. "Dos novelas de Alejandro Morales." *Maize: Notebooks of Xicano Art and Literature* 4, nos. 1–2 (Fall–Winter 1980–1982): 6–8.

Molinaro, Mary. "Review of *The Rag Doll Plagues. Library Journal.*" 117, no. 2 (January 1992): 180.

Newman, María. "He Does It All—for Love of the Written Word." *Los Angeles Times*, September 26, 1991.

Nieto, Margarita. "Chicano History Brick by Brick: *The Brick People* by Alejandro Morales." *Los Angeles Times*, September 18, 1988. https://www.latimes.com/archives/la-xpm-1988-09-18-bk-3143-story.html.

Parotti, Phillip. "Review of *The Rag Doll Plagues.*" *Texas Review* 12, nos. 1–2 (Spring–Summer 1991): 141.

Plaza, Galvarino. "Reseña de *Caras viejas y vino nuevo.*" *Cuadernos Hispanoamericanos: Revista Mensual de Cultura Hispánica*, no. 312 (June 1976): 783–85.

Ramírez, Arthur. "Review of *Old Faces and New Wine.*" *Revista Chicano-Riqueña* 10, no. 4 (Fall 1982): 65–67.

Ramírez, Arturo. "El desmoronamiento y la trascendencia." *Caracol: Revista de la Raza* 3, no. 2 (July 1977): 22–23.

Ventura Sandoval, Juan. "Testimonios de la literatura chicana." *La Palabra y el Hombre* no. 17 (January–March 1976): 98–99.

Wildermuth, Kurt. "Review of *The Rag Doll Plagues* by Alejandro Morales." *MELUS: Multi-Ethnic Literature of the United States* 19, no. 1 (March 1994): 121–23.

Wong, Oscar. "Caras vemos . . . Chicanos no sabemos." *Vida Universitaria*, June 11, 1976, 18.

Xelina. "Review of *Caras viejas y vino nuevo*." *Nuestro: The Magazine for Latinos* no. 7 (October 1981): 50–51.

Zermeño, Francisco. "Review of *Reto en el paraíso*." *Lector* 2, no. 3 (November–December 1983): 29–30.

DOCUMENTARIES

Kirsch, Michael, Alejandro Morales, Alessandra Morales-Gunz, and Art Kirsch, dir. *The Brick People*. Irvine, CA: OCShowbiz, 2012. Available at https://www.youtube.com/watch?v=u3ucv0TLCF4 and https://www.uctv.tv/shows/The-Brick-People-27723.

Mancha, Luis, and Alejandro Morales, dir. *Inner Borderlines: Visions of America through the Eyes of Alejandro Morales*. Brooklyn, NY: Films Media Group, 2014.

ONLINE SOURCES

Albaladejo Martínez, Manuel. "La presencia del español en la literatura escrita en los Estados Unidos: La Literatura CHICANA." *Ars Creatio: Revista Cultural Digital*, 58 (2020). http://www.arscreatio.com/revista/articulo.php?articulo=358.

"Alejandro Morales." Contemporary Authors Online, Gale, 2005. Accessed January 20, 2021. http://link.galegroup.com/apps/doc/H1000070140/LitRC?u=csumb_main&sid=LitRC&xid=c44a4846.

"The Curing Woman." *Short Stories for Students*, Encyclopedia.com. Accessed December 15, 2020. https://www.encyclopedia.com/education/news-wires-white-papers-and-books/curing-woman#criticism.

García, Mario T. "Writer Alejandro Morales to Receive Luis Leal Literature Award." Accessed April 10, 2020. https://wiki2.org/en/Alejandro_Morales.

Sedano, Michael. "Brick That Built Pasadena." *La Bloga: The World's Longest-Established Chicana Chicano, Latina Latino Literary Blog*, August 21, 2018. https://labloga.blogspot.com/2018/08/brick-that-built-pasadena.html.

——. "Chicano Literary Classics: *Barrio on the Edge*." *La Bloga*, March 10, 2020. https://labloga.blogspot.com/2020/03/chicano-literary-classics-barrio-on-edge.html.

———. "Spotlighting Chicano Novelist Morales: Review of Alejandro Morales' *The Captain of All These Men of Death*." *La Bloga*, April 23, 2019. https://labloga .blogspot.com/2019/04/spotlighting-chicano-novelist-morales.html.

ACADEMIC DISSERTATIONS

Albaladejo Martínez, Manuel. "Hacia una cartografía de Los Angeles a través de la literatura chicana." PhD diss., Universidad de Alicante, 2007. See chapter 6, on *Caras viejas y vino nuevo*, *La verdad sin voz*, *Reto en el paraíso*, *The Brick People*, *The Rag Doll Plagues*, and *Waiting to Happen*.

Fortes, Mayra. "Identidades sin frontera: Rupturas y continuidades en la literatura de la Onda y la narrativa chicana." PhD diss., Vanderbilt University, 2009. See chapter 4, on *Caras viejas y vino nuevo*.

Flores, José Roberto. "Raza especulativa: Reimaginando el discurso racial en la narrativa mexicoamericana (1970–2010)." PhD diss., Arizona State University, 2017. See chapter 5, on *The Rag Doll Plagues*.

García-Martínez, Marc. "Artesano at Work: The Flesh-and-Blood Aesthetics of Alejandro Morales." PhD diss., University of California, Santa Barbara, 2008.

Gamber, John Blair. "Trickling Down: Waste and Pollution in Contemporary United States Minority Literature." PhD diss., University of California, Santa Barbara, 2006. See chapter 3, on *The Rag Doll Plagues*.

Garza, José. "Social Turbulence as Reflected in Alejandro Morales' Novelistic Techniques." PhD diss., Indiana University, 2006.

Georgi, Sonja. "Bodies and/as Technology: Counter-Discourses on Ethnicity and Globalization in the Works of Alejandro Morales, Larissa Lai and Nalo Hopkinson." PhD diss., University of Siegen, 2010. See chapter 4, on *The Brick People* and *The Rag Doll Plagues*.

Lamb, Jeffrey Norman. "Identities on the Margin: Perspectives on Cisneros, Conde, Crosthwaite and Morales." PhD diss., University of California, Los Angeles, 1997.

Lee, James Kyung-Jin. "Multicultural Dreams, Racial Awakenings: The Anxieties of Racial Realignment in American Literary Works of the 1980s." PhD diss., University of California, Los Angeles, 2000. See chapter 1, on *The Brick People*.

Li, Baojie. "Borderland Narrative in Contemporary Chicano Literature." PhD diss., Shandong University, 2009. See chapter 1, on *The Rag Doll Plagues*.

López González, Crescencio. "La urbanización de la conciencia chicana." PhD diss., University of Arizona, 2011. See chapter 4, on *Caras viejas y vino nuevo*.

Martinsen, Eric Lars. "Global Moments: Spectatorship, Violence and the Urban in Contemporary Fiction." PhD diss., University of California, Santa Barbara, 2010. See chapter 5, on *The Rag Doll Plagues* and general discussion of technologies and disease in Morales.

Medina, Félix, Jr. "The Mexican Worker: A Marxist Reading of Labor Struggles in Californian Chicano/a Literature." PhD diss., Michigan State University, 2017. See chapter 4, on *The Brick People*.

Morton, Michelle E. "Utopian and Dystopian Visions of California in the Historical Imagination." PhD diss., University of California, Santa Cruz, 2005. See chapter 4, on *Reto en el paraíso*.

Nez, Ana Arellano. "Consciousness and Resistance in Chicano Barrio Narratives." PhD diss., University of California, Santa Barbara, 2016. See chapter 5 on *Barrio on the Edge / Caras viejas y vino nuevo*.

Ortega Martínez, Danizete. "The Chicana/o Grotesque: National Origins, Subversive Traditions, and Bodies of Resistance in U.S. Southwestern Literature." PhD diss., University of New Mexico, 2009. See chapter 3, on *The Rag Doll Plagues*.

Perreira, Christopher Michael. "Empires of Disease: Criminal Encounters, Contagious Nations, and Archives of U.S. Culture and Literature." PhD diss., University of California, San Diego, 2015. See chapter 5, on *The Captain of All of These Men of Death*.

Ramírez Macías, Greta Ximena. "Alejandro Morales en la construcción de la identidad chicana a través de la literatura." PhD diss., El Colegio de Michoacán, A. C. Centro de Estudios de las Tradiciones, 2014..

Ramírez Méndez, Alejandro. "Trans-Urban Narratives: Literary Cartographies and Global Cities in the Urban Imagination of Mexico and the U.S." PhD diss., University of California, Los Angeles, 2018. See chapter 3, on *The Rag Doll Plagues*.

Rodríguez del Pino, Salvador. "La novela chicana escrita en español: Cinco autores comprometidos." PhD diss., University of California, Santa Barbara, 1980.

Rosales, Jesús. "La narrativa de Alejandro Morales: Encuentro, historia y compromiso social." PhD diss., Stanford University, 1995.

Sánchez Jiménez, Juan Antonio. "La evolución narrativa en la obra de Alejandro Morales." PhD diss., Universidad de Alcalá de Henares, 2001.

Spires, Adam. "Writing Acadia and Aztlán: The Novels of Claude LeBouthilier and Alejandro Morales." 2001. PhD diss., University of Alberta, 2001..

CONTRIBUTORS

ADINA CIUGUREANU is a professor emerita of American culture at Ovidius University Constanta, Romania. A Fulbright research grant recipient, she has published six books and over forty articles in edited volumes and prestigious academic periodicals. She has served as president of the Romanian Association of American Studies (2012–2016) and treasurer of the European Association for American Studies (2012–2020).

SOPHIA EMMANOUILIDOU is affiliated with the Department of American Studies at Aristotle University of Thessaloniki in Greece. She has published several articles on Chicana/o literature and identity-focused theories. She is the coeditor of the volume *Transnational Interconnections of Nature Studies and the Environmental Humanities, Ex-centric Narratives: Journal of Anglophone Literature, Culture, and Media*, vol. 3 and a special issue of *Revista Canaria de Estudios Ingleses*, vol. 81.

ELENA ERRICO is a research assistant professor of Spanish and translation studies at the University of Módena, Italy. She is the author of *Lo spagnolo in contatto: Uno studio empirico su adolescenti gibilterrini* and coauthor of *La qualità in interpretazione: Ricerca, didattica e pratica professionale*. She has also published work with the UCLA Chicano Studies Center.

MARC GARCÍA-MARTÍNEZ is a professor of English at Allan Hancock College in Santa María, California, and a lecturer in the Department of Chicana/o Studies at the University of California at Santa Barbara. He is the author of *The Flesh-and-Blood Aesthetics of Alejandro Morales: Disease, Sex, and Figuration*, the first full-length scholarly study in English of the innovative novels of Alejandro Morales.

MARÍA HERRERA-SOBEK is a professor emeritus of Chicana and Chicano studies at the University of California at Santa Barbara. She specializes in theories and analyses of folklore, gender, culture, oral tradition, feminism, film, as well as ethnic construction. Her books include *The Bracero Experience*, *The Mexican Corrido: A Feminist Analysis*, *Northward Bound: The Mexican Immigrant Experience in Ballad and Song*, and *Chicano Folklore: A Handbook*.

AMAIA IBARRARAN-BIGALONDO is a lecturer at the University of the Basque Country, where she teaches North American ethnic literatures and cultures. Her research involves the study of Chicano literature, art, and culture. She is the author of *Mexican American Women, Dress and Gender: Pachucas, Chicanas, Cholas*. Her work appears in the *Journal of the Spanish Association for Anglo-American Studies* and the *International Journal of English Studies*.

LUIS LEAL was a distinguished professor of Chicana and Chicana studies at the University of California at Santa Barbara. He was the author or editor of forty-five books and four hundred articles on Mexican, Latin American, and Chicano literatures. He was awarded the Aztec Eagle in 1991 by Mexican President Carlos Salinas de Gortari, and in 1997 he received from President William Jefferson Clinton the US National Medal for the Humanities.

BAOJIE LI is a professor of American literature in the Department of English Language and Literature at Shandong University in China. She researches Hispanic, modern, and comparative literatures, with a focus on cultural studies.

FRANCISCO A. LOMELÍ is a professor emeritus of Spanish and Portuguese and Chicano and Chicana studies at the University of California, Santa Barbara. He has edited *The Routledge Handbook of Chicana/o Studies*, *The Historical Dictionary of U.S. Latino Literature*, and *Chicano Literature: A Reference Guide*. He is the recipient of the Luis Leal Award by Hispa-USA and was elected to the North American Academy of the Spanish Language.

MARGARITA LÓPEZ LÓPEZ is a professor emeritus of Spanish at the California State University at Channel Islands. Her research interests are Mexican literature, Chicana/o-Latina/o literature, gender and feminist studies, and Latin American literature. She has presented scholarly work internationally on writers Alejandro Morales, Tomás Rivera, Juan Rulfo, Rosario Castellanos, Carmen Boullosa, Élmer Mendoza, Miguel Cervantes, and Graciela Limón.

MANUEL MARTÍN-RODRÍGUEZ is a professor at the University of California at Merced. He is the author of *Cantas a Marte y das batalla a Apolo: Cinco estudios sobre Gaspar de Villagrá* and *With a Book in Their Hands: Chicano/a Readers and Readerships Across the Centuries*. He is a member of the Academia Norteamericana de la Lengua Española and sits on the editorial board of the *Bilingual Review / Revista Bilingüe*.

STEPHEN MILLER is a professor of Hispanic studies at Texas A & M University. He specializes in Hispanic literatures of the nineteenth century through the contemporary period. His work appears in *The Cambridge History of Spanish Literature*, *The Feminist Encyclopedia of Spanish Literature*, *The Encyclopedia of Contemporary Spanish Culture*, *The Encyclopedia of World Literature in the 20th Century*, and *The Dictionary of the Literature of the Iberian Peninsula*.

DANIEL A. OLIVAS is a Chicano playwright, book critic, interviewer, and author of nine books, including *The King of Lighting Fixtures: Stories*, *Crossing the Border: Collected Poems* and *Things We Do Not Talk About: Exploring Latino/a Literature through Essays and Interviews*. His work has appeared in the *New York Times*, *El Paso Times*, *Los Angeles Times*, *Los Angeles Review of Books*, and the *Huffington Post*.

JESÚS ROSALES is an associate professor of Spanish in the School of International Letters and Cultures at Arizona State University. Specializing in Chicano literary history and Chicano literature written in Spanish, he is coeditor of *Spanish Perspectives on Chicano Literature: Literary and Cultural Essays*, the editor of *Thinking en Español: Interviews with Critics of Chicana/o Literature*, and the author of *La narrativa de Alejandro Morales: Encuentro, historia y compromiso social*.

ADAM SPIRES is an associate professor of Spanish and Latin American studies at Saint Mary's University in Canada. His scholarly works and presentations analyze Acadian, Latin American, and Chicano culture and literature. He is the translator of Morales' 2005 Spanish-language book *Pequeña nación* into English (*Little Nation*, Arte Público Press) and has published his work in the *Canadian Journal of Latin American and Caribbean Studies*.

DONALDO W. URIOSTE is a professor emeritus of Spanish language and Hispanic literatures and founding director of the Institute for World Languages and Cultures at California State University at Monterey Bay. Prior to coming to CSUMB as a founding faculty member, he taught at Colorado College and at California Lutheran University, where he taught Spanish language, Latin American literature and culture, and Chicano literature and culture courses.

INDEX

Acosta, Oscar Zeta, l; *Autobiography of a Brown Buffalo*, 1, 10; *The Revolt of the Cockroach People*, 194
aesthetic/aesthetics, 4, 5, 9, 14, 20, 24, 31n1, 36, 37, 38, 136
Agamben, Giorgio, 137; "homo sacer," 137
Aguirre, Eugenio, 228
Agustín, José, 4
AIDS, 248, 253–55. *See also* HIV
Albaladejo Martínez, Manuel, 215, 225
Aleph, 271; "sitio totalizador" (all encompassing), 280. *See also* Borges, Jorge Luis
Alford, Fred, 86
Alianza Federal de Mercedes (Federal Alliance of Landgrans), 283. *See also* López Tijerina, Reyes
alien culture, 136
All Quiet on the Western Front (film), 240
Almaguer, Tomás, 39; internal colony, 39
Althusser, Louis, 146
Alurista, 39
Alvarez, Salado, 243
American Dream, 79
American Protective Association (APA), 148
Anaya, Rudolfo, l; *Bless Me, Ultima*, 1, 10
Anders, Allison, 144
Anderson, Benedict R., 146, 149. *See also* "imaginary community"

Anglos, 134–35, 138, 183, 185–86, 188–89, 282; and Mexicans, 77, 104n10, 130, 190–91, 193, 237–39, 254, 257
anthropomorphosis, 77
antihistory, 35
Anti-Oedipus: Capitalism and Schizophrenia, 71. *See also* Deleuze, Gilles; Guattari, Félix
Anzaldúa, Gloria, 83, 185–86; *Borderlands/La Frontera: The New Mestiza*, 82, 180; and "la facultad," 271, 275. *See also* "mestiza consciousness"; thirdspace; "consciousness of duality"
archetypes, 42, 164, 253
Arias, Ron, 2; *The Road to Tamazunchale*, 2, 10
Arte Público Press, 279
autobiography, 57, 111, 228
Aztlán, 120, 123, 163, 166, 170–72, 175, 207; and heterotopia, 161, 165, 168, 170, 181, 183

Bardovi-Harlig, Kathleen, 218
Barrera, Mario, 39; internal colony, 39
barrio, 1, 5, 10, 35, 79, 81, 85, 143, 150; as alienating milieu, 35; hard-core barrio, 1, 37, 38; as liminal space, 81; localism in, 73, 80; Los Angeles barrio, 240; translocality of, 85; as war zone, 41–42; X-ray of the barrio, 37–38
"barrioization," 94, 190. *See also* Villa, Raúl Homero

Barrio on the Edge, 6; apocalyptic ambience in, 48, 144–45; chaos and disorder in, 37; and cumulative chaos, 39; dreamlike iterations in, 35; environment of inverted values, paradoxes, and contradictions in, 40; as eschatological, 39; graffiti mural of, 37; ground zero in, 41; as minimalist, 37; as naturalist, 37; and "pornography of violence," 45; and *"pretérito imperfecto"* vs. *"pretérito indefinido"* (Imperfect past vs. indefinite past), 216; X-ray of the barrio in, 37. See also *Caras viejas y vino nuevo*
Barthes, Roland, 9, 10
Baudrillard, Jean, 179
Bentley-Adler, Collen, 244
Bhabha, Homi, 35; and "decentered subject," 179–80, 186. See also hybrid: "hybrid zones"
Bierce, Ambrose, 20–24
bigotry, 172, 255
Blanco S., Antonio, 234
blood (or bloody/bleeding), 19–20, 26–27, 46, 48, 100, 184, 202–3, 221–22, 248, 253; Aryan, 24, 134; Mexican, 127, 243, 257–58; mixed, 186–87
Bloom, Harold, 10
body, 46, 76, 100–101, 119, 163, 202, 214, 253, 258–60; attack on, 20–22; transformation of, 18, 26, 249–50
Body Work: Object of Desire in Modern Narrative, 259. See also Brooks, Peter
borders, 76, 134, 140; and borderlands, 82; and borderland as metaphor, 83, 181; and borderlines, 75; and hegemonic centrism, 75; San Diego–Tijuana border, 176
Borges, Jorge Luis, 271, 280
Bracero Program, 166, 257
Brés, Jaque, 217
The Brick People (book), 6, 11, 179–85, 229, 272–73
The Brick People (film), 194
Brito, Aristeo, 1; *El diablo en Texas*, 1
Brooks, Peter, 251. See also *Body Work: Objective of Desire in Modern Narrative*

brown skin/faces/people, 134, 166, 191–92, 186, 254, 260n10. See also *The Brick People*
brown insects, 182–3
Buell, Lawrence, 84
Buñuel, Luis, 46, 47, 49
Burgess, Anthony, 43
Bursik, R. J., Jr., 151. See also *Neighborhood and Crime: The Dimension of Effective Community Control*
Byatt, A. S., 141; ans "political desire," 141

California, 55–56, 59, 91, 94–95, 104n10, 112, 138, 164–65, 167, 171, 173, 198, 202, 204, 227, 234–36, 238, 241, 243, 273; and Aryans 134, 138–39, 140, 191; as heterotopia, 111–13, 122, 168, 173; Southern California, 7, 16, 30, 54, 72, 162–65, 174, 180, 227, 231, 243, 256, 272–73; (Spanish) myth of, 92
Candelaria, Nash, 228
The Captain of All These Men of Death, 7, 11, 273
Caras viejas y vino nuevo, 1, 4, 6. See also *Barrio on the Edge*
Carpentier, Alejo, 271
castas (castes), 251; and racial inequality, 251
Catholic/Catholicism, 58, 65, 101–2, 168–69, 183, 185
Cela, José Camilo, 4, 40. See also *La familia de Pascual Duarte*
Chávez, César, 283
Chavez Ravine, 93, 95, 98, 105n11, 149
Chicano sensibility, 273, 280. See also *rasquachismo*
children, 47, 68, 121, 134–35, 155, 207, 224n6, 251; killed, 31–32n3, 119–20, 147–48, 184; Mexican, 91, 112, 185, 190; miscegenated, 192
Chinese Exclusion Act of 1882, 181
Cisneros, Sandra, 283
"City of Angels," 13, 95, 128, 140
Clementine theory, 149, 152
A Clockwork Orange (film), 35, 40–41, 42, 44–46, 49. See also Kubrick, Stanley
Coatlicue (Aztec goddess of Life and Death), 253, 254

colonialism, 4, 75, 180
coming-of-age immigrant tales, 4
Comrie, Bernard, 224
Concentrated Poverty Neighborhoods (CNP), 143
consciousness, 123, 205, 265; and barrio, 48, 82; cultural, 134, 162, 180–81, 186–88; environmental, 72, 79; historical, 115, 170
connotation, 28, 31n1, 37–38, 46, 48, 217
connotative, 13–15, 25–27, 30, 31n1, 65
"consciousness of duality," 188. *See also* Anzaldúa, Gloria
Corpi, Lucha, 269
Cortázar, Julio, 4, 280. *See also Rayuela*
Cortés, Carlos, 260
criollos (Spanish born in the Americas), 254
cultural admixtures, 2; mestizo, 258
cultural nationalist, 1; nationalism, 2, 41
Cummins, Jeanine, 268
curanderismo (popular healings), 136
Cyland River Barge Transport Company, 131

Dalí, Salvador, 40; *Un Chien Andalou*, 40, 46–47, 49
Darwin, Charles, 247
Death of an Anglo, 8, 11, 227–28, 229–31, 224n6, 281. *See also* Ginsberg, Judith
The Death of Artemio Cruz (*La muerte de Artemio Cruz*), 280
The Decline of the Californios, 234. *See also* Pitt, Leonard
Deleuze, Gilles, 71, 72
dialectic/dialectical, 17, 24, 131
Díaz, Porfirio, 229, 241
Diccionario panhispánico de dudas, 214
Dickinson, Gordon, 87
Dietrich, Lisa C., 157
Dimock, Wai Chee, 84
disease, 35–36, 53–54, 138, 185, 189, 193, 200–205, 247, 252, 255, 258–59, 278; in the form of tuberculosis and polio, 60–69
"Documentos para la historia de California, los cuales pertenecían al Archivo Particular de Don Antonio F. Coronel por él depositados en el Bancroft Library, 1878," 244
Donoso, José, 4
Dos Passos, John, 4
Duisit, Leonel, 9, 10
dystopia, 4, 35

ebola, 248, 260
ecocritical, 72–73, 75, 85n7, 208; ecological criticism, 248. *See also Ecological Literary Criticism*
Ecological Literary Criticism, 247
ecology, 71; and the association and the ecotone, 73, 74, 82; biotic and abiotic factors of, 73; and Chicano ecothinking, 71, 74, 84, 85; and ecospaces, 76; and ecosystem of barrio cohesion, 81; and ecosystems, 73; and environmental consciousness, 72; and localism and translocalism, 74; Mexican Indian concept of, 131, 247, 256; and Native American ecological concepts and beliefs, 131; natural, 131; and relationship between man and nature, 131; and tropes of ecological discourse, 71
El Clamor, 236
el cuerpo de la gente, 18
El Movimiento, 85
El Pueblo de Nuestra Señora la Reina de Los Ángeles de Porciúncula, 95, 136, 176, 189, 273
epidemic diseases, 2; "apocalyptic diseases," 4, 247; pollutants, environmental contamination, and virulent epidemics, 257
Episodios nacionales, 243
epistemophilia, 247–48, 258–59
esperpento, 7, 103n4
Esteva-Fagregat, Claudio, 260
Estok, Simon, 84
eugenics, 4, 138; American Eugenics Association, 138; and Aryan blood, 134; and Aryan Club, 137; Aryan Club of Southern California, 138, 191; and Aryan fatherland, 138; and Aryanism, 191; and Darwinists,

Index **313**

eugenics (continued)
138; and ethnic and capital hegemony, 133; and ethnic discourse, l41; eugenicists' austere codifications, 82; and inferior race, 139; and miscegenation, 189; and mixed-blood people, 186; and "mongrel races," 138; movement, 192; and neonativism, 140; Southern California Eugenics Club, 139; and supremacist notions of whiteness, 83; theory, 192

exotic metanarratives, 2

experimentation: aesthetic/novelistic, 2, 3, 5, 9, 35, 49, 213–14, 219. *See also* noir narratives

extreme poetics, 4, 35, 37

extreme surrealism, 37

Fan, Li, 129

fantasy of accuracy, 55

Faulkner, William, 4

Federación de las Mujeres de las Tijeras (Federation of Women with Scissors), 155

feminist/feminism, 116, 120, 143, 145–46, 152, 155–57, 204

filth, 24, 27, 134, 189, 200, 249–52, 256

flesh-and-blood, 2

Fondo de Cultura Económica (publisher), 38

Foucault, Michel, 36, 111, 165, 172, 179, 271. *See also* "other spaces"

Franco, Dean, 135

Frémont, John C., 238

Frente la tranquilidad la locura, 233

Freud, Sigmund, 258

Fuentes, Carlos, 4, 103n1, 199, 228, 265, 280. *See also Where the Air Is Clear; The Death of Artemio Cruz*

futurism, 4

Gabrieliño (Gabrieleño)-Tongva, 86

gangs (*clicas*), 144; and *cholos*, 146, 153; "gang cleaning," 152–53, 155. *See also* Vigil, James Diego

García, Robert, 157

García Lorca, Federico, 255

García Márquez, Gabriel, 4; *Crónica de una muerte anunciada*, 216, 228; *One Hundred Years of Solitude*, 239, 248, 260, 280

García-Martínez, Marc, 8, 10n1, 36, 51n13, 65, 68n9, 68n13; *The Flesh-and-Blood Aesthetics of Alejandro Morales: Disease, Sex and Figuration*, 8, 10, 33n9, 68n13, 103, 106n28

Garrard, Greg, 85

Gebser, Jean, 265

geography, 27, 79, 129, 163, 165, 174, 176n6; "consequential geography," 96–97; geocultural, 73, 111, 141

Gersdorf, Catrina, 74. *See also Nature in Literary and Cultural Studies: Transatlantic Conversations and Ecocriticism*

ghettoizing, 150

Gili Gaya, Samuel, 225

Ginsberg, Judith, 6. *See also Death of an Anglo*

Gold Rush, 130

Gonzales, Rodolfo "Corky," 39, 283

Goucher, Candice, 85

Grasmick, H. G., 151. *See also Neighborhood and Crime: The Dimension of Effective Community Control*

Great Depression, 29, 47, 80–81, 190, 240; Crash, 80; post-Crash, 81

grotesque, 3, 47, 100, 103n4, 106n27

Guattari, Félix, 71, 72

Guernica, 3, 41, 45

Gurpegui, José Antonio, 3, 8, 10, 11, 244, 260

Gutiérrez, José Angel, 283

Gutiérrez, Ramón, 4

Hackford, Taylor, 144; *Blood In, Blood Out* (film), 144

Halley's Comet, 241, 245

Hemingway, Ernest, 4

Hearst, Randolph, 241. *See also* "robber barons"

Herrera-Sobek, María, 4, 44

heterotopia, 4, 35–36, 67n7, 90, 111–15, 121–23, 170–74, 179, 181, 269

heuristic voice, 9
Hill, Sabrina, 150–51, 157
Hinojosa, Rolando, 1; *Estampas del Valle y otras obras*, 1, 10
historical novels, 127–28
historiography, 181
history, 30–31, 42, 71–72, 75, 84, 90–91, 96, 103n6, 104n10, 110–14, 117–24, 139, 150, 203–4, 208, 227, 240–42, 263, 265, 272–73, 276, 280–81; antihistory, 36; and California, 231–35, 238–39; Chicano, 89, 93, 95, 97, 99, 147, 180, 199, 243, 267; ethnohistory versus official history, 3; intrahistory, 36, 270–71; intrahistory versus antihistory, 3; of Los Angeles ("city"), 128–35, 141, 189; personal history, 5; of social stigma and stereotyping, 38; of tuberculosis, 57–59, 65
Hopper, Paul, 218
Huerta, Dolores, 283
Hurtado Albir, Amparo, 224
hybrid/hybridity/hybridities, 3, 121, 130, 140, 144, 180–81, 193, 204, 268, 270; and "hybrid zones," 36, 179, 181
hyperrealism, 4, 444, 448

iconoclast, 4
identity, 83, 95, 103n5, 110–11, 121–22, 124, 152–53, 161, 163, 168, 179, 200, 209n2, 209n13, 229; Chicano/Mexican, 82, 90, 104, 131–32, 191, 913, 203, 208n2, 223, 258; cultural/ethnic/racial, 72, 76, 81, 102, 141, 143, 180, 190, 198–99, 268; self-identity, 74, 78
"imaginary community," 146. *See also* Anderson, Benedict R.
"immunized blood," 257; and "breeders," 257
Imperial Eyes: Travel Writing and Transculturation, 260
Indigenous lands, 83
indios (Indians), 250, 254
infrarealism, 3
Inquisition, 251
intercalated (-sections/-stories/-short narratives), 56–60, 64, 67n6, 239

intrahistorical, 3
Islas, Arturo, 23–24, 238. *See also The Rain God*

Jackson, Helen Hunt, 234. *See also Ramona*
Jiménez, Francisco, 245
Jirón-King, Shimberlee, 58, 67n3
Joseph Simons Brick Factory, 183, 190, 240–41
Joyce, James, 4
Jung, Karl, 265
Jurmain, Claudia, 87

Kanellos, Nicolás, 279
Kaup, Monika, 266. *See also* neobaroque
King, Martin Luther, 283
Klein, Emily, 258
Kroeber, Karl, 247. *See also Ecological Literary Criticism*
Kubrick, Stanley, 35. *See also A Clockwork Orange*

"La Cucaracha" (the cockroach) (song), 194
La familia de Pascual Duarte, 40, 47, 49
La hija de la ataraxia, 233
La Llorona, 169, 176
Lamex (Los Angeles-Mexico), 5, 243, 256, 257
La narrativa de Alejandro Morales: encuentro, historia y compromiso social, 8. *See also* Rosales, Jesús
"landguage," 187–88
"langscape," 187–88
language, 49, 74, 76–77, 90, 114, 135–36, 166, 168, 187–88, 208n1, 213, 215, 218, 220, 224n2, 239
La Onda group, 4, 38
Las sergas de Esplandián, 233
Latin American Boom, 4, 38, 39
Latin American fiction, 229, 23l
Latour, Bruno, 85
Laughlin, Harry H., 191
La verdad sin voz, 6. *See also* Ginsberg, Judith; *Death of an Anglo*
Leal, Luis, 4
Lefevere, André, 216, 223

Index **315**

Lefebvre, Henri, 129; "space of spaces," 129; "mental space," 129; neocapitalism, 133, 135
Leguin, Charles, 85
Li, Baojie, 127, 142
lizard people, 136, 182–84
lloronas, 40, 47
Löbus, Triin, 217–18
Lomelí, Francisco A., 4, 6, 8, 50n1, 103, 113, 213–16, 219–20, 222, 224n5, 244n1
López, Alma, 279
Los Angeles Star, 236
Los Angeles Times, 237, 247–48
López Tijerina, Reyes, 283. *See also* Alianza Federal de Mercedes
Lowenthal, David, 129
Luis Leal Award for Distinction in the Arts, 4, 6, 7, 85

magical realism, 2, 128, 179, 181
Márquez, Antonio, 3, 10
Martínez, Max, 6, 8, 215, 219–20, 222, 224
Matsunaga, Michael, 143
Mayer, Sylvia, 74. *See also Nature in Literary and Cultural Studies: Transatlantic Conversations and Ecocriticism*
marginalized (people, communities, characters, etc.), 7, 37, 93, 109–10, 115, 120–23, 133, 175
MAYO (Mexican American Youth Organization), 283
Méndez M., Miguel, 1; *Peregrinos de Aztlán*, 1, 11
"mestiza consciousness," 180. *See also* Anzaldúa, Gloria
mestizaje, 197–201, 204, 206–8, 209n2, 209n15; and mestizo, 258
Metahistory: The Historical Imagination in Nineteen-Century Europe, 271. *See also* White, Hayden
metanovels, 4
metaphor, 1, 30, 39, 46, 54, 65, 83, 93, 149, 165, 172, 217; metaphoric/metaphorical, 9, 14–16, 22, 24, 26, 44, 100, 184, 194n2, 204, 222, 225n14, 227

Mexican American, 6–7, 9–10, 13, 18–19, 59, 81, 89, 91, 94–95, 111, 127, 140–41, 197, 254, 264, 283
Mexican-American War, 2, 50n8
Mexican migration and immigration, 6
Mexican Revolution, 257
miscegenation, 189. *See also* eugenics
Misión de San Gabriel, 148
Molina, Lucía, 225
monstrous figures, 277
Montebello, 59, 89, 92, 94–95, 111, 127, 147, 181, 229, 232, 240
Moore, Joan W., 158
Morales, Alejandro D., 1; *The Brick People*, 6, 11; *The Captain of All These Men of Death*, 7; *Caras viejas y vino nuevo*, 1; *Death of an Anglo*, 6, 11; *Rag Doll Plagues*, 247–60; *Reto en el paraíso*, 6, 11; *River of Angels*, 7, 11; unrepentant individualism, 6
Morrison, Toni, 271, 275
Mortiz, Joaquín, 6, 38, 39
mulattos, 254
multiple marginality, 144
Murguía, Alejandro, 27–29
Murphy, Kevin, 87
Murray, Ixta Maya, 35, 144; *Locas*, 144
"mystic(al) realism," 3, 41, 49

Nature in Literary and Cultural Studies: Transatlantic Conversations and Ecocriticism, 74
Neighborhood and Crime: The Dimension of Effective Community Control, 151
neobaroque, 265. *See also* Kaup, Monika
new criticism, 247
new historical novel, 227
noir narratives, 2, 5
nonconformist, 5
"novelas totalizadoras" (all encompassing novels), 280–81
Nouveau roman, 38
nuance: linguistic, 216; narrative, 9, 222; temporal, 223

Oedipal romance, 258
Old Faces and New Wine, 6. See also Martínez, Max
Olmos, Edward James, 144
Onetti, Carlos, 38; El pozo, 38
Orange County, 112, 163–64, 170–71, 174, 252, 254–55, 272
Ordóñez de Montalvo, Garci, 232. See also Las sergas de Esplandián
"other spaces," 179, 271. See also Foucault, Michel; thirdspace
Our Lady Queen of Los Angeles, 147

pachuco, 190. See also Zoot Suit Riots
Padilla, Genaro, 4
palimpsest, 75, 181
Paris Commune, 152
Peña, Devon, 74, 79. See also ecology: and localism and translocalism
Pequeña nación (Little Nation), 7, 143–57, 278
Pérez Galdó, Benito, 243. See also Episodios nacionales
Pérez-Torres, Rafael, 206–7, 210n17
Picasso, Pablo, 42, 265
Pitt, Leonard, 234. See also The Decline of the Californios
The Place of the White Heron, 161–62, 167, 174–75
Plumwood, Val, 76, 85
Popular Voice, 237
postcolonialism, 4
Pratt, Louise, 260. See also Imperial Eyes: Travel Writing and Transculturation
Pressman, Michael, 144
PRI (Partido Revolucionario Institucional), 229

Quinto Sol (publisher), 38, 267
Quinto Sol Generation, 1–2, 267
Quiseo de Abasolo, 7, 242

racism: racist violence, 18, 22, 26, 190; racist beliefs/views, 27, 29–30, 82, 138, 200, 250, 255, 266

Rag Doll Plagues, 7, 11, 227, 247–60, 277
A Rainbow of Colors, 276, 277
The Rain God, 22, 238. See also Islas, Arturo
Ramona, 234. See also Jackson, Helen Hunt
rasquachismo (Chicano sensibility), 265. See also Ybarra-Frausto, Tomás
Rayuela, 280. See also Cortázar, Julio
Rechy, John, 2; The Sexual Outlaw, 2, 11
religion, 41–42, 77, 122, 163, 168, 170, 252
"Relación de sus recuerdos" (manuscript), 245
Reto en el paraíso, 6, 227, 229, 231–40, 266, 272–73
revolución, 143, 146, 156
Revueltas, José, 229
Reyes, Graciela, 217
rhetoric, 19–22, 30, 73, 250
The Rhetoric of Ecology: Colonial Discourse in Journalism, Travel Writings, and Imperial Administration, 250. See also Spurr, David
Río de Porciúncula, 78, 86, 94, 103, 130
Ríos, Isabella, 2; Victuum, 2, 11
Rivera, Tomás, 1; ". . . Y no se lo tragó la tierra," 1, 11
River of Angels, 7, 71–87; and eugenics and neonativism, 75; and palimpsest, 75, 79, 127–42, 185–95, 265, 274–75, 276, 278
Robbe-Grillet, Alain, 4
"robber barons," 241. See also Hearst, Randolph
Rodríguez, Luis J., 35, 144
Roosevelt, Theodore, 241
Rosales (May), Jesús, 6, 7, 11, 145
Rough Riders, 241
Ruiz de Burton, María Amparo, 228. See also The Squatter and the Don

Sábato, Ernesto, 38; El túnel, 38
Sáenz, Gustavo, 4
Said, Edward, 129
Saldívar, Ramón, 6, 11
Sánchez, Juan Antonio, 144, 244
Sánchez, Phil, 2; Don Phil-O-Meno sí la Mancha, 2, 11
Sánchez, Ricardo, 39

Index **317**

Santa Ana Scribner, 237
Santiago, Danny, 35
Schreiner, Daniel, 9, 11
Siglo Veintuno (publisher), 35
Simons Brickyard, 5, 127, 176n4, 181, 193, 194n1
social disorganization, 151. *See also* Bursik, R. J.; Grasmick, H. G.
sociospatial, 94, 190
Sodom and Gamorrah, 41
Soja, Edward, 35. *See also* thirdspace
somatic encodings, 2
Soper, Kate, 153
Southern California Aryan Club, 134, 138–39, 191
southwest, 92, 147, 257, 283
spatial (re)locations, 189
spatiocultural, 72
Spires, Adam, 7, 8; *Little Nation and Other Stories*, 11, 279
Spurr, David, 250
The Squatter and the Don, 228. *See also* Ruiz de Burton, María Amparo
Stand and Deliver (film), 144
Staples, Robert, 150
Steinbeck, John, 38; *Tortilla Flat*, 38
suffocation, 22, 31, 32
Sun Construction Company, 131, 186
surrealism, 3, 4, 45, 47, 49, 103
symbolism, 129, 132, 206

Tally, Robert T., 187. *See also* "langscape"
testimonial, 3
Texas, 104n10, 105n13, 227–28, 230, 244n6, 281–82
thirdspace (third space), 36, 179. *See also* Foucault, Michel
Tlatelolco, 6
Tongva, 32, 77, 86n11
topopoetic, 188
totalizador, 89, 103, 280
totalizing, 5, 145
trauma, 21, 64, 139

Treaty of Gudalupe-Hidalgo, 77, 227
trialectics, 179, 184

Unamuno, Miguel de, 270
Un Chien Andalou, 40. *See also* Dalí, Salvador
Urioste, Donaldo W., 8
US-Mexico War, 130
utopía, 35

Vargas Llosa, Mario, 4, 38; *La ciudad y los perros*, 38; "literatura es fuego," 284
Venuti, Lawrence, 216
victim(s), 25–26, 37, 40, 69n17, 94, 144–45, 156–57, 237; Chicanos and Mexican Americans as, 42, 95, 150–51; of disease, 56, 61–64, 200, 205, 248–49
"vida loca," 48, 146
Viejo Vilmas, 239
Vigil, James Diego, 143, 145, 147, 149, 157; and macroviolence of institutions, l57; and microviolence of gangs, l57
Villa, Raúl Homero, 190. *See also* "barrioization"
violence, 26, 38, 40, 43–44, 47–49, 51n13, 199; gang/barrio, 95, 144–45, 157, 213; Mexico/Mexican, 6, 115–16, 122–23; and racism, 19, 26, 29, 161; sex/sexual, 45, 120
Viramontes, Helena María, 269
Virgin of Guadalupe, 7

Waiting to Happen, 7, 276, 278
Walton, Linda, 85
Wars of Independence, 257
water, 14, 18, 78–79, 98, 130–32; as "natural flow" and divider, 16, 76–77, 128; as symbol, 13, 20–21, 23, 26, 28, 78–79, 131
Where the Air Is Clear (*La region más transparente*), 280. *See also* Fuentes, Carlos
White, Hayden, 271. See also *Metahistory: The Historical Imagination in Nineteen-Century Europe*

"white man's burden," 260. See also *Imperial Eyes: Travel Writing and Transculturation*

Yao, Shi-mou, 132
Ybarra-Frausto, Tomás, 265. See also *rasquachismo*

Zapote Tree, 8
Zinn, Howard, 29–30
Zoot Suit Riots, 190–91. *See also* pachuco
Zúñiga-Lomelí, Sonia, 244

www.ingramcontent.com/pod-product-compliance
Lightning Source LLC
Chambersburg PA
CBHW020327240426
43665CB00044B/725